The Political Economy of Information

Studies in Communication and Society

Vincent Mosco and Janet Wasko, General Editors

Communication and Latin American Society: Trends in Critical Research, 1960–1985
Edited by Rita Atwood and Emile G. McAnany

The Political Economy of Information
Edited by Vincent Mosco and Janet Wasko

Technologies of Control: The New Interactive Media for the Home
Kevin G. Wilson

The Political Economy of Information

Edited by Vincent Mosco and Janet Wasko

THE UNIVERSITY OF WISCONSIN PRESS

The University of Wisconsin Press
114 North Murray Street
Madison, Wisconsin 53715

3 Henrietta Street
London WC2E 8LU, England

5 4 3 2

Printed in the United States of America

Library of Congress Cataloging-in-Publication Data
The Political economy of information.
(Studies in communication and society)
Includes index.
1. Communication. 2. Information science.
I. Mosco, Vincent. II. Wasko, Janet. III. Series.
P91.P6 1987 001.51 87.40369
ISBN 0-299-11570-4
ISBN 0-299-11574-7 (pbk.)

Contents

The Political Economy of Information

1. Introduction: Information in the Pay-per Society

Vincent Mosco

Information Society. Postindustrial Society. Third Wave. Microelectronic Age. Computer Era. Network Marketplace. There is no shortage of reminders that society is changing and that these changes have something to do with communication and computer technologies. This book is an effort to analyze these changes by looking at information, the principal product of computer/communication systems. We call it *The Political Economy of Information* because one particularly useful way to understand social change today is to examine how *power* is used to shape the production, distribution, and use of information as a *commodity*.

Technology itself, even such seemingly powerful forces as the computer, does not determine or even shape social relations and social institutions. It is, rather, more useful to see technology as opening up a number of social potentialities. Those who have power to advance certain of these determine or shape the use of technology. This is not to suggest that all uses of technology are a function of power; rather, power sets the pattern for the principal direction of production, distribution, and use.

A fundamental source of power in capitalist society is profit from the sale of commodities in the marketplace. In fact, a basic driving force in the development of capitalism has been the incorporation of things and people into the commodity form. Capitalism was forged in clashes over making land, raw materials, finished products, and human labor commodities to be bought and sold for their *exchange*, as opposed to their *use*, value. The articles in this book consider the process of incorporating information into the commodity form.

As this suggests, power and commodity are inextricably linked. The division of academic disciplines into politics and economics reflects a distortion of this necessary connection. *The Political Economy of Information* is one among a number of efforts to return to the original unified field of such classical political economists as

Smith, Marx, and Ricardo. Such a perspective can advance our understanding of the social relations of information (see Mosco, 1986).

The first part of the book addresses ways of seeing, or, as Dan Schiller puts it, "How to Think About Information." This is followed by studies that identify specific domains in the political economy of information. These include how corporations are making information a marketable commodity, how the state advances that process, the implications for access to information and the wider class structure, and the impact on the workplace and the home. The concluding articles—studies of developed and Third World societies—consider the international significance of transforming information into a commodity.

The remainder of this introduction will be taken up with two tasks. First, I offer a particular perspective on the political economy of information and trace the implications of this way of seeing for central issues confronting people today. The idea of the Pay-per Society provides another way of thinking about social life—about our social relationships in the home, the workplace, and the wider world of political upheavals. The introduction concludes with an overview of the remaining thirteen chapters.

THE PAY-PER SOCIETY

These days everyone seems to have a catchword for the new computer/communication technology: the Postindustrial Society, the Information Age, the Computer Era, the Second Self, the Third Wave, the Fifth Generation. These slogans embody general attempts to glorify the technology and gloss over the fundamental problems it creates or accentuates. They are what I like to call Pushbutton Fantasies (Mosco, 1982). As fantasies they are important because they, explicitly or not, seek to occupy the image space that people turn to when they think about what the new information technology means. Consequently, I have decided to enter this catchword contest by offering an image that captures better the spirit of computer communications today: the Pay-per Society.[1]

We see evidence of the pay-per society all around us. There is pay per call in telephone, pay per view in television, pay per bit or screenful of material in the information business. Advertisers refer to pay per reader, per viewer, or per body when they place an advertise-

---

1. The pun on "paper" contributed to my choice of the term. It unnerves the high-tech advocates among my colleagues who, ignoring the contents of their own offices, think that paper is on the way out.

ment. In the workplace, word processors know about pay per keystroke. And so on.

The essence of what is happening is this: new technology makes it possible to *measure* and *monitor* more and more of our electronic communication and information activities. Business and government see this potential as a major instrument to increase profit and control. The result is a pay-per society. Let's take a closer look at some of these examples and what is behind them.

First pay per call. The rise of digital technology has led to a concerted business effort to deregulate phone service in North America and Europe. Part of this effort is a move to introduce local measured service or pay per call. Many U.S. and European jurisdictions permit charging by the call or per second of phone use. Canadian companies such as Bell Canada are eager to introduce the service. The principal reason for pay per call is that it gives companies the opportunity to offer attractive deals to their business customers and maintain their profits from individual customers and small businesses. With the historical commitment to universal service deregulated or privatized out of existence, companies would use pay per call to shift their cost burden to those who lack the power to contest such a shift (Mosco, 1985; Pike and Mosco, 1986).

Second, pay per view. We have come a long way from the time when most television viewers paid for the service indirectly, through the increased cost of products advertised. We have moved rapidly from indirect payment to a monthly cable television charge, to pay-per-channel schemes with such services as Home Box Office. Now we hear more and more about pay per view. Pay per view is made popular by videocassette rentals but is appearing as well on interactive systems. According to one executive, "Pay-per view is the next grand frontier" (*Newsweek*, 1985).

How about pay per bit? The power of computer technologies to measure and monitor each transaction opens the door to charging for information by the page (or screenful, as it is increasingly called), by the bit, or by the minute of phone use. All sorts of information, from news stories to our shopping habits, from textbooks to performance data on the workforce, are now being packaged and repackaged in marketable form. As a result, as Demac and the Schillers point out in Chapters 7 and 8, these stores of information, or databases, which were once distributed by governments at no charge or a nominal fee to individuals and libraries, are now sold by private companies on the private market. Indeed, as Dan Schiller describes, companies have initiated a new position, the Information Resources Manager, whose job it is to successfully market data on customers and employees, data that might otherwise be stored away or discarded.

Pay per call, per view, and per bit are complemented by what advertising people call pay per body. Advertisers have always known that the cornerstone of electronic media is the process of buying and selling audiences (Smythe, 1981). The new technology deepens and extends this process. The computerized credit card, the home computer, and the sophisticated television system that permits home banking, shopping, opinion polls, and so on also allow corporations to collect massive amounts of information on users. One analyst estimates that within five years 40 million so-called smart cards for automating banking, shopping, and other services will be in circulation in the United States alone. (Glaser, 1986, p. 35). How much money you have, what you like to buy, your views on capital punishment, your preference for president or for laundry detergent—the new technology is used to draw detailed marketing profiles of individual households for what is called (using appropriate military language) precise targeting of potential buyers. Indeed, advertisers are testing systems that use these profiles to direct different commercials to homes in the same neighborhood. These same advertisers go on to pressure program producers to shape their work for an audience of likely consumers. There is little resistance in the media. As one newspaper executive for the eighties put it: "Newspapers are in the information business, but at a more basic level their product is influence—the ability to help advertisers influence consumers" (Mosco, 1982, p. 104).

It should come as no surprise, then, to read daily newspaper accounts of the mania for mergers and joint ventures that has seized the computer communications industry. Companies see the profit in the pay-per society and are joining their respective strengths to take advantage of these money-making opportunities (Bernstein, 1986; Rothmyer, 1985). Take, for example, a recently announced joint venture among RCA, Citicorp, and the regional telephone company Nynex. RCA, now a subsidiary of the giant General Electric, itself owns the major television network NBC and is a leading arms manufacturer. Citicorp is one of the world's largest banks, with over a thousand offices in more than 90 countries. It has pioneered in electronic, particularly home, banking. Nynex is one of the largest telephone companies spun off in the AT&T case. It serves New York and most of New England. These companies have joined to form a home information service that would provide banking, shopping, information, and other services for a pay-per fee over a re-equipped television set. This development mirrors an earlier joint venture among Sears, IBM, and CBS. There is no guarantee that such ventures will achieve short-run success. In fact, such so-called teletext or videotex systems have been slow to develop, in part because of the cost of making such services worthwhile, but also because of their technical complexity. Nevertheless, one might see such ventures as testing grounds for future systems differing somewhat from their forerunners, but rooted in similar principles. In Chapter 9 Eileen Meehan describes a good example of this pattern. The interactive video system QUBE attracted a good deal of media and academic attention, both for what it tried to do and for its failure in business terms. But as Meehan skillfully points out, QUBE succeeded as a testing ground for a range of now lucrative systems (including Music Television, or MTV) and pioneered in developing the means to make profitable use of information gathered on subscriber choices.

The same technologies that extend the pay-per society into the home are used extensively to create a pay-per workplace. Hence pay per keystroke. Secretaries now work on machines that monitor when they begin work, when they take a break, how many keystrokes they type, and whether or not the number meets a minimum quota (10,000 strokes an hour is common). Telephone operators are driven to complete a phone call every 26 seconds. In addition to regular monitoring of Average Work Time, operators are presented with a computer printout on over 60 activities, including the amount of time they spend in the washroom. These same computer systems now control skilled telephone craft workers, who can be found in front of the same screens that confront operators. They are expected to complete a precise number of jobs each day; the computer that parcels out their work also monitors their performance (Mosco and Zureik, 1987). One result is a growing incidence of stress-related problems in the workplace. Or, as Jean de Grandpré, chairman and chief executive officer of Bell Canada, put it: "I have no stress. I impose stress on others" (*The Whig-Standard*, 1985). Grocery checkout clerks work with optical character readers that compute the number of items they ring up over a period of time. Workers in the insurance industry are given a fixed amount of time to handle phone inquiries based on the type of claim. The fast-food industry is preparing a generation of young workers for the rigors of a work world in which the machine embodies relentless supervision (Reiter, 1986).

Let's sum up where we have come to thus far by identifying what is driving this pay-per society. First, there are developments in technology: the integration of digital computers for processing information with cable and communication satellite systems for distributing it, and the linking of these to high-definition screens for display. These make up computer-communication systems that measure and monitor information transactions and permit the packaging and repackaging of information into a marketable commodity.

Driving the technology are large businesses that would use computer communications to increase profit and extend control over workers and consumers. Businesses have a lot to gain in the pay-per society. They stand to gain simply by making information a commodity for sale rather than a public good, necessary for the maintenance of democracy. Though information has been a commodity from the earliest days of capitalism, the new technology deepens and extends opportunities for selling information by transcending the boundaries that space and time impose on the packaging and repackaging of information in a marketable form. A newspaper story can be repackaged in a number of saleable forms, including radio, television, cable, teletext, magazines, computer databases, educational "courseware," and so on—each package brings its own return for essentially the same content. It is no wonder that a company like Time, Inc., or ABC would like to be involved in most of these businesses. It is an opportunity to be paid several times over for the same story. Similarly, information about our credit purchases, vacation choices, opinions about society and politics, can be packaged and sold several times over. Again, it is no wonder that companies like Sears and American Express would like to be involved in this range of businesses.

Beyond the increased profit from the sale of information, as Andrew Clement describes in Chapter 11, there is the use of information technology to slash labor costs by eliminating jobs or deskilling them and thereby cheapening their value. Automated operator services, diagnosis and repair, and record keeping and filing have eliminated tens of thousands of jobs in the North American telephone industry. Membership in the largest phone union in the United States, the Communications Workers of America, dropped from 500,000 to 440,000 between 1981 and 1984. (*New York Times*, 1984). Since the telephone industry is looked on, in the words of a Science Council of Canada report, as "a paradigm for automation in other parts of the service sector," it is likely that we will see this pattern grafted onto other industries, such as banking, insurance, education, and social services (Cordell, 1985, p. 37). The jobs that remain in these industries are shorn of their skill content and thus cheapened beyond the need for further automation. This has been the case in the fast-food industry. One of the reasons why fast-food employment is growing so rapidly and unlikely to experience severe automation is that labor costs are too abysmally low to justify the cost of extensive automation. But it certainly makes sense to eliminate a well-paid branch bank manager. Here is how one responded to the drive to automate, deskill, and centralize information and authority:

> A Canadian local bank manager pointed out that his regional vice-president knows precisely the state of his branch, at any point during the day, by pressing the appropriate buttons. He can know the state of deposits in the bank, the state of withdrawals, the state of payments of loans, defaults on loans, everything that is put in the data banks, the bank's central place. So I asked the branch manager, "What is your role?" His response was "I'll be damned if I know." (Cordell, 1985, p. 41)

So the telephone operators and craft workers that remain see themselves as automatons responding to the dictates of a video display terminal that displays precise orders and just as precisely monitors their conformity. One consequence of this is that consumers bear more and more of the workload. Customers now go to the phone store to pick up a phone. Customers plug it in. Customers find phone numbers. Customers take the phone out to be repaired or, more likely, toss it out and buy a new one. Since the company does not pay customers for their labor, it saves money that used to pay a phone worker's wages.

But beyond this, as Gerald Sussman points out in Chapter 13, companies want to use the new technology to expand their control internationally. This technology allows a company to centralize key finance, marketing, research, and planning decisions in a headquarters office kept up to date with a regular stream of information brought in by a global network of computer communications systems. The company can then use the world as its market for products and labor, taking advantage of low-cost regions, antiunion policies, and political conditions that oppress resistance. Consider Digital Equipment's boast in a management publication about the company's World Computer:

> DIGITAL'S WORLD COMPUTER
>
> - keyboards made in Boston
> - display monitors made in Taiwan
> - system boxes assembled in Westfield, Mass.
> - floppy disk drives made in Singapore and assembled and tested in Springfield, Mass., and in the future will also be assembled in Singapore

- disk drive heads are made in Westboro, Mass., with plans to move this operation to Shrewsbury, Mass.
- integrated circuits are fabricated in Hudson, Mass., sent to Taiwan to be cut and packaged, then sent to Marlboro, Mass., to be made into hybrid circuits, then tested and sent to Westfield, Mass., to be incorporated into the Professional 350 processor
- computer memories made in Hong Kong and Singapore
- circuit memories assembled in Albuquerque, N.M.
- power supplies made in Phoenix, Arizona
- some circuit modules subcontracted in Puerto Rico
- at the Westfield plant, "Gus" the robot works around the clock loading and unloading circuit modules from a "Smart Burn-In" system which tests the reliability of the modules
- robot manufacture of disk drive heads is being developed for Westboro or the Far East
- "for flexibility," DEC wants to build monitors not just in Taiwan but also in Hong Kong

SOURCE: Decworld, March 1983.

The new technology makes possible a truly international division of labor. But, just as important, it is a flexible one. In response to changing political or economic conditions, companies can relocate with relative ease to a more stable or a cheaper location (Fuentes and Ehrenreich, 1983).

CENTRAL PROBLEMS IN THE PAY-PER SOCIETY

One can identify three central problems of the pay-per society. The headlong drive to expand the profitable uses of new technology deepens and intensifies some of the thorniest social and moral concerns: class divisions, threats to civil and human rights, global warfare.

We have been so caught up in what I call the Pushbutton Fantasies of the computer society that we have lost sight of a growing class of people who cannot afford the price of admission to the information age. As business and the Pentagon work toward the fifth-generation computer, the U.S. government acknowledges that about one-third of its adult citizens are functionally illiterate. What does this mean? They cannot read a help-wanted ad. They cannot address an envelope well enough to guarantee delivery. They cannot figure out how much change they should get back at the grocery store.

Here is what one man told Jonathan Kozol for his recent book *Illiterate America*:

> "I've lost a lot of jobs," one man explains. "Today, even if you're a janitor, there's still reading and writing . . . They leave a note saying, 'Go to room so-and-so . . .' You can't do it. You don't know."
> "The hardest thing about it is that I've been places where I don't know where I was. You don't know where you are . . . You're lost."
>
> "Like I said: I have two kids. What do I do if one of my kids starts to choking? I go running to the phone . . . I can't look up the hospital phone number. That's if we're at home. Out on the street, I can't read the sign. I get to a pay phone. 'Okay, tell us where you are. We'll send an ambulance.' I look at the street sign. Right there, I can't tell you what it says. I'd have to spell it out, letter for letter. By that time, one of my kids would be dead . . . These are the kinds of fears you go with, every single day . . ."
>
> "Reading directions, I suffer with. I work with chemicals . . . That's scary to begin with . . ."
>
> "You sit down. They throw the menu in front of you. Where do you go from there? Nine times out of ten you say, 'Go ahead. Pick out something for the both of us.' I've eaten some weird things, let me tell you!" (Kozol, 1985, pp. 27–28)

and a mother talks about trying to read to her five-year-old:

> "I can't read to them. Of course that's leaving them out of something they should have. Oh, it matters. You believe it matters! I ordered all these books. The kids belong to a book club. Donny wanted me to read a book to him. I told Donny: 'I can't read.' He said: 'Mommy, you sit down. I'll read it to you.' I tried it one day, reading from the pictures. Donny looked at me. He said, 'Mommy, that's not right.' He's only five. He knew I couldn't read." (Ibid., p. 28)

Today you can add to the familiar "Why can't Johnny read?" the increasingly familiar "Why can't Johnny and Jane afford a dial tone?" U.S. government policies known by such euphemisms as "deregulation," "privatization," and "return to the marketplace" are increasing the price of phone service to the point where large numbers of people are forced to give it up. AT&T itself predicts that deregulation and the divestiture, both emanating from the pressures on large corporations to keep down the price of long-distance service, will cause local rates to jump 200 to 300 percent over the next five years, forcing three out of ten U.S. households to do without telephones (Pike and Mosco, 1986).

As the chapters by Terry Curtis, Oscar Gandy, Donna Demac, the Schillers, and Eileen Meehan indicate, deregulation of the phone service is part of a wider attack on public information institutions in North America. The public interest commitment in broadcasting is going the way of universal telephone service. Public education, libraries, the postal service, are all eroded by the tidal wave of defunding and privatization.

The growing class division between those who can afford computers and pay-per-view television in stereo and those who cannot read or afford the price of a phone is reinforced by the growth of a two-tiered workforce. According to Russell Rumberger and Henry Levin (1985), we are dividing into a society characterized by a high-tech minority at the top and a mass of people at the bottom whose work has suffered the ravages of automation and deskilling. Extrapolating into the future, the U.S. Bureau of Labor Statistics identifies the five largest growth occupations to 1995 as building custodian, cashier, secretary, office clerk, and sales clerk. These are optimistic projections. The last four jobs mentioned are under explicit attack from automation. But more to the point, they are part of what is known too politely as the pink-collar ghetto: jobs that women have moved into in huge numbers over the last 20 years, but also jobs with little or no mobility potential.

According to the economist Lester Thurow:

> A bi-polar income distribution of rich and poor is replacing the wide expanse of the middle class. . . . From the point of view of technical economics, a shrinking middle class is of no concern. One business magazine recently noted that the growth of high-income households would be a great opportunity for companies producing high-income leisure products. They are right. . . . But it is a cause of concern for political democracy. (Thurow, 1985, p. F-3)

Of equal concern is the new technology's potential to violate fundamental rights to privacy and permit the widespread political management of our lives. Buying into the pay-per society means more than instant shopping or movies. It means providing private companies and governments with enormous amounts of information on how we conduct our daily lives. The laws that protect against the misuse of such information are popguns against an elephant. Since it is increasingly essential for us to use the new technology to bank, shop, or even work, we resign ourselves to the loss of privacy. If you need a job you keep quiet about the relentless monitoring. Companies are now experimenting with identification cards for washrooms that compute who is using the facilities and for how long (*Canadian Business*, 1985; *Los Angeles Times*, 1987).

But there is a wider danger than the threat, however real, against individual privacy, and that is social management. A good example of social management is contained in a rarely quoted passage of Orwell's *1984*. He describes the Lottery:

> "Oh, pack it in!" said the third man. They were talking about the Lottery. Winston looked back when he had gone thirty meters. They were still arguing with vivid, passionate faces. The Lottery, with its weekly pay-out of enormous prizes, was the one public event to which the proles paid serious attention. It was probable that there were some millions of proles for whom the Lottery was the principal if not the only reason for remaining alive. It was their delight, their folly, their anodyne, their intellectual stimulant. Where the Lottery was concerned, even people who could barely read and write seemed capable of intricate calculations and staggering feats of memory. There was a whole tribe of men who made a living simply by selling systems, forecasts, and lucky amulets. Winston had nothing to do with the running of the Lottery, which was managed by the Ministry of Plenty, but he was aware (indeed everyone in the Party was aware) that the prizes were largely imaginary. (Orwell, 1961, p. 73)

The pay-per society can go well beyond Orwell's *1984*. It can offer instant electronic lotteries and maintain their power to manage large numbers of people by offering real prizes. That is social management. Social management is also information systems that chart networks of contacts among phone and computer users, irrespective of communication content. Such contact networks can pinpoint groups of people who may be acting against the interests of top management. The mathematician who pioneered these "block-modeling" techniques, overwhelmed by inquiries from government agencies, corporations, mental institutions, and prisons, now warns of misuse (*New York Times*, 1983). That is social management. Social management is also changing your behavior to conform because you know the technology can monitor your behavior whether or not it is actually doing so. Hence, the greater fear is not that we will give up our privacy, but that we will keep it and live in a society in which privacy is not worth having.

Class divisions. Social management. Now, the threat of nuclear annihilation. The military have been the driving force in computer communications from the earliest primitive computers that were used to compute artillery firing tables and decipher enemy codes. The major project to develop supercomputers in the United States is a $600 million program, the Strategic Computing Initiative (SCI), which will produce driverless tanks and a computer co-pilot for the military (U.S. Department of Defense, 1983). The significance of computers in nuclear warfare is not lost on George A. Keyworth II, who as President Reagan's chief science advisor testified at congressional committee hearings on the Star Wars program. His language speaks volumes on science research in the United States:

> It has been the incredible leaps in data processing, as much as any single area, which has fueled this explosion. And it is not just that we no longer need mammoth warehouses to contain the radar and computers necessary to the ABM of the 1960s. The very existence of today's and tomorrow's ability to solve complex problems on incredibly small machines, and fast, has opened up the development of our entire national technical base. . . . It was data processing which overcame John von Neuman's skepticism of ever making the ICBM work in the first place. It was data processing at the heart of the move to MIRVing. It was data processing which tied ICBM fleets together for coordinated execution. It was data processing which has provided the ICBM accuracy necessary for preemptive strikes. And it is data processing which will be at the heart of any defense against ballistic missiles. (U.S. Congress, 1984, p. 8)

Computer communications systems are now at the heart of nuclear weapons systems—so much at the heart that people fear the consequences. Precision-guided nuclear weapons, like the Cruise, combined with even a leaky Star Wars defense system, make first-strike strategies more tempting, particularly when the enemy itself is seen as irrational enough to strike first (Ford, 1985). Then there is the danger of an erroneous reading from a sensor as occurred once, when a computer misread the rising moon for a Soviet attack, leading to a major alert (Computer Professionals for Social Responsibility, 1984). No less a beneficiary of military computers than Thomas J. Watson, Jr., long-time head of IBM, has expressed his fears about a strategy of launching an attack based on a computer warning:

> the more the whole philosophy of launch-on-warning becomes attractive, the greater the danger. And as machines of war and missiles become more prey to preemptive strike, the more temptation there is to put more and more of the data in the hands of a computer and take the human being out of the equation. To the extent that you do that, you are indeed putting the U.S. into a position where a computer could trip us up pretty badly. (*Computerworld*, 1983, p. 15)

Trip us up badly indeed.

But can the generals be trusted any more than the computers? Joseph Weizenbaum has reported that during the Vietnam War computers in the field were specifically programmed to tell Pentagon computers that raids over neutral Cambodia were actually raids over Vietnam. Highly placed Washington insiders who were permitted to see the summaries produced by Pentagon computers wrongly believed that they were getting a privileged insight into field action. As Admiral Moorer, then chairman of the Joint Chiefs, put it: "It is unfortunate that we had to become slaves to those damned computers" (Weizenbaum, 1981, p. 560). One wonders about resting the fate of humanity in the hands of someone who programs computers to mask a war and then claims to be enslaved by these same computers.

But it is not simply a question of fixing the technology or reining in the generals. Military projects like Star Wars are the only legitimate means of providing direct government funding for corporate projects. Multi-billion-dollar contracts would be criticized as improper government intrusion into the free marketplace if the money were earmarked for civilian projects. In this basic sense military programs such as Star Wars and SCI will work well for major arms manufacturers like Rockwell, McDonnell Douglas, Ford Aerospace, and Hughes, and companies with a stake in artificial intelligence like Boeing, Martin Marietta, Texas Instruments, and Bell Helicopter (Mosco, 1987). As Table 1.1 suggests, the same companies that have benefited most from Pentagon research and development contracts are the chief beneficiaries of Star Wars contracts.

In return for this largesse, the government receives the support of its corporate constituents in convincing a skeptical public. According to an executive with Rockwell's Space Transportation System Division:

> When people ask how much is enough for military spending they compare it to welfare or education or something else we're doing. I can't understand that . . . the United States could win in a technological competition with the Soviets if we were committed . . . if we set our minds to it we could get a decisive advantage. (Karas, 1983, p. 59)

RESPONDING TO THE PROBLEMS OF THE PAY-PER SOCIETY

How do we respond to these problems? Let me start by turning the clock back to 1947 and share with you the thoughts of the man most closely identified with the development of computing science, Nor-

Table 1.1. Top 10 Recipients of Pentagon Star Wars (Strategic Defense Initiative) Contracts, Fiscal Years 1983–1984

Company	SDI Awards (in $ millions)	Total 1984 Awards (in $ millions) and Rank
Boeing	364.3	4,563.8 (5)
Lockheed	240.1	4,967.5 (4)
McDonnell Douglas	236.8	7,684.2 (1)
L.T.V.	211.0	1,655.3 (14)
Teledyne	115.4	425.8 (44)
Rockwell	88.7	6,219.3 (2)
T.R.W.	76.4	982.5 (24)
Hughes Aircraft	34.8	3,230.5 (7)
AVCO	30.6	872.8 (27)
Litton	25.3	2,440.7 (10)

Sources: Council on Economic Priorities, *The Strategic Defense Initiative: Costs, Contractors, and Consequences; Aerospace Daily,* 26 April 1985.

bert Weiner. Weiner struggled to formulate an answer to these same problems at the dawn of the computer age:

> The answer, of course, is to have a society based on human values other than buying or selling. To arrive at this society, we need a good deal of planning and a good deal of struggle, which, if the best comes to the best, may be on the plane of ideas, and otherwise—who knows? I thus felt it my duty to pass on my information and understanding of this position to those who have an active interest in the conditions and the future of labor, that is, to the labor unions. I did manage to make contact with one or two persons high up in the C.I.O., and from them I received a very intelligent and sympathetic hearing . . .
>
> Those of us who have contributed to the new science of cybernetics thus stand in a moral position which is, to say the least, not very comfortable. We have contributed to the initiation of a new science which, as I have said, embraces technical developments with great possibilities for good and for evil. We can only hand it over into the world that exists about us, and this is the world of Belsen and Hiroshima. . . . there are those who hope that the good of a better understanding of man and society which is offered by this new field of work may anticipate and outweigh the incidental contribution we are making to the concentration of power . . . I write in 1947, and I am compelled to say that it is a very slight hope. (Weiner, 1948, pp. 28–29)

What is left of that hope today?

The first source of hope comes from the very problems that current uses of the technology present. The pay-per society is a far from stable world. There is the accelerating gap, increasingly clear to more and more people, between the potential of the technology for giving control to all of us and the current drive to use technology to centralize control. This gap between potential and reality makes it hard to maintain the charade that we need elite rule.

Next are the tremendous social costs of using technology to further concentrate wealth and power. I am thinking here of the enormous stress that the new technologies inflict (for secretaries, Nussbaum, 1984, p. 244 indicates, it is now greater than for air traffic controllers). People are responding to these problems by rebelling against the authority of the machine. One study showed that when management removes control over the pace of work from office workers and transfers it to machine systems, error rates increase from 40 to 400 percent. As a clerical worker put it "Maybe when they see how bad the information is, they'll give us back our jobs" (Gregory, 1982, p. 98).

Nor is it easy simply to shift such work overseas, because workers in the Third World are increasingly reacting against oppressive working conditions — as Control Data learned when workers in a microchip plant in Seoul kidnapped a couple of CDC executives sent from headquarters to look into labor problems in a plant. Similar incidents have prompted many U.S. firms to speed up automation and bring the robot-run plants back to the United States.

But that raises a more fundamental issue. The pay-per society is built around massive amounts of individual consumption. Yet computer communications are eliminating the jobs that provide the income necessary to keep consumption going. Certainly there are ways of maintaining an economy based on concentrating consumption in a fabulously wealthy elite. But how will that society control the millions who are denied? For example, will the millions of women and racial minorities who have struggled for years for some degree of economic, political, and social equality yield easily to deepening inequalities? I think not.

Recent events have taught us that a high-tech world is a very fragile one indeed. Around the same time that the Challenger space shuttle took seven people to their deaths, a computer malfunction mistakenly shifted several billion dollars from one U.S. bank to another. Such developments make it harder to convince people that they can rely on computer programs thousands of times more complicated to provide a military defense system that can never be tested.

Finally, the very danger of a highly competitive, militaristic world has led more and more people to consider the peaceful alternatives. The peace movement will have its peaks and valleys, but it cannot be denied as one of the most significant social developments of our time. So the very promotion of an elite-controlled high-tech world is itself creating serious problems.

Just as important, the problems and the potential in the technology are providing new bases for joint action. Fewer and fewer people can escape the problems of the pay-per society. Even computer programmers find their jobs subject to automation (Howard, 1985). Moreover, as people close to the problems of the computer age, they are reacting more and more strongly against them. I am reminded of Winston, the hero of *1984*, who rebelled because as a government employee charged with rewriting history, he could observe that government at its most corrupt. Similarly, Winston's real-life counterpart Daniel Ellsberg, writing an official history of the Vietnam War for the U.S. government, was radicalized by what he learned and played a major role in ending the war. I thought of Winston and Ellsberg as I read the account of 30 computer workers in the Philippines who walked out of the official election counting office, some carrying discs, all refusing to give in to Marcos' orders to rig the count.

In *Pushbutton Fantasies* (1982), I tried to identify what Stavrianos (1976) called green shoots of grass on a very bleak landscape. These included examples of media networks set up by U.S. trade unions, a feminist radio network of 80 stations, the National Federation of Democratic Radio Stations in Italy, a plan to use computer information systems to expand true workplace democracy in the mines and factories of Salvador Allende's Chile, and a public interest group's proposal to build a grassroots computer network in the United States.

Today I might add the massive grassroots literacy campaign in Nicaragua that would be a model for North America, the creation of worker protections and increasing worker influence, if not control, over the implementation of new technology in Scandinavia, and the nationwide struggle of organized labor and community activists in North America to protect universal telephone service. *The Political Economy of Information* is itself one small part of this effort.

THE POLITICAL ECONOMY OF INFORMATION

The first group of papers in this volume address conceptual and theoretical issues in the political economy of information. Dan Schiller begins by presenting three perspectives in this area. The first, *information theory*, identified information as a measure of organization or structure. Its proponents, chiefly mathematicians, engineers, and systems theorists, saw information theory as an instrument for understanding complex systems, from telephone networks to biological organisms to entire societies. Schiller takes this view to task for, among other things, failing to account for the social and historical determinants of information. The second, or *postindustrial*, view tried to account for the social dimension by defining information as a resource that makes for a radical break in historical development. Schiller criticizes this perspective for its lack of concreteness ("a resource is anything of use, anytime, anywhere, to anyone") and situates the postindustrial view in its ideological context. Against these perspectives, Schiller offers the view that information is a *commodity*. As such, it "bears the stamp of society and of history in its very core." Schiller outlines a conceptual scheme for understanding the information economy. In the course of doing so, he challenges the established political-economic view, contained in the work of Baran and Sweezy, for example, that dismisses the economic role of information in capitalist society. Schiller proceeds to build a political-economic theory that makes information central to capitalism.

In Chapter 3 Kevin Robins and Frank Webster also identify three perspectives on information. However, they situate their position between what they identify as a traditional political-economic perspective and one that insists on the relative autonomy of the cultural domain. The former, reflected in the work of Nicholas Garnham, stresses the economic underpinnings of information technology and the significance of market forces for shaping the communications revolution. The latter, presented most explicitly in Ian Connell's critique of Garnham, claims that political economy offers an overly reductionist view of the cultural domain. It stresses the ideological dimension and makes claims for the potential contained in new technologies to offer greater diversity in content and control. Though aligning themselves more with Garnham than with Connell, the authors see the need to move the debate forward by starting from the *political* rather than the economic in political economy. Specifically, they see developments in computer/communications technology leading to a major restructuring of social and political life that cannot be captured by either strict economic or cultural analysis. Their work is true to the spirit of Lukacs' notion of totality in that they identify the ways in which the new technologies are transforming all spheres of everyday life, creating a new micropolitics of society.

Ben Bates is less ambitious, but his contribution provides an interesting angle of vision that complements others in the book. In "Information as an Economic Good," Bates offers an economist's perspective on what he calls this "peculiar commodity." After reviewing the work of a range of information theorists, Bates concludes that information is, even from a traditional economic perspective, a "distinctive good" whose value is determined by the expected returns from the use of that information. Bates contends that returns from future use may go to others rather than the direct user of the information, creating what he calls "ancillary value." Ancillary value results from changes in the social and economic environment for information goods. He contends that many difficulties within established economics can be traced to a failure to consider and indeed make central to economic models the political-economic notion of ancillary value. Bates uses the concept to critique the notion that the privatization of information markets will lead to their optimal performance.

Terry Curtis rounds out this set of theoretical chapters with an analysis of a bifurcation in classical political economy between two different values in the production and distribution of wealth: liberty and equality. He examines the history of this bifurcation and contends that contemporary political economists have focused all too exclusively on the idea of liberty. Consequently, when they turn their attention to policy matters, it is the threat to liberty, the fear that we will lose individual privacy, that receives foremost attention. He calls for more attention to the other side of traditional political economy—the concern for equality. In doing this, he argues that the use of detailed information about individuals for market segmentation and the use of targeted communications media pose substantial threats to equality and challenge the very notion of the democratic community that is the foundation of equality.

In Chapter 6 Oscar Gandy offers a concrete analysis of the threat to equality contained in the use of new communication technologies. Gandy reviews research on the distributional impacts of new technology and suggests that in several vital areas a substantial portion of the population in developed societies such as the United States lacks the competence to communicate in a technologically sophisticated world. Contrary to certain analysts, he suggests that class and race may matter more in the information society than they did in the industrial world because the powers of data gathering for surveillance, market manipulation, and general social control are greater in a society marked by computer communication systems.

Gandy's review of research on government information control provides a good introduction to Donna Demac's chapter on the information policies of the Reagan administration. Demac extends arguments developed in her book *Keeping America Uninformed.* In it she identified specific restrictions that the U.S. government, particularly under President Reagan, has imposed on the free flow of information within the United States. These include tightening secrecy laws, invoking national security to restrict cultural exchanges, increasing the price of information enormously by privatizing government information programs, and using the cover of reducing paperwork to cut back on government oversight activities and programs that encouraged citizen access to information. The overall effect of these activities, Demac concludes, is to strengthen executive branch power and stifle debate on significant national issues. In Chapter 7 Demac builds on these points by analyzing what she calls the administration's "practice of conditioning assent," which, in her view, is "every bit as essential to extending government controls as the content of the restrictions imposed." Such strategies as floating trial balloons, letting the storm blow over, imputing guilt by association, browbeating the media, and waging disinformation campaigns have been used effectively to condition assent for government policies that would limit democracy.

Demac's work adds an important dimension to international as well as domestic policy debates. For at the very time that the U.S. government was imposing severe restrictions on the flow of information within the United States, it decided to withdraw from the United Nations Educational, Scientific and Cultural Organization, ostensibly because UNESCO was promoting policies that would restrict international communication systems. In fact, the U.S. withdrawal curtails its participation in international programs that would democratize information flows worldwide.

In their chapter, Anita and Herbert Schiller identify the impact that restrictive government policies have had on the U.S. library system. They situate their argument within the general historical process whereby information has come to be a more and more vital commodity for transnational business. Libraries are in a particularly sensitive position because they rely on government support to survive and grow. At the same time, private companies are increasingly coveting what they perceive to be a source of enormous private profit, the very information that libraries identify as a public good. Their article therefore takes up one of the fundamental struggles of our time, the conflict over the social definition and use of information. As they conclude, the stakes are high:

> Transforming information into a saleable good, available only to those with the ability to pay for it, changes the goal of information access from an egalitarian to a privileged condition. The consequence of this is that the essential underpinning of a democratic order is seriously

damaged. This is the ultimate outcome of commercializing information throughout the social sphere.

In Chapter 9 Eileen Meehan takes us to the front lines of the information/entertainment industry with an analysis of how the only substantial project implementing interactive cable television in the United States—Warner's QUBE system—was shaped by the economic constraints discussed in previous chapters. As Meehan shows, for Warner "interactive" meant a system for testing products and developing program formats, such as music videos, that would sell products. Even the venue for QUBE, Columbus, Ohio, was chosen because its demographic characteristics precisely fitted the needs of advertisers. Moreover, QUBE employed a monitoring system tailored to identify the link between subscriber choices and demographic characteristics, thereby providing an invaluable database for future development. Much has been made of the fact that QUBE failed to generate enough income to survive in Columbus. A reading of Meehan's chapter suggests that this is a very shortsighted view. QUBE was not intended to achieve commercial success. Rather, it was a testing ground for future interactive networks, paving the way for the kinds of information delivery systems that will generate the most income. In essence, absent significant political change, if the library system described by the Schillers is a thing of the past, the interactive video systems described by Meehan are the wave of the future.

In Chapter 10, Tony Tinker, Cheryl Lehman, and Marilyn Neimark present another dimension of corporate control over information, here the information generated by business accountants. In "Bookkeeping for Capitalism," they challenge the popularly accepted image of accounting information as an objective report of business activity. They show that, like other forms of information, accounting is a set of social practices that reflect and reinforce a dominant ideology—in this case the belief that a capitalist economic system is the only acceptable and successful way to conduct commerce. To do this, they present three case studies from diverse sources of accounting information. The first examines four decades of the published financial statements of Delco, a multinational company that operated in the colonial and postcolonial state of Sierra Leone. Here they provide a literal accounting for imperialism. The second is an analysis of 60 years of annual reports from General Motors that identifies changes in the way American business accounted for itself in a changing society. The authors highlight the growing role of the explicitly ideological "nonfinancial" dimension of these reports and show how they reflect and seek to mold the changing culture of American capitalism. The third source of evidence comes from professional journals and magazines aimed at practitioners (the *Journal of Accountancy*), academics and researchers (*Accounting Review*), and corporate managers (*Fortune*). Here accountants account for their place within the system. This chapter takes an important step in the process of demystifying the content and professional ideology of accounting and thereby adds a new dimension to critical communications research.

From corporate information, we turn to the use of information in the workplace. In the next two chapters Andrew Clement and Jörg Becker examine the impact of changing computer communications systems on a changing work world. In Chapter 11 Clement focuses on the use of office automation to centralize control of the workplace. He identifies three specific processes. First, automation is used to deskill information workers like clerks and computer professionals. Second, he shows how computerization puts in place sophisticated moniitoring and surveillance systems that further centralize control. Finally, he describes the ways in which office computer systems are used to limit access to information, providing upper management with a deep view of the organization while keeping lower-level information workers in the dark. Clement's work confounds the postindustrial thesis that the information society increases the power of information workers and generally decentralizes control. Rather, Clement suggests, it deepens and extends patterns of centralized control that have characterized capitalist society since the Industrial Revolution.

Jörg Becker's "Electronic Homework in West Germany" assesses a phenomeonon that writers like Alvin Toffler (1980) have claimed will transform the nature of work: the ability to work at home electronically. Becker situates his work within Habermas' theoretical perspective on the decline of the public sphere in capitalist society. He reviews critically the work of those who fantasize about how homework will end the drudgery of factory and office. Becker concludes that electronic homework still resides largely within the realm of fantasy. A great deal more has been said about it than put into practice, largely, he contends, because the practice is very risky for both labor and capital. The risks to labor, particularly to organized trade unions, are not difficult to ascertain. Individual workers cut off from a collective workplace lose many of the basic material and social benefits that office workers enjoy. In addition to having to purchase or rent their own equipment, homeworkers are often paid piece or hourly rates without medical and social security benefits. For trade unions, homework enormously complicates the organizing process. But Becker points to a factor that has not been given much research attention: management is unaccustomed to maintaining social control at a distance. In the current state of technology, management must extend a degree of trust in its workers that makes it decidedly uncomfortable. As a result, Becker forecasts that electronic homework will develop slowly. This is for him a hopeful sign, because it provides the time to develop the social policies that might ameliorate some of the dangers inherent in the home workplace.

The final two chapters also address international concerns. In Chapter 13 Gerald Sussman examines the proliferation of information technologies among the Association of Southeast Asian Nations (ASEAN), principally Indonesia, Malaysia, the Philippines, Singapore, and Thailand. He identifies major policy trends, principally privatization, and projects taking place in the region, discusses the major users of the new technologies, and considers the likely social-structural consequences for these countries. Sussman is particularly concerned with the impact of programs developed by transnational financial and industrial firms, aided by international bodies such as the World Bank, implemented through local companies and political authorities, and designed to incorporate these nations into a globally integrated production and service economy and a new international division of labor.

The final chapter of the book examines the emergence of the Intergovernmental Bureau of Informatics, an international body that, as Eileen Mahoney writes, "provides a unique prism" for examining "the social and technological forces, economic actors, and political maneuvers fashioning the role of an international organization within the emerging world political economy." Mahoney suggests a number of lessons to be learned from the failure of the IBI to provide Third World elites with an opportunity to play a major role in the global political economy of information. These include the complete dependency of international business on global communication networks, with the result that business cannot permit its dependency to be exploited by international bodies over which it lacks control. Organizations like the IBI cannot achieve stability in the international communication power structure because they cannot reconcile the needs of Third World societies and those of international business. Mahoney's political-economic analysis, combining as it does the themes of domination and instability, provides a fitting conclusion to this collection of studies on the political economy of information.

REFERENCES

Bernstein, L. (1986). "Why Sell RCA at All?" *New York Times,* 19 January, p. E-23.

Canadian Business (1985). "I Saw What You Did and I Know Who You Are." November, pp.77–83.

Computer Professionals for Social Responsibility, (1984). "Strategic Computing: An Assessment" CPSR, Inc., P.O. Box 717, Palo Alto, Calif. 94301.

Computerworld (1983). "In Depth: An Interview with Thomas J. Watson, Jr." 15 June, p. 15.

Cordell, A. J. (1985). *The Uneasy Eighties: The Transition to an Information Society*, Ottawa: Science Council of Canada.

Demac, D. (1984). *Keeping America Uninformed.* New York: Pilgrim.

Ford, D. (1985). *The Button.* New York: Simon and Schuster.

Fuentes, A., and B. Ehrenreich (1983). *Women in the Global Factory.* Boston: South End Press.

Glaser, S. (1986). "Smart Cards." *High Technology* 6, July pp. 34–43.

Gregory, J. (1982). "Technological Change in the Office Workplace and the Implications for Organizing." in D. Kennedy, C. Craypo, and M. Lehman (eds.) *Labor and Technology: Union Responses to Changing Environments.* University Park, Pa.: Pennsylvania State University Press.

Howard, R. (1985). *Brave New Workplace.* New York: Viking.

Karas, T. (1983). *The New High Ground.* New York: Simon and Schuster.

Kozol, J. (1985). *Illiterate America.* New York: Doubleday.

Los Angeles Times (1987). "Raising Your Hand Just Won't Do." 1 April.

Mosco, V. (1982). *Pushbutton Fantasies: Critical Perspectives on Videotex and Information Technology.* Norwood, N.J.: Ablex.

Mosco, V. (1985). "Regulation and Deregulation." In *Proceedings of the National Economic Conference.* Ottawa: Federal Department of Finance.

Mosco, V. (1986). "Marxism and Communications Research in North America." In B. Ollman and E. Vernoff (eds.) *The Left Academy*, vol. 3. New York: Praeger.

Mosco, V. (1987). "Star Wars Is Already Working." *Science as Culture* 1.

Mosco, V., and E. Zureik (1987). *Technological Change in the Telephone Industry.* Report to the Federal Department of Labor, Ottawa, Canada.

New York Times (1983). "Big Brother and Block Modeling." 20 November.

New York Times (1984). "A Union Copes With Deregulation." 18 November.

Newsweek (1985). "Hollywood Tries for a New Hit." 8 April, p. 56.

Nussbaum, K. (1984). "Office Automation: Jekyll or Hyde." In V. Mosco (ed.) *Policy Research in Telecommunications.* Norwood, N.J.: Ablex.

Orwell, G. (1961). *1984* New York: Signet.

Pike, R., and V. Mosco (1986). "Canadian Consumers and Telephone Pricing." *Telecommunications Policy,* 9 March, pp. 17–32.

Reiter, E. (1986). "Life in a Fast-Food Factory." In C. Heron and R. Storey (eds.) *On The Job: Confronting the Labour Process in Canada.* Kingston and Montreal: Queen's-McGill Press.

Rothmyer, K. (1985). "Hot Properties: The Media-Buying Spree Explained." *Columbia Journalism Review* 24, November/December, pp. 38–43.

Rumberger, R. W., and H. M. Levin (1985). "Forecasting the Impact of New Technologies on the Future Job Market." *Technological Forecasting and Social Change,* 27, pp. 399–417.

Smythe, D. W. (1981). *Dependency Road.* Norwood, N.J.: Ablex.

Stavrianos, L. S. (1976). *The Promise of the Coming Dark Age.* San Francisco: W. H. Freeman.

Thurow, L. (1985). "The Disappearance of the Middle Class." *New York Times*, 5 February.

Toffler, A. (1980). *The Third Wave.* New York: William Morrow.

U.S. Congress, Senate Committee on Foreign Relations (1984). *Strategic Defense and Anti-Satellite Weapons*, 98th Cong., 2d sess., 25 April. Washington D.C.: Government Printing Office.

U.S. Department of Defense (1983). *Strategic Computing.* Washington, D.C.: Defense Advanced Research Projects Agency.

Weiner, N. (1948). *Cybernetics.* Cambridge: MIT Press.

Weizenbaum, J. (1981). "Once More, the Computer Revolution." In T. Forester (ed.) *The Microelectronics Revolution.* Cambridge: MIT Press.

Whig-Standard (Kingston) (1985). "Bell Canada Enterprises." 4 November.

2. How to Think About Information

Dan Schiller

> *[O]ur product is information. . . . Information that charges airline tickets, hotel rooms, dining out, the newest fashions and even figures mailing costs for a travel magazine; information that grows money funds, buys and sells equities and manages mergers; information that pays life insurance annuities, figures pricing for collision coverage and creates and pays mortgages. . . . information that schedules entertainment on cable television and electronically guards houses; information that changes kroners into guilders, figures tax rates in Bermuda and helps put financing together for the ebb and flow of world trade.*
>
> —American Express, 1982

Thus did the American Express Company herald its elevation, in 1982, into the select group of thirty corporations making up the Dow Jones Industrial [sic] index.

American Express is not unique. Companies engaged in information-intensive services in banking, communications, data processing, engineering, advertising, law, and so on play an ever more critical role in overall U.S. investment, employment, and international trade. Major manufacturers, such as General Motors, McDonnell Douglas, and General Electric, have diversified far into the field of commercial information services. A new administrative discipline known as "information resource management" is finding broad application across the business world. This discipline attempts to treat information "as a resource like other resources such as money, personnel and property, which have values and costs and are used in achieving program goals" (Horton, 1983, pp. 1,24). In short, as one authority declares, we "can no longer deny that information is becoming a commodity" (Spero, 1982, p. 152).

Not just *any* commodity, either, but a fundamental source of growth for the market system as a whole; information, some say, has become the essential site of capital accumulation within the world economy.

Yet the source and the real character of this general shift in the social definition of information themselves remain obscure. Where is the common ground shared by a college course in anthropology and computerized credit data—between a front-page newspaper account of a city council meeting and genetically coded messages? How, when, and why, futhermore, does information become economically valuable?

Throughout the postwar era, many writers have grappled with such questions. At least three broad, often overlapping, conceptual approaches to the subject have emerged. In spite of serious flaws, each tradition may be utilized critically as a means to explore how to think about information.

INFORMATIONAL THEORIES

As late as 1933, the *Oxford English Dictionary* gave no hint of the profound shifts beginning to occur in the conceptualization of information. The *Dictionary* revealed only that "information" had been in currency in English since Chaucer, when it denoted an item of training, an instruction; and that the word then found several additional meanings: an idea; the communication of news; a complaint against a person presented in court (*Oxford English Dictionary*, 1961, p. 274). By the end of the following decade, however, mathematicians and engineers had forced a dramatic break with these past usages (*Oxford English Dictionary Supplement*, 1976, pp. 300–301). Their development of statistical formulae for measuring the amount of "information" within a system proved of immediate utility to communication engineers trying to design cost-efficient transmission channels of appropriate bandwidth, or information-carrying capacity (Wiener, 1961, p. 11). Yet the "mathematical theory of communication" depended upon a dramatic redefinition of information itself—a redefinition which transformed "information" into an encompassing category of apparently sweeping relevance and explanatory potential (Shannon and Weaver, 1959; Weaver 1949). Information, these theorists asserted, was a measure of organization, pattern, structure, or—in Krippendorff's recent treatment (1984)—of a potential for organizational work. "[T]here is a widespread feeling," wrote one scientist receptive to information theory's universalistic ambition, ". . . that information theory is basic to a thoroughgoing consideration of all organized systems" (Branson, 1953, p. 84).

The new "information theory" promised to unlock the inner workings of diverse systems—collections of related entities—"from steam engines to human societies," as one of the eminent participants in a conference underwritten by the Macy Foundation put it (von Foerster, Mead, and Teuber, 1955, p. 70). In 1950, for example, an article in the *American Scientist* declared that "consideration of the effects of information storage and information transfer on physical, chemical, biological, psychological, and sociological systems" might well "help in understanding and predicting many of the aspects of our universe" (Raymond, 1950, p. 278). Early confirmation of the value of this approach appeared evident in a contemporary breakthrough in biology: the discovery of the precise sequence of the DNA molecule, which formed "the code which carries the genetical information" (Watson and Crick, 1953, p. 965; Yoxen, 1984, p. 18). A hitherto-undetected but potentially vital informational component of physical, chemical, biological, and even social systems could be sought after and, it was believed, explicitly specified.[1]

However, despite significant refinement and conceptual augmentation (e.g., von Bertalanffy's [1950] "open systems" concept), information theory encountered difficulties when applied to social "systems." These difficulties were due largely to an overwhelming tendency to operationalize the system concept in mechanistic terms. To yield the secrets of their structure, systems required rigorous codification: of input and output "variables," their "values," and above all, their behavioral relationships. This process of codification tended in practice to impose a formal, mechanistic order on the contingent, conditional, and often unclearly interrelated historical realm of human social agency.

Compared with telephone networks and even with biological organ-

---

1. Ten renowned conferences on "circular causal and feedback mechanisms in biological and social systems"—"cybernetics"—sponsored by the Josiah Macy, Jr., Foundation, did much to familiarize researchers from engineering, mathematics, physiology, psychiatry, anthropology, chemistry, philosophy, and other fields with emerging concepts of information theory. A considerable portion of the conferees' time was spent attempting to discern the relevance of notions of "control," "feedback," "homeostasis," and other concepts associated with information theory for their host fields. This early conviction that the search for an informational component of analysis might be extended usefully to *any* system in fact facilitated development of increasingly precise knowledge of the informational workings of diverse systems. To biology, especially, information theory has proven a powerful stimulus to improved understanding. And, on the other hand, growing knowledge of biological information processing suggests that such "natural systems" may offer vital clues to problems currently faced by designers of "artificial" information networks. As one researcher puts it, "[i]nformation processing is ubiquitous in natural systems," and computer scientists seek to deepen understanding of "architecture, data structures, and algorithms" by "viewing them in both natural and artificial settings" (Sampson, 1984, pp. 4, 5).

isms, societies appeared to be "exceedingly complex systems," whole chunks of which had, of necessity, to be relegated by theorists to "black boxes," whose internal workings "cannot be comprehended," but should be explained at some point further along (Beer, 1958, p. 286).[2] This point, however, never really arrived. Even more damaging, any possible *social* determinants of information had a tendency to drop out of the analysis. "[W]ithout materials there is nothing and without energy nothing happens," wrote one borrower from this tradition, "But without information, nothing has meaning: materials are formless, motion is aimless" (Oettinger, 1980, p. 192). Were there really *no* irreducibly *social* agencies and *historical* relationships conditioning the organization and use of information, energy, and matter? Information theorists implicitly identified the essential structuring agency of all systems in information itself. They not only sought an informational *component* of organized systems, that is, but also hoped to develop a unique informational *plane of analysis* to explain its operative features. Therefore they sidestepped the possibility that information—at least in social "systems"—might be a systematic *product* of social institutions. Though matters of indifference to information theorists, the following questions must be, in fact, critically relevant: What social forces structure information? How have they developed? Over what range of "systems" do they operate?

A quite different school of thought *did* attempt to elucidate a social framework for information. By the late 1960s and early 1970s, theorists of an emerging "postindustrial" or, later, "information" society became prominent. Postindustrialists argued that new "intellectual technologies"—above all, the computer—were dramatically discontinuous with earlier systems of information processing and control. The new technologies would be as central to the emerging society as "machine technology" had been to its industrial predecessor. Postindustrialists often claimed to find a "new class" of white-collar employees—"knowledge professionals" or "information workers"—constituting the preponderant segment of the workforce in the developed market economies. Finally, they argued that information itself had become the transforming resource of social organization. For Daniel Bell, and for those generally lesser thinkers who followed him, the postindustrial society broke with and transcended the elemental re-

2. "The most complex situations we have heard discussed are the stabilities engendered by inverse feedback in social structures of isolated communites reported principally by social anthropologists" (von Foerster, Mead, and Teuber, 1955, p. 74).

lations including, most crucially, the opposition between capital and labor, which had shaped its antecedent (Kumar, 1978). Knowledge was supplanting capital and labor as the decisive factor of production.

There were ideological advantages to be derived by declaring that postindustrial society constituted a radical break with the past. By emphasizing discontinuity, however, it was the rather dismal visage of the *present* that was obscured. Notable were the selective silences in the writings of the postindustrialists and their successors: about the crisis of empire occasioned by the devastating political and economic impacts of the U.S. war in Vietnam; about the abrupt economic slowdown—to which intensifying international competition both contributed and responded—that threatened to undercut the brief "American century"; and about the unprecedented transnationalization of the entire market economy. Rather than attempting to contextualize the important changes in the information sector that they did identify within these determining historical circumstances, the postindustrialists chose to abstract from them. Information society analysts such as Harlan Cleveland carried this tendency to yet greater lengths. Cleveland (1985, p. 20), ironically, even criticized Daniel Bell for his coinage, the "postindustrial society," on the grounds that the term put too little distance between a promising future and a somewhat rusty past:

> Can't we find a term for the future that goes beyond saying it comes after the past? Surely *postindustrial* is too reductionist a tag for so different and exciting a prospect, and too economic a name for a period in which the discoveries of science, the innovations of technology, and integrative thinking about politics, culture, and psychology will be at least as important as economic analysis to an understanding of what's going on.

Yet an even more basic conceptual flaw was also evident throughout the writings of the postindustrialists. They commonly pinpointed the source of information's economic value in supposedly intrinsic attributes of information itself. "The information resource," claimed Cleveland (ibid, p.33), "in short, is different in kind from other resources"—as if, in finding that a shoe is not a table, he had somehow fixed at last on the former's essential economic nature. Not subject to the laws of thermodynamics, according to Cleveland (ibid, pp. 25, 34), information is "expandable, compressible, substitutable, transportable, leaky, shareable." These "inherent characteristics" were held to furnish the vital clue to information's mounting economic importance (ibid, p. 29). Such claims have grown frequent; Jane Yurow, for example, warns that because information is different from other goods, "markets for information products may not operate in the same ways as markets for tangible commodities" (Yurow et al., 1981, p. 54).

This reasoning resurrects a longstanding economic fallacy. As Hilferding pointed out at the beginning of the 20th century, such a theory of economic value invalidly relies upon categories that "are natural and eternal entities" (Hilferding, 1984, pp.132–133). It substitutes for the essential historical development of social relations *among persons* the purportedly immanent qualities of things. Why was not the status of information a major topic of economic theory in 1700, 1800, or 1900? Why was it only in the postwar period that the economic role and value of information took on such palpable importance?[3] With such questions the advocates of information's innately distinctive economic role are, of necessity, unconcerned. They find it difficult to explain the history of their own subject without retreating into technological determinism: the "computer revolution" becomes responsible for the unprecedented visibility and economic significance of information. But this is no answer. For why was there a "computer revolution"? Why only in the postwar era? Why predominantly in the developed market economies? And what kind of an upheaval did this "revolution" actually portend?

We will not comprehend why and how information becomes economically valuable by beginning from its own supposedly intrinsic attributes; we cannot uncover its real social framework in this fashion. What if, however, quite the contrary, we suppose that information is *not* inherently valuable? What if, that is, only a profound social reorganization can permit information to become valuable? What sort of historical changes would be required for such a sweeping and dramatic revaluation?

To answer these questions we will introduce a key distinction of our own: between information as a resource and information as a commodity. Using this elemental distinction we may grasp the nature of information in society.

---

3. A fourth tradition of thinking about information did in fact emerge as an outgrowth of conventional economic theory, at the same time that businesses began systematically to confront the issue of costs associated with early generations of digital computer technology. Associated with analysts such as Kenneth Arrow, Kenneth Boulding, Fritz Machlup, Marc Porat, and George Stigler, the tradition of conventional economic theory concerned with information cannot be evaluated here, other than to note that it overlaps at points with the postindustrialists' treatment of information, developed below.

A resource is something of actual or potential use. That is all. The soil, the sea, and the spectrum are resources. But all resources are not commodities. Only under particular conditions can they be transformed into commodities. A resource is anything of use, anytime, anywhere, to anyone; but a commodity, as we shall see, bears the stamp of society and of history in its very core.

Lacking this distinction, the information society theorists lead on to an erroneous consideration of how information is innately different from other resources. Employing it, however, permits us to consider how information is socially identical to other commodities. For the moment we begin to study the production and use of information resources within history, we find that they have experienced the same series of changes in social organization as other resources claimed by capitalism and transformed by it into commodities: *all are produced increasingly by wage labor within and for a market.*[4] Oblivious to this social transformation, information society analysts evince an implicit willingness to treat *all* resources, including information, as commodities. Employing it, however, we enter the domain of political economy, which seeks to comprehend the historical evolution of the market economy itself.

It might have been assumed that political economy would be at the forefront of the social analysis of information. Yet the third major way of thinking about information, stemming from political economy, paradoxically dismisses an economic role for information altogether. This line of reasoning holds that activities such as advertising, market research, law, financial services, and other information-intensive pursuits are simply not productive. As with the two previous schools of thought, this theoretical tradition yields useful insights upon investigation.

Advocates of this view assert that informational functions such as advertising are unnecessary—even harmful—and that, therefore, they should not be treated in the same fashion as such clearly beneficial pursuits as farming, steel production, and automobile assembly. Prominent exponents of this position are Baran and Sweezy (1966, p. 125), who, after arguing trenchantly that advertising "constitutes as much an integral part of the system as the giant corporation itself," go on to claim that, nonetheless, advertising expenses "are manifestly unrelated to necessary costs of production and distribution—however broadly defined" (ibid.,p.122).

4. It is to the historical explication and analysis of this fundamental claim that my forthcoming work, *The Information Commodity*, is devoted.

These writers justify their argument on both moral and theoretical grounds. Baran and Sweezy echo a longstanding concern to differentiate and support "useful" as against "unuseful" social labor. In the early 19th-century United States, this distinction was central for journeyman artisans who contrasted their own productive crafts with the connivings of "monopolists" and "speculators." The latter, personified by lawyers and bankers, were hastening the expansion and rigidification of wage relationships (Wilentz, 1984). But the distinction between producers and nonproducers has persisted down to the present as a widespread mistrust of "parasitic" paper-pushers and other members of information-intensive occupations.

A theoretical argument seems to lend this suspicion credibility. When reduced to its essentials, the argument runs as follows: no matter how important to the functioning of the market economy, virtually all of the information-intensive employments fall within the sphere of circulation of capital and not of production. Once assembled, a car must indeed be advertised, marketed, and financed, but these functions are ancillary to the production of the automobile itself. They add no new value to it in their own right. To the older strata of "surplus eaters"—unproductive participants in the economy—are added, in this view, a virtual host of new ones: "corporate and government bureaucrats, bankers and lawyers, advertising copy writers and public relations experts, stockbrokers and insurance agents, realtors and morticians, and so on and on seemingly without limit" (Baran and Sweezy, 1966, p.127). All are part of a vast social wastage created by the need to dispose of a mushrooming economic surplus under conditions of monopoly capital.

This logic, however, is flawed—on three counts. First, the occupations comprised by the category of circulation clearly do not constitute the entire information sector. Scientific research, engineering, and development, for example, cannot be included in circulation; and what about the labor of journalists, teachers, and librarians? The information-intensive occupations evidently cannot be conceptualized as existing solely within the domain of circulation. Second, it can be argued that the distance between circulation and production has itself narrowed dramatically. Advertising, market research, research and development, even financing, have today grown ever more tightly coupled to production and distribution, particularly in the consumer goods sector. Toothpastes, detergents, and deodorants, for instance, are not produced today until exhaustive research has identified which product features, market locations, and demographic groups should be targeted to facilitate maximum sales. For this reason it is increasingly impossible in practice to disentangle "circulation" from "production," as the activities that make up both tend to fuse ever more tightly together. Finally, the occupations consigned to circulation by these analysts have themselves changed fundamentally since the mid-19th century, when the dichotomy between productive and unproductive labor first took shape. This crucial issue requires amplification.

"[F]or labour to be designated productive," wrote Marx (1977, p. 1044), "qualities are required which are utterly unconnected with the *specific content* of the labour, with its particular utility or the use-value in which it is objectified. Hence labour with *the same content* can be either productive or unproductive.

> For instance, Milton, who wrote *Paradise Lost,* was an unproductive worker. On the other hand, a writer who turns out work for his publisher in factory style is a productive worker. Milton produced his *Paradise Lost* as a silkworm produces silk, as the activation of *his own* nature. He later sold his product for £5 and thus became a merchant. But the literary proletarian of Leipzig who produces books, such as compendia on political economy, at the behest of his publisher is pretty nearly a productive worker since his production is taken over by capital and only occurs in order to increase it. A singer who sings like a bird is an unproductive worker. If she sells her song for money, she is to that extent a wage-labourer or merchant. But if the same singer is engaged by an entrepreneur who makes her sing to make money, then she becomes a productive worker, since she *produces* capital directly. A schoolmaster who instructs others is not a productive worker. But a schoolmaster who works for wages in an institution along with others, using his own labour to increase the money of the entrepreneur who owns the knowledge-mongering institution, is a productive worker. (Emphases in original)

That labor is productive, in other words, which creates a surplus for a capitalist over and above the wealth which it consumes in order to be capable of producing at all (Roll, 1956, p. 129). No matter how repellent the function of a given kind of labor, it is productive if it "is taken over by capital" so as to contribute to accumulation by means of the wage relationship and market exchange.

As late as the mid-19th century, the majority of the information-intensive activities dismissed as unproductive by Baran and Sweezy were performed, if at all, by self-employed individuals. Law, finance, accounting, advertising, research and development, and so forth were neither organized as autonomous capitalist enterprises, nor yet assimilated within the division of labor of the giant firm. Instead they were carried out almost exclusively by individuals or partners brokering their services to capital in exchange for money; no capitalist directly appropriated their own surplus, and thus they did not contribute to capital's productive self-expansion. For this reason Marx himself dismissed them as "peripheral phenomena" that can be ignored when considering capitalist production as a whole" (Marx 1977, p. 1048).

Information services were not, however, to be left permanently to the realm of self-employment (Garnham, 1979). Marx left open the possibility that the definition of productive labor could broaden with the historically expanding arena of capitalist production: "for the most part, work of this sort has scarcely reached the stage of being subsumed even formally under capital, and belongs essentially to a transitional stage" (ibid, p. 1044; see also Harvey, 1982, pp. 104–5).

Today, these once "peripheral phenomena" have become profoundly more important. The complex historical processes that contributed to the ability of capital to impose wage relationships on an ever-increasing proportion of all social labor cannot be adequately explored here. Technical innovation, however, especially in the areas of information storage, processing, replication, and distribution, hastened the separation across a growing range of employments, of the producer from both the product and the process of production. The expanding scale of capitalist enterprise in turn demanded and made possible both continuing technical innovation in information technology and a colossal expansion of the whole gamut of business services performed by Baran and Sweezy's "surplus eaters." The latter, however, were not surplus eaters at all. Drawn into the giant firm or entering the employ of specialized service corporations, formerly self-employed professionals were instead increasingly transformed into directly productive wage laborers. Their labor not only contributed to the value of the automobile, to put it another way, but also, more importantly, produced a surplus for the owners of accounting firms, advertising agencies, research and development laboratories, public relations companies, and corporate marketing departments. This trend is continuing—indeed, accelerating—across the fields of education, librarianship, and medicine, among others.

In contrast, Baran and Sweezy abstract from the elemental and historically dynamic relationship that *is* capitalism—the wage relation—in favor of a Sisyphean attempt to distinguish productive from unproductive labor in terms of a hypostasized set of productive activities. They first confuse socially useful or desirable activity with economically productive labor, and then try to determine whether a given pursuit is productive on the basis of its contribution to a now quite arbitrarily truncated "basic" sector of the economy. Their argument is thus essentially ahistorical and comes perilously near to advancing a modern variant of the fallacy introduced by the economists known as the Physiocrats in the late 18th century: that only that labor is productive that works on the land, in agriculture. In its modern form, the argument stresses both agriculture and manufacturing; it may even allow that the zone of productive labor comprises the "material" production of goods as a whole. In either case it is only by fiat that information-intensive (and a range of other) labor is consigned to the unproductive realm. Such a view takes totally insufficient account of the fact that capitalism, in its essence a dynamic form of social organization forever dependent on identifying and exploiting new areas of social labor, has moved from agriculture to manufacturing *and beyond* over the course of its own history.

Such an argument, finally, also engenders a profoundly misleading analysis of the basic changes now taking place in the economy. In a recent issue, the editors of *Monthly Review* published an article documenting the so-called "strange recovery" of 1983–1984 (Sweezy and Magdoff, 1985). The article presented data on investment in producers' durable goods—the machinery, equipment, and transportation apparatus, as well as structures, whose use undergirds the entire U.S. economy. The data showed that investment in "high-tech" products, including computing, accounting, and office machines, communication equipment, and instruments, far outstripped investment in traditional agricultural and manufacturing equipment over the 1979–1984 period.

This portrait of capital investment trends cannot be challenged. By 1985, in aggregate (1982 dollars), corporate outlays for such high-tech products made up an astounding 36 percent of nonresidential purchases of producers' durable goods; this proportion had increased steadily since the 1940s, but accelerated markedly in the wake of the 1974–1975 recession (Schiller, forthcoming; U.S. Department of Commerce, 1986a, 1986b). Electronic products moved ahead of factory machinery and mobile equipment to become the largest single category of capital equipment spending in 1985 (Winter, 1986). The crucial question is what to make of these striking facts.

Sweezy and Magdoff view this spectacular change in the overall character of capital investment as "for the most part concerned with making money rather than with making goods" (Sweezy and Magdoff, 1985, p. 6). The billions upon billions of dollars invested in computers, telecommunications networks, office equipment, and advanced instrumentation of every kind "have less to do with production than with finance" (ibid.), and merely "sustain and foster speculative fevers in the process of servicing customers, designing strategies for investment and speculation, and inventing new instruments for speculation" (ibid., p. 7). In contrast to some of the technological revolutions of the past, which "have served to lift capitalist economies out of a stage of stagnation and to set in motion a long period of rapid growth" (ibid., p. 9), information technology yields scant economic promise. This is because the new electronic and communication technologies ostensibly have had but "minor secondary effects" in the areas of manufacturing and construction—"the basic industries" (ibid.). Far from heralding a new wave of capitalist expansion, information technology in this view betokens only a more serious phase of stagnation giving rise to rampant speculation.

Neither the general tendency to chronic economic stagnation nor the specific "speculative fevers" so much in evidence today, both of which the editors of *Monthly Review* have done so much to document and analyze, can be doubted. However, owing to their a priori assignment of productive labor to one historically antecedent segment of the overall economy—the "basic industries" of agriculture, construction, and manufacturing—Sweezy and Magdoff simply refuse to recognize the empirically observable and continually escalating contributions of the new information technology across and throughout all economic sectors. This refusal is made simpler, and more palatable, because in the article under review the authors treat the United States economy strictly in national terms. That the prime unit of economic activity is today the transnational corporation—a fact of which these authors are well aware, having written eloquently about it elsewhere—in this analysis disappears from view. So too does the fact that these transnationals, by far the most important source of demand for the high-tech capital investments described above, are employing the latter precisely to unify, control, and further expand their productive profit-making activities on a global scale.

By the 1980s satellites were being utilized to interconnect computerized printing facilities of newspapers such as the *Wall Street Journal, USA Today,* the Toronto *Globe and Mail,* and the *Financial Times,* permitting them to garner advertising revenues in national and transnational markets. Research and development laboratories shared data and sophisticated information-processing capabilities across borders by means of "packet-switched" computer networks. Book publishers deployed computer systems to facilitate tighter inventory control and to expedite distribution among publishers, wholesalers, retail chains, and libraries. Credit reporting and financial information services migrated to electronic networks to deliver data, "treasury management" programs, and even money itself, to corporate subscribers. Manufacturers like General Motors and Boeing moved to link engineering and design directly to production, and to integrate "islands" of automated machinery, through transnational computer-communications systems. Agribusiness combines and energy companies relied on satellite remote sensing to monitor global harvests and to search out oil and mineral deposits. Are these manifold evidences of the integration of information technology into production and distribution simply to be dismissed as economic waste?

And what about the labor of the millions of wage-earners today engaged, directly and indirectly, in the use of these new information technologies? Utilizing the new productive processes supported by continuing massive capital investments in such technology, these workers create both conventional goods and, especially, information products and services. Heavily concentrated in the United States and other developed market economies, information services employment is one of the fastest-growing segments of the labor force. Employment in computer and data processing services between 1974 and 1984 more than tripled; job growth in advertising—a comparative laggard in the area of the economy known as business services, which includes most contract information services—was still more than twice as large as the overall industrial average (Howe, 1986, pp. 29, 33). Over this same decade, the number of nonsupervisory employees in the entire business services industry doubled, to just over 4 million (ibid., p. 34)[5]—showing a rate of growth no less than four times that of the nonagricultural economy as a whole. And this of course does not include the additional information service workers laboring within diversified transnational corporations as inhouse employees. Can these millions of wage-earners continue to be thought of merely as unproductive laborers?

First in agriculture, then in manufacturing, and subsequently elsewhere, capitalist forms of economic organization have continued to take hold of production (Mandel, 1978). To claim otherwise is to reveal an arbitrary blindspot to the fundamental trends within the political economy, centering on the crucial role of communications and information, that Dallas Smythe (1977) identified a few years ago. Al-

5. It must be added at once that the business services category lumps together very disparate kinds of jobs, including both computer experts and janitors, management consultants and watchguards. Nevertheless, the segment of the business services job category devoted to information-intensive services—and it is a very substantial component, probably more than half the total—itself registered employment gains generally far in excess of those characteristic of the overall economy (Howe, 1986).

though the prospect of a national economy whose role in the emerging transnational division of labor centers on services (and military industries) may be abhorrent, that economy has only extended capitalist commodity production to new spheres. It therefore remains economically productive. Indeed, it could be argued that, despite the tendency to stagnation so evident today, an emerging information industry exhibits exactly those features characteristic of previous leading-edge sectors, such as the railroad, electrical, and automotive industries, each of which spearheaded sustained economic expansion in its era.

CONCLUSION

Wage labor and markets are themselves always incomplete products of human social organization. Neither burst suddenly on the scene in finished form; indeed, their constant expansion has been the chief task confronted by capital. Wage relations emerged very unevenly, often the result of protracted struggles over the character and control of production in particular trades. The development of the market into an increasingly encompassing and integrated mechanism for commodity exchange has also been a slow process. To it, the state, communications and transportation technologies, and an intensifying need to dispose of surpluses made decisive contributions. The penetration of capitalism has thus always been and today continues to be a dynamic and unfinished process.

It is a process that has two basic dimensions: as new peoples are brought under the wage relationship, new products, services and productive processes facilitate the self-expansion of capital throughout growing segments of social life. Its "endpoint," assuming that neither Armageddon nor basic social transformation intervenes, can come only where *all* social labor is waged and *all* products and services are exchanged only as marketed commodities. What is significant today is, above all, the "progress" toward this theoretical endpoint. The wage form *is* far more universal than at any previous time, the impact of automation notwithstanding; over the course of the present century it has been imposed globally, making especially impressive inroads in the so-called less-developed countries. Within the developed market economies the wage has also continued to advance, extending lately to embrace formerly independent professionals and an unprecedented proportion of women. Over this century, at the same time, the world market has been woven ever more tightly, to the point where now it is made extraordinarily difficult—politically, economically, and, frequently, militarily—for any country or region to extricate itself or to maintain itself after its initial extrication.

This then is the historical and analytical matrix within which the contemporary transformation of information must be situated. As against the information theorists' claim that information denotes organization, we say yes, but information *itself* is conditioned and structured by the social institutions and relations in which it is embedded. These social relations are today creating a very specific form of organization—capitalist organization—across an unprecedented range. As against the postindustrialists' assertion that the value of information derives from its inherent attributes as a resource, we counter that its value stems uniquely from its transformation into a commodity—a resource socially revalued and redefined through progressive historical application of wage labor and the market to its production and exchange. The wage has been imposed continually on new fields of social labor including, particularly over the past century, information. Markets have been developed as the determining exchange mechanism for an ever-expanding spectrum of commodities including, especially since the Second World War, information. For these reasons, finally, as against those political economists who dismiss the information sector as unproductive, we insist that the information commodity has become the prime site of contemporary expansion within and for the world market system.

REFERENCES

American Express (1982). Advertisement. *Wall Street Journal,* 25 October.

Baran, P., and P. Sweezy (1966). *Monopoly Capital.* New York: Monthly Review.

Beer, S. (1958). "The Irrelevance of Automation." *Cybernetica*, 1, 4, pp. 280–95.

Branson, H. R. (1953). "Information Theory and the Structure of Proteins." In H. Quastler (ed.) *Essays on the Use of Information Theory in Biology*. Urbana: University of Illinois Press.

Cleveland, H. (1985). *The Knowledge Executive.* New York: Dutton.

Garnham, N. (1979). "Contribution to a Political Economy of Mass-Communication." *Media Culture & Society,* 1, pp. 123–46.

Harvey, D. (1982). *The Limits To Capital.* Chicago: University of Chicago Press.

Hilferding, R. (1984). "Bohm-Bawerk's Criticism Of Marx." In P. Sweezy (ed.) *Karl Marx and the Close of His System: Bohm-Bawerk's Criticism of Marx*. Philadelphia: Orion.

Horton, F. W., Jr. (1983). "Rethinking the Role of Information." *Government Computer News,* April, pp. 1, 24.

Howe, W. (1986). "The Business Services Industry Sets Pace in Employment Growth." *Monthly Labor Review,* 109, 4, pp. 29–36.

Krippendorff, K. (1984). "Information, Information Society, and Some Marxian Propositions." Paper presented at the 34th Annual International Communication Association Conference, San Francisco, 24–28 May.

Kumar, K. (1978). *Prophecy and Progress: The Sociology of Industrial and Post-Industrial Society.* New York: Penguin.

Mandel, E. (1978). *Late Capitalism.* London: Verso.

Marx, K. (1977). "Results of the Immediate Process of Production." In *Capital,* vol. 1 New York: Vintage.

Oettinger, A. (1980). "Information Resources: Knowledge and Power in the 21st Century." *Science,* 209, 4 July, pp. 191–98.

Oxford English Dictionary (1933/1961). Vol 5. Oxford: Clarendon Press.

Oxford English Dictionary Supplement (1976). R. W. Burchfield (ed.) vol 2. Oxford: Clarendon Press.

Raymond, R. (1950). "Communication, Entropy, and Life." *American Scientist,* 38, pp. 273–78.

Roll, E. (1956). *A History of Economic Thought.* 3d ed. Englewood Cliffs, N.J.: Prentice-Hall.

Sampson, J. R. (1984). *Biological Information Processing: Current Theory and Computer Simulation.* New York: John Wiley & Sons.

Schiller, D. (forthcoming). *The Information Commodity.*

Shannon, C., and W. Weaver (1959). *The Mathematical Theory of Communication.* Urbana: University of Illinois Press.

Smythe, D. (1977). "Communication: Blindspot of Western Marxism." *Canadian Journal of Political and Social Theory,* 1, 3, pp. 1–27.

Spero, J. (1982). "Information: The Policy Void." *Foreign Policy,* no. 48, Fall, pp. 139–56.

Sweezy, P., and H. Magdoff (1985). "The Strange Recovery of 1983–1984." *Monthly Review,* 37, 5, pp. 1–11.

U.S. Department of Commerce (1986a). *Survey of Current Business,* vol. 66, no. 7, table 5.7, p. 60. Washington, D.C.: Government Printing Office.

U.S. Department of Commerce (1986b). *The National Income and Product Accounts of the United States, 1929–82,*table 5.7, pp. 234–35. Washington, D.C.: Government Printing Office.

von Bertalanffy, L. (1950). "The Theory of Open Systems in Physics and Biology." *Science,* 111, 13 January, pp. 23–29.

von Foerster, H.; M. Mead; and H. L. Teuber (eds.) (1955). *Cybernetics: Circular, Causal, And Feedback Mechanisms In Biological and Social Systems.* Transactions of the 10th Conference, 22–24 April, Princeton. New York: Josiah Macy, Jr., Foundation.

Watson, J., and F. Crick (1953). "Genetical Implications of the Structure of Deoxyribonucleic Acid." *Nature,* 171, pp. 964–67.

Weaver, W. (1949). "The Mathematics of Communication." *Scientific American,* 181, 1, pp. 11–15.

Weiner, N. (1961). *Cybernetics.* Cambridge: MIT. (Originally published in 1948.)

Wilentz, S. (1984). *Chants Democratic.* New York: Oxford University.

Winter, R. (1986). "Forecast for '86 Capital Outlays Improves." *Wall Street Journal,* 30 April.

Yoxen, E. (1984). *The Gene Business.* New York: Harper & Row.

Yurow, J., et al. (1981). *Issues in Information Policy,* Department of Commerce, publication no. NTIA-SP-80-9. Washington, D.C.: Government Printing Office.

3. Cybernetic Capitalism: Information, Technology, Everyday Life

Kevin Robins and Frank Webster

There are some who still fondly imagine that knowledge, casting the clear light of awareness, inspires and contains goodness within itself.
—Dora Russell, *The Religion of the Machine Age*

BEYOND THE ESTABLISHED PARADIGMS

How are scholars interested in communications to make sense of the sea-changes currently taking place there consequent on the arrival of cable, satellite, and other computer-communications technologies? Not unexpectedly, the established paradigms have been drawn upon. Thus Nicholas Garnham, approaching from a perspective of political economy, raised many important points about the historical transformation and the growth of new media/information markets. Emphasizing the strategies of transnational corporations, the current crisis and recession as the contexts within which the new media technologies are being born, the industrialization of culture, and the colonization of leisure, Garnham's approach is conceptually familiar. To the fore is a stress on the economic underpinnings of recent developments and the significance of market principles for shaping the "communications revolution." The function of new technologies is "to develop the market for so-called information goods and services as a new growth sector" that expresses both "the needs of the corporate sector for enhanced communications facilities and the increasingly desperate national search for a share of the international market in high technology products." At the core of analysis and explanation of developments is "the expansion of price and profit" (Garnham, 1983, pp. 11, 14). To Garnham, the economic factor is primary, and it is evidently shaping and indeed intruding deep into the culture and polity.

Perhaps predictably, Garnham's account was soon criticized by someone unsympathetic to his economic reductionism. Ian Connell (1983), insisting on the relative autonomy of the cultural, lays stress on the ideological dimensions and possibilities of the "communications revolution." Starting from the principle that communications are essentially matters of interpretation and that there are limits to the ability of economic forces to shape consciousness, Connell regards Garnham's analysis as an "irrelevance." He is prepared to forego Garnham's structural account, deal "with the potential of things as they are and as they will soon become," and to welcome the potential diversity of programming heralded by new technologies. Taking as given the new technologies and the economic influences bearing upon them, Connell's interest is at an altogether different level, the sphere of consumption, of responses and attitudes toward programs, rather than the sphere of production.

This is an altogether familiar terrain—the ideological versus the political-economic perspective. It is one that we contend is conceptually and empirically inadequate to appreciate present developments. Therefore, this chapter is an attempt at once to criticize and go beyond the presently dominant paradigms by which communications are theorized and at the same time to draw attention to important dimensions of the "communications revolution" that are overlooked by both political economy and textual accounts.

It should be admitted that we are not agnostic as regards the two approaches. We are skeptical about the relevance of Connell's ideological focus on the media to an analysis of the upheavals that we are now experiencing. Indeed, we find naive his faith that the expansion of productive forces (the new technologies) by corporate capital is in some way aloof from social values yet able to proclaim an era that will celebrate the values of abundance and diversity. To some extent, then, this article is intended as a defense and support of Garnham's analysis and argument. Like him, we believe that the "communications revolution" can best be theoretically understood from the perspective of political economy. But having said this, we do not want entirely to align ourselves with Garnham's position. At the heart of our differences with him is the question of what actually constitutes a political economy of the media. For all its value, Garnham's approach comes, in our view, close to being a purely economic analysis of the new technologies. Although it identifies much in the dynamics of the process whereby the "information revolution" is being manufactured, it does not in fact constitute a *political* economy. Garnham's interpretation does not fully explain the transformation we are currently witnessing, and his argument should be pushed further. In the following discussion we seek to sketch some of the elements that are absent in Garnham's analysis in an attempt to offer a more adequate political economy of the new information and communications technologies.

Our hope is that doing this will make it possible to move the argument beyond what has become a sterile debate within, especially, British media studies: the standoff between the advocates of textual/

ideological analysis, on the one hand, and the camp of political economy, on the other. Thus Connell's critique of Garnham—which extends his earlier criticism of the work of Graham Murdock and Peter Golding (Connell, 1978)—grows out of, and reinforces, this theoretical schism. The same polarization is insistently present in Carl Gardner's criticism of Garnham's "reliance on a grossly overdetermining economic analysis"; Garnham, it is suggested, is guilty of "privileging the moment of production and the commercial intentions of the producers." Against this is counterposed a "politics of representation," a consideration of "struggles around meaning" (Gardner, 1984, p. 45). Thus we have two distinct theoretical approaches and emphases glaring at each other across the chasm of the base/superstructure divide (Robins and Webster, 1979; 1987b). Each undoubtedly has its own important insights and truths, and each identifies real weaknesses in the other "school." In our view, however, this theoretical rift has become an obstruction to theoretical bearings. Is there really only a choice between economic analysis (ownership, control) and the "politics of representation"? We believe that both a narrowly economic perspective and a reliance upon ideological/textual analysis fail to bring out some of the most salient aspects of the communications "revolution."

How, then, can we move the debate on? First, and most generally, it is necessary to reject the idea that the current transformation is *simply* an economic/technological process, that it is *simply* a struggle to establish new products and markets in the face of recession. Our approach suggests, against this, that the upheaval we are undergoing is very much a social and political matter: that is to say, the "communications revolution" represents a profound restructuring of social, political, and cultural relationships in the face of a crisis that is very much more than an economic recession. Second, and more particularly, we believe that this approach allows us to identify significant patterns of social change that are inaccessible to textual/ideological theory and to economic analysis in terms of price and profit. There is an important social space that is invisible to any simple base/superstructure conceptions of society, a space hardly explored in British media theory. There is a sphere in which capital seeks to influence, not ideas or profits, but the very rhythms, patterns, pace, texture, and disciplines of everyday life. Within our wider focus upon power relations in society, this represents—to use Foucault's term—the terrain upon which operate the "systems of micro-power." For us, the "communications revolution" is socially significant insofar as it represents a recomposition of the microstructures—and of the experiences—of everyday life. And crucially important here is a consideration of how technologies invest and inform the patterns of culture, of the whole way of life.

In the following discussion we seek to explore some aspects of this approach to the new media/information industries. The analysis is by no means exhaustive; it remains a sketch of some of the crucial issues that are neglected in the articles of Garnham, Connell, and Gardner—issues that center upon the relations between information, technology, and everyday life.

MOBILIZATION, TECHNOLOGY, EVERYDAY LIFE

The present mutation of the culture industries cannot be understood in isolation. We can only develop an adequate political economy if we situate these industries within a wider social and historical context. We seek, therefore, to understand the more momentous changes that are now reverberating through society by reinstating the concept of totality (cf. Jay, 1984) as essential to grasp their significance, scale, and meaning, and we situate these changes within the historical trajectory of the search for capital accumulation and obstacles placed in the way of this endeavor.

The first thing that ought to be emphasized is that the transformation of broadcasting and the mass media is just part of a far wider restructuring of society and social relations, one that has been occasioned by the strategic exploitation of microelectronics (and, to some extent, other new technologies) as an economic and political escape route out of the present crisis. We are witnessing not just the convergence of various new media/information technologies (video, cable, satellite, videotex, personal computers), but also, and more importantly, the convergence and integration of broader, and hitherto discrete, sectors of the electronics industry (particularly data processing and telecommunications). Along with this comes a collision of the interests of corporations operating till now in relatively safe and separate areas (IBM, AT&T, Xerox, RCA, Exxon, etc.). We are talking, then, not simply of sizeable tremors in the media landscape, but, in fact, of a more fundamental restructuring and recomposition of the industrial landscape and, consequently, of the existing pattern of capital accumulation—a transformation that has been described by sociologists like Daniel Bell in terms of the emergence of a new social era, that of "postindustrial society" (see Webster and Robins, 1986, and Robins and Webster, 1987a). What we must be aware of is the fact that the new microelectronics/information technologies are changing not just entertainment and leisure pursuits but, potentially, *all* spheres of society: work (robotics, office technology); political management; policing and military activities (electronic warfare); communication; consumption (electronic funds transfer, retailing technology). If the combined, though disaggregated, forces of multinational corporations and political interests succeed in the systematic introduction of these new technologies—from robotics and data banks to cable television and personal computers—and, particularly, in laying an integrated national electronic grid (the "wired society"), then social life will be transformed in almost all aspects. And two key areas may be highlighted as being of particular political significance: the reconfiguration of the relation between work and leisure (the so-called leisure revolution) and the exploitation of data banks and surveillance technology for control purposes.

The strategic development of microelectronics and information technology will, then, have reverberations throughout the social structures of advanced capitalist societies. The real meaning and significance of this can be more fully grasped if we situate the present upheaval and restructuring in its historical context. But in terms of what kind of history? The history of "technological revolutions"? The economic history of "long waves" in capitalist growth (as theorized by Kondratieff and Schumpeter)? Neither of these, in fact. For the purposes of our political economy we want to draw upon the work of Jean-Paul de Gaudemar (1979), who periodizes capitalist development in terms of the ways in which capital uses labor power and "mobilizes" populations for the production of surplus value. Gaudemar refers to the early 19th century as the period of "absolute mobilization." At this time the traditional way of life of rural populations is systematically undermined in order to create a docile and disciplined factory workforce. This process involves disciplinary efforts, both within the factory and across the fabric of everyday life: on the one hand, the division of labor, waged employment, time-thrift, and the discipline of the "factory-prison"; on the other hand, the undermining of traditional culture (fairs, sports, etc.), the control of social space, and the moralization of the workforce through religion and schooling.

During the course of the 19th century, absolute mobilization is replaced by "relative mobilization." In this process the earlier form of "external" discipline and control—the "policing" of workers—is replaced by an internal factory discipline in which technology now plays a central role and in which control coincides with the goal of productivity and surplus-value extraction: the machine as dual instrument of control and of increased productivity. This line of development finds its apotheosis in the early 20th century with the scientific management of Frederick Winslow Taylor and, particularly, the automated assembly line of Henry Ford. In the Fordist factory the worker is divested of particularity and skill and subordinated to the logic of the machine. In the words of a contemporary American sociologist, "the task of the worker requires simply speed, dexterity, alertness and nervous endurance to carry the 'robot' through dull, monotonous, fatiguing, relentlessly automatic operations" (Dunn, 1929, p. 62). The Fordist plant becomes an integrated and automated complex, a mega-machine that paces and disciplines the workforce. Control is then truly structural. The time-clock and the assembly line prevail. Relations of power, subsumed into the functioning of technology, become automatic and invisible.

Fordism represents, then, the culmination of relative mobilization as a regimen within the factory. But (as with absolute mobilization) relative mobilization, particularly in its Fordist apotheosis, entails more than control over the immediate process of production: it necessitates a restructuring of the relation between factory and the outside world, and, consequently, an extensive recodification of the microstructures of everyday life. In this sense, "Fordism" designates not just a "revolution" in the factory, but also the creation of "a whole way of life." And it is this latter aspect that concerns us particularly for the purposes of our present argument.

What, then, are the components of Fordism as a social system? Four broad and interrelated areas may be identified in what must be a rather cursory overview. First, Fordism entails the progressive intrusion into the sphere of reproduction—leisure, the family, and everyday life—by capitalist social relations.[1] This has occurred largely through the growth of *consumerism as a way of life*, for where there is mass production there must necessarily be mass consumption. As John Alt has argued, "the early social context where social relations and consciousness were largely mediated by the conditions of working class experience has been largely superseded by a socially-private existence mediated by consumerism" (Alt, 1976, pp. 68–69).

Where there once existed a relative independence (pig-rearing, smallholdings, weaving and sewing, etc.), there now exists a thorough dependence upon capitalistically produced and marketed com-

1. Although we refer specifically to Fordism—which evolved during the first half of the twentieth century—we are, of course, describing changes that were emerging throughout the whole period of relative mobilization.

modities (Trachtenberg, 1982). The reproduction of social life is fuelled by the products of capitalist factories—not only its material reproduction, but also, and increasingly, its psychic reproduction.

A second characteristic aspect of Fordism has been the increasing *state intervention in the management of society*. There has been a tendency toward "a more directly political control over the production and reproduction of daily life, extending methods of factory discipline into the state's management of the social totality" (Levidow and Young, 1981, p. 5). Under the conditions of Fordist production—an intricate and technologically mediated division of labor, the integration of conditions of production and reproduction/consumption, the erosion of traditional forms of social integration—society becomes more complexly interrelated and interdependent and also increasingly susceptible to fragmentation and disintegration. In order to ensure the conditions of social integration and cohesion, state management and regulation become indispensable. And this intervention, as Joachim Hirsch has suggested, may take two distinct forms: the state as "both the materially supporting 'caretaker of existence' and the controlling, repressive 'surveillance state'." On the one hand, the state undertakes "bureaucratically organized regulation" in order to guarantee not only the conditions of material production (e.g., economic planning, fiscal policies, scientific research and development), but also those of social reproduction (welfare, social policy). On the other hand, it becomes increasingly implicated in those surveillance and intelligence activities appropriate to what Hirsch calls the "security-state" (Hirsch, 1981, pp. 83, 82, 87).

The third and fourth aspects of Fordism are related and involve the attempted *capitalist annexation of time and space* respectively. Fordism extends and deepens that process through which capital has sought to impose its rhythm and tempo upon time and time-consciousness. The period of relative mobilization has been characterized by "a gradual separation of work time from personal time . . . in which, paradoxically, work time and "leisure" time [have] gradually become more alike" (Thrift, 1981, p. 64).

The times of production and reproduction have become increasingly continuous—an integrated time subject to a calculating and external time-discipline. Time is segmented and compartmentalized according to the different tasks of production/reproduction, divided and subdivided to be used as productively, intensively, and deeply as possible. As Foucault has suggested in another context, "power is articulated directly onto time; it assures its control and guarantees its use" (Foucault, 1979, p. 160). And, like time, so too have space and spatial relations been colonized by capital. For, to quote Foucault again, "discipline proceeds from the distribution of individuals in space" (ibid., p. 141). Under Fordism this has primarily entailed the centralization of social structures in order to ensure monopolization and the efficient functioning of power: the concentration and centralization of productive units, of communications systems, of bureaucratic organizations, of urban structures, and so on. Complementing this is the increasing privatization and marginalization of everyday life, symbolized in the serial mobility of the private car and the isolation of televiewing.

Our argument, then, is that Fordism puts social life under the dual regimen of productivity and discipline. The reign of capital, which began as a revolution in the "manner of production," has become a revolution in the "manner of living" (Granou, 1974). Now, it may appear that the account we have given so far is somewhat functionalist and determinist in the way it presents the unrelenting domination of capital over social life. But let us be clear that we are describing a *tendency*. Let us emphasize that mobilization invokes counter-mobilizaton: the attempt to discipline populations is the struggle to contain and unify an always potentially disruptive and unstable "self-mobilization." Indeed, the present crisis, we would argue, is the consequence of a struggle between the forces of mobilization and counter-mobilization. Characterized by Garnham as essentially an economic matter, it is in fact a crisis of, and a challenge to, Fordism as a way of life. Although Fordism (supported by Keynesian economic strategies) produced a period of economic prosperity and comparative social detente, it also produced other, less desirable, consequences ("side-effects"): ecological pollution, the overexploitation of natural resources, the threat of nuclear annihilation, and so on. In the face of these threats, opposition has been mobilized by diverse social movements (socialists and trade unionists; ecologists; the women's movement; blacks; antiwar campaigners; health campaigners; etc.). Through the current crisis capital struggles to absorb and defuse these movements of protest. So evident now is the devastation wrought by the Fordist "revolution" that it has become necessary to restructure the mode of accumulation and the way of life. And the "information revolution" promises to do exactly this. It offers the possibility of assimilating demands related to the quality of life as the motor of a new phase of accumulation; the new information technologies promise to meet and satisfy the clamor for more freedom, democracy, leisure, decentralization, and individual creativity. According to one observer, "the revolution in telematics is a great *human* revolution, something capable of transforming all our lives as workers, consumers, citizens and individuals" (Butler, 1981, p. 4). That, at least, is the sales-pitch: the reality, as we shall indicate in a moment, is somewhat different.

This long preamble brings us to the crux of our argument. We are now in a position to draw together the threads of our discussion—to assess what is likely to be the real direction of the current restructuring process and the real impact of the new technologies. Thus far we have sketched out a historical context within which to situate these technologies. It is, however, a contextualization that is informed by a particular theoretical and conceptual emphasis: it is through the concept of "mobilization" that we can explore the historical impact of capital—especially through the exploitation of technology—upon the way of life. And it is this theoretical emphasis that allows us to critically examine the probable consequences of information technologies and to ask what the "great human revolution" really adds up to. Our argument is that the so-called information revolution in fact represents a significant new stage in the strategy of relative mobilization—one in which technological domination becomes extensively and systematically used in spheres far beyond the workplace. This "revolution" is both an intensification and, in important ways, a reconfiguration of Fordism as a way of life. Against Garnham's economic emphasis and Connell's stress on ideology and signifying practices, we want to suggest that this seismic shift is important insofar as it represents a restructuring and reorganization of relations of power. What we feel is lacking in most accounts of the new information/communications technologies is consideration of the ways in which they will articulate and express power relations. Particularly important for us is the question of what Foucault calls the "microphysics of power": the ways in which information technologies will provide the filaments through which power and control will invade the social body as a whole; the extent to which integrated cable systems, particularly, will assist and support the "capillary functioning of power" (Foucault). Our concern is with the new technologies as cultural and political forces, ones that will shape and inform the microstructures of everyday life.

WORK AND LEISURE

We can concretize this argument by looking at some of the ways in which social and cultural processes will be transformed by the new technologies; in so doing, we can bring out the nature and significance of those changes that have a bearing on the present recomposition of the media /communications industries. As we have already indicated, information technologies will have a profound impact on work and leisure, and, particularly, on their interrelation. It is clear that, in the "information society," the deskilling of much work will continue under various forms of automation (Shaiken, 1984; Wilkinson, 1983). Moreover, this tendency will extend increasingly to jobs in the service sector, with accelerating office automation and the Taylorization of much intellectual labor. The force of these developments will be felt perhaps most acutely by women workers; whether they work in the factory, the office, or the home, the quality of their daily lives is likely to deteriorate (Huws, 1982, 1984).

Beyond the intensification of work discipline, however, there is another issue that is of more consequence for the present discussion. Here we are referring to the prospect that, as a consequence of rising technological unemployment, the whole relationship between work and leisure may be transformed, and along with it the quality of our everyday lives. André Gorz has argued that "salaried work will by the end of the century have ceased to be the main occupation"; in the "microelectronics revolution," he suggests, "economy of time (of work, of personnel) is the primary objective" (Gorz, 1983, pp. 216, 212).

Gorz pushes the argument further: "In the context of the current crisis and technological revolution it is absolutely impossible to restore full employment by quantitative economic growth. The alternative rather lies in a different way of managing the abolition of work: instead of a society based on mass unemployment, a society can be built in which time has been freed" (Gorz, 1982, p. 3). The choice, he explains, is "*either* a socially controlled, emancipatory abolition of work *or* its oppressive, anti-social abolition" (ibid., p. 8). Gorz confronts the question of how, in a world of disappearing (waged) work and expanding "leisure" time, we shall use the time that has been "liberated." In the "postindustrial society," what will be the content, the experience, the quality, of our everyday lives? We have doubts about Gorz's optimistic faith in our ability to appropriate information technologies for socialist goals (Webster and Robins, 1986, Ch. 4), but we agree with him when he says that the socialist use of time should be defined by our ability to "relearn to apply ourselves to what we do, not because we are paid to do it, but for the leisure of creating, of giving, learning, of establishing non-market and non-hierarchic, practical and affective relations with others" (Gorz, 1983, p. 216).

This objective is important in the face of what capital has in store for us. For what it enthusiastically and ideologically dubs the "leisure revolution" will be quite another matter. If capital has its way, the likelihood is that the realm of "leisure" and "free" time will be further subsumed under the regime of consumerism; the trends apparent in Fordist society will expand and deepen. The more (or less) affluent redundancy of enforced leisure will be serviced from the factories of the culture industry; commodified entertainment and services will be pumped into the individual household in a steady, metered flow. And the tendency will be towards increasingly privatized and passive recreation and consumption. In this consumer Cockaigne, an increasing number of social functions and activities will be mediated by the domestic television console: not just entertainment, but also information services, financial and purchasing transactions, communication, remote working, medical and educational services. Through the television console, and it alone, we shall gain access to what has been called the "network marketplace." In order to become socially and culturally enfranchised, the individual household must necessarily become heavily capitalized, investing in the essential video, communications, videotex, and computing technologies. Technologies will proliferate in the homes to mediate the work of consumption and reproduction, to facilitate the increasingly demanding and complex experience of everyday living. As one enthusiast puts it, "for many consumers, the daily business of living has become sufficiently complex, costly, and labor intensive that some machine assistance is not only feasible but necessary." The answer, she believes, is that "the family's information, record keeping, and communications needs must be responded to electronically through the new technologies of the 1980s" (Jones, 1983, p. 152). Another, more critical, commentator cuts through this bunkum when he suggests that this process is, rather, subordinating the domestic sphere to "the productivist criteria of profitability, speed and conformity to the norm." Through the "information revolution" capital invades the very cracks and pores of social life: "the industrialisation, through home computers, of physical and psychical care and hygiene, children's education, cooking or sexual technique is precisely designed to generate capitalist profits from activities still left to individual fantasy" (Gorz, 1982, p. 84).

TIME AND SPACE

These are forms through which the reach of capital is extended throughout society. And fundamental, now, to these strategies is the exploitation of information technologies. Crucial here is the way in which these technologies can, potentially, extend and deepen capital's hold on temporal and spatial relations. What the "information revolution" means, in the case of time, is the acceleration of that process, which we have already outlined, whereby the sphere of "leisure" and reproduction becomes better subject to time-discipline. Increasingly, "leisure" will become amenable to arrangement by capital, which can now access the consumer via electronic/information consoles capable of penetrating the deepest recesses of the home, the most private and inaccessible spheres to date, offering entertainment, purchases, news, education, and much more round the clock—and priced, metered, and monitored by corporate suppliers. In these ways "free" time becomes increasingly subordinated to the "labor" of consumption.

The great virtue, however, of the new technologies lies in their capacity to transcend the limitations of Fordist time-discipline. For, under Fordism, with its rigid division of the day into work time and reproduction time, there develops both a constraining inflexibility in the exploitation of time and also a limitation on the depth and intensity of (productive) time use. With the combination of work, leisure, and consumption functions in the domestic information terminal, however, the rigid distinction between production (work time) and reproduction ("free" time) may be eroded. Domestic cable networks facilitate the restructuring of patterns of time use on a more flexible and individual basis; they provide the technological means to break the times of working, consumption, and recreation into "pellets" of any duration, which may then be arranged in complex, individualized configurations and shifted to any part of the day or night. The objective is, of course, to intensify and de-rigidify the exploitation of both labor power and "consumption power."

Related to the annexation of time is the colonization of geographic and social space. The impetus of Fordism as a social system was based upon control through the centralization and concentration of spatial structures and relations. The most insistent claim from the architects and ideologues of the "information society" is that the new technologies can halt this centralizing tendency and inaugurate a new era of decentralization. Thus the influential Nora Report argues that information technology "allows the decentralisation of even the autonomy of basic units," such that we can expect the passage "from an industrial, organic society to a polymorphous information society," one that is composed of "innumerable mobile groups" (Nora and Minc, 1980, pp. 126–27). It is, indeed, the case that decentralization is on the agenda. This is apparent in the new "demassified" media (cable, video, citizens' band radio, videotex) that are now undermining those patterns of centralization, synchronization, and standardization characteristic of the *mass* media. These new media, it is suggested, provide tailor-made communication and recreation, promoting thereby greater diversity, choice, and freedom. In the sphere of production, too, there are signs of disillusionment with massive (Fordist) corporations and bureaucracies, and of a growing aspiration toward small, federated enterprises. The new communications technologies are the key to the disseminated factory and enterprise, for they allow productive (and bureaucratic) structures to become fragmented and dispersed—on both a national and international scale—without losing the ability to oversee and coordinate activities. As one techno-enthusiast has commented, "the multinational can now use its communications network to coordinate the activities of decentralised units." This, he suggests, means that "the organisation can have responsiveness *and* control": "decentralised activities can be coordinated as if they were centralised" (Keen, 1981, pp. 149, 141). Flexibility has been gained in production and administration without the loss of control.

Decentralized activities can be coordinated as if they were centralized. This is the important insight. Centralization and decentralization do not represent alternative paradigms of social organization. Rather than representing the road to freedom and democracy, decentralization refines and streamlines the effective exercises of power. First, it should be stressed that the disseminated electronic "cottage industry" or "electronic home" will in fact be embedded within a social structure increasingly subject to the centralizing and managerial tendencies of bureaucratically organized regulation. Large-scale systems for the coordination of national statistical data will promote social modeling, policy making, and management; and centralized mechanisms of administration and regulation will be reinforced by the formation of integrated intelligence systems handling, for example, welfare, social security, or tax data. A further, and crucial, area of centralization is to be found in the formation of police and military information systems. A second point to be made—and to be made emphatically—is that decentralization complements and reinforces such overarching tendencies toward centralization. Decentralization, dissemination, fragmentation, individualization, privatization, isolation, marginalization—these are the modalities through which power will flow through civil society in the "information age." Decentralization of the spaces of production and consumption/reproduction: mobilization and, simultaneously, immobilization.

Our argument, then, is that the "communications revolution" is taking place within a much broader restructuring of social life, one that can be seen—historically and theoretically—as both the extension and the reconfiguration of Fordism. As such, this "revolution" marks a significant extension of relative or technological mobilization to spheres of life beyond the workplace. Through information technologies, with their wide-ranging applications, social life opens up to more effective colonization; the rhythm and social space of everyday life become, potentially, subject to a more certain and effective codification according to the prevailing relations of power. It is this possible mobilization of the time, distribution, and manner of everyday life that constitutes, in our view, an important political and theoretical space between economic analysis (Garnham), on the one hand, and ideological/textual analysis (Connell), on the other. (See Robins, 1983, Robins and Webster, 1983a.)

SOCIETY UNDER SURVEILLANCE

We want now to extend the argument by focusing upon one crucial dimension of the new communications technologies that is usually ignored by media analysts. It is a perspective that allows us to assess the real power and political implications of information technologies, particularly in their impact upon the fine grain of daily life. We are referring here to the intelligence and surveillance capacities of these technologies—an area more familiar, perhaps, to investigative journalists and civil libertarians.

We approach this discussion, to which we have already briefly alluded, by way of a further historical detour. At the end of the 18th century, Jeremy Bentham outlined his plans for an institutional architecture of control. What Bentham devised was a general mechanism—applicable to prisons, asylums, schools, factories—for the automatic and uninterrupted functioning of institutional power and control. This mechanism, the Panopticon, is a building of circular structure with a series of individual cells built around a central "well"; at the center is an inspection tower from which each of the cells could be observed and monitored. A calculated illumination of the cells, along with the darkening and masking of the central tower, endows the "inspective force" with "the unbounded faculty of seeing without being seen" (Bentham, 1843, p. 80). The essence of the Panopticon, Bentham suggests, consists in "the centrality of the inspector's situation, combined with the well-known and most effectual contrivances for *seeing without being seen*." What is of importance, he argues, is "that for the greatest proportion of time possible, each man should actually *be* under inspection"; but it is also desirable "that the persons to be inspected should always feel themselves as if under inspection," for "the greater chance there is, of a given person's being at a given time actually under inspection, the more strong will be the persuasion —the more *intense*, if I may say so, the *feeling*, he has of his being so" (ibid., p. 44). The inspector is apparently omnipresent and omniscient, while the inmates, cut off from the view of each other, are reduced to the status of "solitary and sequestered individuals." The inmate is marginalized, monitored, and, ultimately, self-monitoring: "indulged with perfect liberty within the space allotted to him, in what worse way could he vent his rage, than by beating his head against the walls?" (ibid., p. 47).

Jeremy Bentham considered the Panopticon to be an architectural paradigm capable of generalization. This insight has been developed most fully by Michel Foucault in his historical and philosophical exploration of forms and relations of power. For Foucault, the Panopticon, as a mechanism and edifice for channeling the flow of power, amounts to a major landmark in the history of the human mind. Historically, it represents a bulwark against the mobile disorder of the swarming crowd, against forbidden circulations and "dangerous mixtures." The Panopticon is a form of mobilization—and here Foucault's work intersects with that of Gaudemar—the production of an architecture of control and supervision, eliminating confusion through the elaboration of a permanent grid of power. What Bentham did was to crystallize a sea-change in the social economy of power: his contribution was part of a wider "effort to adjust the mechanisms of power that frame the everyday lives of individuals; an adaptation and a refinement of the machinery that assumes responsibility for and places under surveillance their everyday behaviour, their identity, their activity, their apparently unimportant gestures; another policy for that multiplicity of bodies and forces that constitutes a population" (Foucault, 1979, pp. 77–78).

This policy, according to Foucault, was implemented through the creation of spaces that are at once architectural, functional, and hierarchical. The Panopticon contains "so many cages, so many small theatres, in which each actor is alone, perfectly individualised and constantly visible" (ibid.; p. 200): "the crowd, a compact mass, a locus of multiple exchanges, individualities merging together, a collective effect, is abolished and replaced by a collection of separated individualities. From the point of view of the guardian, it is replaced by a multiplicity that can be numbered and supervised; from the point of view of the inmates, by a sequestered and observed solitude" (ibid.; p. 201). Within the Panoptic machine, the individual "is seen, but he does not see; he is the object of information, never a subject in communication." The inmate is subjected to "a state of conscious and permanent visibility that assures the automatic functioning of power" (ibid.). So insidious are the relations of power that the individual becomes self-monitoring:

> He who is subjected to a field of visibility, and who knows it, assumes responsibility for the constraints of power; he makes them play spontaneously upon himself; he inscribes in himself the power relation in which he simultaneously plays both roles; he becomes the principle of his own subjection. By this very fact, the external power may throw off its physical weight; it tends to the non-corporal; and, the more it approaches this limit, the more constant, profound and permanent are its effects: it is a perpetual victory that avoids any physical confrontation and which is always decided in advance. (Ibid., pp. 202–3)

The Panopticon, then, is a machine that ensures the infinitesimal distribution of power, one that turns the monitored individual into a visible, knowable, and vulnerable *object.* It is a generalizable "type of location of bodies in space, of distribution of individuals in relation to one another, of hierarchical organization, of disposition of centres and channels of power, of definition of the instruments and modes of intervention of power" (ibid.: p. 205). According to Foucault, the Panoptic machine, "at once surveillance and isolation and transparency" (ibid.: p. 249), is an integrated system of surveillance/intelligence and discipline/control.

We believe that Foucault is right in seeing Bentham's Panopticon as a significant event in the history of the human mind. We want to suggest that the new communication and information technologies—particularly in the form of an integrated electronic grid—permit a massive extension and transformation of that same (relative, technological) mobilization to which Bentham's Panoptic principle aspired. What these technologies support, in fact, is the same dissemination of power and control, but freed from the architectural constraints of Bentham's stone and brick prototype. On the basis of the "information revolution," not just the prison or factory, but the social totality, comes to function as the hierarchical and disciplinary Panoptic machine.

If we consider the loops and circuits and grids of what has been called the "wired society" or "wired city" (Aldrich, 1982; Martin, 1978), we can see that a technological system is being constituted to ensure the centralized, and furtive, inspection, observation, surveillance, and documentation of activities on the circumference of society as a whole. Cable television networks, for example, can continuously monitor consumer preferences for programming material, along with details of any financial or communicative transactions. We have the now innumerable, and increasingly interlinked, networks of bureaucratic and commercial data banks that accumulate and aggregate information on the activities, transactions, needs, and desires of individuals or social groups. And, of course, this is the age of the, now mundane, surveillance camera, of telephone tapping, and of ever more sophisticated and integrated police computer systems (Manwaring-White, 1983).[2] This is the real achievement of cable! The population becomes *visible* and *knowable* to the different computerized "inspective forces." Here, as Foucault suggests of the Panopticon, is "a machine for dissociating the see/being seen dyad: in the peripheric ring, one is totally seen, without ever seeing: in the central tower, one sees everything without ever being seen" (Foucault, 1979, p. 202). The individual becomes the object of surveillance, no longer the subject of communication. And, like the Panopticon, the "wired society" too is a "system of individualizing and permanent documentation" (ibid., p. 250): the observed and scrutinized individual, subjected to continuous registration, becomes the object of knowledge (of files and records). Seen and known. Overcoming spatial and temporal constraints, the electronic grid fulfills the dream of an "infinitely minute web of panoptic techniques" (ibid., p. 224).

We are not suggesting that there is, or will be, a single omniscient and all-seeing "inspective force" in the "wired society." The nodal points on the electronic grid will be multiple and differential. There is, of course, the problem—a pressing political and civil liberties issue—of increasingly centralized state and police surveillance/intelligence activities, which, as David Leigh suggests, represent "a very pure form of bureaucratic utopia: the official is kept invisible, and the citizen is stripped naked" (Leigh, 1980, p. 218). This political and repressive use of the new information and communications technologies must always be kept to the fore. But we are also talking of more ordinary and routine surveillance activities, undertaken from more diffuse and numerous power centers. As opposed to the more active and calculative amassing of data by control agencies, there exists also a more passive and mundane gathering and collation, by bureaucratic and commercial organizations, of what has been called "transactional information" (Burnham, 1983). For *any* electronically mediated activity—cable viewing, elctronic financial transactions,

2. To answer the charge that this is a paranoid and unsupportable assertion, we point skeptics to the considerable body of literature documenting the accumulation of command and control technologies and the abuse of them to surveille large sections of the populace (see, for example, Bamford, 1983; Campbell, 1980; Davies, 1985; Davies and Black, 1984a, 1984b; *Guardian,* 1985; Leigh, 1980).

telephoning, for example—spawns records that can yield up a harvest of information about individuals or groups: their whereabouts and movements; daily patterns of work and recreation; contacts, friends, associates; tastes, preferences, desires. Such information, when accumulated and processed, becomes an invaluable asset to a plurality of corporate and political interests. These different, but related, tendencies point to the increasing importance of surveillance and social monitoring. Joel Kovel has, in fact, argued that surveillance is "a process inherently tied to the development of technology." Surveillance, he suggests, originates in the labor process, where there developed a need for "watching the producer and controlling what was being done" (Kovel, 1983, p. 76). This phase in the development of surveillance techniques, which found its apotheosis in Taylor's scientific management and in the Fordist factory, has now been superseded by more extensive and ambitious surveillance:

> The same craft has been taken over by the state as its target shifts to the domestic population. what began with control of the worker and flourished into the technology of Scientific Management in the early years of the century, has turned to directly political ends. Computerised electronic surveillance has ushered in a whole new phase of domination. (Ibid., pp. 76–77)

Technologies, as they have actually existed, have been constituted to watch and control, to control through watching. Information technologies—*actually existing* information technologies—extend this capacity. In them is perfected the ability to mobilize and control through watching and monitoring: power expresses itself as surveillance and panopticism, on the scale of the social totality. The eye of power; the technology of knowledge and control. The cabled electronic grid is a transparent structure in which activities taking place at the periphery—remote working, electronic banking, the consumption of entertainment or information, tele-shopping, communication—are *visible* to the electronic "eye" of the central computer systems that manage the network(s). The "technical" process of administrating the numerous electronic transactions is simultaneously, and integrally, a process of observation, recording, remembering, surveillance. The electronic worker, consumer, or communicator is constantly scanned, and his or her needs/preferences/activities are delivered up as information to the agencies and institutions at the heart of the network. Decentralized, sequestered, privatized activities and lifestyles are monitored from the diverse centers of power/administration. In the panoptic structure of the electronic grid, we find expressed that pattern of centralization and decentralization—of concentrated power and fragmented impotency—which, we have argued, is at the heart of that emerging configuration of social relations referred to ideologically as the "information society." The lives of those on the periphery are subject to constant surveillance and documentation—and, hence, control—from the central observatories of the social Panopticon.

Jeremy Bentham's Panopticon—as the prototype of a regimen of power relations—is, then, a central figure for understanding the modalities of power in the "information society." In the panoptic machine—whether it is constructed of bricks and mortar, or electronic cables—mobilization is achieved through the (serialized, cellular) isolation of individuals, combined with the development for surveillance and intelligence by centralized agencies. Again we would stress that we are exploring terrain inaccessible to economic theory (Garnham) or ideological analysis (Connell): we are concerned with the implications of the new technologies for the deportment of everyday life, for the way in which capital may come to better discipline the very conduct, rhythms, and spaces of day-to-day existence.

KNOWLEDGE, INFORMATION, INTELLIGENCE

Another important, and neglected, aspect of the communications revolution is of particular significance to those involved or interested in the mass media. Many commentators now see the emerging pattern of capital accumulation, the successor to Fordism, in terms of the evolution of an information economy and an "information society." Information is thought to be the key to a new phase of economic growth. And, more ambitiously, freely flowing information is held up as the means to achieve a future libertarian and communicative democracy. Thus Tom Stonier argues that "in a postindustrial society, a country's store of information is its principal asset, its greatest source of wealth" (1983, p. 12)—"as our knowledge expands the world gets wealthier" (ibid., p. 63). He can then go on to suggest that "whereas material transactions can lead to competition, information transactions are much more likely to lead to cooperation—information is a resource which can be truly shared" (ibid., pp. 18–19). And, more fantastically, "no dictator can survive for any length of time in communicative society as the flows of information can no longer be controlled from the centre" (ibid., p. 203). In the present context of social and economic crisis, information offers itself as the principle of redemption (see Williams, 1985).

Although we remain highly skeptical about this putative information utopia, it nonetheless remains the case that a significant mutation is taking place in the social economy of information/knowledge. We have already indicated that the media industries, and, more importantly, the whole of the electronics, telecommunications, and data-processing industries, are undergoing a process of convergence and integration. This upheaval should also be understood as a transformation in the existing structures of information production and circulation—as an important recomposition of the present social ecology of information/knowledge. The way in which this is significant particularly for an understanding of the current mass media "revolution" is brought out in a recent report by the British government's Information Technology Advisory Panel (ITAP). Here it is argued that:

> new technology is eroding many of the distinctions that have previously distinguished one form of information medium from another; publications, films and news services are now all becoming aspects of an expanding "tradeable information sector." (Information Technology Advisory Panel, 1983, p. 11)

And again:

> There is now an expanding "tradeable information sector" which encompasses the supply of financial and business information, printing and publishing, on-line technical information, consultancies, etc. We consider that the entertainment industry and aspects of education and training services fall within this sector, since many of the same technological influences bear upon these activities as upon more obviously "information" activities." (Ibid., p. 7)

Circumstances, then, make it increasingly impossible and irrelevant to treat the mass media in isolation: the culture industries are increasingly becoming subsumed within a massive and overarching information sector, of which they make up but one constituent part.

According to the ITAP report, this emerging information mega-industry divides into trading and nontrading components. The latter category includes certain activities within the private sector (banking, insurance), along with central and local government operations, and (though ITAP does not mention these) military and policing applications. The greatest component of the industry, however, is involved in the trading of various kinds of information ("packaged," "semi-packaged," transient, permanent, skilled judgment, education and training, entertainment [ibid., pp. 12–16]). As to the noncommercial exploitation of information—the bureaucratic and control applications—we have already touched upon this in our brief discussion of surveillance. Bureaucratic social management and police or military surveillance manifest themselves as the compulsive and incessant gathering of what is called "intelligence." What Joachim Hirsch refers to as the modern "security state" accumulates and processes information for the purposes of regulation and control.

But if information is being marshaled in the political domain, it is also circulating on an ever greater scale in the marketplace. Thus we have a veritable explosion of new media commodities: video games, videocassettes and discs, cable and satellite channels, personal computers. And we also have the commodification of new areas of information: "a much wider range of information has become profitable because it can be flexibly processed, selectively rearranged, and quickly transmitted and disseminated by a virtuoso new technology" (Schiller and Schiller, 1982, p. 461). Thus scientific and technological knowledge, demographic information, education, medical care, public reports and statistical services, libraries, and much more all become transformed into information commodities (Lumek, 1984; National Commission on Libraries and Information Science, 1982). Pushing in this same direction is state intervention that seeks to transform what have hitherto been public resources into commercial enterprises. The liberalization and privatization of British Telecom, for example, is part of the strategy to open up the information sphere to market forces. So too is the attempt to hive off government information services to private organizations whenever feasible, and when not, to introduce commercial criteria into the government's own administration of information and statistical services; according to the recent Rayner Report, all information should be charged for at commercial rates. All of this is bound to have serious social implications. We are likely to see an increasing scarcity of information that is not considered to be commercially viable. The available information will be differentially distributed: "hard" (financial, commercial, scientific) data for the wealthy corporate sector; trivial data, through videotex and teletext channels, for the domestic consumer. And, most important, the principle of public knowledgeability, of the availability of information resources as a public service—an ideal imperfectly realized at the best of times—will be undermined (paralleling, of course, the subversion of public service broadcasting [the British Broadcasting Corporation], the decline of library services, and the dismantling of communication publicly owned communication systems [British Telecom]; see Robins and Webster, 1983b; 1985).

Can this amount to an "information revolution"? Does it put us on the threshold of an "information society"? We think not. This political and commercial annexation of information only appears to be a novel occurrence (Robins and Webster, 1987a). The appropriation of information/knowledge, in our view, has roots particularly in the capitalist labor process. Marx described this phenomenon in terms of the tendential separation of mental from manual labor, suggesting that capital strives to monopolize the intellectual aspect of the labor process in order to increase productivity and to ensure control. It is a development that, again, finds it apotheosis in Taylor's scientific management. With scientific management the project of appropriating the skills and knowledge of workers becomes systematic and compulsive. What Taylor realized was that it was to their traditional skills and rule-of-thumb knowledge that his workers owed their independence and resilience in the face of discipline and control. On this basis he undertook

> the deliberate gathering in on the part of those on the management's side of all the great mass of traditional knowledge, which in the past has been in the heads of the workmen, and in the physical skill and knack of the workmen, which he [sic] has acquired through years of experience. The duty of gathering in of [sic] all this great mass of traditional knowledge and recording it, tabulating it, and, in many cases, finally reducing it to laws, rules, and even to mathematical formulae, is voluntarily assumed by the scientific managers. (Taylor, 1974, p. 40)

All "brainwork" Taylor aimed to concentrate in his centralized "planning department." It is with machinery, however, that this gathering in of skill and knowledge can become truly systematic. It is through technology that we see "the separation of the intellectual faculties of the production process from manual labour, and the transformation of those faculties into powers exercised by capital over labour" (K. Marx, 1976, p. 548). With Henry Ford's assembly line this process reaches its historical culmination. Here the skills of the worker are truly embodied in the machinery: control of the labor process assumes the guise of objective necessity, and domination expresses itself through the form of technological "rationality." In the Fordist factory, as one contemporary observer noted, "automatic machines show a transfer of thought, skill or intelligence from person to machine" (Reitell, 1924, p. 41). In the subsequent history of the labor process, this automatic and impersonal functioning of power through the technological appropriation of knowledge/skill has been intensified and extended, including the Taylorization and mechanization, through information technologies, of certain forms of intellectual labor.

Our argument is that this gathering in of skill/knowledge/information, hitherto most apparent in the capitalist labor process, is now entering a new and more pervasive stage. What we are seeing is the progressive collection, centralization, and concentration of knowledge on a wide social scale, and, thereby, the establishment of what we would call Social Taylorism (Webster and Robins, 1986, ch. 11). In an intensive consumer society, as we suggested earlier, needs—material and psychic—are met by commodities. As Ivan Illich suggests, the "professionally engineered commodity" replaces the "culturally shaped use-value," and we see the substitution of "standardized packages for almost everything people formerly did or made on their own" (Illich, 1978, p. 24). The corollary and consequence of this consumerization is a tendential depletion of social skills, knowledge, self-sufficiency. Jeremy Seabrook has written perceptively of the "plundering of people, the shedding of skills, the loss of human resource" and of "the process of wrenching away from working class people needs and satisfactions they had learned to answer for each other, and selling them back, in another form, as commodities" (Seabrook, 1982, pp. 179, 105). We are talking of a process of social deskilling, the depredation of knowledge and skills, which are then sold back in the form of commodities—or, alternatively, professionally administered through bureaucratic agencies and organizations.

It is just this appropriation and concentration of social knowledge and skill that the new information technologies are designed to promote. They underpin a more extensive, efficient, and systematic colonization of social knowledge. Potentially all social functions are to be incorporated and metamorphosed into information commodities: education, entertainment, health care, communication, and so on. According to Mary Gardiner Jones, whom we quoted earlier, we can look forward to

> a flexible, multipurpose information and communication system [which] could encompass not only information, education and entertainment services but also a series of remote control applications to adjust home temperatures and energy use, setting off alarms at a variety of types of intrusion, fires and other hazards, and handling record-keeping, accounting, and bill-paying. (Jones, 1981, p. 36)

In the new information industries, social knowledge and resources will be annexed and alienated. The mass of traditional knowledge, in Taylor's terms, will be recorded, tabulated, and reduced to laws, rules, and mathematical formulae. Through data banks and information services we shall have to buy the information necessary to function in a complex industrial society, or be deprived of it if we are too poor. With the new information technologies, previously dispersed, and inaccessible, information/knowledge can become processed and possessed. We shall see the "migration of information from the home to the organisation," and much of this information, until recently, "would not have been collected at all, but would instead have been stashed away in our homes" (Burnham, 1983, pp. 12, 11).

More than this, people themselves will increasingly be relegated to the status of data; their actions and transactions will be recorded as digits and ciphers by the ubiquitous and always watching information machines. Already credit agencies, finance houses, and large retailers are constructing databases on customers and potential customers, categorizing them, analyzing them, scrutinizing their movements, that they might be used to the optimum benefit of the corporation. In advanced capitalist societies online links give instant access to buying patterns, demographic traits, balances outstanding, and other characteristics. The Direct Mail Sales Bureau advises business to build and access these resources. Introducing the concept of "Precision Management," it observes that "vast sums are being invested by far-sighted marketers to create complex data bases which contain a vast array of information about our various target markets. Thus armed, we can speak to people about that which is relevant [what is saleable] and ignore that which is not relevant [the poor] to their [sic] needs and interests" (advertisement, *Financial Times*, 16 October 1985). The size and scale of these databases can be awesome. For example, in Britain Infolink, the biggest agency of its kind in the United Kingdom, boasts an information bank that includes the entire electoral register of 42 million voters, whom it can review at a rate of 48,000 transactions an hour (Wiltshire, 1986). Increasingly, people are objects of surveillance: objects of knowledge and information.

It is worth adding that, although this surveillance has been developed chiefly as an extension of market endeavors, capital has not been entirely responsible for its spread. The growth of the modern state, integrally connected as it is with the rise of corporate capitalism, has contributed independently and massively to the maximization of surveillance. Anthony Giddens (1985) has recently reminded us of the importance of nationalism, citizenship, war, and the preparation for war as key factors stimulating heightened surveillance (and its converse, control of information dissemination). Inexorably the state has amassed files, increasingly computerized and interlinked, on health, taxation, social security, employment, education, vehicle ownership, housing, crime, and intelligence. In the present period, when the state has noticeably raised its coercive profile in response to social unrest and in order to facilitate the necessary restructuring to regain competitiveness, Giddens' warning of the risks of totalitarianism inherent in states that so intensively scrutinize and manipulate their people deserves close heed (cf. Campbell, 1986; G. Marx, 1985).

As Bentham's Panopticon expresses the social relations of surveillance and control, another figure expresses the social relations of generalized Taylorism. We are referring to H. G. Wells's conception of the World Brain or World Encyclopaedia—the dream of an unlimited, concentrated, and accessible reservoir of knowledge. According to Wells,

> an immense and ever-increasing wealth of knowledge is scattered about the world today, a wealth of knowledge and suggestion that—systematically ordered and generally disseminated—would probably . . . suffice to solve all the mighty difficulties of our age, but that knowledge is still dispersed, unorganised, impotent . . . (1938, p. 47)

The knowledge systems of the world must therefore be concentrated in the World Brain, in the creation of "a new world organ for the collection, indexing, summarising and release of knowledge" (ibid., p. 59). Wells ponders "the creation of an efficient index to *all* human knowledge, ideas and achievements . . . the creation, that is, of a complete planetary memory for all mankind" (ibid., p. 60); "the whole human memory," he believes, "can be, and probably in a short time will be, made accessible to every individual" (ibid., p. 61). For Wells, "the time is ripe for a very extensive revision and modernisation of the intellectual organisation of the world"—(ibid., p. 26): "this synthesis of knowledge is the necessary beginning to the new world" (ibid., p. 64). The world "has to pull its mind together" (ibid.) through this new kind of "mental clearing house," the World Brain (ibid., p. 49).

Nowadays the figure of the World Brain is not an ideological mirage to be mocked and peremptorily dismissed. Like Jeremy Bentham's Panopticon it is a utopian proposal, but one that should be taken seriously. The World Brain is an intellectual "invention" with considerable social and political resonance. It is one that tunes well with the aspirations of police and surveillance agencies; with business corporations like Telerate, Datastream, Reuters, or the now defunct International Reporting Information Systems (IRIS), which sought "to gather in, sort and increase in value by sophisticated analysis the vast amount of information floating around the world" (Saint Jorre, 1983); and with the purveyors of videotex information, who realize that this "can be seen as a system in which the basic structuring imposed on the information according to amount of detail and place in the subject hierarchy . . . makes the Wellsian dream practicable" (Fedida and Malik, 1979, pp. 166–67). The World Brain anticipates what we can now see as an emerging new regime of information production, circulation, consumption, and control; as a new economy and politics of knowledge.

Wells, of course, sees this "new encyclopaedism" as an entirely benevolent phenomenon. His is the Fabian ideal of knowledge as a social resource: knowledge is neutral and contains all goodness within itself. In reality, however, things are somewhat different. What we have in the World Brain is the utopia of technocratic planning, administration, and management. The encyclopaedic dream represents, in fact, a technocratic consummation and travesty of what has been termed the public sphere. In the place of informed debate and interchange and of public knowledgeability (as aspirations, at least), we are left with nothing but the commerce, collation, and manipulation of data. As Jürgen Habermas has demonstrated, the (bourgeois) public sphere has undergone a long process of decline. Historically, we have seen the replacement of a political public sphere by a depoliticized consumer culture that erases the difference between commodity circulation and social intercourse, and by social engineering through the massaging of "public opinion." Critique has become integration, acclamation, consumption (Habermas, 1962, chs. 5–6). The public sphere becomes publicity and public opinion. And now publicity and public opinion assume the diminished and alienated form of the "world encyclopaedia" or "information society." Public debate and discourse have given way to the mindless, avaricious, and indiscriminate amassing of information. For the Fabian Wells—as for the masseurs and diagnosticians of public opinion—it seems self-evident that the free and bountiful flow of information will bring people together. In reality, information can divide them, render them ignorant, silence them, manipulate them, monitor them, alienate and isolate them. For the majority of us, as André Gorz has argued, the "information explosion" does not promise greater freedom or independence:

> The expansion of knowledge rather has gone in parallel with a diminution of the power and autonomy of communities and individuals. In this respect, we may speak of the schizophrenic character of our culture: the more we learn, the more we become helpless, estranged, from ourselves and the surrounding world. This knowledge we are fed is so broken up as to keep us in check and under control rather than to enable us to exercise control. (Gorz, 1976, p. 64)

What is missing in most accounts of the "information society" is an understanding of the way in which knowledge and information mediate relations of power. As we have already suggested, a society of routine and procedural surveillance is one that also, necessarily and automatically, gathers and processes information. Surveillance is also continuous and perpetual intelligence, the recording of existence, and the accumulation and the annexation of knowledge. Surveillance, knowledge, power: in the "information society" there is no one central "planning department" as there is in the Taylorized factory. The centers of power are multiple and differential; the archives of commerce and control are relatively dispersed. But in each of them social knowledge and resources are appropriated and transformed into power and capital. The store of collective knowledge, and of popular memory and tradition, is tendentially displaced by the estranged objectivity of data banks and information reservoirs (Lyotard, 1980). Moreover, information, when it is harvested on a massive and systematic scale, becomes intelligence. Information on natural resources, or on the activities and transactions of individuals, becomes politically significant when it is held in large quantities that can be processed and aggregated by technological means. What we are suggesting, in fact, is that in the "information society" the intelligence function is the paradigm for all information gathering. In the words of one information apparatchik, what we are seeing is

> the maturation of the intelligence function from its origins as a government spy service to full growth as an intellectual discipline serving the private and public sectors alike. . . . Today's proliferation of information banks and analytical centers for investment counselling, political risk assessments, and "futures" estimates are witness to the growth of the intelligence discipline outside traditional government circles. (Colby, 1981, pp. 67–68.

Information is not a thing, an entity; it is a social relation, and in contemporary capitalist societies it expresses the characteristic and prevailing relations of power.

The information industries, then, are undergoing a process of massive institutional transformation, convergence, and integration. Behind the myth of the "information society" there is the reality of a growing commercial and political exploitation of social knowledge and information. What we need in order to respond to this initiative by capital is not a policy for cable, nor simply a media policy, but a politics of information.

CONCLUSION

In this discussion we have tried to outline our difficulties with the approaches of Nicholas Garnham and Ian Connell to the new media technologies and industries. Each grasps particular and important aspects of the new communications "revolution,"and, in our own view, Garnham's work represents an important starting point for research. But crucial dimensions of this "revolution" are overlooked by both Garnham and Connell. We have sought to open up some of these in order to explore the social meanings of the new technologies.

What we have suggested, first, is that media analysts must try to understand the wider social, political, and economic restructuring process that is now shaping the communications "revolution"—a process that entails a significant recomposition of the forms of social mobilization (for example, a transformation of state regulation and "preventive" surveillance). Circumstances now conspire to undermine parochialism, making it impossible for us to be media specialists alone. We have then gone on to argue that this disconcerting "revolution" cannot be understood simply in terms of ideological or economic issues. These aspects *are* important, but we must also understand the current upheaval in terms of the mobilization and transformation of *everyday life*. Of particular interest is the growing importance of technology beyond the workplace—the increasing technological mediation of everyday life; far from being socially neutral, information technologies are beginning to shape the whole way of life and assume a profound cultural significance. The category of "everyday life"—which has led a kind of half-life in the interstices of cultural theory, in the work of such different thinkers as Leon Trotsky, Fernand Braudel, Henri Lefebvre, and Agnes Heller—can help us to see the pervasive and intrusive nature of the "information revolution." For it points to the ways in which the rhythm, texture, and experience of social life—the very segmentation of time and space—are being transformed and informed by capital. And, furthermore, it allows us to see how relations of power penetrate and infuse the social body. This emphasis upon power is central to our own analysis of the new technologies: we are concerned with the ways in which everyday, and apparently insignificant, activities, deportment, and interchanges are disciplined and controlled.[3] This leads us to suggest that the development of integrated and systematic information/communi-

3. We are not unaware of the difficulties in theorizing power, particularly in relation to the question of agency. There is always the danger of falling into conspiracy theory. In the exercise of power, as Foucault observes, "the logic is perfectly clear, the aims decipherable, and yet it is often the case that no one is there to have invented them, and few who can be said to have formulated them." Foucault suggests that "power relations are both intentional and nonsubjective." Theoretically this formulation remains inadequate. It does, however, identify the seeming paradox in our perception of power (see Foucault, 1981, pp. 95, 94).

cations networks significantly transforms the economy of power in society. In our view, society as a whole comes to function as a giant panoptic mechanism: automatic and continuous surveillance, along with centralized power and peripheral isolation, conspire to create a climate in which the inmates of society "not only *suspect*, but [are] assured, that whatever they do is known, even though that should not be the case" (Bentham, 1843, p. 66). The panoptic society is a society of routine and compulsive information gathering. It is, we suggest finally, a society in which the nature and composition of knowledge/information undergoes a radical transformation. In the "information society," we have the massive and systematic exploitation of information (intelligence) by commercial and political interests. Information/knowledge becomes a site—and stake—of the struggle for power.

Our response to the information revolution is somber. We are not talking of what information technologies *might* do; of how cable *could* further democracy *if* it was run by the right people; of the *possibilities* for satellite television or viewdata systems or word processors. We are talking *actually existing* technologies—technologies already constituted to embody particular social relations, technologies that threaten to constitute a mega-machine, a systematic and integrated mechanism (and the more integrated and extensive a technological system, the less possibility there is of its flexible use). We must confront the reality of existing technologies, technologies in the present tense. And we must confront the reality of an "information age" that is now being engineered in Thatcher's Britain. We can expect no utopia courtesy of Ms. Thatcher. If we want one we shall have to invent it ourselves, and the new technologies do not provide a short cut.

REFERENCES

Aldrich, M. (1982). *Videotex: Key to the Wired City*. London: Quiller.

Alt, J. (1976). "Beyond Class: The Decline of Industrial Labor and Leisure," *Telos*, 28, Summer, pp. 55–80.

Bamford, J. (1983). *The Puzzle Palace: America's Security Agency and Its Special Relationship with Britain's GCHQ*. London: Sidgwick and Jackson.

Bentham, J. (1843). *Works,* vol. 4., J. Bowring (ed.). Edinburgh: William Tait.

Burnham, D. (1983). *The Rise of the Computer State*. New York: Random House.

Butler, D. (1981). *Britain and the Information Society*. London: Heyden.

Campbell, D. (1980). "Society Under Surveillance," In Peter Hain (ed.) *Policing the Police,* vol. 2. London: Calder.

Campbell, D. (1986). "The Chilling Effect." *New Statesman*, 24 January, pp. 22–24.
Colby, W. E. (1981). "Intelligence in the 1980s," *Information Society* 1, 1, pp. 53–69.
Connell, I. (1978). "Monopoly Capitalism and the Media," In S. Hibbin (ed.) *Politics, Ideology and the State*. London: Lawrence and Wishart.
Connell, I. (1983). "Commercial Broadcasting and the British Left," *Screen*, 24, 6, pp. 70–80.
Davies, N. (1985). "MI5's Surveillance Machine," *Observer*, 10 March.
Davies, N., and I. Black (1984a). "Subversion and the State," *Guardian*, 17 April.
Davies, N., and I. Black (1984b). "Targets for Covert Action," *Guardian*, 19 April.
Dunn, R. W. (1929). *Labor and Automobiles*. London: Modern Books.
Fedida, S., and R. Malik (1979). *The Viewdata Revolution*. London: Associated Business Press.
Foucault, M. (1979). *Discipline and Punish: The Birth of the Prison*. Harmondsworth: Penguin.
Foucault, M. (1981). *The History of Sexuality*, vol. 1. Harmondsworth: Penguin.
Gardner, C. (1984). "Populism, Relativism and Left Strategy," *Screen*, 25, 1, pp. 45–51.
Garnham, N. (1983). "Public Service Versus the Market," *Screen*, 24, 1, pp. 6–27.
Gaudemar, J. P. de (1979). *La Mobilisation Générale*. Paris: Editions du Champ Urbain.
Giddens, A. (1985). *The Nation-State and Violence*. vol. 2 of *A Contemporary Critique of Historical Materialism*. Cambridge: Polity Press.
Gorz, A. (1976). "On the Class Character of Science and Scientists." In H. and S. Rose (eds.) *The Political Economy of Science*. London: Macmillan.
Gorz, A. (1982). *Farewell to the Working Class*. London: Pluto Press.
Gorz, A. (1983). "The Reconquest of Time." *Telos*, 55, Spring, pp. 212–25.
Granou, A. (1974).*Capitalisme et Mode de Vie*. Paris: Editions du Cerf.
Guardian (1985). "The Spymasters Who Broke Their Own Rules." 1 March.
Habermas, J. (1962). *Strukturwandel der Öffentlichkeit*. Darmstadt: Luchterhand.
Hirsch, J. (1981). "The New Leviathan and the Struggle for Democratic Rights." *Telos*, 48, Summer, pp. 79–89.
Huws, U. (1982). *Your Job in the Eighties: A Woman's Guide to New Technology*. London: Pluto Press.
Huws, U. (1984). "The New Home Workers," *New Society*, 22 March, pp. 454–55.
Illich, I. (1978). *The Right to Useful Unemployment*. London: Marion Boyars.
Information Technology Advisory Panel (1983). *Making a Business of Information*. London: Her Majesty's Stationery Office.

Jay, M. (1984). *Marxism and Totality: The Adventures of a Concept from Lukas to Habermas*. Cambridge: Polity Press.

Jones, M. G. (1981). "Telecommunications Technologies: New Approaches to Consumer Information Dissemination," *Information Society*, 1, 1, pp. 31–52.

Jones, M. G. (1983). "The Challenge of the New Information Technologies: the Need to Respond to Citizens' Information Needs," *Information Society,* 2, 2, pp. 145–56.

Keen, P. G. W. (1981). "Telecommunications and Business Policy," In R. W. Haigh, G. Gerbner and R. D. Byrne (eds.) *Communication in the Twenty-First Century*. New York: John Wiley.

Kovel, J. (1983). *Against the State of Nuclear Terror*. London: Pan.

Leigh, D. (1980). *The Frontiers of Secrecy: Closed Government in Britain*. London: Junction Books.

Levidow, L., and B. Young (1981). "Introduction," In *Science, Technology and the Labour Process*, vol. 1. London: CSE Books.

Lumek, R. (1984). "Information Technology and Libraries," *Library Management*, 5, 3, pp. 3–60.

Lyotard, J. F. (1980). "Le Jeu de l'Informatique et du Savoir," *Dialectiques*, 29, Winter, pp. 3–12.

Manwaring-White, S. (1983). *The Policing Revolution: Police Technology, Democracy and Liberty in Britain.* Brighton: Harvester Press.

Martin, J. (1978). *The Wired Society*. Englewood Cliffs, N.J.: Prentice-Hall.

Marx, G. T. (1985). "I'll Be Watching You: Reflection on the New Surveillance," *Dissent*, Winter, pp. 26–34.

Marx, K. (1976). *Capital*, vol. 1. Harmondsworth: Penguin.

National Commission on Libraries and Information Science (1982). *Public Sector/Private Sector Interaction in Providing Information Services*. Report to the NCLIS from the Public Sector/Private Sector Task Force. Washington, D.C.: Government Printing Office.

Nora, S., and Minc, A. (1980). *The Computerisation of Society*. Cambridge: MIT Press.

Reitell, C. (1924). "Machinery and Its Effect Upon the Workers in the Automotive Industry," *Annals of the American Academy of Political and Social Science,* November, pp. 37–43.

Robins, K. (1983). *Cable and Capital.* Cable Working Paper no. 2. Sheffield/London: Sheffield City Council/Greater London Council.

Robins, K., and F. Webster (1979). "Mass Communications and Information Technology." In R. Miliband and J. Saville (eds.) *Socialist Register 1979.* London: Merlin.

Robins, K., and F. Webster (1983a). "Information Technology, Luddism and the Working Class." In V. Mosco and J. Wasko (eds.) *Critical Communications Review, vol. 1: Labor, the Working Class and the Media*. Norwood, N.J.: Ablex.

Robins, K., and F. Webster (1983b). "The Mis-Information Society." *Universities Quarterly,* 37, 4, pp. 344–55.

Robins, K., and F. Webster (1985). "The Revolution of the Fixed Wheel: Information, Technology and Social Taylorism." In P. Drummond and R. Paterson (eds.) *Television in Transition.* London: British Film Institute.

Robins, K., and F. Webster (1987a). "Information as Capital: A Critique of Daniel Bell." In J. D. Slack and F. Fejes (eds.) *The Ideology of the Information Age.* Norwood, N.J.: Ablex.

Robins, K., and F. Webster (1987b). "New Media, Old Problems: The Communications Revolution and Media Theory." *Communication*, 10.

Saint Jorre, J. (1983). "The Information Dream IRIS, Part 1: The Rise." *Observer*, 17 April.

Seabrook, J. (1982). *Unemployment.* London: Quartet.

Schiller, A. R., and H. I. Schiller (1982). "Who Can Own What America Knows?" *Nation*, 17 April, pp. 461–463.

Shaiken, H. (1984). *Work Transformed: Automation and Labor in the Computer Age.* New York: Holt, Rinehart and Winston.

Stonier, T. (1983). *The Wealth of Information: A Profile of the Post-Industrial Economy.* London: Methuen.

Taylor, F. W. (1974). "Testimony Before the Special House Committee." In *Scientific Management.* New York: Harper.

Thrift, N. (1981). "Owners' Time and Own Time: The Making of a Capitalist Time Consciousness, 1300–1880." *Lund Studies in Geography*, series B, 48, pp. 56–84.

Trachtenberg, A. (1982). *The Incorporation of America: Culture and Society in the Gilded Age.* New York: Hill and Wang.

Webster, F., and Robins, K. (1986). *Information Technology: A Luddite Analysis.* Norwood, N.J.: Ablex.

Wells, H. G. (1938). *World Brain.* London: Methuen.

Wilkinson, B. (1983). *The Shopfloor Politics of New Technology.* London: Heinemann.

Williams, S. (1985). *A Job to Live: the Impact of Tomorrow's Technology on Work and Society.* Harmondsworth: Penguin.

Wiltshire, M. (1986). "System Has Details on 1.7 Million Companies." *Financial Times*, 24 March.

4. Information as an Economic Good: Sources of Individual and Social Value

Benjamin J. Bates

Information is, without a doubt, a peculiar commodity. It has resisted numerous attempts at both definition and measurement, generally limiting efforts at quantification to considerations of such external indicators of information as its flow (Pool, 1984) and gross indicators of aggregate value (e.g., Machlup, 1962; Porat, 1978). In the absence of any consensual definitions of information or measures of information, scholarly considerations of information as a discrete good have, of necessity, remained essentially theoretical. Yet even at this level, information has remained a problematic concept. The unique properties of information as an economic good have led to a number of apparent paradoxes arising from attempts to subject information to economic analyses. One basic paradox, for example, lies in the question of whether information is a public (Samuelson, 1954, 1958) or a private (Boulding, 1966; Marshall, 1974; Stigler, 1983) economic good. Another question concerns whether information goods, because of their unique nature, must inherently fail to meet social efficiency and social welfare conditions.

A number of scholars trace the problematic aspects of information in economic analyses to deficiencies in the analytic treatment of information as an economic good. Several (Demsetz, 1967; Lee, 1982; Leff, 1984) argue that previous theoretical considerations have failed to incorporate important aspects of information. Minasian (1967) and Barzel (1977) have argued that traditional treatments of information ignore some aspects of cost and value. Others (e.g., Babe, 1983; Dervin, 1982; Thompson, 1982) argue that many of the problematic aspects of information arise from an improper focus upon the physical manifestations of information rather than upon the information itself. In an earlier paper (Bates, 1985), I addressed the question of the value and cost of information goods and proposed an extension of traditional economic theory that seemed to resolve many of the problematic aspects of information as an economic good. This paper will use that extension/development as the basis for a consideration of more specific issues of value in information goods.

VALUE AND INFORMATION GOODS

The question of value in information has been addressed from many perspectives, across several disciplines. In these treatments, however, many more questions and issues have been raised than have been resolved. Basic issues raised include the following:

The indeterminacy of the value of information

The dichotomy between the value of information per se and the value of the physical good that contains the information

The incompleteness of considerations of valuation of information goods.

Although this chapter will address all three issues, my primary focus will be on complete valuation.

The issue of indeterminacy arises from a thread common to virtually all consideration of the economics of information: the idea that the value of a piece of information is not fixed or constant. The basic approach to the valuation of information taken in recent research can be traced to Arrow (1962), who argues that the full value of information cannot be known until that information has been put to use by its "consumer," since the circumstances of its use affect its value. Hirschleifer (1973), for example, believes that the certainty of the information, its applicability and decision-relevance, content, and degree of diffusion all influence its value to the user. Similarly, Black and Marchand (1982) note that the structural and political factors in the specific context of the information use also affect its value to the user. Others (Hirschleifer, 1971; Marshall, 1974; Paisley, 1965; Stigler, 1983) further developed the concept that the value of information arises from its use, a conceptualization not too different from the conceptualization of value for other goods.

Thus while most researchers have noted, and have in fact focused upon, the uncertain nature of the value of information, there seems to be a general consensus that the value of a piece of information derives from its (future) usefulness. To be precise, the value of information comes from its use at some future point, and is influenced by the circumstances of that use. The root cause of the indeterminacy issue, therefore, lies in the fact that information goods cannot be given a definitive or concrete value prior to their use, and that information goods may be used more than once. The indeterminacy problem, though, lies in the fact that most traditional economic models are deterministic, and cannot easily deal with uncertainty. As a result, some researchers have argued that in the absence of any concrete measures of information or its value, information goods are beyond the scope of economic analyses.

However, by taking the step from a concrete, purely deterministic perspective to a probabilistic framework of analysis, many of the problematic aspects of indeterminacy in valuation may be resolved. The development of the fields of decision analysis and decision theory has provided a theoretical framework for dealing with questions of uncertainty through the application of such a probabilistic approach. A key concept in such analyses is "expected value," which is essentially an average of all the possible values of some good or outcome, weighted by their respective likelihood. The value of some information good can thus be expressed as the average of all the possible values deriving from the use of that information, weighted by the probability that such a use will occur. This allows for consideration for both variations in value due to the context of its use and the possibility of multiple uses of the information. The resulting expected value of the information provides a mechanism that allows the analyst to treat the value of information goods as fixed in subsequent analyses.

Thus the substitution of the expected value of the information good for its true, yet unknown, actual value allows the application of traditional economic analyses and methods to this distinctive economic good. Furthermore, this substitution is not that different from one used for more traditional economic goods, whose utility (or "use") value to consumers has been recognized as varying from consumer to consumer and among the various contexts of the use of that good.[1] That aspect of indeterminacy led early economists to develop the concept of exchange value as a more consistent, or deterministic, measure of the value of goods, a measure that has become the standard for modern economic models.

With the use of the concept of expected value, then, it would seem that information does not behave all that differently from other economic goods, at least with respect to the issue of indeterminacy in value. Thus it appears, as was suggested by Coase (1974), that infor-

---

1. For example, the value of a gallon of water is recognized as being higher for a person dying of thirst in a desert than for people sitting beside a freshwater spring, having drunk their fill.

mation goods can be treated in the same manner as more traditional economic goods and are subject to the same economic forces, laws, and manipulation. Among these are the basic economic efficiency and optimality conditions, and particularly the condition that costs and revenues (benefits) of goods must be equal at the margin.[2]

Information goods have been generally perceived as failing to satisfy these criteria. One basic problem is the perception that for many, if not most, information goods, marginal cost is inherently unequal to marginal revenue, and such information goods are thus incapable of being provided efficiently, or in a manner that would maximize total social welfare. I will argue here that this perception is largely incorrect and is rooted in the failure to consider the full costs and benefits of the transfer and use of information goods. In doing so, however, I will not presume that any provision of information goods is necessarily efficient or would maximize social welfare; rather, my argument is that it is possible for information goods to be produced and distributed in a manner that would meet such criteria.

Whether the provision of information goods would be *likely* to meet such criteria is another question. Some scholars (e.g., Dizard, 1982; Masuda, 1981; Sweeney, 1981), considering the possibility of a new "information society," argue that information goods will meet those conditions in such a society; others (e.g., Krippendorf, 1984; Nanus, 1982) raise questions about the potential outcomes of a shift in emphasis to information goods or contend (e.g., Halina, 1980; H. Schiller, 1984) that the provision of information goods in capitalistic economic, societies is not likely to meet either efficiency or welfare maximization criteria. The question of whether information goods will be likely to satisfy such criteria, considering current trends in the "informationalization" of the United States, will be addressed later.

THE FULL COSTS AND BENEFITS OF INFORMATION TRANSFER

As noted earlier, information is a distinctive good whose unique features are evident even in common, more basic, considerations of costs. As an "ethereal" good (Thompson, 1982), the production of information is characterized by a high fixed cost component (the costs as-

2. Strictly speaking, this criterion is valid under the conditions of perfect competition, although the basic concepts and relationships are extendable to other market conditions.

sociated with acquiring or developing the information) and a very low, in fact arguably nonexistent, variable cost component (the costs associated with the replication of the information). The low variable cost component reflects two distinctive characteristics of information: the fact that it is essentially nonmaterial and thus requires the consumption of no other resource in its replication, and the fact that information is infinitely reproducible. It should be noted, however, that the physical distribution of information requires the use of some communication channel, or medium, and that some costs may be associated with the replication and distribution of the information *good*, the physical embodiment of that information in a discrete, tangible form.

In traditional economic analysis the marginal cost of a good would typically be seen as being equal to the full fixed costs of that good for the first unit, and equal to the variable costs of that good for each subsequent unit. For information, ignoring for a moment any distribution costs, this means that the marginal cost for the first transfer would be equal to the full costs of producing that information, and would be essentially zero for all subsequent transfers. And even if one includes the distribution costs of the information *goods*, there will be cases where the marginal costs of distribution will be zero (for example, broadcasting), thus requiring for economic efficiency and optimality a setting of marginal revenue, or the price of the information good, at zero.

Thus, traditional approaches have led to a number of apparent paradoxes. Most obvious is the theoretical circumstance that, after the first transfer, the marginal cost of information, per se, is zero. Economic optimality conditions would then require that for information to be distributed optimally to more than one consumer, the marginal cost of such information must also be set at zero, making information essentially a free good. However, in the absence of revenues from its transfer, there is no incentive for the private production of nonexclusive information (there would still be incentive for the production of information as long as that information was limited to a single consumer). There would thus seem to be no way in which nonexclusive information, as an economic good, would be produced in the private market in a manner that would be efficient and socially optimal.

A related paradox concerns certain information goods—for example, advertising—whose distribution is subsidized by the information provider. Advertising messages are goods that are costly to produce and distribute, yet are distributed widely without cost to the consumer. Moreover, advertising is often used to subsidize the provision of other information goods, implying that the marginal revenue of advertising messages may actually be negative. Yet traditional analysis does not consider it possible for marginal costs to be less than zero, thus suggesting that information goods such as advertising would necessarily violate economic efficiency and optimality conditions requiring the equality of marginal costs and revenues.

There is also the more basic problem, noted by such scholars as Dervin (1982) and Thompson (1982), which has contributed to these apparent paradoxes: the tendency for the economic value of information to be linked to the medium of distribution (the information *good*) rather than the quality or intrinsic utility of the information itself. The marginal cost of information, after the first unit, has been seen as being determined by the costs of replicating and distributing its physical manifestation, the information *good*. The consumer's demand for information goods, on the other hand, is likened to what Paisley (1965) referred to as the intrinsic utility value of the good, its potential usefulness to the consumer. Traditional economic considerations of information goods in the past have therefore focused on different aspects of the good for the determination of values (prices or revenues) and costs; the value of information goods to the buyers has been determined by information content, whereas the costs experienced by suppliers have been determined by information form. With costs and benefits not being determined by related aspects of the good in question, it is hardly surprising that, under traditional economic analysis, the various efficiency criteria might not be satisfied for information goods.

Other aspects of information's uniqueness as an economic good may lend insights to the resolution of this apparent quandary. Value, for information, has been defined as deriving from the benefits associated with its use. From this beginning, one can extend this conceptualization of value to include the concept that the use of information may create value not only for the user, but for others as well. Further, the value created may be positive (a benefit) or negative (a cost).

Information, in the pure sense, has been defined as a measure of uncertainty, of negative entropy (Rapoport, 1968). The use of information in systems acts upon the system, reducing (or increasing) the level of uncertainty. According to Ludwig von Bertanlanffy (1968, p. 32), "the process of receiving and using information is the process of adjusting to the contingencies of the outer environment." The use of information changes the system, not only for the individual using the information, but for others as well. Clearly, such changes in the system can result in changes in the status, relationships, and opportunities of others within the system, effectively creating (positive or negative) value, ancillary to that received by the user of the information—shifts in value that can, however, be attributed to that use of information.

The most common example of this effect in the economics literature is the use of "insider trading" in the stock market (e.g., Hirschleifer, 1971; Marshall, 1974). In such cases the value of the information depends not only upon the individual's ability to make use of it, but also upon its use by others. Value in this situation lies in the ability to profit from acting on information about the future price of some stock. However, the use of that information, whether by the individual or by others, brings current prices closer to the future price and thereby reduces the potential for profit. Thus the value of information is influenced by the degree to which it is used, both by the individual and by others.

This example demonstrates the creation of some degree of secondary, or ancillary, value through the use of information. This concept of ancillary value may be used (1) to resolve the basic economic paradoxes related to information as a good, and (2) to consider the likelihood of information goods' being produced and distributed optimally in any particular society.

INFORMATION GOODS AND ANCILLARY VALUE

Most people would immediately recognize and accept the premise that the user of a good or product receives some sort of value from the use (or consumption) of that good. This premise is, in fact, a fundamental cornerstone of modern economic theory. Thus the fact that the consumer (user) of information receives some value or benefit from its use can be treated as an obvious, well-established principle. The principle that the use of a good by one individual can create value for others, above and beyond that created for the individual, is not so obvious.

There are some information goods, however, whose creation of value for persons other than the immediate user is generally recognized, therefore providing examples of the existence of such ancillary value. "Price" advertising contains only market information on the price and availability of products, and provides a prime example of ancillary value. There is an abundent supply of such information goods, and most such information is consumed without much impact on the consumer. Occasionally, though, a consumer may make use of "price" advertising for his or her own benefit: for example, by going to Store Z in order to save on the purchase of widgets. This person's use of the information also clearly benefits the advertiser (Store Z), which has not only attracted the consumer for that purchase but might also benefit from his or her patronage in the future. In any case, it is clear that some ancillary value from the use of that information (the "price" advertisement) has been created for someone other than the immediate user.

Yet the ancillary value described above is still of a kind that could be termed "private" value. That is, it is returned directly to individuals in discrete, readily recognizable forms. But economic theory would also argue that such "price" advertising information, and its use by consumers, makes the marketplace for widgets operate more efficiently. The use of such information by consumers thus creates ancillary value to the society at large by making the marketplace more efficient, thereby increasing social welfare. This ancillary "social" value, in contrast to the ancillary "private" value discussed above, tends to be returned more diffusely and indirectly, making it not as apparent or recognizable to individuals. Nevertheless, the benefits derived from the use of "price" advertising can be seen as accruing not only to the user of that information (private value) but to the supplier of the information (ancillary private value) as well as to the society at large (ancillary social value). The existence of positive ancillary private value can resolve the paradox of advertising's apparently negative marginal cost (and revenue) and render the provision of such advertising economically efficient (Bates, 1985).

Another case in which ancillary value in information goods is readily recognized may be found in "education." For brevity, I will define "education" as the set of basic information goods transferred to individuals through the traditional educational process, hopefully to be retained and used throughout the students' (consumers') future. Education, as a set of information goods, has specific value to the individual user (student) resulting from the user's ability to make use of those goods for his or her own benefit throughout the future, both in society and in the workplace. It is also widely recognized that the individual consumer's ability to make use of "education" creates ancillary value to the society at large. For instance, the proper functioning of a democratic society is often said to rely on an educated population that is able to make informed choices (cf. Nimmo, 1985). In that a properly functioning democracy can be said to have some value, "education" can be said to create ancillary social value. And as with advertising, an educated population capable of rational decision making contributes to the efficiency of economic markets, providing another source for ancillary social value.

The fact that education is heavily subsidized by the public sector only reinforces the argument that education's creation of ancillary social value is widely recognized. Although less widely recognized, it can be seen that education also creates ancillary private value. Several sociologists (e.g., Braverman, 1974; O'Connor, 1973) have argued that the current educational structure creates ancillary value for industry by absorbing or reducing training costs. Thus "education" can be seen as creating not only direct private value to the user, but also ancillary private and social value.

Traditional microeconomic analysis has recognized the existence of ancillary value arising from the use of various goods through the concept of externalities, although it has usually considered such ancillary value in terms of costs rather than benefits. The conceptualization of "externalities," however, implies that such costs or benefits exist outside the traditional marketplace and thus do not figure in traditional economic analyses.

In order to deal with externalities within a microeconomic framework, one must be able to bring them into the analysis, to internalize those aspects of economic reality into the models. In most cases this can be accomplished on a theoretical level fairly simply, through the expansion of the scope of the model and the analysis. In the case of information, this is accomplished by simply including expected ancillary value (both private and social), as well as basic expected value, in all value considerations of the production and distribution models for information goods. Although this may be easily accomplished on the theoretical plane, problems emerge when economic models are applied to the real world.

Economic models are based upon the behavior of economic individuals, be they people, firms, or governments. For a model to be realistic, it must be based on a realistic consideration of behaviors and motivations in real markets. Thus the question arises: to what extent is ancillary value considered by various economic individuals in determining their market behavior?

On the basis of consumer behavior in the past and the examples given above, I feel that ancillary value is at least partially considered in current market behaviors, but has been more generally ignored in theoretical models. As noted earlier, several scholars (e.g., Demsetz, 1967; Leff, 1984; Minasian, 1967) feel that theoretical considerations of the economics of information and information goods have failed to incorporate certain aspects of costs and revenues; that value is created through the use of information which is not considered by traditional economic models. Yet it would appear, since information goods are clearly produced in quantity in modern society, that aspects of ancillary value are not ignored in the real markets for such goods. The fact that ancillary private value exists and is widely recognized and incorporated into economic decision making provides, in truth, the only logical basis for the existence of advertising, especially nonprice (persuasive) forms. Thus a strong case could be made that, in the real world, ancillary private value has already been internalized into at least some information markets and that only in traditional theoretical models has that aspect of value been ignored.

However, it would also appear that ancillary social value is not widely or regularly considered in the functioning of real-world information markets. Markets in which the government operates would appear to be the exception to this rule. As the creation of "social" value can be seen as the primary function, and source of validation, for governments, what would normally be considered social value can be seen as having fundamentally the same role for governments as private individual value has in private markets. Thus I feel that one can safely conclude that the ancillary social value created through the use of information goods is generally ignored in both theoretical and real considerations of value, and therefore remains essentially external to information markets and to economic behavior patterns within them. The one exception to this case occurs when governments, or other organizations whose primary concern is with the creation of social value, are primary participants in information markets. In such cases the "social" aspects are privatized by their role in maintaining the rationale for the continuance of such organizations.

MODERN SOCIETY AND ANCILLARY SOCIAL VALUE

Information goods are becoming an increasingly important segment of economic output. One of the distinctive features of information goods is that such goods can create significant levels of ancillary value, returned to both private individuals (or firms) and to society as a whole. Thus, the questions of whether such goods are produced efficiently and who derives both primary and ancillary value from their distribution and use are becoming increasingly vital concerns. And the demonstration of the economic efficiency of information markets, depending as it does on the relationship of relative values at the margin, would seem to call for the inclusion of all sources of value. The maximization of social welfare thus requires the explicit internalization of all forms of value into information market considerations, with particular attention being granted to the consideration of ancillary social value.

Although it seems quite likely (witness advertising) that information producers are aware of the existence of ancillary value for information goods, and have incorporated consideration of ancillary private value into their economic decision making, there remains the basic question of who, if anyone, is taking into consideration, on a regular basis, the ancillary social value associated with the production and consumption of information goods. Certainly the state has some concern for the existence of such value and has taken steps to ensure the production and distribution of some information goods that create ancillary social value. However, it seems unlikely that private firms or individuals take the existence of ancillary social value into account in either their creation or their consumption of information goods, or that they will do so. There is currently no visible incentive for private firms or individuals to be concerned with aspects of ancillary social value.

From a theoretical perspective, then, it would appear that in the United States at least, only governments or other organizations directly concerned with issues of social welfare are likely to pay attention to issues of ancillary social value. And as at least part of the value of information goods (ancillary social value) remains external to the bulk of market considerations in the private sector, it is quite likely that information high in positive ancillary social value will thus be underproduced by the private sector. Further, the failure of economic individuals to consider ancillary social value is likely to have an effect on their consumption of information goods. That is, in ignoring the social costs and benefits of information goods in their decision making, firms and individuals are more likely to overconsume information goods with high ancillary social costs and underconsume those with high ancillary social benefits. This could have severe repercussions in the continuing development of information-based societies.

Scholars addressing the formation of such "information societies" have long been concerned about that transition and the potential effects of having information and information goods as a central focus of a society (see Brzezinski, 1971; Horowitz, 1985; MacRae, 1970; Mosco, 1982; Theobald, 1981). In particular, concern has been expressed not only about the creation of information and information goods, but about the level of availability of that information to all members of the society. The likely effects of the externalization of ancillary social value on the production and distribution of information are two related issues that dominate considerations of "information societies" of whatever form.

Lasswell (1971) has argued that the most likely area of policy/regulation in an "information society" would be the area of information access, although his primary concern is with issues of privacy. Others (see Dervin, 1982; MacRae, 1970; Michael, 1971; O'Brien and Helleiner, 1980) have focused upon the accessibility of information to individuals, and in particular the potential for limited access posed by both economic and noneconomic costs of obtaining information goods. The fear expressed by many of these researchers was that information goods would become so costly as to prevent some segments of society from being able to gain access to that information.

There are undoubtedly costs associated with the consumption or acquisition of any good, be they direct economic costs associated with its price or noneconomic costs (such as time) incurred in its acquisition or consumption (see Lee, 1982). The true net cost to a consumer of information goods, though, consists not only of these well-recognized direct costs, but also the ancillary costs or benefits associated with the consumption of the information goods by such individuals. To the extent that ancillary social value remains external to the market system, those costs, and particularly those benefits, associated with the consumption of information goods will not be incorporated in the access costs faced by potential consumers. That is, it is quite likely that information goods, at least those with positive ancillary social value, will be more costly than would be economically efficient or socially optimal because aspects of true costs and benefits are ignored in the marketplace.[3] Goods that are high in (positive) ancillary social value, those information goods which it should be in society's best interests to have produced, consumed, and utilized, will be less accessible (more costly) in markets in which such sources of value are ignored.

Currently, both public and private markets produce information goods. It would seem, though, that only the public market recognizes and incorporates aspects of the social value of information goods into its production and consumption actions. However, it could be argued that public marketplaces incorporate, or internalize, only selected aspects of ancillary social value: those either commonly acknowledged as fundamental, or those returning value to portions of the society well represented in the political process. For, as Prewitt (1970) notes, the beneficiaries of the new emphasis on information and information systems would most likely be existing

3. It should be noted that it is also possible that the externalization of the social costs of information use would tend to result in costs that are lower than is socially optimal, or could net to a cost that is equal to the true cost of consumption. However, most information would seem to be more likely to produce social benefits through consumption and use, rather than social costs. Thus it would seem proper to focus on the results of ignoring positive ancillary social value.

organizations. It would appear that even in the public marketplace, at least some of the aspects of ancillary social value are apt to remain external to the economic system and lead to suboptimality and inefficiency in information production, distribution, and consumption. Thus, even in terms of social value, it appears that the rich get richer and the poor, poorer.

Public markets can be said to incorporate at least some aspects of ancillary social value, however, and are therefore apt to be generally more efficient and socially optimal than most private markets for information. Access, it is usually argued, would be even more restricted in private markets than in public markets: thus the concern expressed by many over the growing tendency to "privatize" information and information markets. Private markets for information are in themselves nothing new,[4] but recently the role of the private market has been questioned with respect to two issues: the development of new information technologies and systems, and the trend among many governments and other organizations of returning certain operations to the private sector.

Both issues are related in their basic concern with the extent to which private markets are likely to dominate in any future information order. Herbert Schiller (1969, 1983, 1984, 1985), in particular, has expressed considerable concern over the role of the private sector in the production and distribution of information, the recent entry of private firms into traditionally public markets for information, and the "privatization" of various public marketplaces for information. Private markets for information, he argues, have tended to predominate in past communication systems and would seem to be likely to predominate in the new information/communication systems.

This domination, and some would say control, of information and information systems is particularly evident in the United States, and there is every indication that private firms will continue their domination in the future. Dan Schiller (1982) notes that the Federal Communication Commission's Second Computer Inquiry set the stage for the private development of the "information society." The process of the adoption and integration of new information systems, built upon the

4. The emphasis on private production of information can be seen in the development of patent and copyright systems to encourage the development of ideas and information by private individuals. Further, the United States has had a considerable tradition supporting a private press, including support for distribution systems.

convergence of computer and telecommunication technologies, has been dominated by the presence and activities of private firms (see Compaine, 1985; Fombrun and Astley, 1983). Also, the general trend toward "privatization" of government services has resulted in several public markets for information recently turning private (H. Schiller, 1984). All these trends indicate that private markets for information and information goods will continue to dominate in the United States.

Thus, particularly with respect to Herbert Schiller's concern with the privatization of information (1983, 1984, 1985), it is increasingly likely that private firms will serve as the main providers/conduits/creators of information goods. However, private markets are not as likely to incorporate considerations of social value (ancillary or otherwise) in their economic decisions. With potentially significant portions of its value external to the market, information production, distribution, and consumption in private marketplaces will not be truly economically efficient or generate maximum social welfare. Private markets for information will tend to be suboptimal.

CONCLUSIONS

The note that has been sounded so far has been fairly critical. There is, however, a lot of room for argument in an abstract, analytical treatise like this, and I will in face make some of those arguments in considering what I have tried to show in this chapter.

Information as an economic good has definite and distinctive value, value that represents the expected returns from the future use of that information. Those returns, however, may well accrue to people other than the direct user of the information, creating what I have termed ancillary value. This ancillary value results in large part from shifts in value, or potential value, brought about by changes in the economic and social environment, which are themselves brought about by the use of the information good. Further, ancillary value may be created both for individuals and for larger, more abstract groups; that is, ancillary value may be private or social in nature.

Many of the theoretical difficulties with the concept of information as an economic good can be traced to the failure to consider this part of the full value of information. Ancillary value has, to use the economist's phrase, remained external to theoretical models. On the other hand, experience with certain economic goods, such as advertising, suggests that ancillary private value, at least, has in fact been incorporated into many markets for information goods. Ancillary social value, in contrast, seems to have been considered solely in public information markets. The failure to incorporate all aspects of value of a good, in *any* market, means that the production and consumption of that good will likely not occur at levels that satisfy various efficiency and social welfare maximization criteria.

Thus, it was argued, markets for information goods were apt to be suboptimal to the extent that those goods created significant levels of ancillary value that were not incorporated into market considerations. And private markets, those in which information is produced and distributed by private individuals or firms, are more likely to be socially suboptimal than public markets, in that ancillary social value is less likely to be incorporated into private market considerations. With the growing "privatization" of information markets, there is a disturbing possibility that information markets might become *increasingly* suboptimal.

Whether any of these concerns are, in fact, valid hinges upon the conclusions that the ancillary portions of the true, full, value of information goods (particularly ancillary social value) are significant and remain external to the marketplace. If information goods have no ancillary value, the failure to include consideration of such value will not affect the functioning of the market. While there clearly are information goods of this type, there are just as clearly information goods whose ancillary value components are a significant portion of that good's total value. Thus not all information markets are necessarily suboptimal or inefficient, but clearly the potential exists.

While there is every indication that social value is largely ignored in private markets, whether for information or any other good, that aspect need not be external to either the public or private marketplace for information goods. Corporations often speak of "returning something to the community." Government speaks of internalizing social costs through the imposition of fees and taxes, and internalizing social benefits through the granting of subsidies. Although one must grant the possibility that private firms and individuals may recognize the existence of ancillary social value and the commonweal, and may even act upon that knowledge, it seems far more reasonable to place any hopes for the eventual internalization of the full value of information goods in the public sector.

Hence the hopes among many scholars for the transition to an "information society," and the generation of new dominant forms of information systems that might incorporate considerations of all aspects of the value of information. The realization of such hopes, and also the concurrent fears, depends on how these new information systems and technologies are implemented and developed within the social system. To date, the new information technologies appear to have developed primarily from "technological push," the desire to develop the technology and new markets (Horowitz, 1985), rather than from a desire to meet any social goals or needs. Issues such as the internalization of ancillary value into the information systems and markets have yet to be fully addressed in the process of the implementation of such technologies and systems, even though they have caught the attention of some scholars.

If the true value of information can be determined, or even guessed at, the implementation of social policy can act to incorporate consideration of the true value of information goods, both private and social, in the functioning of information markets, be those markets public or private. Then, perhaps, theory and reality will coincide in the functioning of "optimal" markets for information goods. Otherwise the fears of a good many scholars about declines in social welfare and equity in an "information society" may well become real.

REFERENCES

Arrow, K. J. (1962). "Economic Welfare and the Allocation of Resources for Invention." In *The Rate and Direction of Inventive Activity: Economic and Social Factors*. Princeton, N.J.: Universities-National Bureau for Economic Research Conference.

Babe, R. E. (1983). "Information Industries and Economic Analysis: Policy-Makers Beware." In O. H. Gandy, Jr., P. Espinosa, and J. A. Ordover (eds.) *Proceedings from the Tenth Annual Telecommunications Policy Research Conference*. Norwood, N.J.: Ablex.

Barzel, Y. (1977). "Some Fallacies in the Interpretation of Information Costs." *Journal of Law and Economics*, 20, 2, pp. 291–308.

Bates, B. J. (1985). "Information as an Economic Good: A Re-Evaluation of Theoretical Approaches." Paper presented at the 35th Annual Conference of the International Communication Association, Honolulu, 23–27, May.

Black, S. H., and D. A. Marchand (1982). "Assessing the Value of Information in Organizations: A Challenge for the 1980s." *Information Society*, 1, 3, pp. 191–225.

Boulding, K. E. (1966). "The Economics of Knowledge and the Knowledge of Economics." *American Economic Review*, 56, 2, pp. 1–13.

Braverman, H. (1974). *Labor and Monopoly Capital: The Degradation of Work in the Twentieth Century*. New York: Monthly Review Press.

Brzezinski, Z. (1971). "Moving Into a Technetronic Society." In A. F. Westin (ed.) *Information Technology in a Democracy*. Cambridge: Harvard University Press.

Coase, R. H. (1974). "The Market for Goods and the Market for Ideas." *American Economic Review*, 64, 2, pp. 384–91.

Compaine, B. M. (1985). "The Expanding Base of Media Competition." *Journal of Communication,* 35, 3, pp. 81–96.

Demsetz, H. (1967). "Toward a Theory of Property Rights." *American Economic Review*, 59, 2, pp. 347–359.

Dervin, B. (1982). "Citizen Access as an Information Equity Issue." In J. R. Schement, F. Gutierrez, and M. A. Sirbu (eds.) *Telecommunication Policy Handbook*. New York: Praeger.

Dizard, W. P., Jr. (1982). *The Coming Information Age: An Overview of Technology, Economics, and Politics*. New York: Longman.

Fombrun, C. and W. G. Astley (1983). "The Telecommunications Community: An Institutional Overview." In E. Wartella and D. C. Whitney (eds.) *Mass Communication Review Yearbook*, v. 4. Beverly Hills, Calif.: Sage.

Halina, J. W. (1980). "Communications and the Economy: A North American Perspective." *International Social Science Journal*, 32, 2, pp. 264–282.

Hall, K. (1981). "The Economic Nature of Information." *Information Society*, 1, 2, pp. 143–66.

Hirschleifer, J. (1971). "The Private and Social Value of Information and the Reward to Inventive Activity." *American Economic Review*, 61, 4, pp. 561–574.

Hirshleifer, J. (1973). "Where Are We in the Theory of Information?" *American Economic Review*, 63, 2, pp. 31–39.

Horowitz, I. L. (1985). "The Political Economy of Database Technology." In B. D. Ruben (ed.) *Information and Behavior*, vol. 1. New Brunswick, N.J.: Transaction.

Krippendorf, K. (1984). "Information, Information Society and Some Marxian Propositions." Paper presented at the 34th Annual Conference of the International Communication Association, San Francisco, 24–28, May.

Lasswell, H. D. (1971). "Policy Problems of a Data-Rich Civilization." In A. F. Westin (ed.) *Information Technology in a Democracy*. Cambridge: Harvard University Press.

Lee, D. R. (1982). "On the Pricing of Public Goods." *Southern Economic Journal*, 49, 1, pp. 99–105.

Leff, N. H. (1984). "Externalities, Information Costs, and Social Benefit–Cost Analysis for Economic Development: An Example from Telecommunications." *Economic Development and Cultural Change*, 32, pp. 255–76.

Machlup, F. (1962). *The Production and Distribution of Knowledge in the United States*. Princeton: Princeton University Press.

MacRae, D., Jr. (1970). "Some Political Choices in the Development of Communications Technology." In H. Sackman and N. Nie (eds.) *The Information Utility and Social Choice*. Montvale, N.J.: AFIPS Press.

Marshall, J. M. (1974). "Private Incentives and Public Information." *American Economic Review*, 64, 3, pp. 373–90.

Masuda, Y. (1981). *The Information Society as Post-Industrial Society*. Bethesda, Md.: World Future Society.

Michael, D. N. (1971). "Democratic Participation and Technological Planning." In A. F. Westin (ed.) *Information Technology in a Democracy*. Cambridge: Harvard University Press.

Minasian, J. R. (1967). "Public Goods in Theory and Practice." *Journal of Law and Economics*, 10, pp. 205–7.

Mosco, V. (1982). *Pushbutton Fantasies: Critical Perspectives on Videotex and Information Technology*. Norwood, N.J.: Ablex.

Nanus, B. (1982). "Developing Strategies for the Information Society." *Information Society*, 1, pp. 339–56.

Nimmo, D. (1985). "Information and Political Behavior." In B. D. Ruben (ed.) *Information and Behavior*, vol. 1. New Brunswick, N.J.: Transaction.

O'Brien, R., and G. Helleiner (1980). "The Political Economy of Information in a Changing Information Order." *International Organization*, 34, pp. 445–70.

O'Connor, J. (1973). *The Fiscal Crisis of the State*. New York: St. Martin's Press.

Paisley, W. J. (1965). "Extent of Information-Seeking as a Function of Subjective Certainty and the Utility of Information." Ph.D. dissertation, Stanford University.

Pool, I. DeSola (1984). "Tracking the Flow of Information." *Science*, 221, pp. 609–13.

Porat, M. U. (1978). "Global Implications of an Information Society." *Journal of Communication*, 28, 1, pp. 70–80.

Prewitt, K. (1970). "Information and Politics: Reflections on Reflections." In H. Sackman and N. Nie (eds.) *The Information Utility as Social Choice*. Montvale, N.J.: AFIPS Press.

Rapoport, A. (1968). "The Promise and Pitfalls of Information Theory." In W. Buckley (ed.) *Modern Systems Research for the Behavioral Scientist*. Chicago: Aldine.

Samuelson, P. A. (1954). "The Pure Theory of Public Expenditures." *Review of Economics and Statistics*, 36, pp. 387–89.

Samuelson, P. A. (1958). "Aspects of Public Expenditures Theory." *Review of Economics and Statistics*, 40, pp. 332–38.

Schiller, D. (1982). "Business Users and the Telecommunication Network." *Journal of Communication*, 32, 4, pp. 84–96.

Schiller, H. I. (1969). *Mass Communications and American Empire*. Boston: Beacon Press.

Schiller, H. I. (1983). "The Privatization of Information." In E. Wartella and D. C. Whitney (eds.) *Mass Communication Review Yearbook*, vol. 4. Beverly Hills, Calif.: Sage.

Schiller, H. I. (1984). *Information and the Crisis Economy*. Norwood, N.J.

Schiller, H. I. (1985). "Privatizing the Public Sector: The Information Connection." In B. D. Ruben (ed.) *Information and Behavior*, vol. 1. New Brunswick, N.J.: Transaction.

Stigler, G. (1983). "The Economics of Information." In *The Organization of Industry*. Chicago: University of Chicago Press.

Sweeney, G. P. (1981). "Telematics and Development." *Information Society*, 1, 2, pp. 113–32.

Theobald, R. (1981). *Beyond Despair: A Policy Guide to the Communications Era.* (rev. ed) Cabin John, Md.: Seven Locks Press.

Thompson, G. B. (1982). "Ethereal Goods: The Economic Atom of the Information Society." In L. Bannon, U. Barry, and O. Holst (eds) *Information Technology: Impact on the Way of Life*. Dublin: Tycooly International.

von Bertanlanffy, L. (1968). "General System Theory—A Critical Review." In W. Buckley (ed.) *Modern Systems Research for the Behavioral Scientist.* Chicago: Aldine.

5. The Information Society: A Computer-Generated Caste System?

Terry Curtis

The threat to privacy in the information society has been recognized and broadly discussed. The extent of that threat seems equal to the growth in the size of governmental and other institutions. The larger the organization, the greater the need for information for control, for progress, for improvement, and for coordination—all functions that, in one view, tend toward the homogenization of society. This view can be traced back to Nietzsche's "mass man," or perhaps even to Rousseau, who, in order to make possible a society based on a "general will," felt that it might be necessary to force people to be free: that is, to enforce a basic consensus within whose limits a general will could be achieved (book 4, ch. 2 of *The Social Contract*). The modern version of this view is the belief that the intrusive search for information by government and other large institutions will have a chilling effect on individuality, while the monotony of the content of the information distributed through the mass media will have a numbing effect on it. The combined effects of these forces will be an homogenization of society without explicit coercion.[1]

In apparent contradiction to this concern for the evils of mass society, there has been speculation that modern information technology is moving society in the opposite direction, toward a "demassification." Frederick Williams, in *The New Communications (1984),* suggests that magazine market segmentation, radio "formats," narrowcasting, alternative video delivery technologies, and, especially, computerized information delivery systems such as videotex, point to a trend in communications media away from the enforced homogenization of society. Relating this idea to Melvin DeFleur and Sandra Ball-Rokeach's dependency theory of mass communications,

1. The monotony of the mass media is too familiar a theme to require citation. The chilling effect of surveillance and search is covered in Marx and Reichman (1984) and Marx (1985).

Williams suggests that "it seems reasonable to speculate that individuals who have the best access to needed information will be the most successful in the years to come" (ibid., p. 286). This suggestion can be interpreted in either of two ways.

On the one hand, there seems to be the implication that the use of information-gathering and information-distribution technologies for the performance of the functions of large governmental, political, and corporate institutions will no longer have coercive homogenizing effects, explicit or implicit. This interpretation depends on the idea that the leveling forces of mass society grew out of the need of social systems for control and integration. New information technologies seem to allow for control and integration within the context of a larger number of variables; therefore there would seem to be less reason for pressure to reduce the number of variables in attitude and behavior in society. Moreover, DeFleur and Ball-Rokeach's theory that the nature and content of mass media are determined by interaction with the audience and its social structures suggests that variety within the audience and variety in social structures will both maintain and be maintained by technologies that allow greater variety in communications.

A second interpretation is that demassification is apparent but not real. In this view the capacity of new information technologies to handle a greater number of variables does not equate to willingness in society to tolerate greater individuality. Moreover, the segmentation of mass media markets by a variety of channels of distribution and a variety of programming formats may not equate to an acceptance of a variety of meaningfully different social and cultural subsystems. The users of information technology for coordination and control may simply have achieved a new set of techniques by which the search for information about individuals and the delivery of homogenizing socialization messages can be performed in a variety of ways for a variety of segments of society. The operant aphorism in this view is, "A difference which makes no difference is no difference." In fact, from this view the demassification issue may simply be a red herring, distracting attention from the mass society's assault on the individual.

The better view is that the political and economic forces at work have in the past threatened and will continue to threaten two values—individual liberty and social equality. Neither threat can be ignored. Moreover, the nature of both can be illuminated by consideration of the classical core issue of political economy: the relationship between individual motivation and the norms of economic production and distribution. Consideration of the function of information in that relationship is especially helpful.

THE PREINDUSTRIAL PERIOD: THE CLASSICAL VIEW

Political economy originated with the philosophers of the 18th century—Petty, Steuart, Hume, and Smith—who gave birth to the modern study of economics while considering how nations should best control the economic forces at work at the start of the Industrial Revolution. They were thinkers of the Enlightenment, rationalists, and classical liberals. The political message of this period of political economy, ripe with the historical context of their thought, appears in one sentence from Smith's *Wealth of Nations*: "The species of domestic industry which his capital can employ, and of which the produce is likely to be of the greatest value, every individual, it is evident, can, in his local situation, judge much better than any statesman or lawgiver can do for him" (Smith, 1976, p. 456; original: book IV, chap. 2, para. 10). This statement relies on a perception that individuals are motivated primarily by self-interest. Still, Smith's preference for individual over governmental decision making assumes the same human nature that is assumed by the other classical liberals, a basically good nature, though subject to temptation and thus corruptible. The corruptibility of human nature, which was to the classical liberals the justification for the state and also the danger of the mantle of state authority, also defines the nature of such restrictions as the classical economists were willing to see imposed on the freedom of the market. Interestingly, some of these restrictions have specifically to do with the distortion of the information upon which individual decisions are based—for example, laws against fraud (Robbins, 1976, pp. 15–18). Except for such limitations, Smith argued that economic interests could best be served by leaving economic decisions in the hands of the individual. He devoted little attention to corporations as economic decision-makers, although it must be pointed out that at that time there was no limited liability for corporations and therefore much less attraction to them as a business form (ibid., pp. 42–46). The point here is that in the consideration of political economy the focus was the individual and his or her rational capacity to make decisions that were based on information to which the individual had the most direct access and which he or she could best understand.

As a statement of the role of information in economic decision making, the quotation from Smith seems likely to represent an empirical assessment. Smith dealt with an economy of small businesses engaged in trade on a local scale, whose workers, investors, and consumers could know and be known to each other. He also dealt with a distant parliament, whose members had only limited access to information about circumstances in the nation as a whole, much less in any one area. In that context his preference for individual decisions seems quite understandable. The free and universal availability of information to the individual and the individual's unlimited ability to comprehend that information were twin assumptions of Smith's theory. The economic problem, as he saw it, was the distortion consequent to the political practice of denying individuals the liberty to act in accordance with the decisions they could make for themselves.

What remains to be extracted from Smith's statement is some clue as to the norms of economic production and distribution, adherence to which he thought was most likely to follow from individual liberty in economic matters. Three values seem to be posited in Smith and the other classics of political economy. The first is growth, that political-economic panacea through which it is at least possible that everyone can become better off. The second is liberty itself. Given the context of the Whig argument against traditional (on the Continent still royal) restrictions on the economy, it is hardly surprising that liberty should be a principal value and that growth should be promised as a reward. These were the times of the Industrial Revolution, and progress and growth were, for the first time, being argued as the product of freedom from traditional restraint. Finally there is rationality, which in the context of economic decisions meant efficiency or the absence of waste. In the era of the Enlightenment, this emphasis on reason, too, is hardly surprising.

THE INDUSTRIAL SOCIETY

Marx's Criticism

The Industrial Revolution had not progressed far before at least one of the students of classical economics began to doubt the effectiveness of liberty as an instrumental value and the primacy of growth as an ultimate value. From the combined perspectives of urban industrial squalor and personal poverty, Marx rejected reliance on individual motivation. This is not to say that he rejected the inherent rationality and capacity for good of the individual. His belief that the workers would eventually develop a class consciousness and reject and overthrow capitalism attests to his faith in rationality, while his belief that a communal society would result from the revolution attests to his faith in individual good. But, following Rousseau, he felt that the origin of the evil in self-interest (*amour propre* in Rousseau's *Essay*), as well as the origin of inequality, lay in society, and specifically in class conflict. Responding to the deferential attitudes of the working class and the self-serving attitudes of the middle and upper classes (particularly the assertion by the propertied classes that unrestricted enjoyment of individual economic liberty would serve the public good), Marx viewed policy as simply an expression of the economic reality. To say that Marx was an economic determinist may overstate the case (Miliband, 1977). Still, Marx rejects reliance on individual motivation in a capitalist context on the grounds that the context is necessarily competitive and exploitative and the individuals who are socialized into that economic system will necessarily pursue self-interest to the detriment of others and of the whole.

Marx's emphasis on class conflict in understanding individual motivation in economic matters carries over into his view of information and its comprehension. The availability of valid information and the capacity to understand it were not, as he saw it, relevant issues in a capitalist economy, since both the economic information itself and the ways in which it could be understood were meaningless except when viewed as propaganda necessary for purposes of social control. Information in the political economy was part of the superstructure, the system of superficial rationalizations of behavior that was determined by the control of the means of producton by some and the exploitation of the rest. Only the elimination of this economic inequality could make availability of information and its rational use important issues.

As to normative principles, Marx was straightforward. Only one value pervades his political economy: that of equality, which he also calls social justice. Liberty was to Marx a bourgeois fiction, a rationalization of privilege. Rationalism, especially if interpreted as efficiency, was simply a part of the superstructure, a false value used to rationalize exploitation. Although there may be some suggestion that a part of the value of the communal, egalitarian economy that Marx proposed lay in its greater capacity for productivity, suggesting that some value was placed on growth, overall one must conclude that to Marx the only item on the agenda of political economy was the elimination of economic inequality.

The Conservative Response

Since Marx, most discussion of political economy has been labeled economics and has been conservative. This is, of course, not the whole story. Robert L. Heilbroner's "Underworld of Economics" was full of political economists not uncomfortable with the label "political" and not uncritical of the effects of the Industrial Revolution (Heilbroner, 1967, chap. 7). Others have included Veblen, Baran, Sweezy, Magdoff, and Domhoff, to name only a few. Even John Maynard Keynes was iconoclastic, if not actually revolutionary. Keynes was, however, both personally and in the treatment of his ideas by others, "classicized," as Thomas Balogh put it, and made conservative (Balogh, 1982).

The importance of this conservatism is not to be understated. Called economics rather than political economy the discipline is nonetheless intensely political, and its political viewpoint is directly related to the issue here: the nature of individual motivation and the role of information in relating individual motivation to the pursuit of economic goals. The response of conservative economists to the criticisms of Marx was to reaffirm the policy goals of the classical economists but to radically alter—in fact to deny—the principles upon which they had been based. The rationality and efficiency of an unrestrained marketplace continued to be posited as the best means of achieving increased productivity and improved distribution. The mechanism that was assumed to make the unrestrained market work, however, was no longer an informed individual acting out of rational self-interest. Economic institutions had grown large. Economic decision making had grown complex. The image of a market controlled by real individuals with full information and full capacity to comprehend their situations was no longer compelling. If Marx's conclusions were not also compelling, the circumstances upon which he based his criticisms could not be ignored. Individual self-interest was giving way as the force shaping economic developments. It was being replaced by the corporate pursuit of stable growth through technological innovation and planning (Galbraith, 1985).

From the mid-19th to the mid-20th centuries, the individual whose rationality and self-interest had been the key to classical economic theory suffered an abstraction almost into irrelevance. Economies of scale and scope were pushing economic calculations and processess from individual to mass level. In the context of mass production and mass consumption, specific information about individual preference was impossible to gather, store, or use. Information became stochastic—statistical generalizations—while individuals became the units of the mass society, the rational man of microeconomic theory. The complex and imperfect nature of this statistical information, which was the basis for discrediting the individual as a decision-maker, also provided the impetus for mass marketing and the mass media. The process of rationalization of production, which Frederick

Taylor dubbed scientific management, needed a counterpart in consumption. Stability of profits is as dependent on stable revenues as it is on stable costs. Political economists, in reaction to the depersonalizing trends in economics, began to call attention to the sacrifice of the classical political economists' value on individual liberty. That sacrifice came in two forms: first, the intrusion into the privacy of the individual in order to accumulate the statistical information out of which economic information would be generalized; and second, the pressure of socialization into conformity through the mass media and their use for mass marketing. In sum, individual motivation ceased to be something reliable, to which the health of the economy could be entrusted, and became instead something uncertain and volatile, to be monitored and managed to whatever degree was possible.

The conservatism of the modern economists takes an interesting form in the treatment of information. Economists have attempted to reduce the rationality of economic decision making to a purely mathematical cost-benefit analysis. Francis A. Walker, then president of the Massachusetts Institute of Technology, wrote in 1888:

> Political Economy, or Economics, is the name of that body of knowledge which relates to wealth. Political Economy has to do with no other subject, whatsoever, than wealth. Especially should the student of economics take care not to allow any purely political, ethical or social considerations to influence him in his investigations. All he has, as an economist, to do is to find out how wealth is produced, exchanged, distributed, and consumed. (Walker, 1888, p. 1)

Walker's use of the term "Economics" came at the beginning of the trend toward dropping the word "political" from the name of the discipline. This is the period in which economics became what Robert L. Heilbroner has recently called "ideological" (Heilbroner, 1986). He explains that "[w]hat is 'ideological' about [economics] is not its hypocrisy but its absence of historical perspective, its failure to preceive that its pronouncements are a belief system, conditioned as are all belief systems by the political and social premises of the social order." The specific belief system of which Heilbroner is speaking is the view that the production and distribution of wealth, that with which economics concerns itself, is "entirely divorced from any intrinsic political tasks." Information about "purely political, ethical, or social considerations," then, must not concern the economist either. Information, to the modern economist, is simply a cost factor in the economic decision-making process. Hence the efforts of Machlup (1962), Arrow (1974), and Stigler (1983) to quantify and evaluate information and include it in their models of economic behavior.[2] This approach would keep economics free from political, ethical, or social considerations, but at the same time make it rhetorical (McCloskey, 1986), ideological (Heilbroner, 1986), or even irrelevant (Balogh, 1982).

The key to understanding the treatment of information in modern economic policy is the identification of the normative judgments involved. The corporation and the political system that supports it value stable profits, growth, and technological innovation, not necessarily in that order (Galbraith, 1985). Neither the liberty emphasized by the classical political economists nor the equality emphasized by their Marxist critics is of concern. There is a sense in which liberty is discussed, but it is the economic liberty that Heilbroner characterizes as "the absence of political functions in the private sphere and of economic functions in the public sphere" (Heilbroner, 1986). Corporate decision-makers are free to seek stability, growth, and innovation without the imposition of political, ethical, or social externalities. This kind of liberty is not concerned with the individual.

THE INFORMATION SOCIETY: The Segmentation of the Mass?

The new information technology has made possible a reconsideration of individual motivation. Certainly in the United States, and probably in other markets as well, there is a limit to the homogenization of the mass market. Individualism, which de Tocqueville described as a principal characteristic of Americans even in the early 19th century creates a resistance to conformity that confounds stochastic predictions of economic behavior and severely limits the size of the market for indistinguishable goods. Even societies that are not thought of as having a cultural tradition of individualism, such as China, offer evidence of the limited utility of homogenization for control and coordination. In light of this limitation, the communications and information technologies that seem to portend demassification may simply reflect the development of the technological capacity to extend the monitoring and management of consumption beyond the previously cost-effective limits.

If one keeps in mind that the reason for resorting to stochastic knowledge in economic planning was the inability to gather and comprehend the totality of aggregated individual information, the dev-

2. An exhaustive review of the literature on the economics of information and the means by which information has been fitted into economic models can be found in Lamberton (1984).

elopment of bubble memory and supercomputers takes on a new importance. Although no current technology would allow for cost-effective collection, storage, and processing of information about every individual, matching techniques (Marx and Reichman, 1984), modeling techniques (Gandy and Simmons, 1986), geodemographics (Robbin, 1980), and clustering by Values-Attitudes-Lifestyles (Riche, 1982) all seem to make it possible to have and use "virtually" individualized information in ways that would be cost-effective for some products or purposes. The key is that just as technology made it increasingly possible to know about and to influence individual preferences in values, attitudes, and lifestyles, corporate and governmental interest in coordination and control has provided a market for that technology. There is a clear and rapid trend toward collection, storage, and use of massive quantities of specific individual information for the purpose of discriminating among segments of the public on the basis of differences in their motivations and likely political and economic behavior.

This does not mean that there is no longer a mass society. To the degree that individual motivations can be homogenized, the effects of those motivations will continue to be more easily planned for and managed. In some markets, especially in relatively uncommercialized markets in the Third World, the efforts to rationalize consumption will continue to depend on the mass media and mass marketing for some time to come. But where marginal productivity in coordination and control by homogenization begins to decline, greater cost-effectiveness is now possible through the new technologies for market segmentation. The uses of information and communications technologies for homogenization of the market have raised concerns over the conflict between the corporate and governmental values of stability and growth, on the one hand, and the social value of liberty, on the other. The uses of the new information and communications technologies for segmentation of the market should raise concerns over the threat posed to the social value of equality.

The ideology of modern economics, as described by Heilbroner, treats as worthy of consideration only that which has an effect on costs and revenues and is thereby relevant to efficiency. It sees "the market as a 'mechanism' for the rational allocation of resources," and is therefore "able to speak about its workings without the encumbrances of guilt that inhibited or cramped economic understanding in earlier times" (Heilbroner, 1986, p. 47). This pursuit of an "economic understanding" of "rational allocation" is what motivated Francis Walker to enjoin students of economics "not to allow any purely political, ethical, or social considerations to influence" them. What, then, will be the result of the collection, storage, and use of information about individual values, attitudes, and lifestyles for the purpose of economic rationalization through market segmentation?

Mass marketing has operated on the assumption that opinion and belief are elements of individual motivation, capable of being monitored and managed by information and mass communications technologies. Market segmentation relies on separating individuals into "clusters" according to their opinions and beliefs. Differences among these groups are the key factors in understanding differences in the motivations of individuals within the groups. Monitoring those differences poses the familiar threat to privacy and other individual liberties that has received much attention. Managing those differences raises another issue altogether. The media that carry segmented marketing messages, just like the ones that carry mass marketing messages, and even the marketing messages themselves, are socialization agents. Values, attitudes, and lifestyles are learned from the content of communications media, whether those media are mass media or not. Moreover, the capacity to socialize different portions of society into different values, attitudes, and lifestyles, and to do so from one generation to the next, seems to offer considerable stability to market segmentation as a technique for the rationalization of consumption. This means that the demassification of society may actually be a powerful reinforcement of social stratifications that could be hereditary and, because they would work through individual motivation, self-enforcing.

As to the question whether segmentation of the market is necessarily stratification of society, the early evidence suggests that it is. It is, of course, possible to imagine market segmentation using variables that have nothing to do with a status hierarchy. But the reality of the political and commercial marketing that has used these techniques is that economic, racial, and ethnic variables have been used in stratification that is explicitly conscious of status. Donnelley Marketing Information Services and Simmons Market Research Bureau developed a system called ClusterPlus^{SM} that divides the mass market into "47 distinct lifestyle clusters" (Arbitron Ratings, 1983). If one knows that cluster Z01 indicates Top Income, Well Educated, Professionals, Prestige Homes, and that cluster Z47 indicates Poorly Educated, Unskilled, Rural, Southern Blacks, it is quite clear that these clusters are stratified explicitly according to status. A similar development for political marketing by the Claritas Corporation in 1980 (since much refined) used 40 clusters (Robbin 1980). More clearly geographically defined than ClusterPlus^{SM}, they are nonetheless equally status-oriented. Cluster number 11 is called "Dixie-Style Tenements," and its members are described as residents of the lowest-class city neighborhoods, mixed black and Hispanic, families and singles, with some high school education and very low socioeconomic status. Cluster number 28, however, is "Blue Blood Estates," a suburban community of the highest class, consisting of predominantly white college graduates with families. The theoretical possibility that segmentation need not mean stratification seems unworthy of too much consideration.

This is not to suggest that there could be, in these clusters, a replacement for the concept of social class based on kinship and property. Daniel Bell has suggested that "as the traditional class structure dissolves, more and more individuals want to be identified, not by their occupational base (in the Marxist sense), but by their cultural tastes and lifestyles" (Bell, 1970, p. 20). This perception reinforces the idea that individuals may be willing to accept identification with the clusters into which they can be put and may therefore be manipulated by them. It does not, however, mean that these stratifications would necessarily be related to differences among the groups in regard to property ownership. Though social class is a concept in need of redefinition, the stratification under consideration here does not seem relevant to it.[3] The forces maintaining these stratifications would be the beliefs of the members. Socialization into them would probably be kinship- and peer-group-related, both explicitly and through learned patterns of media usage. Such stratification might be more usefully characterized as a caste system: a system based on differentiations among individuals that may function to reinforce economic divisions in society. In Marx's view, caste stratification functioned to obscure the relevant, property-based divisions in society, being based on perceived differences among groups and not necessarily on any objective differences.

Why would individuals be receptive to their stratification into distinct divisions of society? Robert Bellah and his associates, in their exploration of the modern form of American individualism, *Habits of the Heart,* assert:

> The sectoral pattern of modern American society has thus often been able to contain potential conflicts by separating those who are different without impairing the economic linkages of sectors within the larger economy. . . . The concept of one's "peers" concomitantly un-

3. For a discussion of the redefinition of social class that dealt (rather stridently) with the use of values and lifestyles in defining social stratification, see Anderson (1974).

derwent a subtle, but important, shift of meaning. It came to signify those who share the same specific mix of activities, beginning with occupation and economic position, but increasingly implying the same attitudes, tastes, and style of life.(Bellah et al., 1985, p. 44).

And although they warn that "where history and hope are forgotten and community means only the gathering of the similar, community degenerates into lifestyle enclave" (ibid., p. 154), they conclude that there is a yearning in modern culture for a sense of community that could give greater meaning to individualism. If the segmentation of communications media could be so complete as to provide for each "cluster" within the market a separately defined, elaborately produced "history and hope," these segments of society could become powerful sources of identification, satisfying the yearning for the sense of community that Bellah and his colleagues suggest is needed, if not "Transforming American Culture," as their concluding chapter is called, precisely as they would hope.

CONCLUSION

Political economy has been concerned with the protection of at least two different values in the production and distribution of wealth. The classical political economists argued the case for individual liberty. Marx argued the case for equality. In their considerations of the role of information in industrial society, political economists have focused almost exclusively on the threat to liberty, especially privacy, posed by the gathering of statistical information and the use of the mass media for the distribution of information. In an information society a corresponding threat to equality may be posed by the use of information about individuals for market segmentation and the use of targeted communications media for distribution of information. The study of political economy should address both concerns.

REFERENCES

Anderson, C. H. (1974). *The Political Economy of Social Class*. Englewood Cliffs, N.J.: Prentice Hall.

Arbitron Ratings (1983). "TargetAID: A Whole New Way To Define The Broadcast Audience." Publication no. GN-0105, 8, 83. New York: Arbitron Ratings Company.

Arrow, K. J. (1974). *The Limits of Organization*. New York: W. W. Norton.

Balogh, T. (1982). *The Irrelevance of Conventional Economics*. New York: Liveright.

Bell, D. (1970). "The Cultural Contradictions of Capitalism," *Public Interest*, no. 21, Fall, pp. 16–43.

Bellah, R. N.; R. Madsen; W. M. Sullivan; A. Swidler; and S. M. Tipton. (1985). *Habits of the Heart.* Berkeley: University of California Press.

Galbraith, J. K. (1985). *The New Industrial State.* 4th. ed. Boston: Houghton Mifflin.

Gandy, O. H., Jr., and C.E. Simmons (1986). "Technology, Privacy and the Democratic Process," *Critical Studies in Mass Communications,* 3, pp. 155–68.

Heilbroner, R. L. (1967). *The Worldly Philosophers.* New York: Simon and Schuster.

Heilbroner, R. L. (1986). "The Murky Economists." *The New York Review of Books,* 33, 24 April, pp. 46–48.

Lamberton, D. M. (1984). "The Economics of Information and Organization," *Annual Review of Information Science and Technology,* 19, pp. 3–30.

Machlup, F. (1962). *The Production and Distribution of Knowledge in the United States.* Princeton: Princeton University Press.

Marx, G. T. (1985). "I'll Be Watching You." *Dissent,* 32, Winter, pp. 26–34.

Marx,G. T., and N. Reichman (1984). "Routinizing the Discovery of Secrets." *American Behavioral Scientist,* 27, pp. 423–52.

McCloskey, D. N. (1986). *The Rhetoric of Economics.* Madison: University of Wisconsin Press.

Miliband, R. (1977). *Marxism and Politics.* Oxford: Oxford University Press.

Riche, M. F. (1982). "VALS: Values + Attitudes + Lifestyles." *American Demographics,* 4,3. pp. 38–39.

Robbin, J. (1980). "Geodemographics: The New Magic." *Campaigns & Elections,* Spring, pp. 25–45.

Robbins, L. C. (1976). *Political Economy Past and Present.* London: Macmillan.

Smith, A. (1976). *An Inquiry into the Nature and Causes of the Wealth of Nations.* Oxford: Clarendon Press.

Stigler, G. J. (1983). "Nobel Lecture: The Process and Progress of Economics." *Journal of Political Economy,* 91, pp. 529–45.

Walker, F. A. (1888). *Political Economy.* London: Macmillan.

Williams, F. (1984). *The New Communications.* Belmont, Calif.: Wadsworth.

6. The Political Economy of Communications Competence

Oscar H. Gandy, Jr.

To understand and to be understood is the most basic human right, one which must be secured for all as we emerge into this postindustrial, information society. It is the right upon which all other human rights ultimately come to depend, and it may be shown to have always been central, at least in theory, to the functioning of democratic society.

Although it is becoming increasingly fashionable to question whether democracy is in fact possible (even if begrudgingly recognized as desirable), this essay proceeds from the assumption that we are all better off if each person enjoys the possibility of maximizing his or her full potential, and having done so, enjoys the benefits such a society produces. In the ideal, at least, democratic social organization represents the best alternative when recognition of the complexity of social reality demands a self-correcting system of rules and procedures.

Movement toward an idealized democracy which maximizes both the contributions to and the satisfactions to be derived from active participation is severely constrained whenever a host of nonrandom factors determine that certain groups and individuals never achieve social or political equality. "Equality of opportunity can't be said to exist as long as associated group characteristics are correlated with economic position, intellectual achievement, social status, or other important socially valued goods" (Guttman, 1980, p. 109).

Of course, at this point in an academic's chapter about technology and the future, it is generally expected that an author will identify polar extremes in order to locate one's views comfortably in the middle, neatly balanced astride technologies with outcomes determined not by their inherent character, but by the character of their users (or the user systems into which they emerge). But at the risk of appearing naive or, worse still, ideological, this essay will argue that a substantial and growing disparity in communications competence is at the heart of this constraint, and that the new communication and information technologies, as presently designed and introduced into social use, are likely to exacerbate the problem.

Because of the increasing commoditization and privatization of information, and because of mounting personal and social deficits, the poor, especially among black and ethnic minority groups, are largely unable to utilize information resources to improve the quality of their lives. This aspect of communications competence, the ability to understand the world so as to act to change it, is only one variable in the equation of inequality.

Market structured limits on conscious awareness are almost matched by similar limits on the ability of the poor to articulate their concerns and to present their demands effectively in the relevant policy centers. Racial and economic segregation appears to be heightening critical forms of social and cultural differentiation, making alliances within and across class lines all the more difficult.

At the same time that the poor are losing ground in this struggle to see and define the world in their own best interests, information elites find their competence enhanced at every turn. For those with the financial and intellectual resources, there is ready access to highly specialized information processing and retrieval services. Not only do microcomputers now provide this technical elite with enhanced analytical capacity, but many systems produce sophisticated multicolor graphic representations, which help to decompose the growing complexity of daily life and present it in ways which are compelling, if not entirely true.

Virtually unlimited access to information about consumers and markets allows these bureaucratically organized interests to segment their relevant markets and to deliver specialized, targeted messages to some while avoiding or ignoring others. The implications of these trends for the future are powerfully disheartening.

THE PROBLEM OF DEMOCRACY

In the contemporary political arena, it appears that belief in the market, rather than the state, is in the ascendancy. James Buchanen (1986, p. 268), as a leading theorist of this school, suggests that "to the extent that markets work, there is no need for the state. Markets allow persons to interact, one with another, in a regime that combines freedom and order, provided only that the state supply the protective legal umbrella." What Buchanen and others fail to consider is that common descriptions of markets ignore the reality that some participants in the market have incentives and resources which allow them to influence how others understand their interests, and the benefits they may derive from purchases or trades in the market. And the state is more often than not led to intervene on behalf of those with greater resources, rather than on behalf of those with the greatest need.

Even where the state is seen to be more democratic in its intent, its organization appears to have antidemocratic consequences. "A welfare state increases the opportunity for bureaucracies to usurp unsanctioned authority, subverting the ends of that state, and also increasing the dependency of citizens upon bureaucratic rather than upon democratic (participatory) institutions" (Guttman, 1980, p. 209).

John Burnheim (1985, p. 3) suggests that pessimism about the democratic possibility may be traced back at least as far as Aristotle, who argued that democracy "inevitably degenerated into rule by the orators and ultimately into tyranny." More contemporary critics like John Rawls also recognize the importance of oratory and debate and the contemporary limits on popular participation. "The liberties protected by the principle of participation lose much of their value whenever those who have greater private means are permitted to use their advantages to control the course of public debate" (Guttman, 1980, p. 138). I wish to suggest that this is a problem of communications competence.

Jonathan Kozol (1985) argues that nearly one-third of the U.S. population is essentially denied full participation in the process of governance. Because upwards of 30 percent of adults living in the United States are functionally illiterate, they are incapable of participating effectively in those institutions which society had developed to ensure its democratic character. Illiterates are unlikely to vote, and "those that do are forced to cast a vote of questionable worth" (ibid., p. 23). When an illiterate is allowed to serve on a jury, Kozol suggests that such a juror is easily won over by the opinions of an articulate but selective reader. Illiterates are not even able to influence their schools in a way that might lead the educational establishment to avoid producing the next generation of illiterates:

> Those. . . who do not possess the competence to read and write, to analyze, to research and draw the right conclusions from that research, cannot turn their intuitions into criticisms that the school will hear. . . . Administrators. . . find it easy to defend the school against the accurate but imprecisely stated protests of the neighborhood or community they serve. Devoted parents, starved of information that otherwise informs their sensitivity with vision and concreteness, find themselves disarmed before the jargon that the school employs to guard the gates and reinforce the walls. (ibid., p. 70)

Although fraught with understandable controversy, there is a suggestion by the linguist William Labov (Morse, 1985) that because of continuing patterns of racial segregation, urban black speech has become increasingly divergent from that of other English speakers. In addition, the continued use of "Black English" is said to delay the development of skill in the use of Standard English. Failure to achieve a command of Standard English represents an almost insurmountable barrier to economic self-suffiency. The sorting processes that select individuals for opportunity and advancement are sensitive to speech, treating language as an index of intelligence, capacity, or potential.

This group has significantly less opportunity to develop competence and skill in the new information technologies because the same social and economic constraints bar their access to such systems. Milton Chen examined the pattern of adoption of microcomputers by elementary schools and determined that adoption rates were "lower for schools with low socioeconomic status (SES) and schools serving [a] predominantly minority student population. Predominantly white schools had twice as many computers as predominantly minority schools" (1986, p. 2). When he looked at the data on households with computers, median income for these homes was $27,000, whereas median income for the nation was $12,000. A study of ethnic minorities in Texas (Shoemaker, Reese, and Danielson, 1985) suggested that members of these groups were likely to expect a technology gap to emerge between people like themselves and the majority of Americans. Harris data (1984) suggest that while race is not an important predictor of computer literacy, income is strongly related to knowledge and expertise.

In describing this population in their report to the Ford Foundation, Carmen St. John Hunter and David Harmon (1979, p. 108) suggest that "their problems are inextricably interwoven with class, race and their access to power. By the time they are adults, those who are caught in a complex of social and economic disadvantages suffer multiple impediments that cannot be removed by learning to read and write." Indeed, the hard-core, stationary poor whom Dahrendorf (1984) identifies as the *lumpenproletariat* are largely invisible:

> They may live in the very shadow of major institutions of health-care or education, yet receive no benefits from those institutions. Their interaction with the majority culture is minimal. Encounters with bureaucracies set up to serve them—employment, housing, health services, their children's schools, the welfare system, the courts—all contribute to their sense of defeat and help perpetuate the cycles of deprivation and alienation. (Hunter and Harmon, 1979, p. 113).

In Dahrendorf's view, it is an error even to call this large and growing group an underclass. He suggests that "it is a misleading term; it is not a class. There is no solidarity among its members because there is no shared reason why they end up in it. Being part of it is a matter of individual fate. . . .The members of the underclass, therefore, are not caught in a common destiny; they are a mass of individuals, each with personal problems" (1984, p. 22). Although we may offer clear and explicit reasons to suggest why these people end up where they do, such as a cultural deficit reinforced by social history (Lemann, 1986), the point to be taken from Dahrendorf's warning is that people do not perceive or understand their class connections, and do not recognize the potential benefit of collective action. And as Ben Bagdikian (1983, p. 46) suggests, the news media play a critical role in defining a political reality which maintains unquestioning support of capitalism. "The result of the overwhelming power of relatively narrow corporate ideologies has been the creation of widely established political and economic illusions in the United States with little visible contradiction in the media to which a majority of the population is exclusively exposed." Although broad reading of newspapers and journals of opinion might provide some Americans with alternative visions, the great majority, and certainly all the illiterates, are relegated to the electronic media, which provide only dim impressions of reality (Gandy and ElWaylly, 1985).

A recent series of articles on the youth of America (Schmidt, 1986) offers some evidence that social understanding has taken a significant hegemonic shift to the right, which may in fact explain the remarkable passivity of the poor in the face of the Reagan-inspired dismantling of the social safety net:

> These unemployed and often undereducated young people do not demand or expect much help from their government. They do not feel cheated or wronged. In contrast to young people in past generations, they respect authority. . . .there are no common goals among young people. . . .and no feeling of allegiance toward their own age group. Poor and unemployed young people see no cause for dissent. . . . "There's a passive acceptance by people of their condition. . . . They're seen as failures, and it's seen as their fault." (ibid., pp. 1, 12)

This army of unemployed and unemployable are systematically (structurally) excluded from the democratic process, and as the new information technologies transform the nature of work, their numbers are bound to grow still larger.

HIGH TECHNOLOGY AND THE EMPLOYMENT CONSTRAINT

Sanford Lakoff (1964) offers an insightful analysis of the problems of equality and the social order. For him, the achievement of socialist equality is possible only at a time when technological advance provides for abundance, where the relations of production have been so substantially transformed that they no longer form the basis of class antagonisms. Some readings on the nature of a future information society suggest that there will certainly be significant movement in a direction of transformed relations of production.

Those analyses that focus primarily on the nature of employment (Jones, 1982; Watts, 1983) suggest an eventual and necessary delinking of work and participation in the economic system. However, many, like Patricia Arriaga (1985), call our attention to the paradoxical nature of such an industrial trend. As more and more human resources are linked with essentially nonproductive labor (information work), and fewer and fewer are associated with the production of actual wealth or value in society, dislocations will occur with potentially disastrous social and political consequences.

Optimistic futurists expect that some new, as yet unidentified, product or use value will be identified which will absorb both excess labor and inflated demand, but Barry Jones suggests that we may enter a period of social dislocation far worse than that which we experienced in the 1970s:

> The decade was marked by an exhaustion of intellectual curiosity, growing pessimism about education, spiritual apathy and social anomie, a rise in irrational cultism, a retreat to privatized experience and drug dependence, a loss of historical perspective (with increasing emphasis on "now time"), dropping out and alienation. (1982, p. 45)

As evidence that we are moving toward a disjunction with the present growth curve, Jones (ibid., pp. 38–39) identifies the following characteristics of the information age: (1) we are witnessing a decline in manufacturing; (2) there is a decline in the cost of technology relative to the costs of labor, for which capitalist rationality demands substitution of one for the other; (3) the new technology has greater range, capability, and reliability and enjoys rates of development, adoption, and diffusion which far outdistance those of any previous technological era; (4) fed by the action of transnational corporations, there is a widespread internationalization and integration of the world's technological and economic systems, involving an international division of labor; (5) this technology is different from other technology in that it is not only strong, fast, and inexhaustible, but also smart and, as a result, largely labor-displacing, rather than complementary; (6) at the same time, the ideological and political controls over the process are being superseded by administrative, bureaucratic, and technical rather than political or social decision making.

UNDER SURVEILLANCE

Perhaps as a defense against the uncertainty and dislocations which analysts like Jones predict, the state and the private bureaucracies have begun to increase their investment in a variety of information-based responses to the challenges of the future. Gary Marx argues that:

> The information-gathering powers of the state and private organizations are extending ever deeper into the social fabric. The ethos of social control has expanded from focused and direct coercion used after the fact and against a particular target to anticipatory actions entailing deception, manipulation, planning and a diffuse panoptic vision. . . . surveillance increasingly involves more complex transactional analysis, interrelating persons and events. (1985, p. 26)

These new surveillance methods differ from traditional means in several ways identified by Marx (ibid., pp. 30–31): (1) they transcend distance, time, darkness, and physical barriers; (2) they are capital rather than labor-intensive; and, very important (3) they represent a shift from targeting a specific suspect to broad categories of suspects. As a major departure for the new surveillance, Marx notes that (4) "one of its major concerns is the prevention of violations," and because it is so decentralized, (5) it triggers self-policing. (6) It is largely invisible and (7) probes beneath surfaces, "discovering previously inaccessible information." He suggests that not only has the "new surveillance been generally welcomed by those in business, government and law enforcement," but "Americans seem increasingly willing, even eager, to live with intrusive technologies because of the benefits they expect to result" (ibid., p. 31).

Priscilla Regan and Fred Weingarten of the Office of Technology Assessment (1986) offer a similarly detailed description of the "surveillance revolution." They note that these "new surveillance tools are technically more difficult to detect, of higher reliability and sensitivity, speedier in processing time, less costly, more flexible and adaptable, and easier to conceal because of miniaturization and remote control" (ibid., p. 5). They note further that most of the information available about the use of such technology is based on government reports, and they conclude the "many forms of private sector electronic surveillance go undetected, and if detected, go unreported" (ibid., p. 6).

The difficulty we face is that law enforcement interests tend to outweigh civil liberties or social power interests when decisions have to be made about surveillance. And we see clear evidence that concerns for economic and social efficiency are gaining similar priority. Whereas court orders are required to place a tap on a telephone in order to investigate a crime, federal welfare agencies appear unrestricted in their ability to search government files to detect cases of persons who might be in violation of government regulations.

Pete Earley recently (1986) presented a frightening if apocryphal story of a government bureaucrat who utilized his desktop terminal to identify and then gather a massive amount of personal and financial information about a potential weekend date on the basis of an automobile license he recorded after becoming attracted to her at a traffic light. Earley notes that the massive amounts of detail in files which can be assessed by government workers will grow substantially in response to demands by the Office of Management and Budget (OMB) "to reduce fraud in federal welfare programs by requiring states to investigate the backgrounds of welfare applicants before adding them to the federal benefit rolls" (ibid., p. 10). These "income verification programs" represent an extension of administrative programs which were field-tested in "Operation Match" before they were recommended to the states. In 1985 the General Accounting Office (GAO) suggested the great variety of possible computer matches which could be pursued utilizing data on recipients of Aid to Families with Dependent Children. These matches, which utilized public and private databases, included credit bureau records, school records, bank records, motor vehicle registrations, a variety of retirement accounts, as well a major federal benefit programs, including Social Security and Employment Security programs (*Privacy Journal*, 1985). With changes in the interpretation of the Privacy Law, none of these matches would be illegal because they had been redefined as "routine use" of government data, and the concept of "reasonable" is no longer binding because such searches do not involve physical and forcible entry (Plesser, 1984).

Although OMB responds that these programs represent no threat to the privacy of American citizens, Earley carefully notes that these systems will in fact create a "de facto national data bank through state governments" (1986, p. 11), which not only has the capacity for interconnection, but is all-inclusive in that it is not limited to those who apply for government services, but to all persons who have machine-readable records.

As Marx (1985) has suggested, the new systems developed by the state are not limited to those necessary to detect crime, but can be used to deny persons access to government services (and eventually, a variety of commercial services). This new extension is what the emerging industry calls "front-end verification." It makes more sense, from the perspective of government and its corporate advisors (e.g., the Grace Commission), to stop crime before it occurs. It is likely that the logic and the technology which represents a new gate at the door to the welfare state will perform a "stop and frisk" on each person attempting to pass through, delaying or refusing entry to any whose profile adds up to a high-risk score.

We should note that at the same time that the government is increasing its surveillance of the average citizen, a program of privatization and classification is making it increasingly difficult to keep our eyes on the government (see Chapter 8 in this volume). The American Library Association has noted a number of disturbing trends which mark a growth in barriers to access to government information (1985). Among these is the tendency of the government to contract with commercial firms to gather and process government information and then to make it available only in electronic formats.

The government bureaucracy, in its determination to reduce inefficiencies in the operation of the welfare state, is clearly more visibly active than the private sector in its use of the new information technology to reduce uncertainty about just who we are, and what we may or may not be entitled to. Yet because there remains some degree of legally guaranteed oversight and redress, including a constitutionally mandated shield against certain publicly abhorred abuses of government power, the assault by the state may perhaps be seen as less onerous than those which characterize the corporate sector.

CORPORATE DATA GATHERING

The nature and the extent of the information piracy, which I define as information about us, taken against our will, or without our knowledge, and impressed into service for the benefit of others without just compensation, varies greatly from business to business. Those industries which are involved in the marketing of products and services tend to gather and utilize information in order to deliver persuasive messages most efficiently and effectively. Those industries which sell shared risk, like insurance companies and, to a lesser extent, financial services firms, gather information in order to set prices or to deny service to those who represent limited profit potential. In this regard, these companies and their information suppliers are very much like the government.

The insurance agencies utilize a variety of commercial intermediaries whose sole business is the collection of information about potential clients. The widespread panic about Acquired Immune Deficiency Syndrome (AIDS) is experienced nowhere more acutely than within the health insurance industry. And although schools and employers may have some limits on their ability to gather information about one's probability of being a carrier, a victim of the disease, or a member of a high-risk group on the basis of sexual preference, the health insurers appear to face no investigative barriers in gathering information about insurability. Only explicit government policy, like that in the District of Columbia which forbids discrimination on the basis of presumed risk of contracting AIDS, serves to limit the impact of such data gathering.

In one sense, information gathered by insurance and credit services firms is similar to the kinds of information being gathered by employers about their actual and potential employees. A variety of technical systems are employed to screen, and then to monitor, employee behavior. Polygraphs have been joined by chemical tests of body wastes to determine whether individuals represent acceptable risks or good investments.

Firms which find themselves faced with increasing competition and diversification of their geographic markets are turning rapidly toward research and analysis to generate more insightful approaches to those markets. A series of mergers within the market and audience research industries suggests that some of the trends identified earlier (Gandy and Simmons, 1986) have accelerated. Time, Inc., Burke Marketing, and Arbitron have come together to develop a people meter/scanner approach to research called ScanAmerica (Fannin, 1986).

Like the BehaviorScan approach, which utilizes dual-cable test markets and the universal product codes to evaluate the effectiveness of commercial messages in different editorial environments, the new ScanAmerica system adds a "people meter" to link individual audience demographics more closely to purchases at the same time that it frees the marketers from agreements with individual stores in test communities. Members of the participating households, which are expected to eventually number 10,000, are reminded periodically to key in their personal code when they begin or stop viewing television. The same household, for fees of up to $400 per year, agrees to utilize a pen-like scanner to record the products they bring into the house. By placing the pen into the same device that monitors their television viewing, the system allows Arbitron to "determine the effect that the commercials—and programming—watched by the family has on its buying habits. And, because each family member logs in to the people meter individually. . . .the system permits a demographic analysis of responses to commercials by age, education, race, sex and other characteristics" (*Privacy Journal*, 1986, p. 1).

Joint licensing agreements allow the combination of research databases to provide market researchers with information in varying degrees of detail about the social, demographic, political, and consumer characteristics of most Americans. Many of these new services are available to researchers and decision-makers for analysis in the home office on individual personal computers (PCs). The Pepsi Cola Company has developed an integrated system which allows its market research people to "get on to retrieve the data, put it into a spreadsheet, graph it, report it, link it up in a capsule and then, provide an application that the brand people can use" (Conlon, 1986, p. 170).

Nielsen is said to have 100 customers who utilize PCs to access a common database on a time-sharing basis. They combine national ratings and demographics with the geographic clustering information from PRIZM. This facility allows the matching of viewer profiles with product-use patterns. Special ratings services provide for analyses of special target groups, like high-income households (Zahradnik, 1986). Nielsen's information product mix also includes a unique twist which places it in the category of broadcaster as well as researcher. Fannin (1986) notes that Nielsen's test markets are the "only test markets where test commercials can be inserted into regular programming schedules in homes with or without cable. Nielsen is able to do this because it has set up its own broadcasting facility. The signal is picked up by households with a microcomputer attached to the home tv, and a special antenna on the roof" (ibid., p. 82). These new systems allow the researchers to break the test communities up into multiple groups on the basis of predetermined criteria, either demographic or behavioral. An associated ability to count the number of commercials viewed by any individual allows the researchers to determine "if a consumer viewed a Folger's coffee commercial three times, would it lead them to switch to the brand" (ibid., p. 86).

Simmons Market Research Bureau, Inc., continues to conduct 19,000 annual interviews with adults 18 and over. These interviews generate some 43 volumes of data which are now available to customers on 45 diskettes for analysis on PCs. This enormous dataset includes readership of some 110 magazines, use of newspapers, television, radio, and Yellowpages, sufficient information to generate 27 demographic breakouts, (e.g., self-concept and buying styles, work-related activities) and data on some 4,000 brands in 800 product categories.

If that were not enough, Simmons integrated services offerings include a special targeted survey of 2,000 college students, which, in addition to the traditional values and behavioral indices, asks their opinions of major U.S. corporations (Zahradnik, 1986).

A group called National Demographics and Lifestyles offers a service it calls "Lifestyle Census" which utilizes a database of some 25 million U.S. consumers, listed by name and address, with information about their leisure activities, demographics, and geography. Another service called "VISIONS" segments consumers by postal route and "precisely identifies and locates who best customers and prospects are, where and how they live, and what they read, listen to and watch and how effectively to reach them." It is said to classify *each* of 88 million households on the basis of demographic, socioeconomic, and housing characteristics. The service makes available specialized software which customers can utilize to generate custom maps of the areas where the best prospects are more densely clustered (*Marketing Communications*, 1986b, p. 188).

Several smaller firms concentrate on particular market segments or subpopulations. The growing population of affluent two-earner families represents a special challenge to the marketers, who recognize that more information is needed to reach this target population successfully:

> Two households, each earning the same income, will live very differently depending upon a number of characteristics such as social class, education, aspiration levels and lifecycles because each of these factors determines how they see their options and who they consider their peers. Ultimately these factors alter how and why they spend their income. (*Marketing Communications*, 1986a, p. 41)

Black advertising agencies are said to be just beginning to develop their research capacity to target the nearly 30 million black Americans with a combined income of some $203 billion. At the moment, these firms are concentrating their efforts on developing advertising content and promotional appeals for media which generally available research has identified as prime locations for finding the black consumer (Parkowski, 1986).

To those who suggest that market research is harmless, merely a way of helping industry respond to the needs and interests of a public which may not have found a way to express those interests, I offer another, less sanguine view. Even if it is true that market research is not directed toward creating tastes and preferences for which there is no tendency, but merely toward identifying potential markets, we must recognize that this approach is inherently conservative and antidemocratic. We might consider the process of market segmentation and targeting similar to that of color image processing. The complex, integrated image of the real world is broken up by dichroic filters in the video camera into coherent bands of light of the same frequency (colors) and sent to different pickup tubes for processing and later recombination into a recognizable image. This recombination takes place only after color correction, modification, or enhancement is performed on these isolated parts of the whole. Although our reflections may have provided the initial basis for the images of ourselves that we get back through the marketplace, they are distorted in a way that is largely beyond our control. Blemishes—or creative, nonconformist hard edges—have been erased by digital smoothing.

OUR RESPONSIBILIY TOWARD THE FUTURE

Many analysts respond to the threats represented by this massive advance in the state and corporate sectors' ability to gather, process, and utilize information about a relatively powerless and clearly outmatched public by appealing to broadly shared concerns about privacy (Gandy and Simmons, 1986). David Flaherty (1985) and others note that traditional definitions of privacy are inadequate to respond to the kinds of wholesale invasions which characterize this high-technology phase. Flaherty speaks to the emerging problem of "group privacy," which "poses some challenges to the traditional privacy claims of individuals. The basic problem occurs when an individual is identified or identifiable as a member of a certain group, by reason of where he or she lives or works, and then receives unwanted attention in the form of solicitations, discrimination, or publicity" (ibid., p. 3). He speaks to the problems which emerge when different firms and agencies create lists, each of which may comply with limited rules restricting their use, but lose control and abandon responsibility when those lists are combined by third parties:

> Using city directories (now automated), postal codes, telephone directories (also automated), mailing lists, and other sources, specialists on geo-coding and target marketing can use computer manipulation to put together very precise information about the characteristics of families living in specific areas. Median-income, voter registration, and data on auto ownership or magazine subscribers in a refined postal area, can produce a fairly precise idea of the consumer and political choices in a particular household. Candidates for election can then di-

> rectly approach specific persons for support. Marketers can aim advertising more precisely. (ibid., p. 6)

Flaherty notes that there have been increasing reports of public resistance to further data gathering by governments in West Germany, the Netherlands, and Sweden. The corporate community in the United States is highly sensitive to the implications that increased public awareness of such a massive erosion of privacy might have. When the Internal Revenue Service (IRS) inaugurated its test of a program to match tax files with commercially available lists which estimated family incomes for millions of Americans (Earley, 1984), the list-sellers, represented most actively by the Direct Marketing Association, appealed to the government not to pursue this path. Alexander Hoffman, chairman of the association, expressed his fears most clearly in his comments to the House committee exploring notions of civil liberties:

> They will come gradually to understand that the IRS is using census data to overlay on the basic mailing lists. And we believe that an inevitable consequence of such a chain of events carried out broadly and nationally would be a tendency of the people to view this as just one more invasion of privacy; just one more step in Government intrusion in our lives; and they would gradually tend to conclude that it is not a very good idea to have your name on a mailing list. And next, perhaps that it is not even a very good idea to be a voluntary participant in marketing research. And next, perhaps, that it is not even a very good idea to be a voluntary participant in filling out your census questionnaire. . . .So this is a process that the public likes and they, at present, have confidence in it and accept it as a legitimate business process. But if they ever came to feel that endangerment of their personal privacy might become a byproduct of this, they could change their attitude entirely. So that is our concern. (Hoffman, 1984, pp. 320–321)

Of course, Mr. Hoffman is right. And it is the responsibility of critical scholars or persons concerned with civil liberties and committed to the ideal of participatory democracy to begin the process of raising public consciousness. This charge represents a difficult, and surely thankless, task because it flies directly in the face of a cultural acceptance of efficiency as the driving moral and social imperative. It almost appears that to miss an opportunity for profit is a more serious crime than to neglect a child, ignore suffering, or deny basic human rights to the indigent.

Raising public consciousness about the growing disparity in communications competence will not be an easy task. Once we recognize the special "event-quality" of collective responses like "Live-Aid" and "Hands Across America," we must see that victim-blaming has been cultivated as the dominant social response to evidence of suffering and need. An army of volunteers has not succeeded in reaching more than 5 percent of those Americans in need of literacy education, yet the federal establishment has not been convinced that the problem deserves more than rhetoric. The earlier success of movements to integrate the broadcasting and print news industries appears to have been stalled in the face of a deregulatory posture in government and a high-stakes fever of acquisitiveness by major economic units.

Privacy legislation appears to be limited to attempts to bring laws governing theft and government intrusion in touch with modern technological realities and is less concerned with the more complicated questions focusing on power relations which are at the heart of a concern with communications competence.

Still, we must persevere. These are important questions, and these are critical times. No opportunity must be lost to make the point that democracy depends upon free and active participation to the fullest extent possible by all who would be a part of society. The widening disparity in the ability to understand and be understood by others makes such participation impossible.

REFERENCES

American Library Association (1985). "Less Access to Less Information By and About the U.S. Government: A 1985 Chronology." *Newsletter on Intellectual Freedom*, 34, 6, p. 192.

Arriaga, P. (1985). "Toward a Critique of the 'Information Economy'." *Media Culture & Society*, 7, pp. 271–96.

Bagdikian, B. (1983). *The Media Monopoly*. Boston: Beacon Press.

Buchanen, J. (1986). *Liberty, Market, and State: Political Economy in the 1980s*. New York: New York University Press.

Burnheim, J. (1985) *Is Democracy Possible? The Alternative to Electoral Politics*. Berkeley: University of California Press.

Chen, M. (1986). "Social Equity and Computers in Education." Paper presented to the International Communications Association, Chicago, May.

Conlon, G. (1986). "Decision Support System for Marketers." *Marketing Communications*, 11, 3, pp. 163–74.

Dahrendorf, R. (1984). "The New Underclass." *World Press Review*, April, pp. 21–23.

Earley, P. (1984). "IRS Uses Marketing Data to Find Non-filers." *Washington Post*, 7 May.

Earley, P. (1986). "Watching Me, Watching You." *Washington Post Magazine,* 11 May.

Fannin, R. (1986). "Researchers' New Know-It-Alls." *Marketing and Media Decisions*, 21, 6, pp. 74–88.

Flaherty, D. (1985). "Cumulative Data Are Not Always Anonymous." *Privacy Journal*, 11, July, pp. 3–6.

Gandy, O., and ElWaylly, M. (1985). "The Knowledge Gap and Foreign Affairs: The Palestinian-Israeli Conflict." *Journalism Quarterly*, 62, pp. 777–83.

Gandy, O. and Simmons, C. (1986). "Technology, Privacy and the Democratic Process." *Critical Studies in Mass Communication*, 3, June, pp. 155–68.

Guttman, A. (1980). *Liberal Equality*. Cambridge: Cambridge University Press.

Harris, L. and Associates (1984). *The Road After 1984*. In U. S. Congress, House, Hearings: "Privacy and 1984: Public Opinion on Privacy Issues." Washington, D. C.: Government Printing Office.

Hoffman, A. (1984). Statement to the House Committee on the Judiciary. U.S. Congress, House Subcommittee on Courts, Civil liberties, and the Administration of Justice, Hearings: "1984 Civil Liberties and the National Security State." Washington, D.C., Government Printing Office.

Hunter, C. and Harman, D. (1979). *Adult Illiteracy in the United States: A Report to the Ford Foundation*. New York: McGraw-Hill.

Jones, B. (1982). *Sleepers Wake! Technology and the Future of Work:* Melbourne: Oxford University Press.

Kozol, J. (1985). *Illiterate America*. Garden City, N.Y.: Doubleday.

Lakoff, S. (1984). *Equality in Political Philosophy*. Boston: Beacon Press.

Lemann, N. (1986). "The Origins of the Underclass." *Atlantic*, June, pp. 31–55.

Marketing Communications (1986a). "Marketing to Aspirations: New Boundaries of Affluence." 2, pp. 33–60.

Marketing Communications (1986b). "Closing in on the Consumer." 3, pp. 177–90.

Marx, G. (1985). "I'll Be Watching You." *Dissent*, 32, Winter, pp. 26–34.

Morse, S. (1985). " 'Black English': Still Seeking Answers." *Washington Post*, 10, December.

Parkowski, M. (1986). "Shades of Grey." *Marketing and Media Decisions*, 2, March, pp. 30–50.

Plesser, R. (1984). Statement to the House Committee on the Judiciary. U.S. Congress, House Subcommittee on Courts, Civil Liberties, and the Administration of Justice. Washington, D.C.: Government Printing Office.

Privacy Journal (1985). Reference to GAO report HRD-85-22, Vol. 11, March.

Privacy Journal (1986). "People Meters and Product Codes = ScanAmerica." Vol. 12, February, pp. 1, 6.

Regan, P. and F. Weingarten (1986). "The National Communications System and Federal Electronic Surveillance." Paper presented at the Telecommunications Policy Research Conference. Airlie, Va., April.

Schmidt, S. (1986). "The Jobless Take the Blame." *Washington Post*, 28 May.

Shoemaker, P.; S. Reese, and W. Danielson (1985). *Media in Ethnic Context: Communications and Language in Texas*. Austin: University of Texas.

Watts, A. (1983). *Education, Unemployment and the Future of Work*. Milton Keynes, U.K.: Open University Press.

Zahradnick, R. (1986). "Media's Micro Age." *Marketing and Media Decisions*, 21, April, pp. 34–50.

7. Hearts and Minds Revisited: The Information Policies of the Reagan Administration

Donna A. Demac

U.S. government information policy has become quite complex. It spins the wheels of the nation's economy, and its domestic and foreign policies and determines the extent to which civil liberties are upheld. In the 1980s, owing to the interwoven objectives of American government and industry, information assumed central importance in well-orchestrated campaigns to significantly lessen the government's regulation of various industries and areas of broad societal concern, including health care and the environment. As information became more profitable, processed and reprocessed by advanced technologies, a laissez faire administration moved to transfer out numerous government information programs to the private sector. In many instances, low-cost federal publications were picked up by private companies that charged several times the original fee. Several agencies contracted out their libraries. The growing profitability of data gathered by remote sensing satellites led Congress to assign management of the Landsat program to the private sector. In addition, large reductions in information programs were carried out under the rubrics of the Paperwork Reduction Act, the national budget, and the administration's cleverly designed programs to restrict the activities of federal regulatory agencies.

Information was also put off limits to much of the American public through controls of a more political nature. Early on, in April 1982, a new presidential classification order was issued, eliminating a requirement adopted in the Carter administration that officials evaluating requests for information should weigh the public interest in disclosure against the government's interest in denying access. This order also for the first time authorized the reclassification of information already in the public domain. There have been numerous examples since then of material that was reclassified long after it was released. James Bamford's book about the National Security Agency *The Puz-*

zle Palace, which he wrote entirely from unclassified material, prompted the government to require that hundreds of documents held by the private library Bamford used be stamped "top secret."

The order on classification and another that authorized the Central Intelligence Agency to conduct domestic surveillance established the ground rules for dealing with public scrutiny. In essence, the public's right to know was converted into the government's right not to disclose.

To those who value public access to information as a means of holding officials accountable, the most important result of the Reagan administration's information policies, economic as well as political, was to dull national debate on contemporary issues. The Reagan administration's innovations in government information policy (broadly defined to encompass the vast territory of information-related economic and regulatory programs, First Amendment practices, and media relations) constitute the most ambitious attempt thus far by the White House to subdue the countervailing forces of participatory government.

ENHANCING EXECUTIVE POWER THROUGH POLITICAL CONTROLS ON INFORMATION

By the time Reagan had been office three years, it was clear that he and his advisors had little respect for the traditions of local activism and robust debate. Rules of secrecy were increasingly embedded in American politics as the administration invoked "national security" claims to justify the imposition of unprecedented restrictions on the flow of information. These included visa denials to authors, dramatists, and political leaders from foreign countries intending to visit the United States, a ban on travel to Cuba, the classification order mentioned previously, and regulations that weakened access under the Freedom of Information Act.

Government refusal to disclose information can be traced back to the country's early years. Historically, official policy on citizen access has changed with the political climate and has included a combination of open procedures, espionage laws, and ad hoc censorship. During the last 20 years, the tug of war between openness and secrecy has intensified. In 1968 Congress passed the Freedom of Information Act, a law that upheld the public right to access to information about the activities of government. Only a few years later, then-President Richard Nixon conducted a secret war in Cambodia. This and other abuses of executive power soon led Congress to strengthen the FOIA. Then in the 1980s, the Reagan administration moved to tip the scale on the side of government secrecy, going much farther than any of its predecessors.

The particular restrictions introduced during this period are extremely important. They proved effective in centralizing control in the White House. In addition, pervasive secrecy, including the selective disclosure of information and misinformation, undermined the oversight powers of Congress and limited the possibility of effective public response to government programs. Many of these restrictions have been written about in books and magazine articles (American Library Association, 1985-87; Demac, 1984; Dorsen et al., 1984; Marro, 1985; Peck, 1985). In this section, however, we will focus on the way such restrictions were introduced and implemented, rather than on the actual restrictions. The intention is to show that the Reagan administration's *practice of conditioning consent* was as essential to extending government control as the content of the restrictions imposed.

Trial Balloons

In December 1985, in an act that Secretary of Defense Caspar Weinberger described as "giving aid and comfort to the enemy", the *Washington Post* printed information concerning a space shuttle flight with a military payload after the media had been briefed on the flight but told to maintain secrecy. In the debate that followed, there was criticism of the government's attempt to curb freedom of the press, but many accepted the administration's justification at face value. The president of the Society of Newspaper Editors was quoted as saying, "I find it a little difficult to believe that, if several major news sources got the information, that it's not available to other nations' agents." *Aviation Week and Space Technology*, the most widely respected magazine in the space industry, editorialized that the real target may have been the American public. Yet virtually no one tied Weinberger's blunderous attempt at censorship to the release that same month by the Defense Department of both the first 10 corporate contracts for work on "Star Wars" research (the Strategic Defense Initiative) and guidelines for limiting information about military payloads aboard the shuttle.

Was the shuttle drama not a test case for things to come? As noted by the novelist Sol Yurick in *Behold Metatron the Recording Angel* (1985), a climate of secrecy was spreading along with a vast expansion of the military sector to create a more militarized environment. The enormous sums being slated for Star Wars research and experimentation were the clearest evidence that this could continue for the long term. Yet Star Wars was still a subject of significant controversy. In this context it seems likely that the Secretary of Defense was looking for signs that the media would bow to his authority on issues of "national security" by providing fewer details about military payloads in space.

On several other occasions the administration floated trial balloons whose objectives went beyond the immediate circumstances. The exclusion of the media during the Grenadian invasion was one example. At the time it was recognized that the administration had broken with established custom. After the invasion, a panel of government officials and media representatives was set up to develop rules covering media access to future military actions. The very existence of this panel was tantamount to a concession by the media, since they thereby accepted that the government would henceforth play a more direct part in determining the movements of reporters during military maneuvers. Furthermore, the panel's conclusions did nothing to clarify the circumstances under which restrictions would be imposed but instead focused on which media organizations *would be allowed in* by the Pentagon during military excursions.

Since Grenada, reporters have been barred from military exercises in Central America on numerous occasions. During the occupation of the Gulf of Sidra off the coast of Libya and the bombing of Tripoli in 1986, the media were kept at a distance, except when the Pentagon organized press polls for selected reporters (more on this below).

None of the later restrictions evoked the intense protest from the media that followed the Grenadian exclusion. The earlier experience had become precedent. In light of this, the fact that the public will never know the full story of the Grenadian invasion is perhaps less important than the fact that the media have conceded a measure of their autonomy and, for the time being, have less public support for independent reporting of critical stages of overseas military combat.

Letting the Storm Blow Over

In other instances, the administration accepted public controversy in the short term in exchange for increased control over the long term.

On 11 March 1983 a presidential directive established the broadest secrecy system in U.S. history. National Security Decision Directive '84 (NSDD 84) required all executive branch employees with access to certain categories of classified information to sign lifetime disclosure agreements as a condition of employment. It specified that these individuals would be required to submit to polygraph examinations when the unauthorized disclosure of information was being investigated.

The initial response from Congress and the public was negative. Hearings were held and a congressional moratorium was adopted that required Reagan to suspend implementation of the directive's prepublication review and lie detector provisions for 12 months. Yet this opposition was short-lived; the moratorium ended in the spring of 1985, and since then Congress has taken no further action.

Moreover, even before the moratorium ended, it was discovered that the White House had violated the clear intention if not the actual language of the moratorium. *Newsday* broke the story in May 1984: "In a remarkable display of duplicity, the Administration has been requiring adherence to an earlier—and almost identical—directive. In addition to facing dismissal for failing to comply, signers risk federal criminal prosecution under a series of statutes and executive orders." (*Newsday*, 1984)

Newsday reported that at least 200,000 federal workers from the departments of Energy, Treasury, and Justice had signed the clone NSDD 84 contracts. Three months later, the General Accounting Office released a study based on a survey of 43 federal agencies, not including the Central Intelligence Agency (CIA) or the National Security Agency (NSA). It determined that some 120,000 people, ranging from top policy-makers to clerks and secretaries, had been forced to sign censorship agreements. It also suggested that this figure was probably low, since a number of agencies, including the Office of Management and Budget (OMB) and the Justice Department, had not responded.

During 1985 and 1986 there were numerous reports indicating that the directive or similar restrictions were being enforced. A congressional study found that more than 20,000 polygraph examinations were conducted in 1985, despite strong evidence that these tests were more effective as tools of intimidation than as a means of detecting untruths. A report released in December 1985 revealed that some of those who had been "fluttered" (undergone testing) had been queried about their religious, political, and sexual preferences (U.S. General Accounting Office 1985). Yet the general response seemed to be "So what else is new?"

If the administration anticipated that a population accustomed to news as entertainment and sensation would quickly grow bored with prepublication review and polygraph testing, it was correct. The storm over NSDD 84 gave way to the eerie quiet surrounding government moves to subject those who "leaked" information to criminal penalties and to extend the rules for military conduct to the civilian sector.

Crime by Association: Espionage Agents and Agency Officials

Whatever the situation in other countries, in Washington, D.C., the "leaking" of classified information has long been an integral part of government operations. This is mainly the result of the enormous volume of material that is classified. Between 1945 and 1963, more than 500 million pages of documents were classified. By 1973, there were several million more. President Nixon once observed that even the White House menu was classified. The disclosure of documents stamped "secret" was therefore quite common.

According to many long-time congressional representatives and Washington-based reporters, the main difference during the Reagan administration was that an even higher percentage of the leaking was done deliberately by the administration. In the days preceding the bombing of Libya, for example, it shared information about the capability of U.S. intelligence to intercept Libyan radio communications. Nonetheless, the administration consistently maintained that Washington was rife with "leakers" who posed a serious threat to the national security.

Here, too, the administration's rationale for increasing its control over the flow of government information was too often taken at face value. Deterring leaks was frequently merely a euphemism for the desire to prevent officials from speaking to the press, a desire no doubt common to many administrations. More significantly, in some instances the ultimate objective of leak investigations was to extend the strict codes of secrecy at such agencies as the NSA and the CIA to the civilian agencies.

At one point in the mid-1980s, there were 11 Americans standing trial for selling information to foreign governments. These trials were well publicized and, along with the similarly publicized reports of international terrorism, bolstered the administration's stance as a government working full time to conquer the enemy—mainly the Russians, but also Qadaffi, antinuclear activists, unpatriotic media reps, and government employees who disclosed information contrary to government wishes.

In addition, the administration anticipated problems in maintaining secrecy that could arise as a result of the vast expansion of sophisticated electronic commiunications networks and the Star Wars program. It invested millions of dollars in the installation of "spy-proof" telephones and imposed nondisclosure rules for unclassified as well as classified research conducted in the early stages of the Star Wars program. Secrecy instructions caused concern in Congress that information needed to judge the feasibility of the program was being suppressed. At a hearing in 1985, Senator Charles Mathias commented that "the latest reports that have trickled out of the X-ray laser program suggest that efforts to promote S.D.I. have gone beyond exaggerating the significance of the results to actually disguising the results."

Frustrating the administration in its efforts to stop leaks was the paucity of sanctions for penalizing those who disclosed information. The United States has no Official Secrets Act. The argument against this kind of law is that it is extremely difficult to determine which type of information is potentially damaging to the national security and which is simply embarrassing to the government in power, which whistle-blowers do a service by forwarding information to Congress and the press and which actually put the country in jeopardy. In a society that views informed debate as the best way to hold politicians accountable, speech-related penalties are acceptable only if they are carefully limited to individuals who pose a direct threat to the nation's interests.

The administration had little patience with such considerations. It sought criminal penalties for those who acted contrary to administration rules for disseminating information. In 1985 its efforts to develop new penalties were rewarded when the Justice Department successfully relied on the Espionage Act of 1917 to obtain a conviction against Samuel Morison, a Navy employee, who gave classified satellite photographs to a London publication.

The Espionage Acts were passed under the impetus of the U.S. entry into World War I. Until the Morison case, they had been used successfully only against actual spies. The Nixon administration attempted to use them in 1971 against Daniel Ellsberg and Anthony Russo, who were accused of leaking the Pentagon Papers, but the case was dismissed because of misconduct by the prosecution. The Morison case was the first to hold that laws initially aimed at espionage could be relied on in cases where people gave classified information to the press.

The Morison decision was potentially relevant to other situations as well. The Espionage Acts were not limited to government employees; they might serve to prosecute researchers and contractors receiving government funds. In theory, after the Morison conviction, any government official who passed defense-related information to a reporter might be committing a crime if the government claimed that the information was secret.

Furthermore, with criminal penalties now applied for leaking, it was reasonable to conclude that the harsher penalties contained in NSDD 84 contracts would also be upheld. Regulations adopted to implement the directive listed numerous sanctions, including removal from one's position of employment, termination of government employment, and assignment to the government of all royalties earned in connection with publication. Moreover, agency reliance on these contracts did not waive the government's right to prosecute under any one of six intelligence laws and executive orders. The Morison conviction gave credence to the notion that such laws could be used successfully.

Browbeating the Media

Within days of the Morison ruling, the White House confirmed a report in the *New York Times* that the CIA had proposed a secrecy law potentially as sweeping as the Official Secrets Act in Britain. The bill would have made it a crime for a government employee to disclose to the press or other unauthorized individuals any classified information "that reasonably could be expected to damage national security." This bill was made redundant after the Morison conviction and was soon abandoned. Yet an important target remained unfettered: the media. There were many indications that the administration was now waiting for a situation in which to test the applicability of the espionage laws to organizations that received classified information.

In its dealings with the media, the administration operated on several fronts. It put considerable energies into achieving high performance standards: timing White House announcements to meet press deadlines; choosing the best locale for a television spot; framing issues in television bites. In *The Triumph of Politics* (1986), David Stockman recounts that the president and his advisors would interrupt a heated policy discussion to watch the evening news broadcasts.

The government also attempted to inhibit Washington coverage by issuing ad hoc restrictions and scheduling fewer press conferences. Reagan's advisors rarely permitted him to speak off the cuff and on several occasions directed reporters not to ask questions during photo sessions. A notable development was the previously mentioned procedure of organizing journalists into press pools during military conflicts.

This new procedure meant that reporters on the scene could be kept completely unaware of what occurred. For example, during the American military exercises off the coast of Libya in the spring of 1986, reporters were taken aboard the aircraft carrier from which the exercises were being directed. For nearly two hours after Libyan missiles had been fired at American planes, the reporters on the ship were told nothing about what was happening and departed ignorant that hostilities were underway. When asked to explain why the media had been kept ignorant, the Pentagon said it feared the information reported might be inaccurate and could mislead the public (*New York Times,* 1986).

A third way that the administration attempted to inhibit media coverage of government was the imposition of restrictions that made information harder to obtain. Government employees were under strict orders not to disclose information, under threat of polygraph tests and even prosecution. New executive orders and regulations that put large amounts of information off limits to the public were sometimes aimed primarily at the media. This was true of the administration's efforts to weaken the Freedom of Information Act through the previously mentioned classification order that placed emphasis on nondisclosure and permitted reclassification. Numerous FOIA requests led to the reclassification or "retroactive classification." Long delays in obtaining responses to requests became legendary at certain agencies. FOIA fee guidelines issued by former Attorney General William French Smith empowered agency officials to evaluate the "public interest" value of a request and to deny fee waivers if a document could be obtained elsewhere.

Over time it became very clear that these forms of deterrence did not satisfy administration officials, who sought to discount the media's influence. Media executives who tried to cooperate—by agreeing to press pools, for example—were much like Little Red Riding Hood handing bread to the wolf and hoping not to be eaten herself. The central issue was whether the White House respected the importance of news operations not controlled by government. Clearly it did not.

To cause further inhibition, the administration engaged in a form of harassment of the media. High-level officials would threaten to take action against a media organization and, though no cases had been brought by the spring of 1986, the newspapers and networks would be forced to spend much time anticipating the possibility *and* reporting the government's allegations in their news about Washington. The latter had the unfortunate result of legitimizing the government's complaints.

The following headlines, taken from the *New York Times* at the beginning and end of May 1986, illustrate what might be called headline harassment:

7 May: "Casey to Consider Prosecuting Publications" (for their use of classified information)

8 May: Justice Department Said to Resist CIA Call to Prosecute News Groups"

9 May: "White House Backing CIA on Prosecuting Publications"

24 May: "Broad Inquiry Ordered in Disclosure of Secrets" (the White House instructed the NSA to begin a systematic government-wide investigation, including identification of ways of preventing the media from disclosing information that would harm national security

26 May: "Casey Asks Justice to Prosecute NBC"

26 May: "Steps Weighed to Limit Access to U.S. Secrets" (these included reducing the number of officials with access to classified information and asking the media to display a more responsible attitude)

29 May: "Spy Trial Brings Warning on News" (news organizations were warned against reporting on the implications of declassified information disclosed at the trial of Ronald Pelton)

31 May: "Debate Is Focused on Responsibility of News Media" (senior Reagan aides attempted to focus the debate over the news media's role in reporting national secrets on the media's responsibilities; the White House backed off from its threat to prosecute media organizations)

By the end of the month, when the White House announced that it was backing off, enough verbiage had been traded to amount to a full-length farce or tragedy or both. A serious charge—that the media were being unpatriotic—had become the basis of government attempts to inhibit media coverage of serious espionage trials, and to further taint the media's already shaky reputation with the public. Indeed, the administration was making press freedom into a docudrama: head of the CIA on the hunt; will he pull the trigger marked Operation Media?

Typically, after several threats, there would be articles and editorials denying (too politely) the government's allegations and drawing the obvious distinction between spies and ordinary individuals who leaked or reported information about the government. But the White House had the upper hand. Not only had it spoken first, but it had the last word on matters of espionage and national security.

Disinformation

One other technique in the administration's secrecy tool kit is actually very old: official deception or disinformation. Deceit, dissembling, and attempts to cover up government stupidity go on in every administration (Chomsky and Herman, 1979). Two distinguishing features of the Reagan team's efforts were its consummate ability to make things appear what they were not and its frequent fabrication of facts to further domestic as well as foreign policy.

For example, prior to the start of the trial of church leaders and staff who were sheltering Central American refugees, the administration issued a White Paper that said people were not being persecuted in El Salvador. This information was directly relevant, since the case would be decided on the basis of whether the people given shelter were political refugees. The White Paper went against all the studies and press reports that had been published over a long period of time. Nonetheless, as the government's word on the subject, it would be used by the federal court in reaching its decision.

Another instance of disinformation was the U.S. Department of Housing and Urban Development's (1984) study on the state of homeless people around the nation. As the numbers grew in cities large and small, the administration maintained that the problem was being exaggerated and attempted to deny any federal government responsibility. HUD's report estimated that the total number of homeless people nationwide amounted to only 300,000, in contrast to estimates of three to four million provided by social welfare agencies and organizations working with the homeless.

Official disinformation is a powerful tool of governmental authority. Budget determinations as well as court decisions may be based on it. False information can *permanently* pollute the record on a given problem or objective, as it often takes years for deceptions to surface, by which time accurate data may be irretrievable. More troubling still, disinformation acts quietly to render public debate meaningless.

In the spring of 1985, the Pentagon announced that it had decided to imitate its adversary by disseminating false documents and press releases in areas of scientific and technological importance. It explained the disinformation policy by referring to the Soviet Union's more closed information practices (*Aviation Week*, 1986). The reference to the Russians could also be viewed as a lame attempt to make disinformation appear new in America. The essence of the Pentagon's announcement was that the rules for government transmission of information to the American public had taken a decisive turn in the direction of censorship.

Reagan is often referred to as the Great Communicator. However, if one takes into account the public relations strategies described here–trial balloons, letting the storm blow over, linking espionage to the disclosure and receipt of government documents, media harassment, and official disinformation–his skills seem less those of a communicator than those of battle captain at war with his own troops.

SHRINKING THE POOL: THE NATIONAL BUDGET, OMB'S INFORMATION COLLECTION BUDGET, PAPERWORK REDUCTION, AND DEREGULATION

To put across goals of tax cuts, a defense buildup, and a balanced budget, Stockman recounted in his memoirs, "called for trench-style political warfare" (1986, p. 8). Stockman's memoirs make frequent use of military terminology. Reagan Administration officials, including Stockman, viewed themselves as warriors on the battlefields of Washington, with right divined by the Marketplace. As the former OMB captain wrote, their plans called for a "frontal assault on the American welfare state . . . risky and mortal political combat with all the mass constituencies of Washington's largesse—Social Security recipients, veterans, farmers, educators, state and local officials, the housing industry, and many more" (ibid.).

Early on, the national budget was the Trojan horse. Large annual increases for military expenditures and large tax reductions created a deficit that would make shrinking the operations of federal agencies, as well as large cuts in domestic spending programs, difficult to circumvent. The budget was also used for introducing "austerities" into research and information-gathering functions that were an integral part of agency operations.

Budget reductions led to significant cutbacks in agency resources for consumer assistance, publications, statistical programs, and research. Several agency research budgets were cut significantly each year. The Environmental Protection Agency was one of those that suffered most. Table 7.1 shows the cuts in the EPA's research funding between 1980 and 1984.

Budget cuts even resulted in reductions in services of the Library of Congress. In fiscal year 1986, a lean budget combined with cuts under the Gramm-Rudman-Hollings Amendment required the Library to operate with $18 million less than in the previous year. This 8 percent decrease led it to reduce from 77.5 to 54.5 hours per week the hours in which the general reading rooms were open to the public. It also meant that there was less money for acquisitions at a time of rapidly rising costs for both governmental and nongovernmental print and computerized information products. The Librarian of Congress, Daniel Boorstin, joined many others in protest and told Congress: "Historians will not fail to note that a people who could spend $300 billion on their defense would not spend $18 million on their

Table 7.1. Cuts in EPA Research Funding (in $ millions)

Type of Research	1980	1984
Air quality	85	59
Water quality	84	24
Toxic substances	38	23

knowledge—and could not even keep their libraries open in the evenings" (Boorstin, 1986; PP. 588–89). As a result of such public opposition, Congress eventually voted funds that would enable the Library to maintain regular hours. Yet this episode indicated an increasing need for a constituency to fight for the maintenance of government information services available to the public.

In a statement before the Senate Committee on Governmental Affairs in 1985, OMB Director James C. Miller III highlighted as a major accomplishment of the administration the elimination of one-quarter of all federal publications. Many were individual publications that are no longer stocked for distribution, but some were series that were no longer being published or new pamphlets and reports that would never be published. The subjects ranged from mundane topics such as growing tomatoes to consumer and health information, statistics on the cost of living in various cities across the country, and annual reports of agencies like HUD.[1]

The Office of Management and Budget

The budget also proved expedient in enlarging the powers of OMB. During the 1980s OMB became one of the leading power centers in Washington, the ultimate authority for programs of great importance to millions of people. Its powers were greatly expanded by the Paperwork Reduction Act of 1980 (44 U.S. Code, sec. 3501 et seq.), which gave it control over government statistical programs, privacy regulations, records management, and the introduction of computer technologies. Moreover, the act gave OMB the means to involve itself in the substantive work of most regulatory agencies by requiring that all

1. Some of the publications that were terminated include: *Health Care Financing Trends* (1982); *Statistical Reporter (1982); Employment and Training Report of the President* (1982); *Election Case Law* (1981); *HUD Newsletter* (1982); *The Energy Consumer* (1981); *Women in Action* (1981); *Urban Mass Transportation Abstract* (1981); and the following reports of the decennial census: "Persons of Spanish Surname"; "Persons of Spanish Origin"; "Household and Family Composition"; "Occupational Characteristics."

forms for the collection of information involving 10 or more individuals be submitted to OMB for approval.

Not surprisingly, each of these powers was interpreted according to the values of the Reagan Administration. The emphasis on efficiency led to a big increase in computer matching and a parallel decrease in the supervision of privacy regulation. Paperwork reduction was incorporated into plans for deregulation.

Backing up the national budget as a tool for implementing the Administration's priorities was OMB's annual Information Collection Budget. Set up under the Paperwork Reduction Act, the ICB enabled OMB to dole out "burden hour" allowances for agency expenditures on reports and regulations. Paperwork "burden hours" provided a coarse but politically expedient measurement tying deregulation to the often stated goal of minimizing the amount of time businesses were required to spend filling out government forms.

One cannot overemphasize the importance of the OMB's combined powers and supervisory authority. An office was established within the OMB called the Office of Information and Regulatory Affairs (OIRA), which became the closest thing the country has ever had to a Ministry of Information. Desk officers at OIRA, assigned to review programs at different agencies, were responsible for seeing that the administration's priorities in the areas of deregulation, privatization, paperwork reduction, and central management were adhered to.

President Carter had also sought to centralize control of the executive branch agencies but lacked the determination of his successor. OMB's authority was enhanced 10-fold by two executive orders issued by President Reagan. The first (Executive Order 12291), issued only two months into Reagan's first term, empowered the OMB to mold and supervise the operations of most of the regulatory agencies. This order required agencies to clear proposed regulations with the OMB before publishing them in the *Federal Register*—the standard procedure for notifying the public until the 1980s, when several agencies, including the Federal Communications Commission and the Nuclear Regulatory Commission, found ways around this rule. In addition, the order required agencies to prepare regulatory impact analyses for most plans for new regulations and to justify any plan in terms of the potential benefits versus the cost of the proposed regulation.

In late 1984 any missing links in OMB's hold on the regulatory process were supplied by a second presidential order (Executive Order

12498). This order established a unified regulatory plan for the entire executive branch and gave the OMB director the authority to review every regulatory activity "planned or under way."

The purpose of these executive orders was to allow the president's aides to intervene at the earliest possible moment in the rule-making process and to stop unwanted plans for allocating resources. A congressional report on the first order said that it established a process that "was redolent with possibilities for secret, undisclosed, and unreviewable communications and contacts by parties interested in influencing the substance of agency action (U.S. Congressional Research Service, 1981). Indeed, the requirement that OMB be notified at the earliest stages afforded possibilities for polling industry groups and halting plans for programs considered undesirable. By injecting itself into agency proceedings, the OMB was able to slow down agency research and investigations in such areas as environmental safety and public health to a crawl.

For example, in January 1986 OMB vetoed plans by the EPA to conduct a new survey of the impact on public health of chemicals in drinking water. The agency sought to determine whether a causal relationship could be established between high chlorine levels in drinking water and health problems and whether increased amounts of calcium or magnesium could have a positive effect on blood pressure. Several studies had suggested that there was a link between chlorine ingestion and organ toxicity or cardiovascular disease. Because drinking water and water softeners contain these chemicals, EPA argued that it was important to investigate whether their presence affected public health.

In refusing to approve this study, OMB asked, "What is the practical utility of the information—what will EPA do with either a positive confirmation or negative confirmation of a relationship in humans?" This question had one particular concern in mind—regulation.

In another example, OMB refused to approve a study proposed by the National Institute for Mental Health to assess the effects of federal budget cuts on patients' use of mental health services and to measure the relationship of outpatient to inpatient care. This study would have gone beyond standard data obtained upon patient discharge from medical facilities by tracking a sample of individuals over a year.

In explaining OMB's reasons for rejecting this study, an OIRA desk officer wrote:

> Disapproved. NIMH has not made a convincing case for the federal need for the data that would be produced from this study. This is particularly true in view of the absence of an administration position to expand mental health services reimbursement under the federal government's health care financing programs. In addition, the NIMH proposal is not designed to "minimize costs to the federal government" as prescribed in [the Paperwork Reduction Act].[2]

OMB and the Privatization of Information

In the Reagan era, proposals that had surfaced in the 1970s to transfer out government information functions moved forward at a steady pace. Privatization of information paid for with tax dollars is obviously a complicated issue, which centers on competing views of government information as a public resource and also involves an assessment of the ways in which scientists, universities, businesses, and the general public will gain access to information in the age of electronically generated information.

This chapter does not tackle these issues. However, in discussing the information policies of the Reagan years it is important to mention the accelerated privatization of agency information programs, as this was an important way in which federal agencies withdrew from providing information to the public and nonfederal agencies. Hundreds of government publications were picked up by private firms.[3] Several agencies distributed notices and decisions through private entities that charged hefty fees.

Since the enactment of the Paperwork Reduction Act of 1980, the executive branch had been obligated to establish uniform federal information policies and practices in order to reduce paperwork, enhance the efficiency of government, and increase the accuracy of agency data and information. As indicated above, the Reagan administration used the Paperwork Act to complement its deregulatory and management objectives.

At the end of 1985, a policy circular by OMB (Circular A-130, "Man-

---

2. A detailed running record of OMB's involvement in agency rulemaking proceedings can be found in monthly reports of the Washington-based organization OMB Watch, entitled "Eye on Paperwork: OMB Control of Government Information."

3. Some of the publications that have been privatized include: *The Car Book (1982); Morbidity and Mortality Weekly Report of HHS* (1983); *Fed-Statistical Directory* (1983); *Decisions of the United States Merit Systems Protection Board* (1985).

agement of Federal Information Resources"), limited agency information programs to those the private sector was unlikely to adopt. The OMB circular served to codify existing policies and to outline future directions. At the time it was released, an editorial in the *Washington Post* observed that the new policy "would likely reduce the number of printed government publications available to libraries free or at low cost and increase the already widespread practice of private outfits interfacing with government computers and providing printouts for users at hefty fees."

In the circular, OMB acknowledges the importance and value of government information to society, the economy, and the management of the government. The free flow of information from the government to its citizens and vice versa is said to be essential to a democratic society. But the circular also emphasizes that government information is itself a commodity with economic value in the marketplace and makes explicit a policy not to compete with the private sector.

The circular includes multiple tests and conditions to be met before agencies will be allowed to collect or create information. Agencies are required to "create or collect only that information necessary for the proper performance of agency functions and that has practical utility, and only after planning for its processing, transmission, dissemination, use, storage, and disposition." Agencies are to "seek to satisfy new information through legally authorized interagency or intergovernmental sharing of information, or through commercial sources, where appropriate, before creating or collecting new information." In addition, complex analysis is required because "the expected public and private benefits derived from government information, insofar as they are calculable, should exceed the public and private costs of the information."

The circular states that the constraints on information collection are not intended to diminish or derogate from the creation or collection of information that is vital to the American form of government. Yet a specter lurks—the danger that the cost-benefit standard will be used by OMB to reject any new agency information programs, that it will constitute too high a hurdle. The circular provides no guidance on how the public benefits of government information could be shown to exceed the cost of generating that information. In keeping with other policy statements of the administration, it gives far more attention to tests and procedures designed to restrict and control government data collection, publishing, and dissemination than to public service.

One part of the circular draws a line between "access to information" and "dissemination of information" in order to limit the responsibilities of federal agencies in providing information to the public. Access is reserved for situations in which the agency's role is passive, merely responding to requests for information to which the public is entitled by law, including requests under the FOIA, the Privacy Act, and other statutes. Dissemination refers to the more active, but controlled, outreach function of distributing information to the public.

This distinction ignores the complicated and often difficult nature of attempts to identify different categories of information collected by and available from the government. The question not answered by OMB is how the public is to know what information is available, particularly once it is available only in electronic form. And how does OMB's new policy of access-on-demand relate to the disclosure objectives of the FOIA and the Federal Depository Library Program? Additionally, as the library community has long argued, making known the existence of information is essential for reaping the greatest benefit from dollars spent on its generation. Widely accessible and low-cost government information stimulates economic, educational, scientific, and technical development in areas ranging from agriculture and art, to solar energy and space technology.

Given its preoccupation with cost cutting, OMB was not the optimal agency to establish the guidelines for government information policy in the new era of electronically generated information. It must be regarded as unfortunate, then, that this agency stepped in to adopt a sweeping new policy and to appoint itself the enforcer of such a program. Though the circular does not have the force of law, it tells regulatory agencies how they should implement laws or presidential policies. Fiscal budget reviews and other measures can also be employed by OMB to ensure agency compliance.

Circular A-130 is one more part of a plan to distance the government from the public and to narrow public expectations, not only for information hitherto furnished by the government, but for what information allows—public participation. Other elements in this plan covered thus far include the interwoven campaigns of deregulation, paperwork, reduction, and fiscal and information budget reviews.

Few realized early enough the way in which such programs could be used to reorient regulatory agencies away from service to the public and toward corporate interests. One government documents librarian (Smith, 1985) has suggested that industry was the party most aware of the consequences of these policies and perhaps was most in control.[4] Certainly budget cuts and information austerities written into agency budgets eroded regulatory programs mandated by law and gradually eroded local programs and citizen initiatives. Such far-ranging changes were what Stockman referred to in his talk of a "frontal assault on the welfare state" and can also be seen in the censorial practices described earlier.

CONCLUSION

The mood in much of the United States by the seventh year of the Reagan presidency was significantly different from that of 1980. The main difference was the decline of politics. The teflon presidency had disappointed much of the extreme Right and had shut out people of the center and further Left. It had told much of the American population, in addition to the Western Europeans and many others, that their opinions did not matter very much. Politics seemed to be little more than the ratings, whether the president was up or down.

Should the day arrive when ratings truly sum up the preoccupations of Americans, the administration or another demogogic ruler will have succeeded in changing the rules of American politics. This has not happened yet. Citizens' groups of all stripes, social, political, and religious, remain active, though faced with new and more complicated obstacles. Groups in opposition to government policies have not been defeated entirely. It is, in fact, impressive how they have carried on in a virtual vacuum of foundation and media interest. Even the right-wing religious groups and antiabortionists, frustrated by Reagan's failure to follow through on their complete agenda, have bonded together in well-funded campaigns as they head for the next presidential race.

Nonetheless, the damage inflicted by the administration must be assessed. Though the targets of information cutbacks, paperwork reduction, and more stringent classification rules may be difficult to identify, their combined impact is clear. Government control over the amount and substance of information available about matters of widespread interest has been employed to deprive people of necessities, including disability benefits and health care, and to erode constitutional freedoms.

---

4. Diane Smith writes: "No single agency has control over the situation. In fact, the situation seems to be one in which the industry is capturing the activity rather than capturing the regulatory agency" (1985 pp.61).

Secrecy builds like compound interest. More rules lead to more intense penalties imposed on a broader range of people. In addition, rising levels of fear and social intolerance are the stepchildren of a closed environment. The result is the undermining of the normal give and take between various departments of government and the public, on the one hand, and, among different groups in society, on the other.

In the 1980s this matter was made a far more serious one as a result of the assiduous efforts of one administration to put important information off limits and to criminalize behavior necessary to open society. A growing reluctance to criticizing government programs could be seen in the increased timidity of the mainstream media. In important areas of controversy, including the covert war in Nicaragua and the government's case against churches providing sanctuary for Central American refugees, the mainstream media tended to stay well within the parameters set by Washington.

Additional research, not attempted here, will be necessary to determine to what extent the shift to the Right by the television networks and mainstream newspapers during this period was due to the regular browbeating they received from the White House, to the return by high-level officials to anticommunism as a means to defeat their adversaries, or to the prosperity of media companies facilitated by large corporate tax reductions in 1982. Similarly, the precise connection between the administration's militarism and the return of vigilantism in certain communities has yet to be determined. It is the difficulty in pinpointing the precise objectives and results of government actions that makes censorship in a so-called free society more pernicious than in a society that is less free.

REFERENCES

American Library Association (1985-87). "Less Access to Less Information By and About the U.S. Government." Washington, D.C.: ALA.

Aviation Week and Space Technology (1986). "U.S. Using Disinformation Policy to Impede Technical Data Flow." 17 March, p. 16.

Boorstin, D. (1986). *Congressional Record.* House of Representatives, 132 (23), 4 March.

Chomsky, N., and E. Herman (1979). *The Washington Connection and Third World Fascism.* Boston: South End Press.

Demac, D. (1984). *Keeping America Uninformed: Government Secrecy in the 1980's* New York: Pilgrim Press.

Demac, D. (1985). "Making Washington Safe for Business." *Business and Society Review*, Spring, p. 29.

Dorsen, N. et al. (1984). *Our Endangered Rights: The ACLU Report on Civil Liberties*. New York: Pantheon.

Marro, A. (1985). "When the Government Tells Lies." *Columbia Journalism Review*, March/April, p. 29.

Newsday (1984). "Editorial: Hoodwinking Congress, Gagging Federal Workers," 17 May.

New York Times (1986). "Handling of Press During Libya Fighting Faulted," 7 April.

Peck, K. (1985). "A Freeze on Facts." *Progressive*, April, p. 28.

Smith, D. (1985). "The Commercialization and Privatization of Government Information." *Government Publications Review*, Spring, p. 61.

Stockman, D. (1986). *The Triumph of Politics: Why the Reagan Revolution Failed*. New York: Harper & Row.

U.S. Congress, Office of Technology Assessment (1983). "Scientific Validity of Polygraph Testing." Washington, D.C.: Government Printing Office.

U.S. Congressional Research Service (1981). "Presidential Control of Agency Rulemaking: An Analysis of Constitutional Issues That May be Raised by Executive Order 12291." Washington, D.C.: Government Printing Office.

U.S. Department of Housing and Urban Development (1984). "A Report to the Secretary on the Homeless and Emergency Shelters." Washington, D.C.: Government Printing Office.

U.S. Department of Justice (1983). "Attorney General Guidelines on General Crimes, Racketeering Enterprises, and Domestic Security/Terrorism Investigations." Washington, D.C.: Government Printing Office.

U.S. General Accounting Office (1985). *Department of Defense: DOD's Training Program for Polygraph Examiners*. Washington, D.C.: Government Printing Office.

Yurick, S. (1985). *Behold METATRON the Recording Angel*. New York: Semiotext.

8. Libraries, Public Access to Information, and Commerce

Herbert I. Schiller and Anita R. Schiller

An economic struggle with major cultural implications, underway for 20 years, and now intensifying, goes relatively unnoticed in the national media. It pits the fundamental principle of American libraries—free access to information—against the interests of the private information suppliers and their advocates in government. The privateers seek profit from the sale of information to those who have the means to pay for it.

There are two main arenas of action in this ongoing conflict. *Inside* the library system itself, a combination of forces is weakening the historic principle of free, socially underwritten access. *Outside*, great efforts have been exerted in recent years, by private interests, to capture the information stockpiles built up from tax-supported outlays on research and development and general governmental activities that produce data.

If current trends continue, the nation's major libraries[1] may be on their way to becoming information emporia—places that sell goods, in this instance, information, to those who can afford to purchase it. At the same time, the country's informational resources increasingly are being appropriated by for-profit firms for processing and dissemination.

These developments are the subject of this chapter. It should be evident at the outset that far more than the library system, important as that is, is involved. We take it for granted that what affects the library touches as well on the general well-being of the nation at large.

1. In this chapter we will be analyzing the changes occurring in major university and research libraries. The local, public libraries constitute, by far, the greatest number of libraries in the country. Yet it is in the large institutions that the changes that are overturning historic arrangements are first observable.

The changes that have occurred in the American economy since the Second World War have transformed the national economic and cultural landscape. The impacts are experienced everywhere, and for many the effects are wrenching.

For reasons that will be elaborated as we proceed, one of the keys to understanding what actually is happening to the American economy is to appreciate the increasingly significant role of information in personal, institutional, and national life.

Attention here is on libraries because historically they have been associated with information collection, organization, retrieval, and dissemination. Another reason for a focus on libraries is that the public library has long been regarded, justifiably, as one of the most impressive achievements, and steadfast institutions, of the American democratic experience. In this sense, as libraries fare, so fares the commonwealth.

THE CONTEXT OF THE DISCUSSION

Libraries, and the nation's system of production, have been deeply affected by three powerful and interactive developments in the last 40 years.

There has been, first of all, since the Second World War, and initially as a consequence of waging that struggle, an explosive increase in scientific and technical information. Enormous federal outlays during the war for research and development (Adkinson, 1978) led to, among other results, the creation of powerful computers. These expenditures also created the infrastructure of the governmental-scientific complex that would be maintained and strengthened in the postwar years (Dickson, 1984).

In the interval between 1960 and 1978, for example, over 400 billion federal dollars were spent on research and development (Arthur D. Little, Inc. 1978). In 1985, not taking into account the inflation since 1978, United States R&D expenditures totaled $49.5 billion, and the estimate for 1986 amounted to $52 billion (*Science*, 1986, p. 785). These are *federal* expenditures. In recent years *private* corporate outlays have roughly equaled the government's. The *total* annual R&D outlay currently, therefore, is in the vicinity of $100 billion.

Since 1945, and with cumulative impact, the amount of information and data acquired from these massive outlays has been stupendous. Not surprisingly, one of the most pressing needs experienced by the engineering, scientific, and administrative sectors is for access to this vast data supply. Access, in turn, is dependent on the organization of the material and the availability of suitable means of retrieval and dissemination.

Numerous official commissions were appointed in the postwar years to consider what were termed Scientific and Technical Information (STI) issues. A review of the work of these panels indicates how much attention was given to these problems. A report prepared for the National Science Foundation in 1976 (the Mitre Report), listed 13 major studies between 1958 and 1976 on scientific and technical information issues (Whalen and Joyce, 1976, p. 3).

Each of these, in varying degree, agreed that STI was a very important sector; that STI is "big business" and that the stakes are very high; and, most pertinently, that severe STI handling problems existed. The Mitre Report quoted a 1969 study by the National Academy of Sciences-Engineering, referred to as the SATCOM Report:

> the proliferation of useful research together with the burgeoning increase in the numbers of trained people involved in science and technology has overcome the capacity of the classical information services to respond effectively. To avert a crisis of major proportions, the only present alternative is a strong effort to accelerate the utilization of modern computer-aided techniques for handling information. (Whalen and Joyce, 1976, p. 2)

The Mitre Report, and the studies it reviewed, considered the growing national information output as essentially an STI problem. Yet it was not long before it came to be seen, in more comprehensive terms, as an issue of *general* information abundance and access.

An Arthur D. Little report in 1978 concluded that STI should be regarded as general, systemic information. "STI—has to be supplemented with society-related objective information to provide a more complete universe, including economic, demographic, political, occupational, health, legal, regulatory, sociological, cultural, environmental information, etc. We call the expanded information set Scientific-Technical and Societal Information (STISI)" (Arthur D. Little, Inc. 1978, p. 6).

In a word, the outpouring of information in the country extended beyond scientific and technical data. It included information about the entire social organism. Its effective organization and management thereby constituted a still greater challenge.

While the growing information and data stockpile provoked a flood of studies and recommendations—among which was the recurrent demand for a national information policy—a technological development, proceeding simultaneously, appeared to many to supply the providential answer to the information explosion.

THE COMPUTER AND THE EMERGENCE OF THE INFORMATION INDUSTRY

Developed during the war into an operational, if still somewhat cumbersome, instrument, the computer was undergoing continuous technical refinement and capability enhancement at a remarkable speed. As one generation of computer succeeded another, the size and cost decreased substantially while the processing capacity expanded greatly.

Unevenly but rapidly, computers were installed in many branches of the economy, to handle special functions of industrial and governmental operations—for example, payrolls and personnel and other records. The banking and insurance sectors were among the first heavy users and transferred the bulk of their transactional activities to the new instrumentation.

The expanding market for, and the rapid installation of, computers has created an information industry whose firms produce, distribute, retail, manage, and process information products and services. The hardware producers constitute a different but related and powerful sector.

An American Federation of Information Processing Societies (AFIPS) study gives an idea of the rapidity of these developments: "The computer manufacturing and services industries have grown steadily since 1971; estimated revenues approximately doubled in the five-year period ending 1976 and are forecast to again double in the 5-year period ending 1981." Also noted was that 1981 revenues of U.S. computer manufacturing and service firms amounted to $64 billion (1976 base), of which $51 billion were for equipment and supplies and $13 billion for computer services (Nyberg, McCarter, Erickson, n.d.).

The Information Industry Association (IIA), a trade organization established in 1968, heralded the emergence of a new and dynamic sector of the economy. An indication of the speed with which some branches of this sector are growing is an *Industrial Outlook* report of the U.S. Department of Commerce:

> 900 firms were responsible for generating revenues of $1.9 billion in the electronic database industry in 1985 (with an estimated growth to 2.2 billion in 1986). 2600 databases were available online, compared to 362 in 1977. The number of customers served by online vendors totalled 784,900 in 1984 compared to 17,000 in 1977. (U.S. Department of Commerce, 1986, p.48).

The information industry is understandably an increasingly influential voice in the overall economy. No different from private firms in other sectors in their objective of engaging in profit-making enterprise, information companies advocate and promote a private and commercial context for the expanding informational activities and information products increasingly available in the computer-serviced economy.

Yet it is the new information sector's striving for profitability, along with its capability of producing a hitherto unimaginable range of processed information, that is changing radically the American social landscape. And it is also, as will be evident later in this discussion, creating the economic-cultural environment in which information issues are defined, considered, and decided.

As computerization and information processing extend throughout the economy, the influence of the for-profit information companies widens. Correspondingly, questions about the production, organization, storage, and dissemination of information are considered and decided upon at sites in which the public has no presence and the for-profit information sector's perspective receives preponderant attention and support.

THE PRIVATE CORPORATION IN THE POSTWAR YEARS

In addition to the massive data outputs originating in the huge national R&D expenditures, and the rapid computerization of large branches of the economy that fed a vigorous and expanding private information industry, a third and overarching feature of the last 40 years has been the striking growth of the private corporation, already substantial in prewar days.

Grown rich during the war years, several hundred American companies reached out and boldly moved into the international market. Thus appeared the transnational corporation (TNC), a firm with operations in several overseas locales. In a few decades the transnational corporation has become the central organizer of the world economy as well as the dominant economic actor in the United States.

Today, a large and growing share of the global output of goods and services is accounted for by the activities of a few thousand transnational companies, most of which are still privately owned by U.S. capital. These huge economic aggregates are totally dependent on computers and telecommunications (satellites, cable, fiber optics) in their daily global operations. The *Business Roundtable*, an organization of the 500 chief executive officers of the most powerful U.S. (transnational) companies, in 1985 emphasized this condition:

> telecommunications is central to the operations of all multinational business activity . . . [Moreover,] the dependence of multinational corporations—whether they are pursuing intracorporate functions or providing services or both—upon international information transfer is steadily increasing. (*Business Roundtable*, 1985, pp. 6-11).

It is in this context of massive data accumulation, computerization, the growth of a powerful, private information industry, and corporate dependence on information flow and new information technologies that the developments in the nation's major libraries take on special meaning and significance.

Fundamental changes in library principles and organization are inextricably linked to the economy's dynamics. As the American corporate system seeks to move to a higher rung of the international division of labor—the control and distribution of information—the nation's libraries are inevitably involved.

We note an assessment made 10 years ago by Lee Burchinal, at that time Director of the Division of Science Information of the National Science Foundation, on the sources of the changing conditions in libraries. Speaking at a conference concerned with "the on-line revolution in libraries," Burchinal pointed out that "the driving forces" for the changes taking place in libraries—that is, "substitution of nonprint forms of distribution" and extensive use of outside services for accessing large remote sources of needed information"—*lie outside the library field and its on-line suppliers". (Emphasis added)*. "The main impetus." Burchinal found:

> is derived from the dynamics of the major elements comprising the U.S. information economy. Information processing requirements of business, banking, and other commercial enterprises are immense. So are those of the military and civilian sides of the federal government . . . in effect . . . libraries and their on-line service suppliers—are following the lead of other industries.

He concluded:

> On-line developments in the library field will not compel rethinking or reformulation of national information policies. But the converse is true—decisions regarding national communication policies and practices will have profound effects on libraries and their operations. (Burchinal, 1977)

If this is true, why *are* the changes underway in libraries important? Can a sector that is "driven" by more powerful, external forces still have a special significance for the social polity at large and for the quality of individual life in particular?

One reason why this may be so is that although their originating stimuli are external, the changes now occurring in libraries create a dynamic of their own which sets off new currents and directions in how information is, and will be, organized in the economy overall. The library, as a key institution in the information arena, is by force of circumstance at the vortex of the changes now happening.

Relatedly, the arrangements and institutions that eventually preside over these vital information functions will in fact largely determine the tone and character of the general social order, as well as deeply influencing the formation of individual consciousness.

LIBRARY DEVELOPMENTS AND ISSUES FROM 1950 THROUGH THE 1970s

Developments in the library sector, affecting mainly but not exclusively the major research libraries, provide a window on the profound changes already evident in the national information and cultural spheres. For example, questions addressed by the 1979 White House Conference on Library and Information Services suggested that the actual survival of the library could be seen as problematic:

> "Do libraries, the traditional storehouses of information and knowledge," the delegates were asked, "*have a place* in this fast-moving Information Age? *If* so, what should it be? When should information be private, when should it be without cost, and how should freedom of information principles be applied? Is there a need for a national information policy, and, if so, what elements should it include?" (White House Conference, 1980, p. 7 emphasis added)

Despite these indications of deep concern, the years preceding the White House Conference, from the mid-1950s to the early 1970s, were years of relative and unaccustomed affluence for American libraries. Though hardly enjoying the largesse and respect accorded the military or the space enterprises, libraries in this period were at least minimally acknowledged as a contributing source of national strength. For the first time, funds were allocated to the nation's libraries, under a series of Library Services Acts beginning in 1956.

To a considerable extent, this could be viewed as the "Sputnik dividend"—an outcome of the shock felt at the Soviet space successes with satellites. Also a factor, as has been noted above, were the awesome information-organization needs that the mounting stockpiles of data mandated. In any case, a series of legislative measures now made federal funds available for the construction of library facilities for the extension of services to previously deprived rural and, later, urban areas, for school materials, and for fellowships and training for information professionals.

At the same time a National Advisory Commission on Libraries was appointed in 1966 to assess national library service needs. In 1970 a National Commission on Libraries and Information Sciences (NCLIS) was created with a mandate to "maintain a continuing assessment of the adequacy of library and information services to meet national needs and to recommend to the President and to the Congress such policies and actions as may be needed. (Commission on Freedom and Equality of Access to Information, 1986, p. 97).

While national support for libraries was never more favorable than in this brief period, systemic dynamics were producing changes and releasing pressures that would soon bring into question fundamental library values, if not the survival of the library itself in its historical form.

The primary push came from the increasing presence and influence of information technology (IT).

LIBRARIES AS EARLY PROMOTERS OF THE NEW INFORMATION TECHNOLOGIES

If providing a market for new information products and services was only a limited consideration, the library's contribution to the early progress of the information-using society as a center of familiarization, experimentation, and training for a new cadre of professionals, and as a site for accustoming its clientele—students and the general public—to the new IT products and services was nonetheless significant.

A study conducted in 1976–1977:

> For the information industry, the Library is one of many information markets. But it is a key market, because it opens the door to much wider sales of information products and services to the American public. From the perspective of the commercial sector, the library's role is to familiarize the public (both general and specialized) with the new information products and services and disseminate them for a fee. According to the Information Industry Association (IIA), "The principal problem facing the industry is one of educating the public to heighten its awareness of the important benefits and uses of information." (1977, pp. 28–29)

Additionally: "This is instrumental to the IIA's primary goal which is 'to promote the development of private enterprise in the field of information and to gain recognition for information as a commercial product'." (ibid., p. 29).

Here is the source of the unfolding dynamic that is changing America's libraries and the entire role of information in this society. The IIA's primary goal, stated above, is basically incompatible with the underlying and historical, though inadequately fulfilled, principle of public library service—equal access for all to the nation's informational resources.

Transforming information into a saleable good, available only to those with the ability to pay for it, changes the goal of information access from an egalitarian to a privileged condition. The consequence of this is that the essential underpinning of a democratic order is seriously damaged. This is the ultimate outcome of commercializing information throughout the social sphere.

Yet this is not a matter of simple acceptance or rejection. The American library system is in no position unilaterally to decide whether it wishes to accept or decline a participatory role in the information commercialization process. The boundaries of decision-making have been set and promoted by powerful forces *outside* the library field, as was noted by Burchinal in 1977.

These boundaries constitute, in effect, the *social* arrangement that the corporate sector is imposing on the production, processing and dissemination of information and that is transforming a social product into a commercial product. The technology, in this situation, facilitates the process. For this reason, though countless other important questions confront the American library community and the public information sphere, it is, we believe, accurate to claim that the commercialization of information is the transcendent question, affecting systemic, national, and library policy making.

Ten years ago, explaining the developing dynamic between the nation's libraries and the private information industry, one researcher wrote: "The information industry's challenge to libraries to heighten public awareness of information, comes at a price" (Schiller,1977, p. 29).

The study described the ironic situation in which the traditionally marginal position of the library was being changed as information organization and provision became of central importance to all sectors of the economy. At the same time, and here was the irony, in an era in which information can be made available in richness and comprehensiveness formerly unattainable, the institution most associated with informational access—the library—is being transformed into an allocating instrument, charging for services and being stripped of its long-standing role as the public's provider.

The new information technologies, organized and managed commercially, have been the means for effecting the changes underway in the libraries over the last 15 years. In short:

> Traditionally, the library has been caught in a double bind; for at the very moment it begins to achieve its objective of information access, and becomes popular and widely used, it must restrict its services because of insufficient support. In other words, success equals failure because a basic assumption behind extended service is that it cannot be supported. Diminished or stabilized funding for libraries during the current period has intensified the double bind problem, because this has occurred simultaneously (and ironically) with expansion in the information sector, the growth of information technology, and rising demand for information. Seen by some as the only way out of the double bind, fees for service were introduced in the expectation that information delivery effectiveness, and the library's role in providing it, would be enhanced. (1977, pp. 29–30)

But far-reaching and unforeseen effects soon became evident:

> During the initial period, online services, supported in part by user fees (in part by library funding), was often viewed as a single added activity to supplement standard reference service, which would continue to coexist. The interrelationships between the two types of service were recognized. but were not directly visible. The developing shift in library resource allocations from free services to fee services, and with it the redirection of resources from one user population to another was less perceptible . . .
> The introduction of online services for a fee is not simply an added activity for those who can pay, but represents a reallocation of library resources from one set of activities to another, and from one set of users to another. (ibid., pp. 29–30)

The "fee versus free" expression, though it captured the fundamental shift in the character of library service, soon became a reductionist cliché, the broader parameters of which were lost sight of or forgotten.

All the same, the essential nature of the change underway transcends the library sector. To the extent that the commercialization, the sale, of information proceeds, the character of the information-based economy is organically affected. It will determine who will enjoy and who will be excluded from the benefits of the information age.

Given the stakes, and taking into account the strength of the interest groups involved, it was inevitable that commercial information and the library's connection to the rapidly growing private information industry appeared early on as perplexing and urgent matters facing the library community.

COMMERCIALIZATION AND PRIVATIZATION ISSUES IN THE LIBRARY FIELD IN THE 1970s AND 1980s

A brief and selective review of a few of the major studies, reports, and proceedings of the American Library Association and related or concerned bodies and commissions reveals the growing pressure from the private information sector and the resistance to this pressure displayed by the American library community.

In 1975, as the economy's utilization of advanced information technology was moving into high gear, the National Commission on Libraries and Information Science (created in 1970 under the Nixon administration) prepared a report on long-term goals for a national program for library and information services (National Commission on Libraries and Information Science, 1975).

The counter-pressures were already evident. On the basic issue of information equality, the report recommended "Federal legislation that would adopt as its prime philosophical goal equal opportunity of access to the nation's library and information services" (ibid., p. 11). Additionally, "the Federal Government must bear a permanent responsibility for preserving and maintaining the knowledge resources of the nation and for making a specific commitment to their interdependent development" (ibid., p. 78).

At the same time, and indicative of its robust growth in the preceding years, the commission urged a major role for the private information industry in organizing and distributing information and foresaw that "the information industry will exert increased influence on the nation's information services in the years ahead" (ibid., p. 25). Acknowledging its already considerable influence, the commission recommended that "greater collaboration . . . be developed between libraries and the commercial and other private sector distributors of the newer information services when the results are in the public interest" (ibid., p. 24). How that determination would be made was left unaddressed. In conceding an ever-larger role to the for-profit information industry, the commission may have been realistic. Yet, as we shall point out, the information industry was and is interested in collaboration with the public library sector only to the extent that it can use it for furthering its own objectives. Still, the insistence in the

1975 statement that library goals embody the principle of equal access to information must be regarded as an important reaffirmation of these goals.

A year later, a report (not a library document, but published by the NCLIS) prepared by the staff of the Domestic Council Committee on the Right of Privacy, chaired by Nelson Rockefeller, revealed a distinct shift of emphasis. In this report, "public sector interests" are infrequently mentioned, and information supply is almost totally a commercial consideration. The voice and perspective of the information industry are pervasive. Government (public) information is seen as a preserve to be handed over to private information managers and entrepreneurs. The flavor of the report's unabashed private sector tone and approach may be appreciated in the following excerpts.

In a section entitled "Write Rules to Classify the Relationship Between Government and the Private Sector in the Production, Publication and Dissemination of Information," the problem—as it is seen from the private information industry's standpoint—is stated explicitly. In brief, it is how to "dismantle" the national structure of public information supply and enable private information interests to become its expropriators:

> Some of the most difficult issues facing the government result from the growth of a new commercial information sector in the United States. This new industry often finds itself in conflict with governmental dissemination services. It seeks a resolution of these conflicts and a uniform set of policies that will provide a climate for its growth and investment. (Domestic Council Committee, 1976, p. 74)

The report explains why this is a problem:

> The problem is complex, since the dissemination of government-generated information is a legal responsibility of the Federal agencies, either specifically written into the agency legislation, or implied in agency mission descriptions. Moreover, many of the information programs of Federal agencies have grown over the years and have become national and international in scope, making *dismantling* difficult. Several of the agencies have taken steps to turn some parts of their dissemination programs over to private sector contractors, *but the commercial industry believes this effort to be insufficient*. (ibid., pp. 74–75; emphasis added)

One section presents without endorsing "The For-Profit Sector View," which asserts flatly: "While publicly supported library functions providing free information *should not be abolished*, it should be recognized that there is no such thing as *free* information" (ibid.,

p. 76; first emphasis added; second emphasis in text). In the general discussion, the report's authors see the issue as "how to provide information services to the public and at the same time establish policies that will not *penalize* the commercial information sector" (ibid., p. 81; emphasis added).

This report, issued in the waning days of the custodial Ford administration, seemed for a while to have been forgotten. But, as will be evident, the IIA's views contained therein would be more and more forcefully articulated as the industry itself grew in size and influence. In fact, 10 years later, in the mid-1980s, these perspectives provided the rationale for the policy and executive decisions of the Reagan administration's Office of Management and Budget (OMB).

Yet the information industry's ascending influence, and the ability to direct national information policy, has not been without opposition. The public's right to equal information access has been defended all along the way. The problem is not the sudden abandonment of principle but the daily weakening of the principle by the adoption of processes and arrangements that undermine and destroy the social character of information.

Twenty-five years after it was first proposed, the White House Conference on Library and Information Services was held in Washington, D.C., on November 15–19, 1979. Authorized by Public Law 93-568, signed by President Ford on December 21, 1974, the conference's purpose "was to improve the nation's libraries and information centers and their use by the public" (Newsletter, 1980).

The White House Conference was a major event in the nation's library and information history. Its 806 delegates approved 64 resolutions that touched on many important informational matters. Here we mention only one issue—the one central to this discussion. Among its goals and objectives, the White House Conference approved in general session a resolution on National Policy for Free Access, which read as follows:

> Whereas, information in a free society is a basic right of any individual, essential for all persons, at all age levels and all economic and social levels, and Whereas, publicly supported libraries are institutions for education for democratic living and exist to provide information for all, Therefore, be it resolved, that the White House Conference on Library and Information Services hereby affirms that all persons should have free access, without charge or fee to the individual, to information in public and publicly supported libraries, and Be It Further Resolved, that the White House Conference on Library and Information Services advocates the formation of a National Information Policy

> to ensure the right of access without charge or fee to the individual to all public and publicly supported libraries for all purposes. (White House Conference, 1980, p. 42)

In addition to this unqualified endorsement of free public access to information, the White House Conference also recommended, in implementation of this principle, that the "United States Congress continue to foster broad public participation in the Federal Government by substantial subsidies on the sale of basic Federal documents and continue to maintain a system of regional and local depositories for Government information" (ibid., p. 55).

Steadfast as these resolutions were in insisting on an adherence to the social basis for information provision, the deregulated economy, and the private information sector in particular, brushed them aside. This was strikingly evident in another report, issued hard on the heels of the White House Conference, by "an independent Task Force assembled and funded by the National Commission on Libraries and Information Science". (National Commission on Libraries and Information Science, 1982).

The subject of the task force's attention was the interaction of the public and private sectors in providing information services, a topic, as we have indicated, of already great and growing importance. That the library community undertook an examination of this significant issue at a relatively early date is worth noting in itself. What came out of the study is another matter. In any case, the task force was commissioned in June 1979, just preceding the White House Conference, and it issued its report early in 1982.

"The Public/Private Sector Report," as it has come to be known, can be regarded as signaling the turning point in what had actually never been an equal struggle for command of the nation's information resources. With the publication of this report, it was clear that the balance had moved decisively toward the commercial information industry and away from the principle of information as a social good. In fact, the report may be read as a declaration of the industry's triumph in the information arena. (Schuman, 1982)

Collaboration between the public and private information sectors no longer was an aim of the industry, as it had been in the 1975 NCLIS report. The Public/Private Sector Task Force, on which the overrepresentation of private sector members was hard to miss, acknowledged the changed situation and the new relationship of forces:

> Should the sectors be regarded as cooperating in the process of distribution of information? Some members of the Task Force see government and the private sector as cooperating components, each meeting

> needs of society in the way that it best does; others see them either as competitive, or, at most, as complementary, without a pattern of sharing responsibility. *Since many of the previous studies and reports have recommended "cooperation between the public and private sectors," it is especially important to note that this has become an issue of controversy in the Task Force, rather than accepted truth.* (National Commission on Libraries and Information Science, 1982; p. 33 emphasis added)

In fact, the position that emerges in the report is the private industry's challenge to the right of the public sector (government, libraries, universities, etc.) to engage in *any* informational activities the industry regards as its own province. For example: "The most basic issue of controversy, of course, related to the role of government. . . . It's not so much a matter of 'capitalism vs. socialism,' since there seems to be none on the Task Force that would urge that the government should 'take over' any segment of the information industry. It does seem to be a matter of whether or not the government should provide *any* services that could be provided by the non-governmental sector" (National Commission on Libraries and Information Science, 1982; emphasis added).

The report's emphasis throughout is on the encouragement of the private sector and the fullest utilization of the market mechanism—selling for profit—in the collection, processing, and dissemination of government information. Thus, the trajectory of the private information sector in its interaction with the library community and whoever else might uphold the principle of equal access to information for all, financed as a social cost, has been from cooperation to unilateral assertion.

In recent years libraries increasingly are being put in the position of adjunct to, and facilitator for, the commercial information industry. Despite their reluctance to adopt commercial practices—charging users for information, relying on private vendors for databases, contracting out functions to private firms and so on—these activities now are routinely implemented. Meanwhile, the distinction between a library and a commercial enterprise narrows. The library's options for preserving its vital social role also diminish.

Librarians and libraries who lack enthusiasm for the private foundations of the information age become barriers to the full-scale triumph of privatization in the national information environment. Given the commercial dynamic at work, the survival of libraries—at least in their customary form—is by no means assured.

The phenomenal increase in personal computers allows the private information industry to anticipate a time in which libraries may be bypassed altogether. Information provision, in this projected scenario, will either be in the hands of private "information professionals," or be directly available to individual end-users—at a price, naturally.

Already some farsighted "educators" are wondering whether there is a need for library schools in the traditional sense (Berry, 1986, p. 4). Who needs librarians, educated according to a social ethic, if information can be supplied by individual entrepreneurs and private businesses, unencumbered with social principles? In fact, an opaque word, "disintermediation," is coming into use to obscure the very transparent process by which librarians may be eliminated in the time ahead.

The changeover now occurring in libraries is not simply a matter of introducing superior techniques and instrumentation that permit all participants—providers, users, and the general public—to benefit. Along with the new electronic technologies come a set of arrangements, social relations if you will. These, as they have developed in recent years under the pressure of private interests and conservative budget cutting, introduce the mechanics of the market to what had been a public sphere of social knowledge activity.

Compare, for example, Dialog's motive for acquiring databases with the library's long-term goal of acquiring as much of the social knowledge of the world as possible, constrained by limited resources, to be sure. Dialog, a major database vendor, is a subsidiary of Lockheed. Its president informs us: "We can't afford an investment in databases that are not going to earn their keep and pay back their development costs." Asked what areas currently are not paying their development costs, the answer was: "Humanities" (Summit, 1986, p. 1).

By the mid-1980s the commercialization of information—its purchase and sale and the growth of a powerful private information sector—has become the dominant feature of the American information-using economy. The amount of specialized data required to maintain a global system of production and distribution expands continuously. New fields and subfields of enterprise have emerged to service the worldwide business system. Many of these are heavily information-dependent. All the power centers of the nation—the transnational corporations, the federal bureaucracies, the Pentagon, and the leading universities—are agreed on the vital importance of information.

Not surprisingly in the current setting, the views and demands of the information industry are now presented as national goals, inscribed in legislation and executive orders of Congress and the Presidency: For example, the Paperwork Reduction Act of 1980; the

OMB's Circular A-130 on Management of Federal Information Resources (12 December 1985); and an earlier circular (A-76), dating back to the mid-sixties, on using private sector contractors for government functions.

These are but a few of a growing number of measures that have been designed, or interpreted, to establish the primacy and legitimacy of market decision making in the informational sphere and that instruct government agencies to yield their information to private firms.

In April 1986 the Department of Commerce announced its intention to privatize the National Technical Information Service (NTIS) (*Federal Register*, 1986, p. 15868). It asked for comments on various privatization alternatives but did not seek advice on whether privatization itself was desirable. It took that as a settled matter.

The NTIS collection of scientific reports and studies from 2,000 sources, both U.S. and foreign, includes over 1.6 million titles in a permanently available archive. If this is privatized, there is no assurance that the flow of materials into the archive will continue, that foreign information will be forthcoming, that infrequently purchased reports will continue to be stockpiled; and that government-produced information will not be copyrighted.

How far privatization and commercialization already have penetrated the public informational sphere is the message of an extraordinary statement of concern, issued in January 1985, by the Council on Library Resources, a private, 30-year-old organization supported by the Ford Foundation:

> Ways must be found to assure continuing attention for those aspects of culture and learning that are important but, in a commercial sense, not necessarily in fashion. . . . Uncritical adherence to the concept of information as a commodity will distort the agendas of institutions and disciplines alike. . . . Public interest in the principle of open access must appropriately influence the structure of the information system and its components. It is certain that the information needs of society cannot be defined by the market place alone. (Council on Library Resources, 1985)

This statement, in effect decrying some of the ravages of commercialization in the informational and library sphere over the last several years, received the endorsement of the Association of Research Libraries (ARL), an organization whose members include the major research libraries in the United States and Canada. The ARL added its concern over the federal government's "tendency to rely too heavily on commercial organizations to distribute government information" (Association of Research Libraries, 1985).

Commercialization and privatization are means to institutionalize a process whereby information is restricted to those with the ability to pay. Governmental administrative measures assist the process when they are aimed at removing huge quantities of information from the public domain and transferring basic informational functions from the government to the private sector.

In January 1986 the Commission on Freedom and Equality of Access to Information, a broadly based appointed panel, presented its report to the Council of the American Library Association. This document, among other matters, detailed how extensive has been the current administration's assault on popular information access and governmental information holdings:

> There has been a determined effort to limit and control the flow of information from the federal government. This has included reductions in the support of federal statistical and information-gathering programs, decreases in government publishing programs and increases in the price of government publications, stricter and broader programs for classification of government documents, requirements that government employees sign contracts allowing the Government to censor whatever they write for publication for the rest of their lives, limitations on contacts with the press and narrowing of the Freedom of Information Act. (Commission on Freedom and Equality of Access to Information, 1986, p. 13)

The attack is not subsiding. In March 1986, before the Subcommittee on Legislative Appropriations of the House Committee on Appropriations, the director of the Washington Office of the American Library Association described, and sharply criticized, the effects of the latest budget cuts on the public's access to basic congressional documents: closure of House and Senate Document rooms; a dramatic reduction in the number of copies of bills, reports, committee prints, hearings records, and so on, so they become practically unavailable to the general public; and significantly higher prices for government materials, making them, in effect, accessible mainly to those who can afford such outlays (Cooke, 1986).

Daniel Boorstin, the Librarian of Congress, told the same committee that the cuts imposed on the nation's greatest library could be compared to the "burning of the ancient Library of Alexandria in Egypt." The Library of Congress, Boorstin emphasized, is "dedicated to the proposition that free government is based on free, copious, and current access to knowledge."

"Historians will not fail to note," he added, "that a people who spend $300 billion on their defense would not spend $18 million on their knowledge—and could not even keep their libraries open in the evening" (Boorstin, 1986, pp. E5 88–89). As a result of the public outcry, several of the measures were made less stringent and some funds restored for activities threatened with curtailment.

CONCLUSION

Where does this review of developments in the informational environment point? A few conclusions may be stated briefly.

1. The commercialization of information in the United States is proceeding almost uninterruptedly. It has been extended into areas that historically have been regarded as non-profit-making and endowed with a deep public interest.

2. At the same time, the technology continues to change rapidly, and contradictory uses are apparent. In the library, in particular, the new technologies are spectacularly useful.

3. The library community and some consumer, civil liberties, and academic information-users have sought to defend the longstanding principles of free access and social criteria for use of the country's information supply. They have maintained these positions, with some slippage on occasion, against very powerful opposition. Now the existence of librarianship itself, as a *social* profession, is in question. The for-profit application of the new information technologies threatens the survival of the free access principle, a cornerstone of American librarianship.

4. Ultimately, the resolution of the public/private issue will be determined by the presence, or absence, of a strong political force or movement. This force, if it develops, will rally popular support for the defense of equal information access as well as raise to national attention the importance of information in the democratic process.

REFERENCES

Adkinson, B. W. (1978). *Two Centuries of Federal Information.* Stroudburg, Pa.: Hutchinson and Ross.

Arthur D. Little, Inc. (1978). "Passing the Threshold Into the Information Age: Perspective for Federal Action on Information." Basic Findings Report prepared for the National Science Foundation, vol. 1, Washington, D.C.: American Library Association.

Association of Research Libraries (1985). "Access to Information." Washington, D.C.: ARL.

Berry, J. (1986). "ALISE in Wonderland." *Library Journal*, 111, March 15, p. 4.

Boorstin, D. (1986). *Congressional Record.* House of Representatives, 132, 23, 4 March.

Burchinal, L. (1977). "Impact of On-Line Systems: On National Information Policy and on Local, State and Regional Planning." Paper presented at the Conference on the On-Line Revolution in Libraries, Pittsburgh, 14–16 November.

Business Roundtable (1985). "International Information Flow: A Plan for Action." New York: Business Roundtable.

Commission on Freedom and Equality of Access to Information (1986). *Report.* Washington, D.C. January.

Cooke, E. D. (1986). Director, Washington Office of the American Library Association, Letter to Vic Fazio, Chair, Legislative Appropriations Subcommittee, Committee on Appropriations, U.S. House of Representatives, 19 March.

Council on Library Resources (1985). "Scholarship, Research and Access to Information." Washington, D.C.: CLR.

Dickson, David (1984). *The New Politics of Science.* New York: Pantheon.

Domestic Council Committee on the Right of Privacy (1976). *National Information Policy.* Report to the President of the United States, published by the National Commission on Libraries and Information Science. Washington, D.C.: Government Printing Office.

Federal Register (1986). Vol. 51, 81, 28 April.

National Commission on Libraries and Information Science (1975). "Towards a National Program for Library and Information Services: Goals for Action." Washington, D.C.: NCLIS.

National Commission on Libraries and Information Science (1982). *Public Sector/Private Sector Interaction in Providing Information Services.* Washington, D.C.: Government Printing Office.

Newsletter of the Society for Scholarly Publishing (1980). vol. 2, 1.

Nyborg, P. S.; P. M. McCarter; and W. Erickson (eds.) (n.d.). *Information Processing in the United States: A Quantitative Summary.* Montvale, N.J.: AFIPS.

Schiller, A. R. (1977). "Commercial Online Services and the University Library: Some Impacts and Implications." A report to the Council on Library Resources.

Schuman, P. G. (1982). "Information Justice." *Library Journal*, 107, pp. 1060–66.

Science (1986). Vol. 231, 21 February, pp. 45–63.

Smith, D. (1985). "The Commercialization and Privatization of Government Information." *Government Publications Review*, 12.

Summit, R. (1986). *Information Today* (Learned Information Inc.), 3, 5.

U.S. Department of Commerce (1986). *U.S. Industrial Outlook 1986—Information Services.* Washington, D.C.: Government Printing Office.

Whalen, B. G., and C. C. Joyce, Jr. (1976). "Scientific and Technical Information: Options for National Action." Washington, D.C.: National Science Foundation, Division of Science Information.

White House Conference on Library and Information Services, 1979 (1980). *Summary*. Washington, D.C.: Government Printing Office.

9. Technical Capability Versus Corporate Imperatives: Toward a Political Economy of Cable Television and Information Diversity

Eileen R. Meehan

Are First World nations becoming information societies? Many scholars answer this question with a resounding yes and then speculate on the positive effects of restructuring corporate, governmental, and human relationships around the manufacture of information (Bell, 1983; De Sola Pool, 1976; Parker, 1976; Porat, 1977). Such speculation and its attendant research (cf. Compaine, 1981; Rice et al., 1984; Wiley and Neustadt, 1982) rests on a rather utopian vision of a future based on computers, cable television, and telecommunications in which these technologies exist only to make life easier and more fulfilling for the average person. Further, the innovation of technologies and services is directly controlled by personal preferences because it is governed solely by a marketplace where consumer demand determines supply.

Such speculation has been scrutinized closely by critical researchers (Gandy, 1983; Guback and Douglas, 1984; Mosco, 1979, 1982; Schiller, 1981, 1984). Using research into global trends in the military and corporate use of communication/information technologies, critical scholars have injected a strong element of caution into academic discussions of the coming information age. Here an important tactic has been the construction of rival, dystopian visions of the future, based on the same technologies that the utopians celebrate.

The global focus of this debate and its related research is important. However, it conflates military and transindustrial applications of information technologies with personal purchases of home appliances and entertainment services. This suggests that the political economy of information is constituted by a simple, undifferentiated, universal, and unified system of relationships. Methodologically, the implication is that the political economy of information can be explored via a single level of analysis.

Yet the critical research cited above, in concert with the industry-by-industry studies so central to critical communication (e.g., Danielian, 1939; Guback, 1969; Mattelart and Siegelaub, 1979, Mosco, 1979; Mosco and Wasko, 1984, Wasko, 1982) makes that assumption untenable. These case studies suggest that the political economy of information operates on three distinct levels. The first level examines the activities and relationships between the military and the handful of transnational corporations (TNCs) that own the invention factories (e.g., AT&T, RCA, IBM). Here one explores the connections between military demand, appropriation of public funds to TNCs for invention and development, imperialism in a world capitalist system, and so on. The second level deals with relationships between such TNCs, other powerful corporations, and governmental entities. Research at this level has explicated the relationships between media corporations and cultural imperialism, governmental intervention both domestically and internationally to protect corporate interests, and information flows. Finally, research at the third level examines relationships between media corporations and the people who purchase the services and technologies that have been innovated down through the other levels.

Research at each level has contributed significantly to our knowledge of the current state of information. At this third level, however, critical research has a special ability to connect with and validate people's experience. Further, this third level of research can be applied to local situations where progressive intervention may seem more possible to people. This is particularly important because the dominant ideology often manipulates promises of diversity at this level (as in the popular writings of the information utopians) in order to secure support for policies serving the vested interests of particular corporations or the military-industrial complex. By changing the terms of public discourse from consumer choice to corporate imperative, one reveals how capitalism systematically limits and slants the claims, images, and outlets available to people despite the technological potential for diversity. To understand this concretely, let us consider the case of a technology whose performance generally failed to meet its promise and then examine in depth an application of that technology that appears to have lived up to its promises.

LET A HUNDRED CHANNELS BLOOM; CABLE TELEVISION

Why does not cable television routinely present hundreds of channels filled with thousands of new, exciting, and highly differentiated offerings? Why has cable failed to revolutionize the way that Americans shop, bank, learn, interact, and relax? In the sixties, both hard-nosed executives and social visionaries were predicting that cable would inevitably change our way of life and our way of work. Not only would cable bring a cornucopia of cultural offerings into the home, but it would also interconnect us so that we would never have to leave home again. In this vision of a wired nation, cable would replace newspapers, broadcast television, telephony, shopping trips, mail, and banking. Further, it would restructure the human landscape by replacing the megalopolis (and its associated social problems) with a network of individual homes scattered throughout the nation, linked to friends, merchants, employers, schools, and governmental representatives via interactive cable.

Barely a decade and a half after Smith's (1972) articulation of this vision for cable, we find the same prophecy being replayed for an interlocked network of computers, satellites, and cable. Yet as cable achieves nearly 45 percent penetration nationally with systems reporting a 60 percent rate of subscription, cable seems increasingly to function as a television service. That is, cable remains largely a one-way delivery system for familiar goods–movies, sports, sitcoms, adventure shows, weather reports, news–aimed at familiar audiences: women or men between 18 and 49, families, children, and teenagers. We are left with a simple question: why?

This paper begins the process of answering that question by examining the particular implementation of a cable technology closest in capability to fulfilling the utopian promises of a wired nation. By taking the strongest example in favor of those promises, one can demonstrate clearly how corporate imperatives shape the design of the technology and limit its application to the provision of specific, limited forms of entertainment/information. Even when implemented as a multichannel, interactive system in the United States, cable is constrained by the industrial and transindustrial context of information/entertainment production in advanced capitalism. The context within which interactive cable was implemented has been bounded by the relationship between technological capabilities and corporate imperatives, a relationship itself structured primarily by the interpenetration of companies involved in the cable, music, film, and television industries. These corporate imperatives, rooted in a drive to secure both profits and numerous niches in an increasingly unified economic sector, effectively limit applications of interactive cable technology, the use of available channels, the information/entertainment presented over those channels, and the information gathered through interactive capability. To illustrate this, I turn to an analysis of QUBE.

TALKING TO YOUR TELEVISION; INTERACTIVE CABLE

Cable came closest to the utopian vision with the interactive cable system QUBE. Although not the first two-way cable system in the United States, QUBE was the first interactive system to be an entirely commercial venture. In a capitalist economy, such a status enshrines QUBE as the first *serious* interactive system, since it attempted to profit from that technical capability. After sketching QUBE's corporate history, I will examine its implementation to reveal the connections between the interactive capability designed into QUBE and the economic imperatives driving Warner's decisions about and uses of QUBE.

Columbus, Ohio, was one of the first cities to grant nonexclusive cable franchises to competing applicants and to grant one franchise specifically to a black-owned company to serve the predominantly black inner city. Interestingly, this decision freed the other cable companies to concentrate on more profitable areas. QUBE, for example, was originally installed by Warner Communications' wholly owned subsidiary Warner Cable in 1977 in the western franchise areas of Columbus, Ohio, where the University of Ohio at Columbus and its bedroom communities are located. From 1979 to 1985 QUBE was operated as a joint venture of Warner and Amex Cable, itself owned coequally by Warner and American Express. During that period, Warner Amex used QUBE to test various programming formats, resulting in the cable channels Nickelodeon (NIK), for children and teenagers, and Music Television (MTV), for 14- to 34-year-olds, and the pay service The Movie Channel (TMC), all offered nationally through Warner Amex Satellite Entertainment Services.

However, continuing losses from the operation of QUBE and from heavy capital investments for new urban QUBE installations eventually led American Express to begin disengaging itself from the joint venture. American Express first decreased its share of TMC and then accepted a merger of TMC with Showtime, a pay channel owned by Viacom, a firm primarily concerned with the production and distribution of television programming and motion pictures. Finally, American Express offered to buy out Warner with the announced intention of selling both programming and cable operations either to Time, Inc. (owner of the second-largest cable operator and the two largest pay services) or to a joint venture between Time and the largest cable operator, Tele-Communications Incorporated (TCI). Countering this move with its own offer to buy out American Express, Warner retained control of QUBE, but sold its programming services to Viacom, the country's 10th-ranked cable operator.

With this brief history of QUBE's ownership in hand, let us turn to a closer consideration of QUBE's interactive capability.

The feature of QUBE most salient to the utopian/dystopian debate is precisely its ability to send messages through the system and receive feedback from subscribers. Perhaps QUBE's most controversial uses of this interactivity were its opinion polls on national issues and its instantaneous feedback to City Council members during meetings. This "electronic democracy" was hailed as a way for people to express themselves to local politicians and to respond to questions of national and international interest. It was also attacked as representing a geo-economic minority whose reactions to forced choice questions were reported as percentages of an unspecified number of responses from an unspecified number of sets-in-use. A secondary issue in these exchanges was the problem of privacy, a problem endemic to the design of the hardware.

Although political polling was a secondary function of QUBE, billing was not. Warner designed the system specifically to include 10 pay-per-program channels as well as 10 "television" channels and 10 "community" channels. On QUBE, "television" meant local network affiliates, public broadcasting, and independent stations imported from other markets. The community channels featured locally produced programs. The 10 pay channels followed familiar genres—sporting events, self-improvement, rock concerts, arts programming, family movies, screen classics, theatrical feature films, soft-core pornography—and were subject to change if revenues for a particular genre decreased to unacceptable levels. Viewers were allowed to sample an offering for two minutes of cumulative viewing. To keep track of these minutes and of billing, QUBE's computer "read" the entire system every two minutes, recording whether the set was turned on, the channel in use, and the last response button touched. From these data the computer compiled monthly bills that included the name, time, and cost of pay programs watched. Because of this, critics argued that QUBE's data might be manipulated to violate the privacy of individuals whose viewing habits clashed with the public images required by their occupations.

Warner Amex responded with a policy statement promising to protect the privacy of individual subscribers. However, the company reserved the right to sell aggregated information. This is a particularly important decision, given the detailed demographic information required from each household as part of its application for a subscription—an application justified by the high monthly cost of basic service, which in turn was due to the high cost of system operation. Thus, through its billing system and its application form, QUBE provided Warner Amex with detailed information about people living in middle-class neighborhoods and willing to pay premium prices for entertainment/information, as well as detailed information about what these people watched and how they responded to specific questions. Granted that all this was sold in an aggregate form, QUBE's database still represented for advertisers and program-developers more precise information about demographically desirable households than was previously available. And the data were gathered in a situation where participants paid for the privilege of being sold.

The economic impetus for interactivity is further indicated when one considers QUBE's location. Columbus, Ohio, has been frequently used by advertisers to pretest products and commercials. Indeed, on one of its basic "community" channels, QUBE often tested products, magazine covers, advertisements, and so on, disguising the test as an opinion poll or the call-in segment of an interview. This in itself suggests that QUBE's opinion polls also served an economic function. The polls made requests for information a normal part of watching QUBE, thereby increasing the internal validity of viewer responses and avoiding the biases necessarily introduced when measurement is obtrusive.

Further, in 1978 American Express's participation in Warner Amex was presaged by a contract with QUBE for "infomercials," wherein advertisements for American Express were presented as educational programming complete with requests for viewers' opinions. This, combined with local merchants' use of QUBE's "community programming" to sell books, insurance, and other services, suggests lucrative retail possibilities, especially if such vending was connected to payment by credit card or to a subscriber's monthly bill. Again, whether a subscriber used such services or watched such advertisements, all subscribers were billed for them as part of the basic cable fee, and all subscribers could be sold as part of the aggregated database.

In economic terms a very real promise of QUBE technology was the promise of multiple revenues from a single service. On the one hand QUBE promised to become a major testing operation. Using QUBE, stimuli were introduced into the home disguised as "mere entertainment" or "community programming" or "objective information." Responses were collected as "tests of knowledge" or "requests for information" or "public opinion." With its fixed sample and its demographic information on subscribers, QUBE seemed to offer the ultimate in naturalistic observation and panel design for marketing consumer goods. On the other hand, QUBE could avoid the cost of the inducements sometimes necessary to secure participation. Indeed, QUBE essentially charged both participants and nonparticipants by placing such tests on channels included in the basic fee paid by every subscribing household. But this multiplication of revenues was not limited to QUBE's product-testing service; consider QUBE's handling of a perennial problem for cable operators, the "churn" rate.

Because QUBE was a pay-per-view system, it could decrease the costs of repeated connection and disconnection of pay channels ("churn"). However, avoiding that cost required the use of more expensive ways to track and charge for pay products—that is, QUBE's expensive computer monitoring system. Yet this monitoring system, which appears to be an expensive solution to an industry-wide problem, is also a source of revenue: no monitoring, no interaction, no product testing. But beyond this lies QUBE's ability to compile information on viewing habits by program and commercial break for each subscribing household. The marketing applications should be obvious. With this sort of computer capability, one would expect that monitoring data—household viewing habits by particular program and genre, responses to marketing questions, and responses to public opinion polls—could be mapped across demographic categories in order to produce aggregated information for sale to other corporations as well as for internal use by QUBE's parent corporations, American Express and Warner Communications. In this way, the cost of billing became a promise of multiple income. But beyond that, it also promised to serve as a guide for product development by Warner Communications, a major producer, distributor, and licenser in the areas of films, television series, television miniseries, books, records, published music, and (until 1984) toys, marketing campaigns, and software as well as hardware for videogames and home computers.

RATIONALIZING THE MANUFACTURE OF CULTURAL COMMODITIES

Although Warner Amex projected that QUBE would be used to test television pilots by production companies and networks, the major user of such testing was Warner Amex itself. This use took three forms: overt development of a format using interactivity (MTV), covert testing of a format (NIK), and covert generic testing via pay-per-view channels that could feed into Warner's activities in film, television, and pay cable (TMC, later Showtime/TMC). Each of these activities feeds directly into the primary manufacturing activity of QUBE's designer and implementer, Warner Communications, Inc. (WCI). Each suggests a second economic force behind WCI's willingness to accept initially high losses to operate QUBE and then to sacrifice profitable programming services (MTV and NIK) as well as participation in Showtime/TMC in order to prevent American Express from selling QUBE to Time, whose cable interests and pay channels augment its strong position as a manufacturer of books, magazines, television series, and films. Exploring WCI's use of QUBE's three testing capabilities should clarify these claims.

Whose MTV?

The most explicit application of QUBE to the development of a programming format was Warner Amex's use of community channels to gather data on the responding household's forced-choice preferences among limited arrays of rock videos. In a regularly scheduled "community" program, respondents typically selected one of three videos (artist and title specified), with the winner from each array being aired later in the program. QUBE's computers not only tallied the votes but stored the responses, allowing further analysis of the aggregated preference data against aggregated demographic data on responding households. Thus QUBE empirically tested the structured choices made by rock fans whose households were paying consumers of entertainment, as opposed to the ratings that claimed to measure consumers of "free" rock radio stations or "free" rock programs scheduled in fringe times on television (e.g., *American Bandstand* on Saturday). The result in August 1981 was MTV, distributed by Warner Amex Satellite Entertainment and designed for 14- to 34-year-olds, with 14- to 24-year-olds most heavily targeted.

This pseudo-experimental design provided data that could be used to answer two questions. The first was of immediate significance to WCI, given its interests in records and music publishing: how could record sales be increased? The obvious answer, of course, was simply to produce records that fall within the genres that 14- to 34-year-olds were willing to buy. However, operationalizing that answer was by no means simple. Consider the sorts of data available. Requests called in to radio stations reflected a willingness to listen, not necessarily to buy. The entire machinery of radio formats, play lists, and best-seller lists was open to significant influence by promotional campaigns originating from such record producers and distributors as Warner. The belief in the music industry was simply that promotion increased sales. Yet, by the eighties, with promotion increasingly elaborate and expensive, record sales had slumped. For WCI, then, QUBE's tests of rock videos provided a way to circumvent disc jockeys, record store employees, and other middlemen in order to directly measure the generic tastes of households willing to pay for entertainment.

By aggregating household data and video-selection data, WCI could make rational decisions on the saleability of generic categories of artists and generic forms of rock music. By analyzing the patterns of preference across different subcategories of households, Warner Amex could design a rock video service constructed not only to promote Warner records, artists, songs, and soundtracks, but also to attract an audience of consumers for resale to advertisers. While the potential for direct and indirect revenues undoubtedly made MTV an attractive venture for Warner Amex, two other factors combined to make MTV feasible: Warner Amex's excess satellite capability and MTV's relatively low costs of production. Warner Amex owned two idle satellite transponders at a time when demand was very high and supply low. Warner Amex could innovate a new satellite-distributed service without delay, thereby allowing the service to establish itself before rivals could secure transponder space. The technical capability to implement the design that emerged from the QUBE test was already in place.

Also in place was an industry-wide practice that promised to keep the costs of production low: record companies were long accustomed to furnishing radio stations with records and prerecorded interviews free of charge. By designing MTV as radio-with-pictures, Warner Amex incurred the costs of an indoor set, technical personnel, and "VJs"—but paid no fees for the use of videos. From 1981 to 1984 MTV paid nothing for its primary programming. Of course, WCI did incur the costs of video production for its QUBE test, but the videos resulting from those expenditures could be recycled on MTV. In this early phase MTV attempted to secure exclusive rights to use videos without purchasing those rights. Significantly, in 1984, when the channel began paying for use, the tradeoff was a commitment from major labels to grant MTV exclusivity. By then, MTV was established as the major outlet for rock videos and the sole satellite channel distributing them. Warner Amex was also beginning to implement a carriage fee for MTV even as advertising revenues remained high.

The possibility of such advertising revenues raises the second question that QUBE's pseudo-experimental design could answer: what generic artists and musical forms would attract the consumers that advertisers most wanted? The late seventies and early eighties had seen the decline of network television's ability to deliver audiences generally and the 18- to 30-year-old category particularly. Programs like the early *Saturday Night Live* had attracted that elusive demographic category, but had proved problematic and costly (Hill and Weingrad,

1986). In QUBE's pretesting, the patterns of preference evinced by households with members falling into that category could be abstracted as the basis for MTV's format. Warner Amex *could* make such inferences, but did it?

The controversy that surrounded MTV's original format suggests that Warner Amex did indeed make inferences connecting preference patterns and the demographics of responding households. Originally, MTV excluded on a generic basis both black artists and musical forms identified principally with blacks (e.g., soul, rhythm and blues, jazz). This replication of the music industry's long-institutionalized "color bar" was, in MTV's case, based on the QUBE testing data. The data showed that the "the kids" wanted to see white performers and to hear musical forms largely identified as white (e.g., mellow/soft rock, middle-of-the-road rock, hard rock, heavy metal). The racial and class biases that defined "the kids" were not generally discussed. However, it is precisely those biases that made the QUBE test and the resulting MTV format attractive to national advertisers. The racial composition of the national pool of consumers is largely white; hence, audience-producers that target whites respond rationally to advertiser demand. Unless an advertiser has a product designed for nonwhites, there is no demand for such audiences and little impetus for audience-producers like MTV to serve the generic tastes of those audiences. While MTV's color bar was finally broken, that breakthrough was achieved by black performers packaged as crossover artists who had gained significant white followings and whose videos betrayed little cultural connection to either the black experience or any particular black subculture—Michael Jackson (CBS), Lionel Richie (Motown), and Prince (Warner).

Prince's connection to Warner raises again the question of MTV's role in promoting Warner products. In the QUBE tests, Warner Amex clearly needed videos to show, yet the tests predated the widespread production of videos by major labels. Still, in the late seventies, as equipment costs dropped and video-oriented discos opened, independent videos were used by some bands to augment their state shows and to complement the audition tapes they submitted to labels. If the QUBE tests used videos of Warner's performers and independent bands, then MTV's original mixture of known bands in concert, known bands enacting stories, and independent bands (including some progressive and new wave bands) makes sense. Of course, when MTV went on satellite, this would also give Warner a "natural" advantage as other labels scrambled to get their stars on video.

Similarly apparent must have been the advantages of including videos in movies. For example, Prince's independent feature *Purple*

Rain (distributed by Warner) presents a string of videos connected by a rather tenuous plot. The result is a visual soundtrack with breaks for dialogue. This contrasts with a film more directly controlled by Warner, *Against All Odds,* in which the plot stops while the videos play. Clips from the film were also re-edited into a video interspersing shots of Warner's Phil Collins performing the title song with shots from the film. Videos from both of these films ran on MTV's heavy-rotation schedule. The result is an integration of videos, film, and soundtrack where each component is simply stitched together, where each can easily be broken out from the whole to be cycled through different media in order to promote multiple consumption based on the same artifact.

These examples suggest how the array of cultural products can become increasingly narrowed when a single product and its constitutive parts are expected to earn multiple revenues. But just as the same material is recycled over different media, it is also presented via a number of different outlets within the same medium, as we will see in our discussion of Warner Amex's satellite channel for children, Nickelodeon

From Pinwheel To NIK Rocks

For the communities surrounding the University of Ohio and in QUBE's franchise areas, surely one of QUBE's attractions was its noncommercial, nonviolent programming for children. Presented over a community channel and called Pinwheel, this programming mixed entertainment with instruction in a manner that rivaled the best public television programming for children then available. Absent from Pinwheel were Warner's own cartoons, so often characterized as among the most violent programming on television (Gerbner et al., 1978). Instead, prosocial materials designed for children from toddlers to 14-year-olds from both the United States and abroad filled Pinwheel's five-hour slot.

It is important to note that by 1977 research on children and television included not only studies of the effects of violence on children, but also research on prosocial effects, on advertising and consumer skills, on cognitive development and children's processing of television. Indeed, the university's department of mass communication mirrored the increasing sophistication and included some of the pioneers in this area on its faculty. Whether such considerations shaped WCI's original decision to offer Pinwheel or Warner Amex's decision to continue the program is unknown. Suffice it to say that positive programming for children was an excellent selling point to a university community or a city council.

Warner Amex's decision to distribute Pinwheel via its satellite transponders to cable companies involved both the renaming of the service (as Nickelodeon or NIK) and an agreement for time sharing with Alpha Repertory Television (originally ARTS; later the Arts and Entertainment Network or A&E), itself a joint venture of ABC and Hearst Publications. The move to satellite distribution, however, also involved some changes in programming. Although Pinwheel was still featured, NIK was expanded to 13 hours, and much of the programming was typical of commercial entertainment aimed at an undifferentiated group of young viewers. Many of the programs were still imported, but the content was no longer strictly prosocial and nonviolent. For example, alongside scientific experiments (*Mr. Wizard)* and children's classics (*Black Beauty*) was a one-eyed rodent battling a mad frog bent on taking over the world (*Dangermouse*), a Canadian teenager getting slimed (*You Can't Do That on Television*), and an integrated band of British youngsters working with an omniscient computer to save the world from US militarism, dishonest scientists, and parasites from outer space (*The Tomorrow People*). In the transition from QUBE to satellite, Warner Amex's children's channel lost its commitment to age-appropriate, prosocial, nonviolent, educational programming.

The change seemed due largely to economic factors. On QUBE, Pinwheel had been subsidized by all subscribers as part of the basic monthly charge. The important consumption choice turned on subscribing not to Pinwheel but to QUBE. However, Pinwheel could be used to sell QUBE to households with children, especially in a university community. These supports for Pinwheel's prosocial programming disappeared with satellite distribution as the primary decision-maker/gatekeeper, and the definition of the audience changed.

There is little reason to believe that a highly specified demand for particular channels originates in cable subscribers, who voice this need to cable operators. The industry's truism is that cable attracts subscribers by providing improved reception, uncut movies, and sports. Indeed, the notion that kiddie shows do not sell subscriptions has lately been supported by the low rate of initial subscription and the high rate of disconnection experienced by the Disney Channel. This suggests one reason for Warner Amex's willingness to share its NIK channel with ARTS. The package promised cable operators two services and two separate audiences—children in general and viewers of serial and cultural programming in the style of US public television—for the price of one. Whereas NIK charged cable operators 10-15 cents per subscribing household, ARTS was free. Given that any cable operator must balance the cost efficiency of the entire service against the potential of any particular channel for attracting and keeping subscribers, this "two in one" approach made NIK/ARTS more attractive than a competing service, CBS's more elitist cultural channel CBS CABLE. Further, the NIK/ARTS combination duplicated the division of time by audience typical of public television stations, but it did so with a twist: NIK/ARTS sold commercial time.

Here, then, is another impetus for the generalization of NIK's programming. Although educators may be interested in prosocial programming geared to developmental stage, advertisers are interested in reaching a range of children whose households are strongly consumption-oriented. As Warner Amex redesigned Pinwheel to become Nickelodeon, the company could draw upon its QUBE technology to estimate the general interest of programs aimed at children for households of known consumers. By analyzing program selection and demographic data, Warner Amex could separate those programs viewed only in households with, say, preschoolers from those viewed in households with both preschoolers and kindergarteners, and so along the age range. A careful analysis of QUBE data could track the process of tuning in and tuning out (including the program preferred to the Pinwheel segment) across household demographics. Further, if a program was viewed consistently by households without children below 14 years of age, this information was also accessible via an analysis of QUBE data.

The use of such analyses to construct a commercial service targeted toward children seems highly probable on three grounds. First, such information would help sell the service to cable operators, who typically are provided with some time on a channel for local sales. Second, the information would also be useful in selling time to national advertisers and would give NIK a basis from which to compete with the afternoon and Saturday morning programming of networks and independent stations distributed by satellite (e.g., WTBS or WGN). Third, the combination of advertising and carriage charges would allow Warner Amex to earn two distinct sorts of revenue from a single service. The corporate impetus, the market structure, and the available technical capability all argue for this interpretation of Warner Amex's innovation of Pinwheel and NIK.

But NIK not only went commercial; it also became another site where WCI could recycle cultural products. Stripped across the week was a half-hour program called *NIK Rocks* that simply strung together videos shown on MTV. In NIK's advertisements for *NIK Rocks*, these videos originally targeted for 14- to 34-year-olds were touted as "your music" to an audience presumably composed of children under the age of 14. This would seem to ensure the program's appeal to caretakers as well as children. But the program should not be underestimated as a promotional device, since preteens are also consumers of records, movie tickets, fan magazines, posters, and tee-shirts.

In this short history of Pinwheel's transformation to NIK, one finds a format that might be written off as a good-will gesture or public service eventually becoming a commercially viable one. To the degree that Warner Amex correlated household demographic data and use of Pinwheel, the company could chart the generality of appeal exercised by programming specialized by age-grade. Not only could specific shows be so analyzed, but, more important, generic forms of programming were also susceptible to such analysis. The technical capability of QUBE's monitoring system, then, could be applied to ascertain scientifically how to construct a programming service for generic children—rather than age-graded children—and most especially for the generic child within a consumerist household. This sort of proprietorial information could then be used to construct a generic service for national distribution that would rationalize the production of child audiences for advertisers, and do so on a daily basis through a network that identified itself as just for us kids.

Again, one must ask: did Warner Amex do that? The transformation of its programming service for children from an educational endeavor to a capitalist enterprise suggests that it did precisely that. Surely the technical capability was there—the QUBE monitoring system, its computer capability, the unused transponder. Just as surely the possibility of double revenues from such a channel, plus the opportunity to recycle content, particularly content that promoted other products (records, films, MTV), was also there. WCI and Warner Amex's consistent characterization of QUBE as a superb ground for program testing and for disguising promotions as information or entertainment also suggests that neither company was unmindful of QUBE's potential. This analysis suggests one covert manner in which that potential may have been used; the section below suggests another covert use that may underlie much of WCI's willingness to sacrifice profits to retain QUBE.

QUBE'S Pay Per View: Testing Manufacturing Categories

And so we turn to the last moment in this analysis of QUBE—to a consideration of the relationship between QUBE's technical capabilities and the principal manufacturing activities of its designer and implementor, Warner Communications Incorporated. The mechanics of each operation are crucial to understanding QUBE's ultimate value to WCI.

Thus the analysis begins by examining the economic constraints on the mass production of cultural commodities (WCI's principal activity and major profit center) and then contextualizes QUBE's design within the framework of that activity.

WCI's principal activity has long been the mass production of cultural commodities, which are distributed by the company through a variety of media including film, television, records, and print. Starting as a movie company, WCI recognized early the possibility of multiple sales from recycled content. Warner's initial foray into sound film (*The Jazz Singer*) opened the way to new forms of song-plugging and film-promotion through the publication of the soundtrack for home performance and the repackaging of soundtracks as records. Warner's eventual expansion into television, books, and original recording opened new ways for specific content to be recycled. While recycling limited diversity in terms of particular representations, mass production limited the general types of cultural commodities (genres) whose specific content would then be recycled. This becomes clear when mass production is contrasted with the craft production of cultural commodities.

In craft production, work is organized around the creation of a singular artifact. This approach depends on irregular sources of symbolic material (insight) and a peculiar arrangement of that material (artistic expression). Craft production tends to be labor-intensive, expensive, and uncertain. Profitability depends on acceptance by cultural and economic elites, often long after the demise of the producer. With the rise of capitalism, this form of cultural production has continued, but in a more rationalized manner through the producer's exploitation of a star system and through the multiple reproduction of artifacts marketed across classes and subcultures.

In contrast, mass production depends on the regularization of symbolic inputs and their arrangement in order to rationalize demand and secure immediate profits. This regularization into manufacturing categories (genres) allows producers to cultivate a demand for generic cultural commodities in audiences. Such commodities are manufactured according to formulae specifying the available pool of narrative, aural, visual, and human components from which workers select a particular configuration for a particular film, program, book, or album. The profitability of a particular commodity validates both the formulae used in constructing the object and the genre as a whole. In the mass production of entertainment, such a success spurs imitation of the particular commodity as well as a resurgence of production within the genre across different media. For example, a hit film may serve as the basis for a television series, inspire the resurgence of a genre on television, or lead to inclusion of objects from the film in a series from a different genre (cf. the film *Blue Thunder*, the television series *Air Wolf*, the helicopter in the *Riptide* series).

To a certain extent such trends are followed by all content-producers. Although this practice solves some problems, it creates others, especially if too many firms follow the trend. Overproduction within a genre leads to dwindling demand for such products from corporate gatekeepers (bankers, networks, distributors, advertisers) and audiences. However, risks are also involved when a firm attempts to revitalize a genre. Acceptance by corporate gatekeepers is uncertain, especially since there are no direct, reliable predictors of audience acceptance. And that is where QUBE comes in.

Ostensibly, QUBE's monitoring and information storage capabilities were motivated by two needs: billing for the use of pay channels and recording responses from households. The system was designed in such a way that household consoles were read by QUBE's central computer in continuous sweeps with data on all use recorded; consoles did not report to the computer when pay programs were selected or responses entered. But if the consoles had been designed to actively report pay-per-view choices and responses, then the data on overall viewing would have been limited to subsections of the subscriber base. An active console design would mean no data for households that neither watched pay programming nor responded, and limited data (title and time) for households that watched pay programs or used both pay-per-view and interactivity or used only interactivity to respond to specific questions. In contrast, the passive console design that WCI implemented allowed constant monitoring of all households independent of billing or interactivity. The result of that technical capability was a data bank that could be analyzed to determine patterned relationships between generic viewing habits, willingness to pay indirectly or directly for programming, willingness to pay specific amounts for specific genres, and demographic categories of willing consumers.

Each differentiation, is significant because WCI's products appeared on television, on pay cable, and in movie houses. In television, willingness to pay is less important then a genre's ability to attract saleable consumers and to do so more effectively than other genres. Here, QUBE's data bank could be analyzed to determine whether certain genres were more attractive for some types of households than others, to gauge whether some genres were more likely to beat others for viewers within certain time periods, and so on. In pay cable, audiences must be willing to pay directly for access to a channel and discontent when that channel's product leads to disconnection of the service. Here, QUBE's data bank could be used to gauge the saleability of old product from particular genres, to use the pricing barrier as a way to test the limits of consumer willingness to spend by genre and age of product, and so on. Such information might influence the selection of films for WCI's first venture into pay cable (TMC), to guide Warner's input to Viacom on original product for their merged service (Showtime/TMC), and to shape WCI's planning for future films. Such films would have two primary sources of revenue—pay channels (HBO, Cinemax, Showtime/TMC), where showings were not exclusive, and movie theaters. Here, QUBE promised to serve as an "early warning system" for changes in generic acceptability in households whose demographics predicted strong attendance at the movies. Indeed, with WCI's implementation of a security service on QUBE arose the possibility of aggregating data on absences from the home, viewing patterns, pay usage, and demographics—all paid for by security-conscious QUBE subscribers.

But again one must ask: did WCI recognize the possibility of using QUBE as a laboratory? If such information was produced from analyses of QUBE's data banks, it would be worthy of the most impenetrable shrouds of corporate secrecy. Given the proprietary nature of any information on WCI's inhouse use of aggregate data from QUBE, an answer to this question depends on inferences from WCI's actions in the marketplace. Fortunately, recent events have been highly suggestive in this regard.

From 1980 through 1982 WCI enjoyed high revenues and solid profits, due in part to its acquisition of Atari, which dominated home video games, and to generally strong revenues from television and film production, licensing, marketing, and so on, despite the slump in record sales. Although the company absorbed losses from QUBE and the start-up costs of programming channels, it was considered sufficiently solid to retain good ratings from the two major investment rating services, Moody's and Standard and Poor's. This changed in the first quarter of 1983, when WCI posted an unexpected $18.9 million deficit. The firm continued losing money until, in 1984, its total debt had risen to approximately a billion dollars. This led to negotiations with its creditors, lowered ratings with Moody's and Standard and Poor's, law suits from its shareholders, and a takeover bid from its major corporate stockholder (Chris-Craft). Attempting to right itself, WCI began selling off holdings both profitable (e.g., Warner Cosmetics) and unprofitable (e.g., Atari) and decreasing its labor costs, all of which decreased WCI's indebtedness to below $300 million in 1985. In the midst of these troubles, American Express declared its intention to buy out WCI for $400 million (later increased to $450 million) and sell the entire operation to Time and TCI for $750 million (increased to $850, then to $900 million), with the partners assuming Warner Amex's $500–550 million debt.

Superficially, the offer would seem to have represented a golden opportunity for WCI to unload a capital-intensive operation that was continuing to lose money. Practically, American Express had constructed a double bind for WCI: either WCI had to pay off its partner, or American Express would sell QUBE to TCI and Time. Those companies had already announced that they would sell MTV Networks and the partial interest in Showtime/ TMC. Clearly, Time and TCI were after Warner Amex's cable operations, including QUBE. In the hands of that combination, QUBE could become the laboratory in which Time tested its books, book series, magazines, television programs, movies, marketing techniques, promotional campaigns and so on. To retain control of QUBE, WCI sold the profitable MTV and NIK, which had earlier been spun off QUBE as the MTV Network, as well as its share of Showtime/TMC to Viacom. Thus, WCI bought out American Express, protecting QUBE but sacrificing two of its successful products.

Such a decision appears irrational if only immediate profitability is considered. WCI needed money to the point that it was selling its assets. American Express was offering to pay $400–450 million for the entire Warner Amex operation, including its debt. In response to this offer, WCI agreed to pay American Express $450 million and began negotiations to sell the profitable MTV Networks and its portion of Showtime/TMC. The logic of capitalism mandated that WCI act in what it perceived as self-interest. Clearly, WCI had a powerful reason to keep QUBE, since keeping the system required it to endure financial losses. This suggests that WCI was well aware of QUBE's covert ability to measure generic preferences and cost thresholds among known consumers. As a laboratory for content testing, QUBE was matched by none—a fact revealed by analysis of its technical capability and WCI's primary economic activity, a fact supported by the willingness of both WCI and Time to expend significant amounts of money to secure access to QUBE.

CONCLUSION: TOWARD A POLITICAL ECONOMY OF CABLE AND DIVERSITY

This study illustrates how QUBE, the single commercial implementation of interactive cable television in the United States, was shaped by the economic constraints that limit cultural production under capitalism. The system's interactivity was designed as a means of product testing and format development, which translated into multiple revenues from a single service. Computer capabilities were tied to billing and monitoring of generic preferences for cultural commodities. Combined with the demographic data gathered via application for subscription, these data were retained as Warner Amex's property, which it could sell in aggregate form. Further, QUBE was installed in the white middle-class neighborhoods of a city commonly used for product testing. From the start, QUBE's interactivity, monitoring, and subscription base were designed to serve the interests of advertisers. Yet, as suggested by the analysis of QUBE's technical ability to covertly measure genre preferences, QUBE was also designed to serve WCI's own interests in rationalizing content production in film, television, and records. Further, the overt use of QUBE to develop programming formats has facilitated the recycling of the same content across different media and through multiple outlets for each medium. As a laboratory, QUBE was unique in its ability to secure revenues from its subjects as well as from its clients.

In short, QUBE is far removed from the vision of a wired society. Yet, as the closest approximation of that vision in the cable industry, QUBE suggests that cable per se has not failed, but rather that corporate imperatives have limited the design and implementation of cable to serve corporate interests. Just as QUBE became a laboratory for overt and covert product testing, so too has noninteractive cable become a simple delivery system designed to increase revenues through the recycling and resale of cultural commodities. Cable works to deliver more of the same content for a fee to slightly fewer viewers; it also works to promote further cultural consumption, thus serving as an advertisement as well as packaging some viewers for sale to advertisers. QUBE works to rationalize cultural production and promotion. Despite the technological potential for a hundred channels filled with a thousand very different programs, the imperatives of profit and cost efficiency systematically limit the number of channels and the kinds of programs available.

This suggests an underlying logic that connects the development of new technologies with information/entertainment production at the level where people and companies interact. First, only technologies in the direct interest of corporations will be made available to us. Second, elaborate capabilities will be tailored to suit particular corporate interests, and our general access to them will be limited by commercial interests. Finally, the content available over those new technologies, elaborated or simple, will be limited by the content-producer's ability to recycle that information/entertainment over as many other outlets as possible. Such a dynamic, revealed in our analysis of QUBE, does not bode well for either the utopian or the dystopian visions of an information society.

However, when demonstrated concretely, the articulation of this dynamic resonates with people's experiences of cable television: much is promised, nothing is on. It is but a short step from the analysis of old technologies to new technologies, of old promises broken to new promises made, of the wired society to the information age. In taking that step, we begin a journey that leads not simply to debunking the current vision touted in support of capitalism, but to a critical understanding of the economic underpinnings that drive capitalism. From such understandings human beings act to make history, though, as Marx correctly observed, not in conditions of our choice.

REFERENCES

Bell, D. (1983). "Communication Technology—For Better or for Worse?" In J. L. Salvaggio (ed.) *Telecommunications: Issues and Choices for Society,* New York: Longman Press.

Compaine, B. M. (1981). "Shifting Boundaries in the Information Marketplace," *Journal of Communication,* 31, 1, pp. 132–42.

Danielian, N. R. (1939). *ATT: The Story of Industrial Conquest.* New York: Vanguard Press.

De Sola Pool, I. (1976). "Background Report, Session D: International Policy Dimensions," In *Conference on Computers/Telecommunications Policy*, OECD Informatics Studies, no. 11. Paris: Organization for Economic Cooperation and Development (OECD).

Douglas, S., and T. Guback (1984). "Production and Technology in the Communication/Information Revolution," *Media Culture & Society*, 6, 3, pp. 233–45.

Gandy, O. H. (1983). *Beyond Agenda Setting: Targeting Information Subsidies and Public Policy.* Norwood, N.J.: Ablex.

Gerbner, G., et al. (1978). *Violence Profile No. 9: Trends in Network Television Drama and Viewer Conceptions of Social Reality.* Philadelphia: Annenberg School of Communications.

Guback, T. (1969). *The International Film Industry: Western Europe and America Since 1954.* Bloomington: Indiana University Press.

Hill, D., and J. Weingrad (1986). *Saturday Night: A Backstage History of Saturday Night Live.* New York: Beachtree Books.

Mattelart, A., and S. Siegelaub (eds.) (1979). *Communication and Class Struggle, 1: Capitalism, Imperialism.* New York: International General.

Mosco, V. (1979). *Broadcasting in the United States: Innovative Challenge and Organizational Control.* Norwood, N.J.: Ablex.

Mosco, V. (1982). *Pushbutton Fantasies: Critical Perspectives on Videotex and Information Technology.* Norwood, N.J.: Ablex.

Mosco, V., and J. Wasko (1984). *The Critical Communications Review, Volume 2—Changing Patterns of Communications Control.* Norwood, N.J.: Ablex.

Parker, E. (1976). "Background Report, Session A: Social Implications of Computer/Telecommunications Policy." *In Conference on Computers/Telecommunications Policy.* OECD Informatics Studies, no. 11. Paris: OECD.

Porat, M. U. (1977). *The Information Economy.* Department of Commerce, Office of Telecommunications. Washington, DC: Government Printing Office.

Rice, R., et al. (1984). *The New Media: Communication, Research, and Technology.* Beverly Hills, Calif.: Sage.

Schiller, H. (1981). *Who Knows? Information in the Age of the Fortune 500.* Norwood, N.J. : Ablex.

Schiller, H. (1984). *Information and the Crisis Economy.* Norwood, N.J.: Ablex.

Smith, R. (1972). *The Wired Nation: Cable TV, the Electronic Communications Highway.* New York: Harper & Row.

Wasko, J. (1982). *Movies and Money: Financing the American Film Industry.* Norwood, N.J.: Ablex.

Wiley, R., and R. M. Neustadt (1982). "U.S. Communications Policy in the New Decade. *Journal of Communications* 32, 2, pp. 22–32.

10. Bookkeeping for Capitalism: The Mystery of Accounting For Unequal Exchange

Tony Tinker, Cheryl Lehman, and Marilyn Neimark

Why is accounting called "the language of business"? What is incorporated—and what is denied—by this popular construction of "what accounting is"? Is accounting really second to none as a comprehensive lingua franca for business and economic discourse? If so, one corollary is that accounting provides a neutral, independent, and impartial lexicon into which diverse views can be safely translated without loss of their unique contents. Overall, this linguistic view accentuates the technical objectivity of accounting—its role as a reliable purveyor of facts and data.

There are difficulties with the notion that accounting is the sovereign business language. The social and historical context in which accounting is embedded and the discipline's involvement in social struggles and conflicts are taken to be nonproblematic in this formulation. Such considerations are conveniently hidden from view by construing symbolism, in accounting and other media forms, in a purely mechanical, engineering-oriented, and realist manner. The quintessence of this perspective is that which epitomizes accounting as "objective bookkeeping."

In contrast to this asocial and technocratic vision of accounting, this paper is in the recent tradition of exploring the subject's role as an ideological weapon in social conflict (cf.Armstrong, 1985; Berry et al., 1985; Burchell et al., 1980, 1985; Cooper, 1980; Hopwood, 1985, 1987; Hoskins and Macve, 1986; Johnson, 1978; Knights and Willmott, 1985; Loft, 1986; Merino and Neimark, 1982; Miller and O'Leary, 1987; Tinker and Neimark, 1987; Tinker, 1980; Tinker et al., 1982). Here, accounting symbols do not merely reflect the world but represent it in structuring the meanings and commonsense notions through which individuals engage social reality. Linguistic, cultural, ideological, and other symbolic activities are not independent of economic and other terrains of conflict; they are prior to them in that they dictate the terms of access to these realities. Such a view gives a preeminent position to accounting as a contested symbolic form.

The breadth of discursive accounting practices, and the diversity of ways in which the subject participates in conflicts over the distribution of social wealth, is highlighted in the three empirical areas that we have chosen to exemplify our arguments: (1) financial disclosure and colonial exploitation, using 40-odd years of published financial statements of a multinational called Delco that operated in the colonial and postcolonial states of Sierra Leone; (2) annual reports, using material from some 60 years of General Motors annual reports; and (3) literary and research discourses, using professional journals (1960 through 1973) aimed at practitioners (*Journal of Accountancy*) academics and researchers (*Accounting Review*), and corporate managers (*Fortune*).

The following section stresses the importance of the symbolic realm in general, and accounting symbolism in particular. Symbolic forms are not mere reflections of "real" phenomena; they enjoy an independent status of "relative autonomy" in that no absolute truth or final meaning can be attributed to signs. Symbols are loosely tied to their referents and can be "made to mean" in ways that serve different social interests. The symbolic realm merits privileged attention for another reason: it has assumed major prominence because, increasingly, the capitalist state has assembled an ideological apparatus for producing the social cohesion needed for capital accumulation. We argue that accounting's discursive practices are vital components of this ideological apparatus. The implications of the following section —that accounting is potentially a powerful weapon in social conflict— are illuminated in the three examples presented in the section entitled—Illustrating Discursive Practices. The implications of the work are reviewed in the final section.

SYMBOLS, IDEOLOGY, AND SOCIAL CONTROL

Two related arguments underlie our claim that accounting is important as a practice that reconstitutes the world by endowing it with meaning. The first maintains that language—a primary vehicle through which individuals are socialized—enjoys a certain autonomy relative to the phenomena to which it refers. This relative autonomy is illustrated by observing that language symbols—signs—are arbitrary in that the meaning associated with the same words can change with the speaker, the receiver, the situation, and previous articulations, creating a history of expressions (Coward and Ellis, 1977).

Second, we argue that accounting ideology is important, not

merely because of its affiliations with "ideas" or "social thought," but because it is a signifying social practice. In an Althusserian perspective, ideologies are viewed as practical, commonsense ideas and beliefs, supplying the institutionally appropriate rules of conduct for citizens. The above arguments are drawn together into a third subsection ("Accounting and Social Control") that focuses on the way that the capitalist state makes special use of symbolic forms such as accounting in displacing social conflict.

The Autonomy of Symbols

The importance of semiautonomous symbol systems is underlined by work in semiology. This literature treats the symbolic (and thus the ideological) realm as socially constituted by recognizing that the subject's subconscious is formed by presignified cultural themes and premises—that is, a prior socialization. The prior socialization brackets and sustains what is considered natural, meaningful, and immutable (Barthes, 1972; Coward and Ellis, 1977; Saussure, 1960).

Ferdinand Saussure's (1960) principle of the arbitrary nature of signs highlights the independence (autonomy) of signification from the economic realm, thus requiring that signs be dealt with as an independent force. Saussure's principle stresses that the sign is independent of any specific material object, and there is no natural connection between the signifier (sound) and the signified (concept).

The autonomy of all systems of representation (writing; enunciation; music; pictorial, architectural, graphic presentation; etc.) elevates meaning-production (cultural) systems to a new status: they are independent terrains of conflict whose outcomes cannot be resolved "reductively"—that is by referring to an economic "base" or some other primary realm (Blumler and Gurevitch, 1982; Curran et al., 1982).

Saussure's arbitrariness-of-signs principle represented a major break with earlier rationalistic and representational traditions in structural linguistics. Claude Lévi-Strauss, and later Roland Barthes, further developed the implications of the principle by viewing language as the medium for producing meaning: as a structure of variant possibilities, the arrangement of elements in a signifying chain, as a practice, not for expressing the world, but for articulating it, articulating upon it (Hall, 1980, pp.29—32). Consequently, in symbolic exchange "the world must be made to mean,"and all symbolic interaction is a culturally modified mode of influence and exchange where social norms and conflicts are embodied in communication (Bird, 1982; Wood, 1979).

Discourse attains its effect on the subject's subconscious by what

Lévi-Strauss (1977) "calls the logic of arrangement."[1] In Freudian-Lacanian terms, ideological statements are made subconsciously palatable by defense mechanisms of displacement (metaphor) and condensation (metonymy). Thus, by generating a recognition effect in the recipient, by bracketing and sustaining certain closures about what could be taken for granted, "natural," "eternal," and immutable, discursive (and ideological) practices maintain a primacy in reconstituting the world (Hall, 1982, pp.72–80; Laclau, 1977).

Ideology as a social signifying practice

Antonio Gramsci, in his *Prison Notebooks* (1971), couples the functioning of the capitalist state with cultural and ideological discourse. In doing so, he elevates cultural forces to a special status and challenges economistic views that relegate symbolic phenomena to a derivative sphere of appearance (rather than essence) (cf. Jessop, 1980, 1982: Jessop et al., 1984; Miliband, 1969). Gramsci's arguments lead us to examine accounting as a cultural and ideological discourse that, first and foremost, can only be meaningfully interpreted as a "real" social practice.

The amplitude of Gramsci's insights increases when linked to the work of Stuart Hall and Louis Althusser (Hall, 1982). Althusser rejects notions of ideology as "ideas" and "false consciousness." Instead, he construes ideology in terms of themes and representations through which people mediate the world (Althusser, 1971). Althusser sees ideology as the "social cement"—the commonsense notions through which conscious subjects engage and construct their worlds. Ideology has a material existence that is inscribed in traditions, institutions, customs, apparatuses, and practices; it functions to interpellate individuals as subjects, "hailing" them through the apparently obvi-

1. Early work in structural linguistics failed to explain the human subject's moment of initiation into language and ideology; it failed to problematize the subject (the source of enunciation). Emphasis in contemporary semiotic research has shifted from the study of systems of symbolic representation and communication to an attempt to explain how the subject (and therefore the subject's practices) are constituted. In this reformulated version of semiotics, symbolic discourse has a material relation in that it invests life (practices) with an imaginary relation; but in contrast with earlier work, the processes by which the "imaginary relation" is produced are now a central part of the analysis. The unconscious is seen as a reservoir of themes and premises: folk taxonomies or presignified cultural inventories that represent a historically sedimented deep structure for orienting discursive practices (Hall, 1980, p. 31).

ous and normal rituals of everyday living, playing a significant role in how individuals make sense of day-to-day life (Curran et al., 1982, pp. 20–26; Althusser, 1971).

The view of accounting adopted in this study corresponds with the broad Althusserian view of social practice indicated above. Accounting here embraces the full gamut of practices that putatively adjudicate in social conflicts over the allocation of scarce resources. These include record keeping, tax advisory services, auditing, legal services, head-hunting activities, certification, management accounting, budgeting, education and training, special investigations, public service projects, and management consulting.

In Althusserian terms, however, ideology, including accounting ideology, is more than a social practice; it is a signifying social practice —a medium through which people interpret, experience, and engage the world. Ideologies take on a real, material force in that they enter experience, shape perception, alter conduct, and shape beliefs. In this signifying sense, ideology is logically prior to other life spheres (economic, political, social, etc.) because it mediates all other experience (Bennett, 1982, pp. 48–50).

The media are regarded as a primary force in shaping public consciousness in semiotic studies. The media are a site of struggle involving conflicting interest groups, including the state. Ultimately, they help invent "the news," "the issues," and "the sides," and do so by orienting and embedding issues in familiar and traditional themes and configurations of meaning. By signaling forward conclusions, bracketing issues and events, imposing closures, and echoing associative themes, the media construct what is commonsense, natural, and immutable.

Our selection of accounting for special consideration is not motivated by the profession's mass appeal (as in the case of television, films, or other media forms). Rather, the accountant's privileged access to key decisional areas in economic and civil society, together with the profession's linguistic near monopoly (as indicated by the epithet quoted at the start of the paper), warrants a thorough scrutiny of the discipline.

Accounting and Social Control

The power of accounting resides in its capacity to individuate its symbolic interventions for specific subjects and to do so on a mass scale by resuscitating themes that are deeply embedded in the social subconscious—what Gramsci calls a shared "commonsense" (macro level) (Althusser, 1971; Curran, et al., 1982, pp. 20–26; Edgley, 1984). When an ideology like accounting is combined and synchronized in a rational manner by the capitalist state, then its importance is heightened still further.

For Gramsci, Althusser, and Hall, the state reproduces the conditions necessary for the valorization of capital: it is a sometimes active, and sometimes subtle force in conforming civil society (social and political life) to economic life (Gramsci, 1971, pp. 246–47). The social democratic state accomplishes this conformity by working through its cultural apparatus to obtain ideological cohesion. By supervising and organizing various blocs and alliances—through arbitration and conciliation procedures, immigration policies, social compacts, and industrial relations legislation—the state seeks to provide the trajectory for capital accumulation.

The "normal" social democratic state struggles to supply conditions necessary for the reproduction of capital—not by force or coercion, but by organizing a mode of cultural leadership or cultural hegemony. The state's primary role is one of organizing consent through its policies regarding the family, the media, the poor, welfare, immigration, the judiciary, education, racial minorities, local government and so on. When the state obtains legitimized and undisputed authority over the political struggle, and all this is secured by broad and popular consent, then we can speak of hegemonic domination. Under this decisive leadership, exploitation and struggle disappear from view; hegemony is established, not by coercion, but by cultural leadership, inspiring loyalty and engineering consent.

Accounting forms part of the state's ideological apparatus in a very specific sense. Althusser's phrase "ideological state apparatus" does not refer to a legalistic or property relation (restricted, for instance, to government departments and nationalized industries). The production of consent requires the state to operate through "impartial" institutions and processes that are not tied to specific political parties or economic interests. The state's apparatus is defined by its functional character and incorporates all the ideological institutions that the state deploys in producing consent. The ostensible neutrality and independence from the state of such media forms as accounting are indispensable to their effective operation (Althusser, 1971; 1976; Hall, 1982, pp. 87–88).

Following this argument, we contend that the accounting profession, through its auditing, consulting, standard-setting, educational, and other discursive practices, is integral to the consensus-making business of the state. It is the part played by accounting in legitimizing business and state practices and ideologies that is highlighted by the three empirical examples that follow.

ACCOUNTING PRACTICES: Three Illustrations

The three discursive examples presented below illustrate accounting's role as an ideological weapon in social conflicts. The first case begins with the financial statements of Delco Company, a Scottish-owned iron ore venture operating in Sierra Leone. This research reinterprets the definition of "efficient performance" that these statements disclose. The second case illustrates the social relativity of General Motors annual reports in the 1916-1976 period. The last case examines 14 years of business and accounting literature (1960-1973) in *Fortune* magazine, the *Journal of Accountancy* and the *Accounting Review* and explores accounting's involvement in social ideology in the post-1960s era, its implicit conception of permissible and respectable research, and its impact on the distribution of wealth between different groups and social classes.

Financial Disclosure and the Colonial State

Althusser's claim that the state's ideological practices are essential in forming social cohesion is illuminated by studying the history of Delco Company, a mining operation in Sierra Leone. The company's 46-year life (1930-1976) covers a period of changing institutional forces in which the state, through ideological, military, taxation, and accounting practices, sought to maintain those conditions necessary for the reproduction of capital. Moreover, because accounting information was a component of the institutional apparatus used to make distributional and allocative decisions, we find the company's evolving social history reflected in its accounting statements.

The study of the Scottish-owned iron ore company begins in 1930, the early colonial period, and traces its expansion through the late colonial period until its collapse in 1976, under the postcolonial state of Sierra Leone (Hoogvelt and Tinker, 1978). Hoogvelt and Tinker constructed a computer simulation model that included all of Declo's financial data for the period. These monetary amounts were then adjusted by an inflation index, thereby expressing monetary amounts in units of comparable purchasing power. All amounts are expressed in 1976 pound-sterling equivalents, including profitability and other measures conventionally used for assessing the success of a venture.

For the shareholders of Delco, the project produced a 10 percent inflation-adjusted, internal rate of return (or 13 percent before inflation). The first two columns in Table 10.1 show how the total 46-year (inflation-adjusted) sales proceeds were distributed between various parties.

For an outlay of £500,000 in 1930 (approximately 3 million in 1976 pounds), the project earned shareholders a net present value of

Table 10.1. Periodization Table: Distribution of Cost Insurance and Freight (CIF) Sales Proceeds by Periods

			Early Colonial Period		Late Colonial Period		Postcolonial Periods			
	1930–1976		1930–1947		1948–1956		1957–1967		1968–1975	
	£1000s	%	£1000s	%	£1000s	%	£1000s	%	£1000s	%
CIF proceeds	424.14	100	55.08	100	94.50	100	171.81	100	102.81	100
European participants										
Shippers	169.66	40.00	22.03	40.00	37.80	40.00	68.71	40.00	41.12	40.00
U.K. suppliers	104.11	24.54	12.86	23.35	27.50	29.11	26.58	15.47	37.26	36.15
Owners and investors	42.70	10.07	5.67	10.30	7.79	8.24	23.37	13.60	5.87	5.71
White directors, management, and employees	31.40	7.40	4.91	8.91	3.88	4.11	15.79	9.19	6.82	6.62
U.K. government	2.51	0.59	0.88	1.60	0.02	0.02	1.44	0.84	0.17	0.16
U.K. leaseholders	0.62	0.15	0.07	0.12	0.20	0.21	0.27	0.15	0.11	0.11
	351.00	82.72	46.42	84.28	77.19	81.69	136.16	79.25	91.35	88.75
African participants										
S.L. government	39.87	9.40	0.96	1.74	12.21	12.92	25.67	14.94	1.08	1.05
Black labor: manual	26.84	6.33	7.61	13.82	5.06	5.35	8.14	4.74	6.01	5.95
Salaried staff	6.16	1.45	—	—	—	—	1.77	1.03	4.30	4.18
Tribal authorities	0.27	0.06	0.09	0.16	0.04	0.04	0.07	0.04	0.07	0.07
	73.14	17.25	8.66	15.72	17.31	18.31	35.65	20.75	11.46	11.25

Note: Figures have been rounded.

£18.9 million at a 3 percent discount rate, after allowing for inflation. In October 1975 Delco (Sierra Leone's second-largest export industry) went into voluntary liquidation, and with it went the several thousand employment opportunities its operations generated. At this juncture, what is of interest are the forces that caused the distribution of income evidenced in Table 10.1 which demonstrated the firm's demise

Table 10.1 is a breakdown of the period into a series of income statements (a periodization analysis). Each income statement in Table 10.1 covers the period in which a particular institutional regime prevailed (early colonial, late colonial, postcolonial) and each regime was designated by its own unique configuration of social and political institutions.

The accounting data in Table 10.1 correlate with historical events of the period. From the early colonial to the late colonial period, we see that percentage share of proceeds collected by the British constituents gently declined (from 84 to 79 percent), and this decline is accompanied by increasing allocations (mainly through taxation) to the colonial state, whose share of the proceeds reaches a peak in the beginning of the postcolonial period (from 1.7 to 14.9 percent). These figures, together with other records of the period, are indicative of the transfer of power, in the form of military, ideological, and other support, from the colonial regime to a growing and increasingly bureaucratic group in Freetown (Hoogvelt and Tinker, 1978).

These changes eventuated notwithstanding the fact that the basic social relations of capitalist enterprises—the relations of production—remained unaltered. The basic relations of deprivation and domination remained constant throughout the firm's history. Thus we see that the returns to the tribal authorities (representing the original owners of the land) and to black labor remain perfectly stagnant throughout the entire period (the declining returns to black wage labor are attributable entirely to a proportionate reduction of the number employed). None of the new and swelling government revenues ever directly or indirectly benefited the native workers, people, and local authorities in the iron-producing province. However, they did serve to secure the continued cooperation of an increasingly alienated indigenous state.

The exploitative relations that persisted throughout the postcolonial period were superficially transformed in one important respect by the appearance of black salaried workers. In response to pressures for indigenization after independence, Delco began to recruit black managerial, clerical, and technical supervisory staff. The agreements of 1967 and 1972 formulated this indigenization program in increasingly stringent terms.

By the time of its closure, Delco employed some 218 supervisory salaried staff, of whom 164 were Sierra Leoneans earning an average annual salary of 3,041 pounds sterling. In 1974 this black salaried contingent received a total income of 422,320 pounds sterling, almost equivalent to the total wage bill of 513,215 pounds sterling for all black manual labor (numbering 2,317).

The explosion in black salaries did not represent an investment in productive employees in the conventional sense. Most of those employed were members of the tribal elite, whose approval and support the company needed if it was to continue operating in Sierra Leone. By the mid-1970s the expanding indigenous pressure, coupled with the prospect of diminishing returns from the mine, induced the Company to leave. In doing so it was simply following a strategy for survival in a market context.

Table 10.1 discloses market appearances but leaves largely implicit the underlying social essence—the exploitative social relations of early and late colonialism. Each regime or era shown in the table is characterized by a configuration of sociopolitical forces that determine the income distribution shown in each period's income statement in the table. A historical continuity underlies the figures shown in the table in that each regime is an outgrowth from, and response to, the contradictions and instabilities of the previous era.

The inability of accounting statements, or any neoclassical economic formulation, to say anything meaningful about "efficiency" and "productivity" has been raised in various theoretical works (cf. Tinker, 1980, for a general survey). The Delco study illustrates how income distribution, reflected in accounting numbers, is shaped by social and political forces rather than marginal productivity considerations.

The Delco study tells a story about the role of accounting in business and social life that is different from the neoclassical parable. This not a fairytale about the "justice" of marginal productivity measured in net present values and accounting rates of return, but the story of a system that was so rapacious and unstable that it failed to meet even the minimum viability test: it did not offer weaker parties (i.e., black employees) enough returns to enable them to reproduce an economic role in the longer term. The fact that conventional accounting failed to beacon the destructive tendencies pursued by a societal entity, but instead blessed it with 'healthy" profitability indices, is a serious indictment of the practice.

General Motors' Annual Reports

Every year since its incorporation in 1916, General Motors (GM) has published an annual report. The report, which is distributed to shareholders and other interested parties, consists of the company's audited financial statements and a discussion of various events and activities involving and affecting the corporation. Over the years, this latter portion of the report has grown in size, relative to the financial statements (e.g., from 28 percent of the annual reports published from 1916 through 1925 to 74 percent of those published from 1950 through 1967). It is this change in overall prominence and in the concomitant variations in the subjects discussed and their treatment that initially led us to examine the nonfinancial portion of GM's annual reports over a 61-year period (1916–1976). (Hereafter the term "annual report" will refer only to the non-financial-statement part of the document.)

This interest in annual reports may seem unusual for accountants, who are typically associated exclusively with financial statements. But those of us concerned with the effects of accounting information and corporate reporting on the distribution of income, wealth, and power no longer view accounting as an assemblage of calculative routines whose only product is a set of financial statements. Rather, we see the subject as a "cohesive and influential mechanism for economic and social management" (Burchell et al., 1985, p.6). From this perspective, financial statements cannot be easily separated from the context in which they are presented and within which they are interpreted. Accounting numbers never exist *in vacuo*. They can only be studied relative to specific meaning contexts—such as annual reports —because these contexts allow economic actors to situate the numbers in schemes of reasoning (deductions, inferences, etc.) that permit the formation of economic expectations and decisions (Simon, 1976).

This case is based on a content analysis that traces the appearance, in GM's annual reports, of 10 themes. These themes, which are summarized in the list below, correspond to a number of technological, social, organizational, and ideological transformations that are widely regarded as characteristic of the 1916-1976 period. It must be emphasized at the outset that the 10 themes are neither independent nor mutually exclusive. They are linked both synchronously and diachronously by a network of interrelationships that the study excavates and explores.

1. *Concentration and centralization of capital:* The process through which the number of autonomously controlled firms decreases through either the expansion of the market power of some firms in an industry relative to others or the fusion of previously autonomous firms through mergers and acquisitions within or across industry boundaries. The concept can be extended to include the coordination of legally autonomous firms through ties that include subcontracting networks, direct and indirect interlocking directorates, joint ventures, minority ownership, common memberships in trade and other business organizations and government advisory boards, and so on.

2. *Internationalization of production and distribution:* The expansion of the firm's operations beyond their national boundaries through the export of domestically produced products, the export of capital, the internationalization of the production process through the international circulation of products within the multinational firm (i.e., the market is superseded internationally by interfirm trade), and the internationalization of the social consumption norm and the homogenization of consumer tastes and preferences.

3. *State intervention:* The collectivity of state activities that support, complement, and promote the accumulation of capital by private business interests. In addition to activities that directly support capital accumulation (i.e., state activities that increase the productivity of a given amount of labor power through spending on physical or human capital and promote profitable private accumulation by lowering the reproduction costs of labor), state intervention also refers to activities that fulfill the state legitimation functions and only indirectly support capital accumulation by maintaining social harmony.

4. *Labor conflict:* Actions that address the social conflict between and the relative strength of capital and labor (e.g., technical control systems, collective bargaining, bureaucratic control systems).

5. *Omnipotence of science and technology:* The ideology whereby science comes to be understood as knowledge, science and technicians are represented as devoted to the neutral pursuit of knowledge, technical efficiency (which emerges as the privileged criterion for evaluating performance), and effectiveness. All questions are reduced to technical problems, and progress and growth are idealized as desirable goals in and of themselves.

6. *Social consumption norm:* The development of a social orientation to career, leisure, and privatized consumption, a structural response to the realization crisis that began to emerge in the 1920s and has been described by Baran and Sweezy (1966, p. 128) as "a relent-

less war against saving and in favor of consumption" which was principally carried out by inducing changes in fashion, creating new wants, setting new standards of status, and enforcing new norms of propriety. Also integral to this ideology is the substitution of consumption and consumer choice for social conflict and political participation.

7. *Social responsibility:* The view that the corporation is responsible for the consequences of its actions (or inactions) to constituencies that extend beyond its legal owners (e.g., to its employees, customers, suppliers, the communities in which it operates, women, minorities, the public in general), whether or not these responsibilities are recognized by law.

8. *People's capitalism:* Reconstituted version of the 19th-century ideology of private property, whereby widespread shareownership is advocated as a necessary condition for (and as evidence of) both economic and political democracy.

9. *Ideology of the market:* The following beliefs: that wages, prices, and profits are set by natural laws acting through consumer utility and a technologically determined production function; that each productive factor is paid for according to its marginal contribution to the production process; that the United States and the world economy are highly competitive; and that only those producers who are the most efficient and responsive to consumer needs will (and should) prosper.

10. *Managerialism:* The ideology whereby management, management skills, planning, and organization are idealized and the corporation is portrayed as a solidary community of constituents (shareholders, consumers, suppliers, creditors, employees, dealers) whose interests will be harmonized (along with those of the community at large) by a managerial elite who share the service and social responsibility ethics of the traditional professions.

The point of view reflected in GM's annual reports is not taken at face value in this study: rather, the reports are interpreted in the light of other sources of information regarding the changing social, political and economic conditions prevailing over GM's history, from 1916 through 1976.

In interpreting GM's annual reports, we reject two common views: that they are neutral reflections of reality, a passive recounting of the year's events, and that they are outright fabrications intended to manipulate a somnolent audience, at best harmless public relations fluff; at worst powerful propaganda that brainwashes a susceptible public.

Contrary to both of these views, annual reports, like all communications vehicles, form a symbolic universe of language, signs, meanings, norms, beliefs, perceptions, and values, through which individuals and institutions define themselves and are defined by others. As the recently developed histories of minorities and women have shown, these definitions and self knowledge carry implicit political commitments; they are thus contested terrains. Annual reports are among the arsenal of weapons companies deploy in political conflicts and in their efforts to maintain the conditions necessary for their continued profitability and growth.

Our task in this study, then, was to discover how GM uses its annual reports to construct meaning systems, thereby influencing the outcome of conflicts with labor, women, minorities, dealers, suppliers, customers, governments, local communities, and domestic and international competitors.

Table 10.2 and the foregoing list of themes and observational variables summarize the results of the content analysis (see Neimark, 1983, for details). Table 10.2 shows the relative proportion of annual report text and illustrations devoted to each of the 10 themes in five distinctive phases of social and economic development during the period. (The phases correspond to recession, depression, recovery, prosperity, and renewed recession within the long waves that have been identified by researchers such as Kondratieff, Kuznets, Schumpeter, and van Duijin, see Graham and Senge, 1980; Mandel, 1978; Mensch, 1978.)

A perusal of Table 10.2 indicates that in different periods different themes assumed prominence in the annual reports: for example, the social consumption norm in the two post World War II periods; labor conflict in the two prewar periods; social responsibility, beginning in 1967; state intervention during the war; and so on. But more important than the relative visibility of each theme in the annual reports are the differences in the ways individual themes are treated among the periods, the ways the themes are interrelated within and across periods, and the social context within which each theme is developed. An example from the history of GM's relations with labor provides a good illustration.

Table 10.2 suggests that a change occurred in GM's labor relations between the pre– and post–World War II decades; and indeed it did. In 1950 GM and the United Automobile Workers union (UAW), signed a historic labor agreement whose provisions "cast American labor relations in their post war mold" (Davis, 1986, p. 111). *Fortune* magazine applauded the contract as a basic "affirmation . . .of the free enterprise system?" citing the following features. First, the contract accepted the existing distribution of wages and profits as "normal," if not "fair." Second, by accepting cost-of-living changes and

Table 10.2. Summary of Themes by Periods

	% of total text and illustrations				
Theme	1916–25	1925–39	1940–49	1950–66	1967–76
Concentration and centralization	20.0	3.0	1.0	0	0
Internationalization	7.7	23.3	2.9	7.2	12.1
State intervention	10.5	9.6	36.7	9.1	8.3
Labor conflict	30.0	31.2	14.8	11.4	7.6
Omnipotence of science and technology	6.0	3.9	12.0	15.6	7.7
Social consumption norm	12.3	9.3	15.0	40.1	41.4
Social responsibility	1.6	7.0	5.6	4.7	17.9
People's capitalism	9.7	8.2	4.4	3.9	0.9
Ideology of the market	0	1.6	0.4	0.2	0.6
Managerialism	2.2	2.9	7.2	7.8	3.5
Total	100.0	100.0	100.0	100.0	100.0
% of total report (including financial statements) accounted for by content analysis	13.8	33.6	42.7	56.8	51.9

productivity as the "basic economic fact " determining wages, the contract threw "overboard all theories of wages as determined by political power, and of profit as "surplus value." and accepted the "macroeconomic principle of the progressive wage." Third, by agreeing to limit negotiations to economic issues, and ceding control over the labor process and product pricing to corporate management, the contract "expressly recognized both the importance of the management function and the fact that management operates directly in the interest of labor"(editors of *Fortune*, 1951, quoted in Davis, 1986, pp. 111–112).

The 1950 contract between GM and the UAW embodied a set of ideological principles that GM had been developing for over a decade in its annual reports. These principles—developed against a backdrop of labor conflict in the 1930s that is described as "arguably the high water mark of class struggle in modern American history" (Davis, 1986, p. 54) —formulate a pluralistic model of the firm in which a responsible, statesmanlike management equitably balances the interests of all participants, within the constraints imposed by the natural laws governing wages, prices, and profits.

The first principle presents the corporation as embedded within a network of interdependent constituencies (employees, shareholders, suppliers, and the public). Throughout the years of labor conflict in the 1930s, GM's annual reports stress the pluralistic basis of the corporation and management's responsibility for harmonizing the interests of various participants. In 1934, for example, GM asserts that "the maximum of progress is possible only by maintaining proper balance between the equities of all parties concerned, including not only those of employer and employees but also those of the public, upon whose continued demand for its products depends the welfare of the Corporation and of its employees themselves" (GM Annual Report [hereafter GM AR], 1934, p. 56).

This effort to establish the apolitical, neutral character of the corporation converages with a second principle: that there is a natural equilibrium of wages, prices, and profits that exists outside management's control. In 1936, GM introduced a new section in its annual reports, titled "Labor Economics." The choice of phrase is important here. A possible alternative heading like "Labor-Capital Relations" would highlight the conflictual relationship between the two; "Labor Economics," on the other hand, implies relations neutrally governed by the laws of economic science. GM's effort to depersonalize the setting of wages is illustrated in its statement that "too many are of the belief that the wage level is at the discretion of management, that there is no ceiling other than that which management seeks to establish arbitrarily" (GM AR, 1937, p. 43). GM attributes the deepening of the depression in 1937 entirely to an abnormal increase in labor costs that "led to the unbalancing of the economic equilibrium, as purchasing power was not evenly distributed in relation to wages" (ibid., p. 11). Throughout the 1930s, GM's annual reports argue that productivity improvements from technological progress and improved operating techniques were the only source of increased wages and reduced prices. (The latter goal was dropped by both GM and the UAW after the war. The success of the postwar agreement between them depended in large part on the company's ability to pass along labors' economic gains to the public through higher prices.)

As World War II came to an end, GM used its annual reports to lay the groundwork for the last principle in the ideological construct that provided the foundation for the 1950 labor contract. It emphasized labor's dependence upon management and the importance of management's organizing and planning activities for both corporate and overall economic growth. The elevation of managerial skills reaches its apotheosis in 1946 with the inclusion of a special section, signed by Alfred Sloan, on "The Importance of Management." In this paean to management, Sloan talks of GM's need for individuals with "talent of the highest order" to determine policy and provide effective administration.There are only a limited number of such individuals available, he cautions, and the demand for them" is always far in excess of the supply. " Moreover,"the standards demanded of the future will be higher than ever before." The cost of attracting and maintaining such talent is "relatively inconsequential": "What such talent may create in terms of more job opportunities, better product values, and additional profits is more important."

American management also has a key role to play in the Cold War, for Sloan. They "must display economic statesmanship of the highest order and demonstrate to the world at large and to our own people in particular that a free competitive economy, stimulating as it does technological progress based on increasing scientific knowledge, insures always an expanding volume of goods and services at progressively lower prices, thus prompting higher living standards and a more abundant life" (GM AR, 1946).

The new regime of labor-capital relations that is represented by the 1950 collective bargaining agreement depended upon, among other factors, the resolution of the realization crisis of the 1930s depression, and the redirection of workers' energies into the pursuit of individualistic and familial consumption. Both objectives were achieved, the first only temporarily, through a combination of Keynesian inspired state spending (largely military) and increased social consumption, a result of the economism of the collective bargaining contracts and a social ideology that made consumption of goods the prime measure of social achievement (Galbraith, 1967).

The building of the new social consumption norm takes a priority place in GM's annual reports in the 1950s and 1960s. Indeed, over 40 percent of the non-financial-statement portion of the reports in these decades is devoted to creating and reinforcing the norm and its accompanying patterns of suburbanization, the idealization of the nuclear family (whose mother has been removed from the wartime factory and returned to the kitchen and laundry room, where she uses GM's Frigidaire appliances, and to the passenger seat in GM cars), and the drive to possess the latest in styling and technology. The latter is reinforced in GM's annual reports through an emphasis on progress and change as universal virtues, characteristic of the American people and American industry.

Keeping up with the social consumption norm required an increasing level of wages, the availability of low-cost consumer and mortgage credit, and government outlays to subsidize housing and suburban development. In addition, in the mid-1960s women and minorities began to press to be integrated into the system in ways that were costly (e.g., lawsuits and affirmative action programs) and threatened both social harmony and political stability. The public, in general, became increasingly aware of the adverse consequences of corporate growth—consequences that contradicted the premises of the social consumption norm. The appearance of social responsibility as an increasingly important theme in this period's annual reports reflects these emerging concerns.

We have argued that annual reports are integral to understanding and interpreting the financial statements they accompany. Nor are the financial statements passive in this process; they bolster a perceptual slant promoted in the annual report and, like it, form part of a network of ideological forces aimed at reproducing the status quo.

Acccounting Research and Business Literature

The critical role of literature in shaping, reconstituting, and reproducing ideas and beliefs is illustrated below using two accounting journals (the *Journal of Accountancy* and the *Accounting Review*) and the popular business magazine *Fortune.* The study spans the 14 year period from 1960 through 1973 and reviews over 1,100 articles, classifying the literature according to content.

Fortune magazine was chosen to represent the discursive field of business because of its wide circulation and the breadth of its opinions and topics. The popularity of *Fortune* is acknowledged by *Magazines for Libraries* (Katz and Katz, 1982, p. 192), which describes *Fortune* as "probably the best-known business magazine in America," also read by students and teachers, who "often turn to it as an indicator of current American thinking about business in general and certain business situations in particular." Thus, *Fortune* can be said to both constitute and represent popular business ideology.

The two accounting journals were selected for their diverse perspectives and their appeal to distinctly different constituencies. The *Accounting Review* is considered a theoretical, academic research publication. Its prominence, command, and influence on what is considered acceptable research has been studied by Paul Williams (1985, p. 300), who concludes that the journal "has the potential to influence the development of ideas in accounting research."

The *Journal of Accountancy* was selected for its practioner-oriented perspective: articles are written by practicing certified public accountants and accounting and government administrators influential in implementing public policies and regulation regarding the profession. As the official publication of the American Institute of Certified Public Accountants, the editorial policy of the journal is closely tied to the institute's affiliation with large accounting firms; in this sense the journal is a deliberately managed media form.

The research analysis of this study stands in contradistinction to traditional content analysis, which, by assuming that communication is objective, ignores its social constitutiveness. To capture the journals' influence on economic and social events, articles were classified into a range of "discourse categories": ideological themes that had the potential to effect a redistribution of income between social groups.[2] (Clearly, this does not imply, or require, intentionality on the part of those contributing to the literature under investigation.)

As a preliminary introduction to these discourse categories, Tables 10.3 and 10.4 list the 18 accounting discourse categories and 25 *Fortune* categories that emerged from analyzing the 1,100 articles (see Lehman, 1985, for details). The tables group the discourse categories into "configurations," which are aggregates of discourse categories that share similar connotations. They are similar to "factors" in a factor analysis, except that here the associations are based on symbolic meanings rather than statistical properties.[3]

The percentage scores, shown in the right-hand column of Tables 10.2 and 10.3, profile discourse activity over the 14-year period. Thus, for instance, 8.3 percent of all *Fortune* articles in this period, focused on subjects and events represented by discourse categories 19,

---

2. Discursive categories were not simply imposed on the data, but were formed after extensive reading and re-reading of the material. The readings aimed to identify the underlying distributional conflict(s) to which articles were addressed. The discursive conflicts so identified formed the basis for the classification of the material. A single researcher performed the classification initially, thereby providing a certain consistency (intra-rater reliability) for the analysis. To assess inter-rater reliability, as well as internal and external validity, six other researchers undertook a parallel analysis of 72 articles. Initially, they formed their own categories, which were then related with those used in the study. The reconciled categorization was then used to classify the 72 articles. A chi-square test of difference was made between the study classification and the test classifications; and a "no-significant-difference" result was found at the .05 percent level.

3. The notion of "statistical significance" and variation when interpreting the results of a study is a relative one (e.g., the universe or population is rarely studied; rather a "sample" is studied). In this study, *Fortune* and the accounting journals are regarded as instruments for affecting and reflecting social disputes; as journals commanding widespread popularity and support, they constitute substantial samples of the discursive population. Therefore, any change in the proportion of discourse categories and configurations for *Fortune,* the *Journal of Accountancy*, and the *Accounting Review* is considered important in and of itself.

Table 10.3. Discursive Activity of *Journal of Accountancy* (*JA*) and *Accounting Review* (*AR*), 1960–1973

	Discourse Category No.	*JA* %	*AR* %	Ave. %
*Accounting configuration A/AA**: Critique of state intervention, promotion of self-regulation, and praise of accountants' professionalism	1	11.3	7.9	9.6
	2	9.4	4.0	6.7
	3	12.6	9.3	10.9
	4	7.8	8.0	7.9
		41.1	29.2	35.1
*Accounting configuration B/BB**: Assertion that accounting benefits business and society by assisting in the efficient allocation of resources	5	10.1	13.3	11.7
	6	3.1	16.1	9.6
	7	3.1	8.4	5.8
		16.3	37.8	27.1
*Accounting configuration C/CC**: Assertion that devotion to the public interest is the profession's natural role, ensured by professional independence, individual ethics, and commitment	8	6.0	0.8	3.4
	9	11.1	5.9	8.5
	10	8.0	4.0	6.0
	11	4.9	2.1	3.5
		30.0	12.8	21.4
*Accounting configuration D/DD**: Advocacy of statistical and accounting expertise in developing CIS	12	0.0	9.8	4.9
	13	4.1	5.1	4.6
		4.1	14.9	9.5
*Accounting configuration E/EE**: Promotion of the international benefits of accounting; praise for its contribution to economic and social freedom, international trade and competition, and global democracy	14	1.6	0.2	0.9
	15	1.2	0.5	0.8
	16	2.1	0.7	1.4
		4.9	1.4	3.1
*Accounting configuration F/FF**: Sundry discourses	17, 18	4.0	3.2	3.6
% Total (rounded)		100.0	100.0	100.0

**Journal of Accountancy* configurations are designated by a single letter (e.g., C); *Accounting Review* configurations are designated by a double letter (e.g., CC).

20, and 21 (these three categories aggregate into configuration G). The tables only summarize the meaning associated with each category; a fuller account of the significance of selected categories will be illustrated in presenting the results of the study.

Our primary thesis is that accounting is part of the broader ideological-discursive sphere of capitalism. The force of accounting research ideology becomes evident when contextualized relative to the political, economic, and social conditions of each era. Thus, we offer a periodization analysis to illustrate how business and accounting literature change over time in response to evolving hegemonic circumstances. This "critical" view of accounting is quite consonant with the popular view of accounting as "serving shareholders." Indeed,

Table 10.4. *Fortune* Discourse Categories and Configurations, 1960–1973

	Discourse Category No.	%
Configuration G: Support for state's role in promoting harmony and consensus:		
Celebration of government assistance to business	19	3.5
Importance of the state's responsibilities to citizens	20	1.7
The state's role as neutral arbiter in effecting social harmony	21	3.1
		8.3
Configuration H: Criticism of state interference and philanthropy:		
State interference as brake on growth; advocacy of deregulation	22	8.9
Criticism of welfare policies as oppressive and impeding growth	23	3.7
		12.6
Configuration J: A consensual view of society and business, emphasizing shared community objectives:		
Managers and wealthy as industrial statesmen, philanthropists	24	1.1
Praise for managerial insights, creativity, and leadership	25	2.9
Pursuit of profit as universally beneficial	26	4.5
Praise for social benefit to all of domestic growth	27	2.1
People's capitalism as means of ensuring that managers are socially responsive	28	5.7
		16.3
Configuration K: Celebration of individualistic and competitive aspects of society and business, and the will to survive:		
Society and business seen as governed by survival of the fittest	29	6.0
Encouragement of individualism	30	4.9
Promotion of material wealth as a measure of success	31	12.3
Essential role of management planning and authority	32	2.0
Monopolies, oligopolies, as advances in competition	33	11.6
Economic rationality as justification for corporate concern for social improvements	34	1.4
Labor strikes as reflections of harsh realities of the market	35	4.7
		42.9
Configuration L: Championing American interests, values, and business practices in international affairs:		
Naturalizing of U.S. international quest for markets and capital accumulation	36	0.7
Description of the U.S. international role as a powerful protector ensuring freedom and averting communist threat	37	0.9
Market capitalism as a benevolent force throughout the world	38	3.5
		5.0
Configuration M: Science and technology:		
Omnipotence of science, technology	39	6.6
Omnipotence of computers.	40	2.9
		9.5
Fortune configuration N: Sundry categories	41, 42, 43	5.2
% Total (rounded)		100.0

the public mandate to attest corporate accounts as "in accordance with GAAP (generally accepted accounting principles)" and to be true and fair is a manifestation of the very role we are ascribing to accounting: that of supplying legitimacy and support to capital accumulation.

The 14-year period of our analysis marks the beginning of the end of the postwar boom. The increase in the pretax and posttax rate of profit and the growth in real wages peaked in 1966, and thereafter stagnation and then stagflation set in, accompanied by falling profits, declining real wages, growing unemployment, and soaring inflation rates.

The early 1960s were a time in which the foundations of postwar consensus were consolidated through a range of political and social strategies; Lyndon Johnson's Great Society and welfare state programs, social contracts, and national economic plans marked this as a period of social cohesion informed by consensus. Such strategies imposed real limits on the efficacy of intervention of the Keynesian state; the inability to deliver the goods precipitated its collapse and ushered in a new authoritarianism in the 1970s (Hall, 1983a, 1983b; Hall et al., 1978). In the results presented below, the discourses of business and accounting can be seen to be participating in changing the socio-economic-political environment of the 1960–1973 period.

The first two aggregations of *Fortune* discourse categories in Table 10.4—configuration G and configuration H—are explicitly directed at the role of the state, and we use them as detailed illustrations below.

The first three discourse categories of Table 10.4 combine to form configuration G. Collectively, they describe the state's involvement in achieving social consensus. They represent the state as responsible for serving, and balancing, a plurality of interests. Additionally, these three *Fortune* discourses envision the state as a positive instrument of change in a wide range of activities. Therefore, configuration G encourages a view of the world in which the state mechanism can be relied upon to assist business through tax policies and to provide fallout shelters to protect its citizens. The state is viewed as an arena where different interests are represented, preserved, and protected in a manner that is not coercive but uses mediation and consensus. Justification for state involvement in a broad range of affairs is expressed in terms of national interests.

Fortune discourse categories 22 and 23, which have been amalgamated into configuration H, cover an array of meaning that is comparable to, yet quite distinct from, that of the first three categories. Configuration H differs from the earlier three in viewing the state negatively: as an impediment to business, creating inefficiencies in business operations through onerous regulations such as antitrust laws.

In addition, the state's bureaucracy and "welfare state" strategies are held responsible for economic inefficiencies and other social ills.

Figure 10-1 presents a longitudinal view of configurations G and H. Although there is a modest increase in state-consensus views (configuration G), this is dominated by a dramatic increase in anti-state-intervention discourses: configuration H rises from 6.6 to 16.2 percent.

What is the meaning of this trend in discursive activity? Earlier, we noted that in the early years of the 1960s, the state had a commitment to maintaining economic growth and economic security and sought to realize these aims by organizing coalitions and consensus between various protagonists. However, these alliances failed–as evidenced in the economic crises and social and political problems of the late 1960s and early 1970s. Thus we would expect to find the abovementioned patterns of business discourse, in that they are sympathetic to the emerging state of affairs: in the early sixties, a primarily supportive view of state involvement, and in the early seventies aggressive denunciation of state intervention.

What is the accounting profession's relationship to the state during this period? Accounting configuration A ("Critique of state intervention . . . ") offers an opportunity to explore the profession's discursive negotiations with the state–that is, the strategies the profession uses in conflicts with state apparatus. Configuration A includes texts that promote and praise self-regulation of the profession, insisting that standards and rules of financial reporting should be under the control of the accounting profession. In contrast to the high regard for accounting that is communicated in these texts, authors claim that society and business are impaired by government involvement in financial matters; state intervention generates inefficiencies and disturbances in the marketplace.

Figure 10.2 traces accounting's discursive patterns relating to the state (configuration A) for the two accounting journals. There is a consistent, substantial increase in criticism of the state over the period: from 36 to 48 percent in the *Journal of Accountancy*, and from 25 to 36 percent in the *Accounting Review*.

These results correspond to those we presented for *Fortune* magazine: discursive practices in the late sixties and early seventies–reacting to welfare state strategies that began to intrude on the accumulation of capital–increasingly present the state as an impediment to social well-being. By juxtaposing *Fortune's* criticism of the state with accounting's denunciation of state intervention, we illuminate the contingency relationship between accounting and business ideologies and various social, political, and economic forces.

Note that the changes in discourse, and our results, contain lags

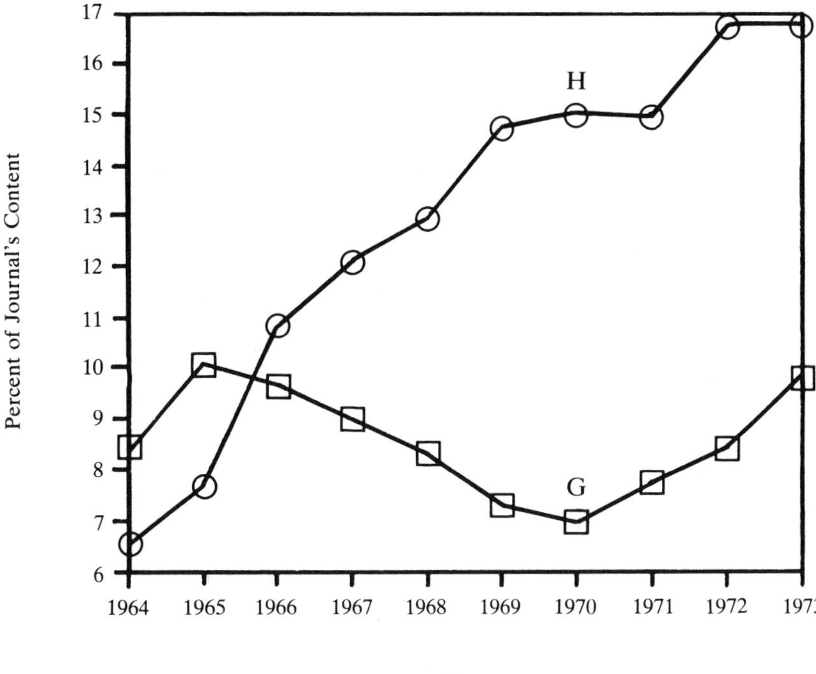

Fig. 10.1. *Fortune,* 1960–1973: Configurations G (support for state's role in consensus making) and H (criticism of state interference and welfare)

and overlaps; as Hall and his colleagues note (1978, p. 219), transition periods are characterized by "structurally different forces developing at different tempos and rhythms." Nevertheless, the power of the media, and the manner in which it can be utilized by social actors, is illustrated in this analysis of accounting and business literature. Accounting participates with the business community, the state, and other coalitions in re-presenting the world (in its literature) in a manner consistent with the changing needs of capital accumulation.

A related implication of the study concerns the role of scientific research in social conflict and specifically its part in producing ideologies that authenticate modes of appropriation. For example, research into standards for financial reporting helps determine the form of communications that society receives from business; research into budgeting and incentive schemes helps management transfer wealth from employees to other constituencies.

Table 10.3 permits us to identify the research themes that the accounting literature promoted and emphasized to the exclusion of others. Configuration B/BB ("Assertion that accounting benefits

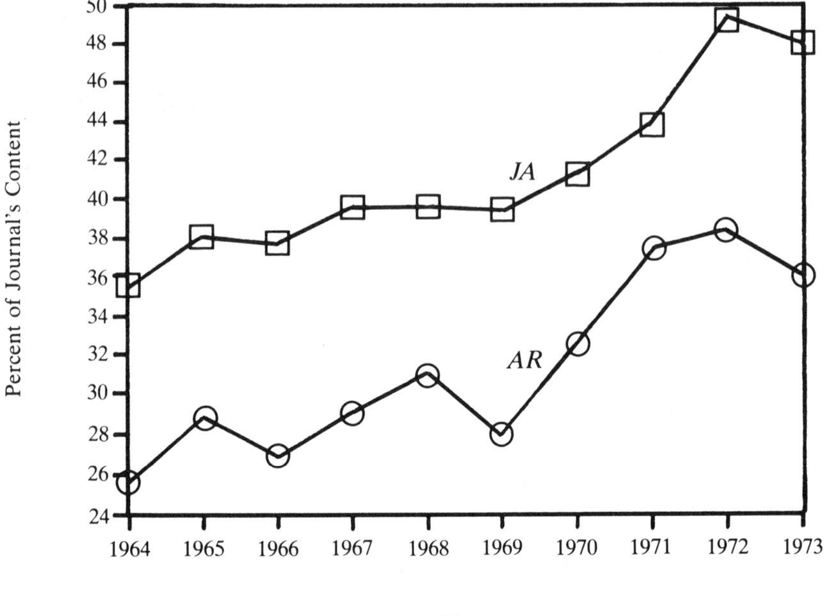

Fig. 10.2. Accounting journals, 1960–1973: Configurations *A (JA)* and *AA (AR),* which are each a critique of state intervention and celebration of professional independence

business and society . . . ") promotes the collective virtues of profit maximization and fails to consider the conflictual underpinnings of this issue (that there are winners and losers). Configuration B/BB equates domestic growth (e.g., industrial and technological growth) with social well-being; the costs of economic growth, and the social sectors that bear those costs, are rarely considered.

Over the period, the two accounting journals devote an average of 27.1 percent of their articles to configuration B, second only to critiques of the state (configuration A). However, if we observe the results for the individual journals, configuration B dominates the academic and research journal the *Accounting Review*–37.8 percent of this journal is devoted to texts promoting accounting's role in the efficient allocation of resources, the benefits to society of maximizing profits, and the importance of devoting resources to industrial and technological growth.

In contrast, consider the results regarding discourse category 8 ("The profession promotes its ethical practices"). Articles in this discourse describe the importance of a formal code of ethics, which all accountants must be committed to upholding, in order to ensure that the public interest is protected and advanced. For the 14-year period under study, the *Accounting Review* devotes 0.8 percent of its articles to this category.

The functionality of these discursive practices lies in the imperative of capital valorization and in an environment of contradictions, antinomies, and changes in discourses and ideologies. Interests groups advance their causes in these journals by putting closure on certain topics, emphasizing others, and situating these divisions as natural and nonproblematic. "Efficient allocation of resources," "social benefits," "self-regulation," "state impediments," are vital rhetorical weapons used by the profession to promote its own distributional advantage.

IMPLICATIONS

The studies of accounting reviewed in this paper are not intended to transport the subject to new heights of scholastic irrelevance; they are intended to provide the groundwork for very practical political objectives. In recent years the Left has been overrun by the bandwagons of Reaganism and Thatcherism. Until the Left understands the makeup of this hegemonic form–termed by Stuart Hall "Authoritarian Popularism"–particularly its cultural and ideological vanguard, there is little hope of the Left's achieving any major political reversal.

We contend that cultural and ideological struggles are pivotal in present-day capitalism, and if the Left is to develop effective counter-strategies, it must abandon the self-indulgence of liberal theoreticism and engage the discursive conflicts of "everyday life" (of accountants, students, workers, women, minorities, academics, etc.). Accounting is one of the last bastions of unpoliticized mystery in this regard. We have used it as an exemplar to show how a specific area of social life might be politicized and effective counter-strategies be developed (Tinker, 1985).

Politicization begins with the analysis of real social relations in their historical, institutional, social, ethical, cultural, and psychological contexts. Detailed analysis of this kind highlights the mutability of the status quo, its rapacious underpinning, and its emerging crises and contradictions. Negating these contradictions is the meat and potatoes of political activity; we have illustrated in this paper the sorts of political interventions developed for one specific microsphere–that of accounting.

References

Althusser, L. (1971). "Ideology and Ideological State Apparatus," in *Lenin and Philosophy and Other Essays*. London: Allen Lane.

Althusser, L. (1976). *Essays in Self Criticism*. London: New Left Books.

Armstrong, P. (1985). "Changing Management Control Strategies: The Role of Competition Between Accountancy and Other Organisational Professions," *Accounting, Organizations and Society*, 10, 2, pp. 129–48.

Armstrong, P. (forthcoming). "The Rise of Accounting Controls in British Capitalist Enterprises," *Accounting, Organizations and Society*.

Barthes, R. (1972). *Mythologies*. London: Jonathan Cape.

Bennett, T. (1982). "Theories of Media, Theories of Society." In M. Gurevitch, T. Bennett, J. Curran, and J. Woolacott (eds.) *Culture, Society and Media*. London: Methuen.

Berry, A. J.; D. Capps; D. Cooper; P. Ferguson; T. Hopper and E. A. Lowe (1985). "Management Control in an Area of the NCB: Rationales of Accounting Practices in a Public Enterprise." *Accounting Organizations and Society*, 10, 1, pp. 3–28.

Bird, J. (1982). "Jacques Lacan–the French Freud?" *Radical Philosophy*, 30, Spring, pp. 7–13.

Blumler, J., and M. Gurevitch (1982). "The Political Effects of Mass Communication." In M. Gurevitch, T. Bennett, J. Curran, and J. Woollacott (eds.) *Culture, Society and Media*. London: Methuen & Co.

Burchell, S.; C. Clubb; A. Hopwood; J. Hughes; and J. Nahapiet (1980). "The Roles of Accounting in Organizations and Society." *Accounting, Organizations and Society*, 5, 1, pp. 5–27.

Burchell, S.; C. Clubb; and A. G. Hopwood, (1985). "Accounting in Its Social Context: Towards a History of Value Added in the United Kingdom." *Accounting, Organizations and Society*, 5, 1, pp. 161–414.

Cooper, D. (1980). "Discussion of Towards a Political Economy of Accounting." *Accounting, Organizations and Society*, 5, 1, pp. 161–66.

Coward, R. and J. Ellis (1977). *Language and Materialism*. London: Routledge and Kegan Paul.

Curran, J.; M. Gurevitch; and J. Woolacott (1982). "The Study of the Media: Theoretical Approaches." In M. Gurevitch, T. Bennett, J. Curran, and J. Woollacott (eds.) *Culture, Society and Media*. London: Methuen & Co.

Davis, M. (1986). *Prisoners of the Dream: Politics and Economy in the History of the U.S. Working Class*. London: Verso.

Edgley, R. (1984). "Comments on Ravetz," *Radical Philosophy*, 37, Summer, pp. 11–112.

Galbraith, J. K. (1967). *The New Industrial State*. Boston: Houghton Mifflin.

Graham, A. K., and P. M. Senge (1980). "A Long-Wave Hypothesis of Innovation," *Technological Forecasting and Social Change*, pp. 283–311.

Gramsci, A. (1971). *Selections from the Prison Notebooks*. London: Lawrence & Wishart.

Hall, S. (1980). "Popular Democratic versus Authoritarian Popularism." In

A. Hunt (ed.) *Marxism and Democracy*. London: Lawrence & Wishart.
Hall, S. (1982). "The Rediscovery of Ideology: Return of the Repressed in Media Studies." In M. Gurevitch, T. Bennett, J. Curran, and J. Woollacott (eds.) *Culture, Society and Media.* London: Methuen.
Hall, S. (1983). "The Great Moving Right Show." In S. Hall and M. Jacques, *The Politics of Thatcherism.* London: Lawrence & Wishart.
Hall, S. (1983) "The Little Caesar of Social Democracy." In S. Hall and M. Jacques, *The Politics of Thatcherism*. London: Lawrence & Wishart.
Hall, S.; C. Critcher; T. Jefferson; J. Clarke; and B. Roberts (1978). *Policing the Crisis: Mugging, the State, and Law and Order*. London: Macmillan.
Hoogvelt, A., and A. Tinker (1978). "The Role of the Colonial and Post-Colonial State in the Development of Imperialism." *Journal of African Studies,* 16, 1, pp. 1–13.
Hopwood, A. (1985). "The Tale of a Committee That Never Reported: Disagreements on Intertwining Accounting with the Social." *Accounting, Organizations and Society*, 10, 3, pp. 361–77.
Hopwood, A. (1987). "The Archeology of Accounting Systems", *Accounting, Organizations and Society,* 12, 3, pp. 207–234.
Hoskin, K. W., and R. H. Macve (1986). "Accounting and the Examination: A Genealogy of Disciplinary Power," *Accounting, Organizations and Society,* 11, 2, pp. 105–36.
Jessop, B. (1980). "The Transformation of the State in Postwar Britain." In R. Scase (ed.) *The State in Western Europe.* London: Croom Helm.
Jessop, B. (1982). *The Capitalist State: Marxist Theories and Methods*. London: Martin Robertson.
Jessop, B.; K. Bonnett; and S. Bromley (1984). "Authoritarian Popularism, Two Nations and Thatcherism." *New Left Review,* 137, Sept.–Oct., pp. 32–60.
Johnson, H. T. (1978). "Management Accounting in an Early Multidivisional Organization: General Motors in the 1920's." *Business History Review*, pp. 490–517.
Katz, B., and L. S. Katz (1982). *Magazines for Libraries*. New York: R. R. Bowker.
Knights D., and H. Willmott (1985). "Power and Identity in Theory and Practice." *Sociological Review* pp. 22–46.
Laclau, E. (1977). *Politics and Ideology in Marxist Theory*. London: New Left Books.
Lehman, C. (1985). *Discourse Analysis and Accounting Literature: Transformation of State Hegemony, 1960–1973,* Ph.D. dissertation, New York University.
Levi-Strauss, C. (1977). *The Scope of Anthropology*. London: Jonathan Cape.
Loft, A. (1986), "Toward a Critical Understanding of Accounting: The Case of Cost Accounting in the UK: 1914–1925." *Accounting, Organizations and Society,* 11, 2, pp. 137-69.
Mandel, E. (1978). *Late Capitalism*. London: Verso.
Mensch, G. (1978). *Stalemate in Technology: Innovations Overcome the Depression*. Cambridge, Mass.: Ballinger.

Merino, B., and M. Neimark (1982). "Disclosure Regulation and Public Policy: A Sociohistorical Reappraisal." *Journal of Accounting and Public Policy*, 1, 1, pp. 33–57.

Miliband, Ralph (1969). *The State in Capitalist Society: An Analysis of the Western System of Power.* New York: Basic Books.

Miller, P., and T. O'Leary (1987). "Accounting and the Construction of the Governable Person." *Accounting, Organizations and Society,* 12, 3, pp. 235–265.

Neimark, M. (1983). *The Social Construction of Annual Reports: A Radical Approach to Corporate Control.* Ph.D. dissertation, New York University.

Saussure, F. de. (1960). *A Course in General Linguistics.* London: P. Owen.

Simon, H. A. (1976). *Administrative Behavior: A Study of Decision Making Processes in Administrative Organizations, 3d ed.* New York: Free Press.

Tinker, A. M. (1980). "Towards a Political Economy of Accounting: An Empirical Illustration of the Cambridge Controversies." *Accounting, Organizations and Society,* 5, 1, pp. 147–60.

Tinker, A. M.; B. Merino; and M. D. Neimark (1982). "The Normative Origins of Positive Theories: Ideology and Accounting Thought," *Accounting, Organizations and Society,* 7, 2, pp. 167–200.

Tinker, T. (1985). *Paper Prophets: A Social Critique of Accounting.* New York: Praeger.

Tinker, T., and M. Neimark (1987). "The Role of Annual Reports in Gender and Class Contradictions at General Motors: 1917-1976," *Accounting, Organizations and Society,* 12, 1, pp. 71–88.

Williams, P. (1985). "A Descriptive Analysis of Authorship in The Accounting Review," *Accounting Review,* 60, 2, pp. 300–313.

Wood, D. C. (1979). "Introduction to Derrida." *Radical Philosophy,* 21, Spring, pp. 18–28.

11. Office Automation and the Technical Control of Information Workers

Andrew Clement

The rapid and widespread computerization of office work raises a host of interrelated issues for those who work with information. Managers have previously used office automation to control more closely the work of clerks. Can the same techniques of control be applied to professionals, middle managers, and technicians as they begin to work increasingly with computers? The longstanding principles of scientific management have historically played a prominent role in the exercise of managerial control. Are they still applicable in automated offices?

Two distinct approaches are being taken to the automation of office work. One relies on terminals connected to centralized computing facilities; the other is based on stand-alone personal computers. How different are they and what are the implications, particularly for workplace control, of these two approaches? Are the personal computers and tightly integrated systems likely to coexist in large corporations, or will one predominate? Can purely technical considerations account for the expected outcome of this competition, or will social factors be significant? These are the central questions that this paper explores.

Much of the attention being paid to office automation revolves around issues of productivity. Vendors advertise systems by appealing to cost-saving potential; workers and unions worry about job security; and economists argue about net employment levels. But the automation of office work is much more than simply a labor-saving technique. Computerization is in its essence *the* technology of control. How it is developed and used has profound implications for who controls office work and how control is exercised. The impor-

---

An earlier version of this paper was presented at the panel session entitled "Impact of Technology on Work," at the Conference of the Society for the Study of Social Problems, San Francisco, September 1982.

tance to management of office automation, as well as the larger political dimension that surrounds it, was clearly expressed by Franco de Benedetti, managing director of the transnational office equipment company Olivetti, at a 1979 conference on office technology sponsored by the *Financial Times*:

> The problems which are usually associated with office automation make up the final chapter of a story which began with the industrial revolution, that is, with the supreme assertion of capitalist production over all preceding types of production and over all those that exist today. . . . Information technology is basically a technology of co-ordination and control of the labour force, the white collar workers, which taylorian organisation does not cover. . . .
>
> EDP (electronic data processing) seems to be one of the most important tools with which company management institutes policies directly concerning the work process and [is] conditioned by complex economic and social factors. In this sense EDP is in fact an organisational technology and, like the organisation of labour, has a dual function as a productive force and a control tool for Capital.
>
> To sum up: the easy adaptability of work to the machine, the diffusion of equipment thanks to technological developments, the measurability of the improvement obtained and finally the increased power which the manager acquires are the cause of the exceptional diffusion of the mechanisation of the office. (Quoted in Albury and Schwartz, 1982, pp. 149–50, and Duncan, 1981, p. 194).

This paper examines the workplace-control implications of recent developments in office technology. The purpose is to show that those who work with information in large organizations are in the process of being subjected to greater managerial control through their use of information systems. Most previous critical research on this theme has concentrated on the work of clerical employees (see Barker and Downing, 1979; Clement, 1986; Glenn and Feldberg, 1980; Gregory and Nussbaum, 1982; Hoos, 1961). As in the work of Ulrich Briefs (1981), and Mike Cooley (1980), the focus here is on middle-level employees. In keeping with these earlier studies, the classic principles of scientific management will be used to explain the way in which office work is being managed. We will further look at how the particular characteristics of office technology present opportunities and constraints for the exercise of managerial control. With special reference to the introduction of desktop microcomputers into corporate offices, we will examine some of the dynamics of decision making about the choice of one technological form over another.

Before discussing the techniques of control and the development of office technologies and how they interact, it is useful to sketch the salient organizational and technical features of office automation.

WHAT IS OFFICE AUTOMATION?

The office is the seat of coordination and control in the modern bureaucratic enterprise. Office workers, whatever their specialized role, directly or indirectly manipulate the abstract, symbolic representations of activities in the outside world for the purpose of regulating them in some way. Since the early decades of the century, this form of work has grown rapidly to assume a large and costly role within business and government operations (see Braverman, 1974, pp. 293–358).

Computers are general-purpose information-processing machines and the closest physical embodiments of the fundamental principles of control (Wiener, 1961). It is because of these attributes and the not coincidental match between the organization of computer systems and that of bureaucracies (Berman, 1986) that business leaders began adopting computerized techniques virtually as soon as computers were invented. As the distinguished computer scientist Joseph Weizenbaum notes, "American managers and technicians agreed that the computer had come along just in time to avert catastrophic crises" (1976, p. 27) in the handling of the financial and logistical transactions upon which burgeoning corporate and military activities depended so heavily.

The initial phase of office automation, which began in the 1950s, was characterized by the computerization of relatively standardized clerical procedures, such as billing, accounting, and payroll. Information was converted to machine-readable form by pools of keypunch operators and submitted in batches to large, central mainframe computers. Generally, computer applications were highly specialized and operated independently of each other.[1]

Although the range and scale of the computerization of functions have grown unabated, the term "office automation" fell into disuse, until recently. Dramatic technical advances, particularly in microcomputing, have brought with them a revival of the term, but with significant new characteristics. Now office automation is associated with *globally distributed, generic, integrated* applications aimed principally

---

1. See the U.S. Congress, Office of Technology Assessment report (1985) for an up-to-date review of the history, technology, and varied implications of office automation.

at computerizing the work of *middle*-level office employees. Whereas in its earlier stage office automation involved the removal of much of the actual work from the office and into centralized data-processing centers, the prevailing trend now is to bring computer equipment to the office worker to use directly. The mechanized processing of information is thus being distributed throughout the organization. It is important to note that while the operations are being decentralized, it is not necessarily the case, as we will discuss more fully later, that effective control is also being decentralized.

Office automation increasingly relies on generic information-processing facilities. Instead of automating procedures that are fairly specific to the business or industry, now much of the emphasis is on computerizing procedures found in virtually every office, independent of its particular industry segment. Just as desks, telephones, filing cabinets, photocopiers, and typewriters are ubiquitous and constitute components of a typical office infrastructure, so too will the emerging office technologies supersede the conventional components. Although there will often be identifiable correspondences between the electronic and conventional components, the transformation will not in general be done on a piece-by-piece basis—for example, replacing a "paper" filing cabinet with an electronic one. Rather, since the shift in the basis for representing information (from marks on paper and analog voice signals to digitally encoded electronic pulses) is a radical change in medium, entire processes will often have to be computerized as a whole.[2]

Access to all the general office "tools," plus others relating to job-specific tasks, is through a "workstation" on an employee's desk. These would be connected to each other (much as telephone sets are) and to shared computing resources. The International Data Corporation projects that by 1990, close to 80 percent of the 60 million white-collar workers in the United States will have computerized workstations, up from 20 million in 1985 (see *Fortune*, 1986).

As computer techniques are being applied more widely, they are also being integrated. This is a dominant theme in the information systems literature at the moment, and its importance is revealed in a statement by the manager of data processing for a major accounting firm:

---

2. The more popular computer-based office services that are generic in nature include: document preparation/word processing; communications via electronic mail, voice messaging, and teleconferencing; personal time management using "electronic calendars"; data analysis with spread-sheet software; database management software; and graphics display packages.

> Integration is the promised land of office automation. While there is some advantage in speeding up document preparation or intra-office messaging, the real payoff comes not from automating individual tasks but from linking a series of components to allow information to flow freely in many forms. (Macfarlane, 1983, p. 102)

Vendors and consultants are actively promoting integration on all fronts—integration of hardware, software, data, and medium of representation.[3] The technical integration is proceeding explicitly in concert with organizational integration. Field operations are being tied more closely with headquarters, factories with offices, and suppliers with producers, and distributors with consumers. The vision is of a seamless electronic web upon which corporations can smoothly, efficiently coordinate and control all of their intricate affairs around the globe.

A final important aspect of contemporary office automation is that it is aimed primarily at middle-level, rather than clerical, employees. This is the somewhat amorphous, hard-to-define stratum containing supervisors, middle managers, technicians, and professionals, the group that in an earlier time George Orwell referred to as the "new indeterminate class of skilled workers, technical experts, scientists, architects, and journalists, the people who feel at home in the radio and ferro-concrete age" (see Kann, 1985, p. 72) and that more recently Peter Drucker (1969) has lumped together as "knowledge workers."

3. Hardware integration involves the physical connection of microcomputers, mainframes, printers, disk drives and the like via communications networks, ranging in scale from intraoffice Local Area Networks (LANs) to global, publicly accessible data networks. Software integration refers to the creation of computer programs that permit several different applications to be handled in a uniform manner. The best examples of this are such popular software packages as Lotus 1-2-3, which permit users to perform spread-sheet analyses of data derived from a database and depict the results as a graph that can be inserted easily into a word-processed document. Related to this is the integration of data, which involves the use of data-structuring techniques, such as the relational data model, to create corporate-wide databases containing the definitive version of every single data item considered to be of importance. The fourth form of technical integration involves the medium of information representation. This finds its most ambitious expression in the proposals for an Integrated Services Digital Network (ISDN), currently being promoted most vigourously by transnational business interests (see Schiller, 1985). As the ISDN name suggests, voice signals, computer data, and video and graphic images would all be coded digitally and transmitted uniformly over a common worldwide electronic network.

Although earlier automated systems have affected middle-level information workers, they have mainly done so indirectly, with emphasis on either reducing clerical labor costs for relatively structured tasks (e.g., payroll) or achieving new processing capabilities not previously feasible (e.g., modeling). Although word processing can be regarded as the leading edge of the current phase of office automation, many observers view it as simply a grab for the "low-hanging fruit." Typing represents such a small fraction (in the range of 2 percent) of office costs that no great savings would be achieved even with its complete elimination. Product announcements and advertising campaigns by equipment vendors, as well as more formal research, point unmistakably to the middle stratum of organizations as the prime target of the promoters of new office technology. Secretarial and clerical support workers will undoubtedly be seriously affected by the automation of office functions; however, this will result not just from their own use of computerized equipment, but also, and in the long run more importantly, from their being bypassed as "higher"-level workers increasingly interact directly with machine systems for carrying out such tasks as document preparation, filing, retrieval, and transmission.

The economic reasons for this are clear, and often repeated by vendors, In 1980, out of $600 billion spent on office personnel costs in the United States, nearly 75 percent went to managers and professionals, with the balance going to the numerically superior clerical and secretarial workers. A widely cited study by the management consulting firm Booz, Allen & Hamilton (Hirschheim, 1985) reported that nearly one-half of "knowledge workers'" time was spent in meetings and over 25 percent was even "less productive" (i.e., wasted). In a climate in which increasing productivity has been declared a national priority and promoted as essential for restoring health and vigor to the American economy, the relatively well paid middle echelons of large organizations have thus been targeted for a major squeeze on their time and energy. In a milieu where the idea that machine calculation offers a ready substitute for human skills has a powerful hold on the imagination of decision-makers and at a time when technology costs are declining rapidly in relation to labor costs, automation is regarded as the obvious and even inevitable answer to the problem (see Strassman, 1985). Office equipment manufacturers of all sizes and specialties (including giants such as IBM, XEROX, and AT&T) have seen in this a market potentially worth $300 billion (*Globe and Mail*, 1981) and are vigorously promoting their solutions to the office "productivity crisis." If these vendors, and the corporate managers they sell to, continue to have their way over the next 20 years, the fundamental infrastructure of office work will have been radically transformed from paper to electronic media. This will have significant implications for information workers at every level.

TECHNICAL CONTROL AND THE SCIENTIFIC MANAGEMENT OF OFFICE WORK

Workplace control—who determines what is done and how—is a significant concern raised by widespread computerization in offices. Office automation greatly increases the ability of managers to extend their control over subordinates in ways that were never possible before. In particular, technical as opposed to bureaucratic forms of control (to use Edwards' [1979] terminology) have become feasible, virtually for the first time. In conventional offices, the facilities of production—the desks, filing cabinets, typewriters, wastebaskets, telephones, and the like—offer few means for managers to direct the execution of tasks, evaluate results, or discipline employees. With an infrastructure based on paper, the devices used for manipulating documents provide little constraint on content or who uses them. They cannot conveniently report to managers which employees are operating them, for how long, and with what output. In order to maintain control over work activities in large office settings, managers have relied on direct, personal supervision as well as more bureaucratic means, such as formal job evaluation schemes, job hierarchies, career ladders, and regular performance reviews. The shift to an electronic infrastructure for office work allows managers to adopt additional control mechanisms that are embedded within the computer systems themselves. Such technical forms of control are well established in some areas of clerical work. For example, online transaction-processing systems typically enforce strict rules over which proposed changes to stored records clerks are permitted to make. Systems have also been programmed to provide managers with such detailed measures of employee performance as average time spent handling a telephone call and number of keys stroked per hour (see Clement, 1984). As automation is introduced at progressively higher organizational levels, there are already signs that sophisticated versions of the same basic techniques are being applied there as well.

Managers have always pursued systematic means to gain effective control over their enterprises. Harry Braverman, in his now classic book *Labor and Monopoly Capital* (1974), has shown how the managerial imperative to exert control over the labor process and the labor force has been a major thrust within the development of modern corporate capitalism. Using "scientific" techniques, management has systematically restructured labor processes to bring them more under its direction. Can the fundamental principles that have guided this effort since Frederick Taylor first formulated them at the turn of the century still provide a useful framework for analyzing the various ways in which managers are shaping office automation in order to extend control over information workers?

As Braverman (1974, pp. 112–21) has stated them, the basic dicta of scientific management are three in number:

1. Dissociate the labor process from the skills of workers.
2. Separate conception from execution.
3. Use management's monopoly over workplace knowledge to control each step of the labor process and its mode of execution.

The application of these three principles has resulted in the following techniques of managerial control that are characteristic of factory organization:

Capturing worker skill under management auspices and embedding it within the mechanized production system

Fragmentation and restructuring of tasks by management

Automated assignment of task sequence and pace

Automated monitoring of worker activity and performance

Enforcement of selective access to information

Management creation of a special corp of "experts" trained in restructuring work processes.

While these do not exhaust established techniques, they are all prominent features of conventional industrial worksites and are becoming more evident in modern offices as information work is increasingly automated. We will examine three techniques—skill capture, automated monitoring, and selective information access—to show specifically how office technology can be used for control as well as for simply enhancing productivity. The focus will principally be upon how, for the first time, middle managers, professionals, and technicians have become subject to these techniques.

Capturing Workers' Skill

Before a process can be automated, it must be understood thoroughly and explicitly. Although many workplaces provide employees with instructions on how to perform office tasks manually, they will almost always be far too general to serve on their own as a basis for automation. Individual workers will know a great deal about specific aspects of their own jobs, but they may be unable or unwilling to express this knowledge formally. Workers could get together to design improvements to the work process, or they could engage consultants to help them, but the results would probably not suit higher levels of the organization. Thus senior management, as a preliminary to automation, has usually initiated its own studies on how work actually gets done in its workplaces. In doing so managers are fulfilling Frederick Taylor's advice of 1911 that "managers assume . . . the burden of gathering together all of the traditional knowledge which in the past has been possessed by the workmen and then of classifying, tabulating, and reducing this knowledge to rules, laws, and forumlae" (see Braverman, 1974, p. 112). However, now they include within their sights even their fellow managers, and the resulting "rules, laws, and formulae" are being expressed as computer programs.

Although managerial and professional work has been studied for some time, the emphasis has usually been on the job as a whole. With the prospect of automation, there has been increased interest in the detailed work activities of these workers. Journal articles with titles such as "Office Automation Provides Opportunity to Examine What Workers Actually Do" (see Jackson, 1984) give an indication of this. Studies have focused on such aspects of professional/managerial work as patterns of communications and time-budget analysis. A major recent study is the one by Booz, Allen & Hamilton mentioned earlier. It was conducted almost like a classic time and motion study. At regular intervals a buzzer would sound, and participants would have to record their activities at that moment. More theoretical research is also being done, involving attempts to describe mathematically general office procedures. Although these studies are posed as determining the "needs" of managers, in fact the results can be used just as easily to tighten the grip on them—to identify and then squeeze out "wasted" activities and to rationalize their jobs further.

Capturing enough information about a work process to automate it reliably is in general very difficult and time-consuming. Even clerical work that is considered routine contains subtleties, often related to the handling of exceptions, that go unrecognized until attempts are made to formalize them. An indication of just how hard this task can be and the lengths managers are sometimes prepared to go to in order to get the information they need about the work process is revealed in the well-known case of the Letter of Credit Section of Citibank's New York head office. Richard Matteis (1979), the Citibank vice-president who headed "Operation Paradise," described how repeated attempts at analyzing the issuing of letters of credit failed until they finally resorted to isolating a long-time clerk in a "white room" and then watched every action she took in handling the various types of transaction the management team presented to her.

The work that professionals and managers do is considered much more difficult than clerical work to automate, in large part because of the greater amount of knowledge involved and the lack of tools available to represent this knowledge conveniently. Recent developments in the field of artificial intelligence, particularly the emergence of "expert systems," promise to alleviate some of the present obstacles and open up hitherto-inaccessible areas of expertise to automation.

In the conventional approach to automation, a systems analyst interviews employees to collect information about the work process and then writes a program that successfully mimics the worker's decision-making behavior. All the rules of action have to be identified explicitly and then coded into a highly structured piece of software that is relatively difficult to change or adapt. In the course of development, the analyst must become something of an expert in the field in order to get the program right. In contrast, the expert systems methodology provides a more flexible way of representing knowledge. The decision rules are stored in a "knowledge base" that is then used by a separate piece of software, known as the "inference engine," in coming up with decisions. Systems are developed through the collaboration of an "expert" and a "knowledge engineer," who does not have to learn the subject matter. In principle, rules are relatively easy to add to or remove from the knowledge base as experience in using the system accumulates.

Although the technology involved is still in its infancy, expert systems have attracted considerable attention from business interests. Edward Feigenbaum and Pamela McCorduck, prominent promoters of artificial intelligence (AI), explain that part of the attraction of expert systems is that they offer managers the means for developing a machine-based "corporate memory." In *The Fifth Generation* (1983, p.80), they describe the vision and identify the chief obstacle to achieving it:

> Over the years, an enormous amount of expertise has been built up, but it is almost all in human heads, not documents. Unfortunately, people die, retire, and forget. Why not a knowledge base that stores the collective corporate expertise, and an expert system that watches over the shoulders of designers and reminds them about what their predecessors already know?
>
> The power of the expert systems comes from the knowledge they contain. That knowledge is, at present, stored in the heads of human ex-

perts, and getting it out—what AI researchers call the knowledge acquisition problem—is the biggest problem that the knowledge engineers currently face.

The technical problems alone in achieving a computerized corporate "mind" are formidable, and many of the claims made for expert systems reflect advertising hyperbole, but this technology cannot safely be ignored. There are commercially viable systems operating in settings as diverse as investment firms (Shearson/Express), computer manufacturers (DEC), oil exploration companies (Schlumberger), and soup manufacturers (Campbells). Major computer companies, (including IBM, DEC, Xerox, Hewlett-Packard, and Texas Instruments) currently offer artificial intelligence products. Sales of expert systems "tool kits" are expected to grow from $74 Million in 1985 to $810 million in 1990 (see Davis, 1986). Although much human knowledge will always remain beyond the grasp of automated devices, the impact of systems of even limited capability upon information workers could be considerable.

When human expertise is embedded into computer software, whether by conventional programming techniques or by more sophisticated means, the effect is much the same. The computer system presents the user with a structured set of possibilities and constraints. Certain actions become prescribed; others become prohibited; and a range in the middle become simply permissible, according to how the system has been designed. In effect a policy of action has been promulgated and put into place. When the user understands what the system is capable of and what its limitations ate, can decide when to use or not use it, and can reliably anticipate the consequences of use, then the user can regard the system as a tool. It is an extention of his or her own capabilities. When all the basic decisions about design and deployment are made by management, then the computer system becomes an automated executor of management policy. The conception of what is to be done and how is management's, and execution is a detail that is relegated to the machine and its operator. In this mode, the system is management's tool for the exercise of workplace control and can confront the employee as an "alien and hostile force," to use Mike Cooley's phrase (1981, p. 47). This can come about because human expertise has been congealed into software, making it an object that can be possessed by others.

Even more critical than what method was used to develop the software and who was involved in its design is the question of who owns the result. As Cooley (1980, p. 9) notes in the case of engineers using stress analysis software:

> the knowledge which previously existed in the conciousness of the [employee], which was part of his or her knowledge, taken home every night and which was part of that person's bargaining power, has now become extracted from them. It has been absorbed and objectivised into the machine through the intervention of the computer and is now the property of the employer, so the employer now appropriates part of the worker himself.

Through exercising ownership rights over software, managers can set in motion the expertise it contains when and where they decide, often without need for the workers from whom it was derived. Perhaps the most dramatic example of the power that owning software gives management over professional employees possessing formerly vital skills comes from the 1981 strike by U.S. air traffic controllers. In preparing for contract bargaining with the Professional Air Traffic Controllers Association (PATCO), the Federal Aviation Administration (FAA) secretly developed automated "flow control" systems that could take over tasks of regulating aircraft movement. The system played a critical role in allowing the Reagan administration to fire 12,000 controllers and still maintain acceptable air service with substantially fewer personnel. The strike was broken and the union decertified (see Shaiken, 1984, pp. 248–58).

Automated Monitoring

The ownership of expertise in the form of software is not the only potent means by which management can use its computerized control of workplace knowledge to control the labor process. Another use of computers in controlling information workers involves monitoring their activities and performance.

Central to the theory of control is the notion of a feedback loop. The behavior of the object of control is sensed on a regular basis so that corrective actions can be effected. The greater the frequency and detail of sensing, the greater the degree of control that can be achieved. This general principle is widely recognized and applied by management. In office work, its most extreme, and in human terms most costly, application has been the electronic monitoring of data entry personnel and telephone operators. Driven by the managerial pursuit of productivity and control, the practice is spreading throughout clerical work and to higher levels of the organization. Electronic monitoring accompanies the growth of automation of production, since raw performance data can readily be obtained as a by-product of the work process, and is rendered less objectionable by an ideology that regards humans as unreliable information-processing machines whose behavior needs to be watched closely.

Detailed monitoring of employees has been carried out using a very wide range of measures, from the mundane to the sophisticated, and at virtually every stratum of the organization. This is illustrated by Intel Corporation, a company well known as a leading manufacturer of microelectronic chips, recognized by *Fortune* in 1980 as one of the five best-managed U.S. firms and heavily dependent on its highly trained professional scientists to maintain its competitive position. According to Robert Noyce, Intel's vice-chairman, the company uses MBO (Management By Objectives) extensively, and "when it comes to performance . . . absolutely everything" is measured (Noyce, 1980, p. 123). This is a task made much easier by computerization. At Intel, a late list is posted to report the percentage of people arriving after 8:10 in the morning. This applies to scientists along with everyone else. Noyce states that the employees like this practice because it shows that the company "cares." One increasingly common way to automate this attendence reporting is through computerized timekeeping/access control devices. Hecon Canada advertised such a product with the question, "IT'S 11:00 A.M. DO YOU KNOW WHERE YOUR EMPLOYEES ARE?" Similarly a New York brokerage firm requires executives to record, on a half-hourly basis, their activities for each time period, broken down by 300 coded task types. A computer-generated Monthly Activity Report then reveals each executive's "productivity" (Garson, 1981). In this case the executives had to fill in the input form by hand. This is time-consuming and potentially a source of irritation and inaccuracy, both deliberate and accidental.

With increased use of computerized devices, many basic activity measures can be collected automatically. The current generation of telephone PBXs (private branch exchanges) have built into them features for keeping track of each number called. Mitel Corp. advertises that its SX-100/SX-200 SUPERSWITCH is a "very thorough informer" that can identify personal use and "long talkers." Electronic mail similarly provides a means for unobtrusive oversight, which was much harder to achieve with a conventional paper-based infrastructure. The analysis of volumes, lengths, times of day, and destinations of mail messages sent by an individual would reveal much about that employee's activities, even without looking at message content. Managers are also beginning to scrutinize their employees' travel activities with the aid of computers. Travel management reporting services, which major credit card companies such as American Express, Diners Club, and enRoute offer to their corporate clients, are being used to check up on travelers' spending practices. Itemized reports of individual expenditures provide the basis for determining whether the employee avoided unnecessary expenditures, took flights with the lowest possible fares, used specified suppliers, and otherwise optimized travel time and expenditure (McArthur, 1986).

So far these examples of monitoring have pertained to measures of activity—what the middle-level employee is doing on company time and with company money. They can help managers to make their subordinates more conscious of their actions and thereby increase efficiency. Also of concern to managers is what the worker actually accomplishes for the employer. It is the measurement of this performance that is at the heart of the current thrust for increased accountability. Computerization is playing an important role here too.

Sales personnel have traditionally been evaluated and paid on the basis of the value of their sales, but automation permits more sophisticated measures of performance. An advertisement for a computer manufacturer in *Fortune* vividly illustrates this. The image depicts a sales prize being decapitated by an axe constructed of computer printouts. The caption reads: "It took Basic Four to show why my 'star' salesman should be canned. No new business. Sky-high travel and entertainment and 43% of his sales were on low-profit items" (*Fortune*, 1979, p. 53).

The job of a life insurance underwriter is considered to be a skilled one, requiring experience and good judgment in deciding whether the company should assume the risks of insuring an applicant's life. When paper-based methods were used, it was relatively difficult to evaluate the performance of individual insurance underwriters in terms of the speed and accuracy with which they processed applications for insurance policies. Short of exhaustive manual searching through stacks of forms, it is hard to locate applications and determine how long they have been waiting to be looked at by the underwriter. At one major insurance company, management attempted to measure the efficiency of underwriters by introducing work-measurement methods based on conventional time and motion studies, but this was successfully resisted by underwriters. However, the installation of an online policy-tracking system achieved much the same end for managers and was more palatable to employees. The system routinely produced reports to management showing, for each underwriter, all the applications waiting at each stage of the underwriting process and compared the performances of all the underwriters. The tracking system also provided the basis for a regular review of cases handled by an underwriter several years earlier (see Clement, 1986).

Another surveillance technique made possible by computerization is the "deep look." Using an online terminal, an executive of a large firm that keeps much of its vital information in a central computer facility can peer far into the operations of the firm. The executive can examine in detail and on an up-to-date basis how the firm and its employees are performing. Powerful computerized query and analysis tools allow the examiner flexibility in determining exactly what to look at and avoids having to depend on reports prepared by subordinates. (Some executives even write their own programs.) The pressure that this form of computerization allows to be put on middle-level workers is revealed in the following quotations from top managers:

> The system provides me with a somewhat independent source for checking on the analyses and opinions presented both by my line subordinates and by my functional staffs. There is a great deal of comfort in being relatively independent of the analyses done by others.

> Frankly, a secondary, but very real, advantage of the use of the system by me is the signal it gives to the rest of the company that I desire more quantitatively oriented management. I want my subordinates to think more analytically, and they are. (Rockart and Treacy, 1982, p. 86)

With the increasing automation of financial transactions, bank headquarters are in a much better position to look over the shoulder of branch managers and reduce their scope of action. This centralization of effective control was revealed at a workshop on the impacts of microelectronics upon work:

> A Canadian local bank manager pointed out that his regional vice-president knows precisely the state of his branch at any point during the day by pressing the appropriate buttons. He can know the state of deposits in the bank, the state of withdrawals, the state of payments of loans, defaults on loans, everything that is put in data banks, the bank's central place. So I asked the branch manager, "What is your role?" His response was "I'll be damned if I know." (Science Council of Canada, 1980, p. 11)

What these examples of monitoring have in common is the fact that when work activities are mediated electronically in some way, they become more open to external scrutiny. Even interpersonal transactions that were previously conducted outside the purview of seniors now become much more visible when conducted via computer. Electronic mail, online calendars, and teleconferencing all allow a superior to "look in" unobtrusively. Such "remote supervison" (see Zuboff, 1982) is impersonal and not subject to the same codes of manners or etiquette that inhibit conventional eavesdropping or snooping. A professor in a well-known computer science department, attempting to discourage the copying of programs by students, developed a procedure called "snoop" to automatically intercept and then view all the electronic mail passing between students. In the discussion of the propriety of this measure, conducted by members of the department through electronic mail, it became clear that many regarded this practice as acceptable. However, it is unlikely that they would have felt it acceptable to open all the notes written and exchanged by students on campus or to install surveillance camera and microphones in the terminal rooms. In a similar vein, a reporter was outraged that her editor had pulled an unfinished article from her electronic file and published it without her permission. She said that this would never have happened if the draft had been simply left, in paper form, in her desk drawer (Lydia Dotto, personal communication).

Working in an automated office may feel like being in an electronic fishbowl because activities and performance are more exposed, but not everyone has the same access to information. At the same time that computer systems make information more available, they also permit management to regulate more precisely just who has access to what information.

Selective Information Access

We have just seen how the capabilities of office automation might be exploited to obtain information about knowledge workers in order to control them. The reverse of this—namely, permitting individual workers only selective access to information about other workers, corporate operations, and so on—is another way of exerting control that office automation offers senior managers. In an environment in which access to information and information-processing resources is increasingly important for individuals exercising discretion in the pursuit of goals, whether personal, corporate, or otherwise, the ability to restrict access is a powerful element in the exercise of control. Louis Mertes of Continental Illinois Bank, project leader of what is reputedly one of the most advanced office systems in the United States, makes clear how he regards information belonging to the organization. In automating office operations at the Chicago bank, the project managers decided to develop a central library to act as "a computerized stronghold of virtually every byte of information that had been captured or stored" (*Datamation*, 1981, p. 32). It seems that Continental will not be alone in this approach.

Access is most commonly restricted through the use of passwords. Layered passwords are employed to prevent unauthorized access to the computing facility as a whole, to particular programs and files (e.g., policy-holder information), to records within files (e.g., particular classes of individuals), and even to certain fields within a record (e.g., a name is obtainable, but not the balance owing). Although these barriers have sometimes been erected as a result of pressure to preserve the privacy of citizens whose records are being held, the restrictions have also been applied quite selectively within the organization. In *Global Reach* Richard Barnett and Ronald Muller (1974) describe IBM's computerized global "tote board." Statistics on sales worldwide are aggregated at several levels by region, and managers are allowed to see only the portions that apply directly to them: they cannot see the "big picture" unless they are at the top of the managerial hierarchy.

In the more fully electronic office, the ability to provide selective access becomes more extensive. In effect it allows for the automatic enforcement of a "need-to-know" policy of information access. Paper-based information that previously was easily accessible because of its proximity or special knowledge of its whereabouts may become effectively off-limits to employees who are not specifically authorized to see it. To an authorized person, however, the same information becomes instantaneously available from virtually everywhere on the globe.

The attention being paid by organizations to monitoring office workers and permitting selective access to information reflects a growing awareness that information is a vital organizational resource and hence must be managed specifically, just as money and personnel are. The systematic approach to doing this has been referred to as "Information Resource Management" (IRM). The breathtaking scope of some data-processing professionals' visions of the future possibilities of IRM is revealed in an article by Robert Landau (Landau et al., 1982). Every possible type of information, regardless of medium, and every possible process that can be performed on it, regardless of device used, would come within the purview of the information manager. We should not overlook the fact that as long as there are still employees in the office, managing information means managing people.

What I have shown is that office automation is making it possible for technical forms of workplace control to be extended to occupational ranks that previously had not been exposed to such techniques. Furthermore, the way in which this is being done is consistent with longstanding principles of scientific management. Skills are being captured by the systematic study of labor processes; conception is separated from execution by the embedding of expertise in software owned by employers; and information workers are being controlled through management's electronic monitoring of their behavior and the regulation of their access to information. Howard Carlsson, a General Motors psychologist, expresses this succinctly: "The Computer may be to middle management what the assembly line is to the hourly worker" (quoted in Braverman, 1974, p. 339). In other words, basic Taylorist principles of management are fundamental and powerful enough to be applicable to professionals and managers in automated offices, a setting far removed from where they were developed. As Mike Cooley (1980) has noted, computerization is "Taylorism's latest disguise."[4]

The extent to which these principles and techniques of managerial control are found in any particular workplace will depend on a host of interacting factors. The size, history, structure, and industrial sector of a firm all have an influence. The organization's environment, including such factors as competition, cost of money, union organization, government regulation, and public attitudes can all affect the degree to which office automation is used as a means for managerial control of the workforce. In addition, much depends on what computerized production technologies are available and how they are configured in the workplace. Not all forms of office automation provide managers with the same opportunities for applying scientific management principles and exercising technical control over office workers. At the moment, the office automation market is in flux, char-

---

4. It is conventional to regard Taylorist principles as leading inevitably to fragmented and routinized jobs. However, as Braverman has formulated them, they apply very well to computerization processes that subordinate workers, without necessarily implying that the resulting jobs are factory-like in the classic sense. With their focus on knowledge and information about the work process, we can regard the principles of scientific management as foundations for an "information economy." This enables us to see more clearly that the "information age," rather than representing a decisive break with the earlier industrial society, is in fact very much part of it. We appear to entering a period of "super-industrialism" and not Bell's "post-industrialism." Toffler is perhaps more correct than appears at first glance when in *The Adaptive Corporation*, (1985) he refers to the coming era as one of "Super-Industrialism," though he switched to the term "Third Wave" when people thought he was talking about "smokestack" industries (Toffler, 1985, p. xxvii).

acterized by the rapid introduction of new products and competing views of how office systems should be structured.

TECHNOLOGICAL ALTERNATIVES

Every technology offers to varying degrees social choices about the way it is developed, deployed, and subsequently used in practice. Thus social organization has an impact on technology before the technology has an impact on social forms. One of the major shaping influences in any technology is the struggle for control—who is going to have a say in how a technology is developed, the ends to which it is put, the way it is used, and so on. The benefits do not accrue to everyone equally in all possible configurations.

Few technologies are as flexible, or offer as much opportunity for people to impress their intentions, as those that underlie office automation. This versatility is illustrated by the fact that the chips at the heart of a word processor may be exactly the same as those in a child's toy, an industrial robot, or a missile guidance system. A good time to observe the range of options offered by a technology in a particular area of application is in the early, formative stages. Once the technology has matured and been solidified, it presents us with an appearance of inevitability that obscures the possibilities that have been closed off. Such an opportune time for studying office automation is now, while it is still full of apparent promise and relatively little is in place—either in real offices or in people's unconscious expectations about what it should be. At the moment two main technological trends are evident. To a considerable degree they reflect significantly different ways control can be exercised in offices and a struggle over control of the electronic office. The outcome of this struggle may be decisive in determining the eventual shape of office automation and the lives of information workers.

Until now the discussion of possibilities for controlling office workers has been based primarily on the capabilities of integrated office systems, as opposed to personal computing. Such integrated office systems evolved directly out of earlier stages of computing, with its reliance upon large mainframe computers. Office automation services would be provided to users through workstations acting as terminals to central host machines. Integrated office systems have the following general characteristics:

Workstations are more or less permanently connected to or at least heavily dependent on other shared computing resources.

The initiative within companies for introducing such systems comes mainly from the data-processing or a similar department with the strong support of senior management

A good deal of planning and coordination precedes and accompanies implementation.

The companies that develop, manufacture, and promote such systems are often very large, even giant, corporations (e.g., IBM, AT&T).

Software is written by the equipment vendors, their affiliates, or by the data-processing department.

The market is growing relatively slowly in spite of massive advertising.

Major obstacles to wider adoption are: difficulty in cost justification, user resistance, management's inadequate detailed knowledge of how an office really works.

Technical control is possible: that is, workers can be managed through the equipment itself.

Personal computing grew out of quite a different tradition and in its early years flourished independently of and in competition with the mainstream of business computing. Its seminal leaders worked outside corporations and viewed their work in clearly antiestablishment terms (see Levy, 1984). Personal computing contrasts sharply with integrated office computing in many of its essential characteristics:

Powerful standalone computers are connected only sporadically to other computing resources.

Initiative within companies for introducing equipment comes from individual users. (Apparently in many cases employees first bring in their personal computers from home or sneak orders for them past corporate purchasing departments by referring to them as "test equipment" or the like [see *Forbes*, 1982].

Relatively little planning and coordination is done prior to purchase; decisions are made individually on the basis of immediate anticipated application or else as an experiment.

Companies originally selling personal computers tended to be newer, smaller, and more entrepreneurial (e.g., Apple, Commodore, Osborne, Grid, Atari).

Software for personal computers used in business is written by many small software firms or else developed by the individual users themselves (even IBM did not develop the software for its Personal Computer, and data-processing departments seldom write programs to run on these small computers).

The market for personal computers is growing rapidly: 80 percent per year between 1980 and 1984. There were eight million in use by 1985, according to International Data Resources (see *Fortune*, 1986). (Personal computers are sometimes referred to as "rabbits" for their apparent breeding properties.)

The major obstacles to expansion are cost and difficulties in interconnection.

The management of users depends on bureaucratic rather than technical means.

In spite of their many differing characteristics, the functional capabilities of personal computing and integrated office systems overlap considerably. Both can be used in the preparation and communication of documents, for data analysis, and for financial planning; in fact, the popularity of Visicalc and its electronic spreadsheet look-alikes is due partly to its superiority to corresponding programs on centralized computing facilities. Although personal computing is not as developed for communications purposes as integrated systems are, the growth of relatively "passive" local and public data networks can be used to overcome this disadvantage considerably. Then the large databases attached to mainframe computers would act as specialized "file servers" rather than the general-purpose central hubs that they are in integrated systems. In other words, integrated systems and personal computing offer two distinguishable and viable alternatives for providing the technical basis of electronic offices.[5]

Where personal computing and integrated systems differ crucially is in the issue of control: who controls the activities in the office, and how is that control exercised? Personal computing leaves much more control in the hands of individual information workers, whereas the in-

5. In practice there is no perfectly clean separation between integrated and personal computing. These terms are used here to represent "pure types" for the purposes of analysis. Furthermore, they do not exhaust the possibilities for viable systems architectures. Democratically run offices (were they to exist) would probably adopt electronic systems sharing many features of both personal computing and integrated systems and at the same time maintain some quite distinctive characteristics too. (See Clement, 1981, for a preliminary discussion of such alternative models.)

tegrated approach implies further concentration of effective control at senior corporate levels. The various ways managers could extend technical control discussed earlier depend heavily on integrated systems. Purely personal systems do not provide convenient means for employers to keep close track of software and data, even when they formally own it, or to monitor the behavior of employees. Collecting the statistics would require extensive manual work.

Personal computing has grown much faster than integrated systems—so much so that it is considered a key element in the shift to so-called end-user computing (EUC), which is generally taken to mean that users have a strong say over the computing resources they use to carry out their own jobs. Throughout the development of personal computing, it has been seen as a challenge to central computing authorities. In spite of often active resistance from this quarter, personal computing/EUC has gained sufficient hold in corporations that it is widely recognized that the former monopoly of data-processing departments on computing has effectively been broken. If personal computing represents "nothing less than the democratization of computing," as Kathleen Wiegner (1982, p. 119) suggests, then it appears as if information workers can look forward to increasing autonomy in the future electronic office. Certainly one of the main attractions of personal computing is the degree of control it offers individuals. As personal computers become easier to master technically, they become increasingly a tool that employees can use for whatever they see fit. The constraints are primarily technical and personal (the individual's lack of expertise), rather than those imposed by the organization in which the individual is embedded. To the extent that middle-level workers do retain an advantaged position in offices, we can attribute the popularity of personal computing at least in part to the relative autonomy it preserves in comparison to integrated office systems. In fact, it is not inconceivable that purchasing personal computers may in some cases be a preemptive act, taken to forestall the imposition of integrated systems. Undoubtedly there are other factors that also account for the present success of personal computing. Personal computers are relatively easy to buy because they have a much lower threshold cost than integrated systems, which can cost hundreds of thousands of dollars in even minimal configurations. Similarly, they do not require a deep understanding of office functions prior to installation. Individuals will often know enough of their own particular situations to justify purchase, and lengthy planning processes can be avoided.

However, there are good reasons for suspecting that personal computing will not continue to have a separate existence in large organizations. Existing barriers to integrated systems are likely to diminish in several ways. Costs are coming down, offices are becoming better understood in a systematic way; and as people become more familiar with computer devices in offices, resistance to the integrated systems may diminish.

Another reason to suspect strongly that personal computing will not become the dominant technical form in large electronic offices stems from the difficulties in centrally controlling their use and the lost opportunity for controlling information workers. A number of signs of management dissatisfaction with personal computing have appeared in the business press. An article entitled "How Personal Computers Backfire" (*Business Week*, 1982) reports that middle managers are using personal computers to maintain their own databases and write their own programs. This poses problems for the company. When a manager leaves, there may be no one else who understands what he or she was doing. Individual databases may not agree with each other or with the company database.

From the point of view of senior data-processing managers, the widely discussed solution to this problem is to centralize control of data and software and tie personal computers into the existing mainframe computers. North American Phillips Corp. insists that all the company's microcomputers be tied into the same large, central information banks. Since controlling the information is as important as controlling the physical hardware, this step represents a reduction in the autonomy of the managers. Bic Corp. went even further and tried to discourage managers from bringing personal computers altogether, though it is unlikely that this prohibition succeeded. One of the ways in which PCs are being integrated into the office is through senior management's insistence that only certain software packages can be used. One company that does this is Home Insurance, whose vice-president for Management Information Systems claims, "With our software we're turning PC's into intelligent terminals" (Ditlea, 1985; p. 86).

Academics have been studying the problems managers face with personal computing. One survey of 39 senior information systems managers concluded that:

> EUC (end user computing) has been a "bottom up" movement. To be effective in the long run, a "top-down" approach to EUC planning and coordination should be undertaken. EUC policies and guidelines and the framework for planning should be established by top management and implemented in organizations. (Alavi, 1985, p. 175)

Kenneth Laudon (1985) drew a similar conclusion from a survey of 25 of the largest corporate users of PCs in the financial industry. He determined that PCs should be connected to corporate information systems, and that the way to do this was for PCs to be more actively managed and decision making more centralized.

Some equipment manufacturers are responding overtly to these control issues. Vector Graphic has advertised a computer that it calls the "Company Computer," which in all other respects appears functionally equivalent to other personal business computers. This suggests that Vector Graphic is trying to take advantage of the fear that knowledge workers have too much independence in their use of "personal" machines. Of course the main company to watch in this regard is IBM.

According to an article in *Datamation*, the days of IBM PC and PC-XT are "definitely numbered." The top-of-the-line PC, the AT, is IBM's "strategic product" and will "ultimately tie individual users more tightly to the IBM mainframe world" (O'Keeffe, 1985, p.74). The key to this integration is the network architecture that is adopted for communication between computing devices. IBM has developed its own set of protocol standards, Systems Network Architecture (SNA), in opposition to the internationally developed standard, Open Systems Interconnection (OSI). The telecommunications expert David Passmore notes:

> In contrast to other computer network architectures, SNA adheres to a principle of strong centralized control of the network by mainframe processors. All session establishment, routing, and network management functions are controlled by one or more host mainframe processors in the network.
>
> IBM's SNA has already become the de facto network architecture standard for most of the Fortune 500 companies. (Passmore, 1985, p. 98)

More recently, *Software Canada* (1986, p. 8) reports that International Resource Development Co. has concluded from recent announcements by IBM that the company

> has reached an internal consensus regarding the integration of PC's into its mainframe environments—PC's will be subordinate to mainframes whenever possible. The promised integration of IBM's new token ring LAN with SNA, as well as the development of LU6.2 are seen to reinforce this view.
>
> Any new products that IBM introduces for micro-to-mainframe com-

> munications can be expected to generate, at least indirectly, the need for more mainframe processing power, the report says.

Partly this is because IBM can earn higher profits from mainframes, but it is also because IBM's phenomenal success in the past has depended on supplying what its principal clients, the major corporations, want from computing.

Although IBM is implementing SNA in a way that makes mainframes essential and discourages direct PC-to-PC communications, this is not because it is technically infeasible to do otherwise. The announcement of the software product AdaptSNA PCcom demonstrates this point:

> It offers high speed micro-to-micro communication and file transfer capabilities without the need for mainframe intervention. [I]t can also be used for large corporate SNA switched networks. In such networks, PC's are typically equipped with [specialized hardware] and don't allow the micros to communicate with each other. Peer-to-peer communication, however, is possible with this software. (*Datamation*, 1985, p. 156)

If IBM can effectively assert its technical/organizational vision, then personal computers in large offices will evolve into powerful workstations strongly connected to corporate-wide computer systems. There will be local processing, but important software and data will be centrally managed. In other words, the prospect is that personal computing will steadily be absorbed into a subordinate role within the centralized hierarchy of corporate computing systems. This certainly is the opinion of Martin Goetz, senior vice-president of Applied Data Resources, the world's largest system software company:

> Mainframes will not go the way of the dinosaur. They are required for executing the mammoth number of batch and online programs and applications. They are, and will continue to be, the central point for the corporation's control of information.
>
> Personal computers tied to mainframes will perfectly complement the mainframes if they are viewed as extensions to mainframes and not as independent and autonomous computers within a corporation. (see *Canadian Office*, 1983, p. 3)

If this comes about, then the current wave of PC's can be seen as Trojan horses. Introduced in the guise of tools offering autonomy to users, they will be turned into extensions of the central computing system and the means for extending managerial control.

Personal computing is not antithetical to large organizations. It can certainly contribute to productivity. Further, it can play a role in maintaining the strategy of responsible autonomy (see Friedman, 1977) and discourage workers from organizing themselves to oppose higher management levels. (According to one business consultant: "An Apple a day keeps the union away" [*Wall Street Journal*, 1981].) However, like the spirit of individualism with which it is allied, personal computing has serious limitations in large organizations. In the long run the integrated systems approach appears to offer more to those in charge of large organizations. Office automation based on highly integrated workstations means that office workers can be monitored more closely, directed in their tasks via a machine, and regulated in their access to information and information-processing resources. This will aid management extracting a deeper understanding of how large offices work and lead to further automation. The extent to which this actually happens will depend on many factors, but there are indications that such a trend is underway. In the absence of organized opposition, office automation will likely be built upon centrally managed, integrated systems accompanied by the hierarchical forms of control this implies.

Because computing and telecommunications provide the potential for decentralized structures and openness of access, it has been argued that new office technologies will result in more egalitarian patterns of communication and use. However, the preexisting strongly hierarchical character of the host organization will discourage this development. We already have powerful media that by their intrinsic nature are nonhierarchical—namely, telephony and mail. The reason that employees do not phone or write to their company president is not some built-in technical bias, but social structure. We may therefore expect the structure and culture of the already centralized organizations in which office automation is embedded to impose centralized patterns of communications and access. Given that the technologies that underlie office information systems are highly malleable in terms of structuring information flows, we should expect them to be designed to reinforce this preexisting pattern. In other words, we may start with technologies that permit openness, but by the time they are deployed in real organizations, their shape owes much to the interests of those who make the purchases.

It could also be argued that personal computing is more productive than the centralized alternative, and that this would be sufficient to ensure its survival in large corporations. However, even though changes in labor process and associated production technologies have typically been brought about in the name of increased productivity, we should not accept this as the sole reason for their development and perpetuation. As Marglin (1974) and Stone (1974) have pointed out, technical superiority and economic efficiency were often secondary to the exercise of power in the emergence of early forms of capitalist organization of production. Noble (1980, 1984) and Shaiken (1984) have made similar arguments in the case of numerically controlled machine tools. It would be extraordinary if a technology as rich in opportunity for extending control as office automation were not seized upon to exploit this aspect of its potential, even at the cost of some loss of productivity.

In the current debates and market competition over what role personal computers should play in large corporations, we can see the joint transformation of social relationships and technological infrastructure in office work. The existing relationship between middle-level employees and their superiors has an influence on the development of office technology. Senior managers prefer highly integrated systems loaded with expertise and based on the IBM model, whereas professionals and middle managers are more likely to opt for independent personal computers. Although the outcome of this contest is not firmly established, it will reflect the relative strengths of the two groups. The advantage that computer users currently enjoy vis-à-vis their superiors, because of the novelty and rapid growth in the desktop computing field, will likely disappear as the pace of innovation slackens and computing becomes ubiquitous, routine, and hence institutionalized. Middle-level employees have asserted their relative autonomy and resisted attempts at regulation, but without organized promotion of their interests they will in the long run be at a disadvantage in the computing arena.

Whichever approach to office automation is successfully promoted to predominance will in turn influence workplace relationships by reinforcing the position of its most active backers. Personal computing would enhance the autonomy of middle-level employees. More likely, however, it is integrated systems that will be installed and used by higher organizational levels to subordinate professionals, technicians, and middle managers. This would mean that the work of middle-level information workers in large organizations will become increasingly bounded in scope and direction. Through this complex interplay of social and technological forces, we see the future of office work being given distinctive shape.

REFERENCES

Alavi, M. (1985). "End-User Computing: The MIS Managers' Perspective." *Information & Management*, 8, pp. 171–78.

Albury, D., and J. Schwartz (1982). *Partial Progress: The Politics of Science and Technology*. London: Pluto Press.

Barker, J., and Downing, H. (1979). "Word Processing and the Transformation of the Patriarchal Relations of Control in the Office." *Capital and Class*, 10, Spring, pp. 64–99.

Barnett, R. J., and R. E. Muller (1974). *Global Reach: The Power of the Multinational Corporations*. New York: Simon and Schuster.

Berman, B. (1986), "Bureaucracy and the Computer Metapher," *Studies in Communication and Information Technology,* Queen's University, Kingston, Canada.

Braverman, H. (1974). *Labor and Monopoly Capital*. New York: Monthly Review Press.

Briefs, U. (1981). "Re-Thinking Industrial Work: Computer Effects on Technical White-Collar Workers." In *Computers in Industry 2*. Amsterdam: North-Holland Publishing Co.

Business Week (1982). "How Personal Computers Can Backfire," July 12, pp. 56–59.

Canadian Office (1983). October, p. 3.

Clement, Andrew (1981)."Community Computing," *Journal of Community Communications*, 4, 3, pp. 10–15.

Clement, Andrew (1984). "Electronic Management: The New Technology of Workplace Surveillance." In *Proceedings of CIPS Session 84*, Toronto: Canadian Information Processing Society.

Clement, Andrew (1986). "Managerial Control and On-line Processing at a Large Insurance Firm." Ph.D. dissertation, University of Toronto.

Cooley, M. (1981). "The Taylorisation of Intellectual Work," In L. Levidow and B. Young (eds.): *Science, Technology and the Labor Process*: *Marxist Studies*, vol. 1. London: CSE Books.

Cooley, M. (1982). *Architect or Bee: The Human/Technology Relationship*. Boston: South End Press.

Datamation (1981). "Changing the Shape of Work," August, pp. 28–34.

Davis, D. (1986). "Artificial Intelligence Enters the Mainstream," *High Technology*, July, pp. 16–23.

Ditlea, S. (1985). "Befriending the Befuddled," *Datamation*, 15 June, pp. 84–90.

Drucker, P. (1969). *The Age of Discontinuity*. New York: Harper & Row.

Duncan, M. (1981). "Microelectronics: Five Areas of Subordination," In L. Levidow and B. Young (eds.). *Science, Technology and the Labour Process*: *Marxist Studies*, vol.1. London: CSE Books.

Edwards, R. (1979). *Contested Terrain: The Transformation of the Workplace in the Twentieth Century*. New York: Basic Books.

Feigenbaum, E., and P. McCorduck (1983). *The Fifth Generation: Artificial Intelligence and Japan's Computer Challenge to the World*. New York: Signet.

Fortune (1979). Advertisement for Basic Four, 12 March, p. 53.

Fortune (1986). "Trends in Computing," A White Paper to Management (special advertising supplement) prepared by International Data Corporation, 23 June, pp. 65–86.

Friedman, Andrew L. (1977). *Industry and Labour*. London: Macmillan.

Garson, B. (1981), "The Electronic Sweatshop: Scanning the Office of the Future." *Mother Jones*, July, pp. 32–41.

Glenn, E., and R. Feldberg, (1980). "Proletarianizing Clerical Work: Technical and Organizational Control in the Office." in A. Zimbalist (ed.) *Case Studies on the Labor Process*. New York: Monthly Review Press.

Globe and Mail (1981). "Providing Paperless Office is a $300 Billion Business," 26 January.

Greenbaum, J. (1977). *In the Name of Efficiency*. Philadelphia: Temple University Press.

Gregory, J. and K. Nussbaum (1980). *Race Against Time: Automation in the Office*. National Association of Office Workers, 1224 Huron Street, Cleveland, OH 44115.

Hirschheim, R.A. (1985). *Office Automation: An Organizational Perspective*. New York: John Wiley.

Hoos, I. (1961). *Automation in the Office*. Washington, D.C.: Public Affairs Press.

Jackson, L. (1984). "Office Automation Provides Opportunity to Examine What Workers Actually Do," *Industrial Engineering* 16, 1, pp. 90–93.

Kann, M. (1985). "The Dilemma of the Technocrats," In L. Lapham (ed) *High Technology and Human Freedom*. Washington, D.C.: Smithsonian Institution Press.

Landau, R. (1982). "Some New Approaches to the Emerging Office Information Systems." R. Landau, J. Bair, and J. H. Siegman. *Emerging Office Systems*. Norwood, N.J.: Ablex.

Laudon, K. (1985). "Organizational Environment and Management Policy" Paper presented at the New York University Symposium on Integrating Systems for End Users—Managers, Micros and Mainframes. New York, 22–24 May.

Levy, S. (1984). *Hackers: Heroes of the Computer Revolution*. New York: Doubleday.

McArthur, Douglas (1986). "Hi-Tech Tattletales." *Globe and Mail Report on Business Magazine*, Spring, pp. 73–74.

Macfarlane, D. (1983). "What You Get When You Buy Office Automation," *Datamation*, February, pp. 102–14.

Marglin, S. (1974). "What Do Bosses Do? The Origins and Functions of Hierarchy in Capitalist Production." *Review of Radical Political Economy*, 6, Summer, pp. 60–112.

Matteis, R. (1979). "The New Back Office Focusses on Customer Service." *Harvard Business Review*, March-April, pp. 146–59.

Noble, D. (1980). "Social Choice in Machine Design," In A. Zimbalist (ed.) *Case Studies on the Labor Process*. New York: Monthly Review Press.

Noble, D. (1984). *Forces of Production: A Social History of Industrial Automation*. New York: Knopf.

Noyce, R. N. (1980). "Creativity by Numbers." *Harvard Business Review*, May-June, pp. 122–32.

O'Keeffe, L. (1985). "IBM's OA Puzzle," *Datamation*, February, pp. 74–78.

Passmore, D. (1985). "The Networking Standards Collision," *Datamation*, February, pp. 98–108.

Rockart, J. and M. Treacy (1982). "The CEO Goes On-line," *Harvard Business Review*, January-February, pp. 82–88.

Schiller, D. (1985). "The Emerging Global Grid: Planning for What," *Media, Culture and Society*, 7, pp. 105–25.

Science Council of Canada (1980). "The Impact of the Microelectronic Revolution on Work and Working." Ottawa. SCC.

Shaiken, H. (1984). *Work Transformed: Automation and Labor in the Computer Age*. New York: Holt, Rinehart and Winston.

Software Canada (1986). "Communications Barriers Hinder Microlink Growth," vol. 5, 4, p. 8.

Stone, K. (1974). "The Origins of Job Structures in the Steel Industry," *Radical America*, 7, 6, pp. 19–64.

Strassman, P. (1985). *Information Payoff: The Transformation of Work in the Electronic Age*. New York: Free Press.

Toffler, A. (1985). *The Adaptive Corporation*. New York: Bantam.

U.S. Congress, Office of Technology Assessment (1985). *Automation of America's Offices*. OTA-CIT-287, Washington, D.C.: Government Printing Office.

Wall Street Journal (1981). "Computer Strike Snags a Bureacracy," 19 May.

Weizenbaum, J. (1976). *Computer Power and Human Reason: From Judgment to Calculation*. San Francisco: Freeman.

Wiegner, K. (1982). "Tommorow Has Arrived," *Forbes*, 15 February, pp. 111–19.

Wiener, N. (1961). *Cybernetics or Control and Communication in the Animal and Machine*, 2d ed. Cambridge: MIT Press.

Withington, F. (1980). "Coping with Computer Proliferation," *Harvard Business Review*, May-June, pp. 152–64.

Zuboff, S. (1982). "New Worlds of Computer-Mediated Work," *Harvard Business Review*, September-October, pp. 142–52.

12. Electronic Homework in West Germany: A Critical Appraisal

Jörg Becker

Jürgen Habermas, in his classic study *Strukturwandel der Öffentlichkeit*, originally published in 1962, described the demise of the liberal-democratic sector. He summarized as follows:

> The domain of discourse that is concerned with the nature of the bourgeoisie has itself become irrevocably divided. The public is split into a minority who are engaged in private intellectual discourse and the majority who are characterized by their overt public consumption. (Habermas, 1969, p. 192)[1]

According to Habermas, "nonpublic discourses" are integrated into the whole system through their "public manifestations" via the culture industry's norms. In another publication Habermas expressed these ideas as follows:

> The political public sphere of a social welfare state is characterised by a peculiar weakening of its critical functions. At one time the process of making proceedings public (Publizität) was intended to subject persons or affairs to public reason and to make political decisions subject to appeal before the court of public opinion. But often enough today, the process of making public simply serves the archaic policies of special interests; in the form of publicity it wins a public prestige for people of affairs, thus making them worthy of acclamation in a climate of non-public opinion. (Habermas, 1979, p. 200)

Such criticism of change in the public sector is not new. In 1950 David Riesman published his classic *The Lonely Crowd*, in which he explores the mentality of the externally directed character whose outlook is a reaction to the values and norms of society. Theodor W. Adorno and Max Horkheimer evolved arguments very close to Riesman's in their study *The Dialectics of Enlightenment*, published in the 1940s (trans. 1972). A great deal of empirical research on differ-

1. Unless otherwise attributed, all translations are mine.

ent themes can be cited to show that these studies are dealing with verifiable realities and that public discussion of the basic problems of democratic societies has diminished. What Adorno, Horkheimer, Riesman, or Habermas could not have seen is the realization and then strengthening of a negative socialization of the individual by the process of informatization. On the one hand, the electro-technical environment penetrates ever deeper into areas of private experience, while the private sphere is ever more controlled and regulated by exterior forces. This results in the apparent contradiction that while electronic goods (home computers and videos) and the electronic service sector (videotex, cable television) are coming on the market in ever-increasing mass, these products and services in themselves promote very individualistic modes of use. Those who uncritically hail the informatization of our societies as a vehicle for strengthening the freedom of the individual, bringing with it an increased individual access to new goods and services, will be proven completely wrong. Privacy, intimacy, and individuality—in short, the general reproductive sector of society—could wind up being externally controlled. It is clear from empirical studies that such developments are not new or unusual. Yet at present they are undergoing an enormous quantitative increase, and it is possible that the informatization of the private domain will lead to a qualitative change in the relationship of the public to the private sector.

Neil Postman (1982) has cited some graphic examples of the effects of informatization on child rearing. When, as happens in the United States, children spend more time in front of the television than in school, when their social awareness is more influenced by the television than by their fathers, and when they are initiated into the world of adult emotions and knowledge through television viewing, then they are no longer able to participate in the process of balancing their experience of the world as children against the alien world of the adult. Thus a necessary component in the process of maturation is lost. The private world of the child is destroyed. If this sanctuary, which is so important for the development of the individual and the democratic potential of society, is reduced or destroyed, then the potential to deal with the world on an individual, autonomous, and independent basis is lost as well. These tendencies are dangerous for both the individual and society.

It is exactly this historical and continually changing relationship between the public and private spheres that ought to be the focus of every democratically oriented theoretical debate concerning the social conditions and consequences of the new information technologies (ITs). Because it blends the public and private domains, the following case study on electronic homework is especially pertinent. It goes without saying that electronic homework is only a small and very specific area of new IT application, yet it must also be seen in the large context of the informatization of our societies.

DISTRIBUTION OF JOBS AND LABOR TO HOMES

In Chapter 16 of his book *The Third Wave* (1981), the American futurologist Alvin Toffler describes the possibilities of the electronically based home workplace as follows:

> Hidden inside our advance to a new production system is a potential for social change so breathtaking in scope that few among us have been willing to face its meaning. For we are about to revolutionize our homes as well.
>
> Apart from encouraging smaller work units, apart from permitting decentralization and deurbanization of production, apart from altering the actual character of work, the new production system could shift literally millions of jobs out of the factories and offices into which the Second Wave swept them and right back where they came from originally: the home. If this were to happen, every institution we know, from the family to the school and the corporation, would be transformed. Watching masses of peasants scything a field three hundred years ago, only a madman would have dreamed that the time would soon come when the fields would be depopulated, when people would crowd into urban factories to earn their daily bread. And only a madman would have been right. Today it takes an act of courage to suggest that our biggest factories and office towers may, within our lifetimes, stand empty, reduced to use as ghostly warehouses or converted into living space. Yet this is precisely what the new mode of production makes possible: a return to cottage industry on a new, higher, electronic basis, and with it a new emphasis on the home as the center of society. (Toffler, 1981, p. 194)

This and similar descriptions are to be found in abundance in popular as well as serious scientific writing. They both display two essential methodological weaknesses: the lack of an empirical basis and the fact that projected or observed social change is deduced by technical-determinist rather than social factors. In order to pinpoint future areas of conflict arising from the growth of the electronically based work place in the Federal Republic of Germany (FRG), it is necessary to describe the social scope and development of this phenomenon, which can be only partially attributed to the process of technical change. Thus we shall briefly discuss the following five parameters:

1. The office in the so-called information society
2. Identity and work experience
3. Unemployment
4. Flexible working hours
5. Female Labor

After this, pilot projects as well as empirical and theoretical work from the FRG will be discussed. The resulting conclusions concerning policy regulations and future research projects will relate back to the five general parameters mentioned above.

SOCIETAL CONDITIONS

The Office in the So-Called Information Society

It is generally accepted by the scientific community that the structure and function of the office will experience a rapid and intensive alteration in the social transition to the "information society." Three highly relevant studies on the development of the office have been carried out in West Germany.

In 1976 the scientific and political community in the FRG was startled by an unpublished internal study by the manufacturer Siemens, Inc. The results of the project known as "Büro 1990" were so alarming that it was impossible to keep them confidential. The project had the following objectives (Siemens, 1976):

To develop possible internal rationalization strategies

To document anticipated changes in the technical hardware of office automation

To pinpoint possible threats to the firm's products markets

To provide catalysts for changes in, and the further development of, its range of products

Taking these objectives into account and reducing them to criteria of economic rationalization and optimization of the company's market position, the study came to the following conclusion. Proceeding from the assumption that information is the subject matter of office work, it distinguished three types of office workplaces:

1. Intensive communications-oriented workplaces (18 percent of the total)
2. Information- and communication-intensive workplaces (66 percent of the total)

3. Labor-intensive workplaces (16 percent of the total)

Because projected rationalization and automation presuppose the standardization of work processes, the degree of standardization of the different types was examined. The proportion of labor that can be standardized for each of the types is as follows: 42.9 percent in workplaces covered by type 1; 38.2 percent for type 2; and 64.9 percent for type 3; the average proportion is 48 percent.

Through the implementation of data and word processing alone, an average of 25 percent of the work relating to all three types can be automated. If we proceed from the premise that in the FRG 40 percent of all jobs are connected to this area (and this is a very conservative estimate), then the 25 percent of the Siemens study can be computed as representing a potential rationalization of 2.5 million workplaces. If we apply this percentage for formalization and automation only to those who are employed in office work, then we come up with the following prognosis. By the mid-1970s, approximately 10 million people were employed in office work, 2.7 million (27 percent) of them in the area of information processing. "Büro 1990" projected that as a result of the formalization of the workplace, 1.1 million people would have to accept jobs that would be more monotonous and less motivating than those which they have at present. Approximately 0.6 million people would be made jobless as a result of automation programs.

The question of job losses in the automated office is also a major concern of a report published by Prognos, Inc., in 1978. According to Prognos, the new information technologies could lead to a reduction of at least 30 to 40 percent of office jobs. The situation in the office is characterized by Prognos in the following terms:

The low amount of investment in the workplace and its environment

The difficulty of measuring the productivity of the office

The fact that the value of an improved information process has yet to be proved in some cases

The lack of Management experience in introducing machinery and hardware into offices

Experts, however, say that the office workplace will be eventually equipped with telephones, teletype machines, keyboards, and machines for display and hard copy. All this equipment will be modularly designed and connected through a broad two-way computerized telecommunication system. Today the investment required for workplace equipment is no more expensive than the annual cost of a normal clerical worker. The amount of productivity gained by the use of this equipment will be very high, but it depends on the acceptance of these machines in an environment that has not, up to now, been characterized by the use of machines. The productivity growth to be realized depends on the integration of these systems into the institution or into society. When this report was published, there were 100,000 display terminals in use in the FRG. By the mid-1980s, experts predict that this figure will have risen to 500,000.

Wolf Dietrich Rauch's 1982 study is a comprehensive theoretical appraisal of modern office information systems. In this cautious and critically balanced investigation, the author describes the contradictory functions and applications of office information systems. Office automation has taken on an ambiguous quality on the level of isolated system functions and separate hardware facilities. Rationalization, for example, can make the office a more humane place to work in and can increase its economic competitiveness. Yet it can also lead to a worsening in the conditions of work as well as to the outright destruction of workplaces. The integration of office functions could result in the enhancement, enrichment, and diversification of work, but it could lead also to specialization, monotony, and further alienation. The general informatization of the office can demystify the decision-making process and, on the widest possible level, allow for the possibility of multilateral participation. It can also destroy personal interaction and submit intellectual work to Taylorist methodology. The introduction of information systems into the office, though fulfilling a basic need, will not necessarily achieve optimum results. "Success," in this instance, relates first and foremost to the function of office information systems and not to the nature of this process or its consequences.

The ambiguity of individual arguments and the lack of practical experience with such systems mean that it is at present impossible to say whether their advantages outweigh their problems, as there is no sound basis for judgment in this matter. Office information systems cannot be analyzed in isolation, because they are inextricably linked to the general informatization of society. Although it is perhaps one of the most important manifestations of the basic innovation of "information through microelectronics," the pros and cons can only be considered in the widest possible context.

Rauch states that for office information systems to fulfill positive and socially beneficial functions, three conditions must be met during the transition to the so-called information society:

1. Access to information must, as a matter of principle, be free.
2. Informatization has to counteract the tendency toward the deper-

sonalization and alienation of human labor.

3. Informatization has to counteract the quantification and specialization (in the Taylorist meaning of the word) of intellectual labor.

Identity and Work Experience

Production is, at one and the same time, work and a utilization process. It is the tangibility and usefulness of the endeavor that gives the work process its value. Work therefore is defined by its purpose and content. In the utilization process, work is reduced to the quantitatively defined timespan necessary to carry out the task. This ambiguity within the production process enables the individual to identify with his or her work, more or less without regard for the utilization process. Individual identification with the work process consists of three elements: the worker's attitude to the product; the worker's attitude to the producer; and the worker's relations to his or her own labor.

Although these three dimensions may differ within the production process, they are of considerable importance to the workers themselves, merging within their work experience. In a report on alienation processes, the psychologist Ute Volmerg (1978) summarizes the results of previous research. The worker's attitude to the product is characterized by work patterns and is calculated without regard to the product itself. The work process is governed by the principle of quantification and the need to minimize the cost of the product. It has come to embody elements of domination. As workers' identification with the idea of the product disappears, so does their relationship with their own individual needs. The attitude of the worker to the producer can only be experienced as one of alienation. Thus the individual loses his or her understanding of the total integration of the production process as well as the social character of work, which is objectified and manifested in the means of production. This, in itself, is no longer personified by a single producer. It is experienced as alienation and subjugation to anonymous power. The individual functions only as a single element in the socialized work process. When individuals are made to work on a cooperative basis that undermines the individuality of the worker, then the cooperation is but a pretense. This cooperation produces isolation, competition, and a defeatist mentality. The last dimension of subjective work experience, the attitude of the individual to his or her own labor, has undergone an irrevocable change in the sphere of industrial production. According to Volmerg (1978), the rationalization of the work process has left no room for individual variation in the shaping of the product. In fact, the opposite occurs: the individuality of the worker becomes a source of error, which can only have a negative effect on the smooth flow of production.

The effects of the industrial labor process on the individual have never been properly researched by orthodox ergonomists. To put it more clearly: the external and tangible effects (e.g., curvature of the spine, blood pressure problems, high adrenalin production) do not give us an exact image of the kinds of sickness that these work processes produce. They act rather as a cover-up. The greatest disorders that are produced by contemporary industrial work, such as stress resulting from continual pressure, tension, agitation, fear, the blocking of emotion and self-confidence, are of a psychosomatic nature and can pass from stages of aggression to those of regression and resignation. Volmerg summarizes research into psychosomatic disruption of the workplace:

> Psychological collapse in the workplace occurs always at the end of a definite pattern of development, in the course of which the individual experiences an undermining of his/her identity. The individual is daily confronted with this process of undermining through the necessity to adapt to the conditions of work. This in itself contradicts his/her own psycho-physical structures. This is especially so in the case of work of a repetitive character or work that requires periods of observation. Its general characteristics are monotony, uniformity, repetition, and a lack of stimulation. According to the theory of activation, in order to fulfill his/her appointed tasks carefully and efficiently, the individual needs constant sensorial activation provided by outside stimulation. If this is not available in the work process itself, then there is a reduction of alertness which cannot be renewed through inner stimulation. (Volmerg, 1978, p. 101)

The knowledge gained from psychology and sociology concerning psychosomatic diseases has, for the most part, come from empirical studies carried out in the area of industrial employment. At this point in time—and this pertains to the very core of this study—the information society is imposing industrial work conditions on information-oriented professions, above all in the office workplace. It is most probable that these industrialized offices will produce their own equivalent of industry-related psychosomatic disease.

Unemployment

It can no longer be denied that the introduction of new ITs will have great middle and long-term effects on employment Yet not only are most studies and data collections under consideration inadequate from a methodological perspective, but the complexity of the issue itself makes it hard to arrive at a valid prognosis on the state of employment. As the microchip, a convergent technology, is the technological core of new ITs, every productive and reproductive sector of any given society will be touched, and thus the effect on employment will be multicausal and accumulative. In the following section, reference is made only to the study of the economist Axel Zerdick (1984), as it stands head and shoulders above the mass of literature that is at present available in this area.

In a four-sided matrix, Zerdick distinguishes two types of producers: media producers (e.g., publishers, broadcasters) and producers of media techniques (e.g., consumer technologies, telecommunications). Zerdick expects a small growth in employment among media producers, but this will pale in comparison with the growth in turnover within the media industry itself. He predicts no growth in employment in the area of media techniques. Even though this area has an above-average yearly growth in productivity of approximately 10 percent, it is also experiencing the earliest and most intensive introduction of techniques that are less dependent on human labor. Moreover, this branch of industry employs 350,000 out of a total of 26 million workers, and any rise in employment in this sector would have very little effect on the overall employment situation.

Zerdick predicts that the effect on employment in the other two sides of his matrix will be qualitatively different. He distinguishes here between (1) electronic homework and (2) electronic self-service (in the public and private service sectors, such as banks and trade). With the full implementation of electronic homeworking, he projects, the introduction of cost-cutting strategies by the producers and long-term social acceptance will mean that 300,000 processing-related workplaces will change location, and one-third of those (100,000) will be lost through rationalization. Zerdick estimates that 1.6 million workplaces can be rationalized by the internal application of word-processing techniques; in the area of self-service (teletex and home computers), he puts the figure at 0.3 million. He predicts a total figure of 2 million unemployed by the year 1990, resulting from the accumulative effects of internal rationalization of business, the industrialization of the office, electronic self-service, and electronic homework. One must see this figure in the context of the basic unemployment of a further 2 million people in the FRG. It does not seem likely that this structural unemployment of 2 million could be lessened by any foreseeable economic growth or demographic development.

One can certainly doubt the wisdom of the speed at which the new ITs are being implemented and question the effects of the rationalization processes that accompany them. There is scientific proof that, on a national level, the negative effects of rationalization will outweigh any possible rise in job opportunities attributable to these technologies. Even if this were not the case, internalization of the fear of being made unemployed would be expressed through the same individual psychosomatic complaints that have been previously described.

Flexible Working Hours

Working hours that are fixed and generally binding for all workers through wage agreements are a result of concerted pressure applied by the organized trade union movement. Yet such arrangements have converted the working day into a time apart, over which the individual has no real control. Because the time spent working has become divided from the totality of the individual's temporal experience, it has come to embody elements of domination. The enormous growth in productivity of many branches of industry in the last decades, as well as the huge rationalization potential of new technologies, makes flexible working hours very attractive for the producer.

Job-sharing, variable working hours oriented toward production capacity, and part-time work are all forms of flexible work practices that are, in reality, bringing us toward shorter working hours. In this area, the concepts of lowering personnel expenditures and raising productivity are one and the same. Such work practices have been introduced during periods of great upward surges in economic growth, when management's potential has been severely stretched. This would be impossible during unproductive periods, in periods when there are large backlogs of orders, or in periods of stagnation. For the workforce in general, but not for the individual worker, overtime constitutes a second form of flexibility. This form of work is an adjustment to the needs of capital-intensive production facilities that operate 24 hours a day. The use of robots on the production line and of data-processing and information systems in administration and the office push the capital cost of each workplace so high that these electronic systems must be used for every single hour of a 24-hour day. Thus the incidence of shift work has been on the rise for years.

Part-time work is of particular interest in the context of this study. It is clearly recognizable as an effective instrument in mastering the problems of the assignment of labor. Producers view part-time work as a flexible hold on the labor force and as a means of raising productivity. Women constitute the bulk of part-time workers, and part-time work serves as a process through which they become partly integrated into the workforce itself. Part-time work also leads to alienation and low pay. There is little possibility of promotion; such positions are threatened much more than others by cyclical fluctuations; and they are on the lowest rung of the hierarchy of professions.

The perception and experience of time must not be discussed only in connection with negotiations concerning wages and working conditions. Such categories must be related to the subjective experience of those concerned. We know from Jean Piaget's work on the personality development of children that time awareness is an elementary component of a person's identity. Space and time are concepts that the child learns how to relate to reality. In this the child learns how to operate in the exterior world, to differentiate between subject and object, to distinguish space and time, and through this to experience himself or herself (Piaget, 1974). Through the reality of repetitive part-time work, stages of psychological development, no matter how intensely learned in childhood, are destroyed by the necessities of the production line. The effects of this kind of work on the perception of time and identity have long been known to industrial psychologists. In their pioneering study of 1957, Heinrich Popitz and his associates wrote as follows:

> In repetitive work the same actions are repeated so quickly that one's consciousness is not able to make patterns out of individual actions that themselves form the individual's awareness of time. Actions threaten to merge into each other and become indistinguishable. The point is reached where one's perceptions are overwhelmed, causing the destruction of the connection between time and place. There is no longer any individual "here and now"; it is completely blurred by the past and future. The subject is no longer oriented on any one point, but only on the continuous flow of time. Temporal consciousness dissolves in the river of time like an oildrop in water.(Popitz et al., 1957: 157–58)

In such a context action becomes meaningless. The active subject has no longer any fixed relationship to time or place and loses his or her identity. The objective conditions for flexible working hours and the subjective experience of the perception of time can only become more and more negative for those who belong to the economically, legally, socially, and psychologically disadvantaged sections of the workforce. These sections comprise part-time, shift, and temporary workers, those who belong to the low-income groups, and above all women. Flexible working hours are more and more subjugated to production timetables. In this way the monotony of increasingly repetitive electronic office work is combined with a weakening of the perception of time.

Female Labor

In a very specific way the so-called information society is a feminine society. Daniel Bell, in his classic study *The Coming of Post-Industrial Society* (1973) has already referred to this phenomenon. In a dramatic change from industrial to post industrial society, the overwhelming majority of white-collar workers are women in subordinate positions in offices and sales outlets. From a feminist point of view, this change can be described in the following manner: in the "information society" the structures of patriarchal domination assume a qualitatively new dimension wherein the emancipated working woman is immediately pacified and integrated in such a way that she is only admitted to the lower sections of the corporate hierarchy. In terms of economics, this change can be described as follows: as product and currency circulations reach a certain point of saturation, they must, in order to stimulate further growth, penetrate the reproductive sector (the family, marriage, women), which must also slowly accept the commodity principle. Certain strands of feminism, in their desire to achieve only career emancipation for women (corporate "feminism") have unwittingly paved the way for this to happen.

Qualitatively speaking, working women fit into the "information society" in the following way in the FRG. Those branches of industry that involve a good deal of information processing employ an above-average percentage of women. For example, women make up 80.0 percent of the service sector (66.2 percent of its temporary work force) 51.0 percent of the trade sector, and 47.3 percent of the finance, banking, and insurance sectors (Mäckle-Schäfer, 1984 pp. 66–77). All these sectors are at the bottom of the salary hierarchy. In any consideration of the professions, it is clear that a majority of women belong to the lower achievement groups. In 1976, 94.5 percent of women in industry were employed as unskilled labor. This is also true for the salaried professions. Even though the percentage difference between male and female employees is not as great, in the same year 58.3 percent of all women salaried workers in trade and industry were not involved in any decision-making process. The fact that on average women have a shorter working week than men is another factor that distinguishes working women from their male counterparts. In 1968, 30.6 percent of gainfully employed women worked less than 40 hours a week, and half had a workweek of less than 21 hours. In comparison, only 2.7 percent of the male workforce worked less than 40 hours a week. When these statistics are examined, it is very easy to discern discrimination against career-oriented women in the workplace.

This can, to a great degree, be explained by the double disadvantage of women's roles as both mothers and supplementary wage-earners.

Women workers will be affected in comprehensive ways by the changes in production brought on by the needs of microelectronics and their enormous effects on new ITs. Those characteristics, described above, that typify the female workforce are in fact "ideal" qualities to be promoted in the push to achieve a breakthrough in consolidating the technical potential of new ITs. In the relevant scientific literture in the FRG as well as abroad, there is a large measure of agreement that the rationalization potential of new ITs will be felt most by women in the form of a probable structural deterioration in the conditions of the female office worker.

EMPIRICAL FINDINGS

It was stated in an extensive study on electronic tele-homework published in 1982 (Ballerstedt et al., 1982) that not one new IT-supported home workplace existed in the FRG. Quantitative data concerning the number of electronic home tele-workplaces in the FRG are hard to obtain. First, it is very difficult to define exactly what constitutes an electronically based home workplace. This problem of definition exists on technical, legal, and sociological levels and is a general one encountered in the area of all new ITs. Second, a whole range of electronically supported home workplaces relate only to internal company structures and thus do not have to be publicly registered. Because of this, it is impossible to compile reliable statistics. Since the appearance of the above-mentioned study from the Batelle and Integrata Institutes in 1982, a number of new empirical studies on this theme have been published. Taking into account the well-known problems of definition and statistical quantification, the German Congress of Trade Unions in Stuttgart estimated that between 100 and 1,000 electronically based home workplaces exist in the FRG.

A technical precondition for electronically based homework is the integrated development of new ITs. The availability of services that can be supplied by the telecommunications network (e.g., teletex, telefax, videotex, data transmission) in principle enables direct communication exchange (online) and thus transfers jobs in those areas directly from traditional locations to new ones. In practice, however, these techniques have enormous limitations in the area of transmission velocity and capacity. At present, teletex is the most efficient way to transmit information. It is possible with a typewriter equipped with memory and transmission facilities using teletex to transfer a text to the storage bank of the recipient's terminal without interfering with his or her ongoing work. In comparison to the traditional telex machine, the character capacity of such machines is larger and the transmission velocity greater. At the terminals of the electronically based home workplace, integration has already begun. But it has not yet fully matured, and depending on the complexity of the sector involved, relatively heavy investment in hardware may be necessary. From a purely technical point of view, it is obvious that only such development will lead toward integrated terminals. Broad-band cabling projects such as the optical-fiber cable system in Stuttgart, the cable television pilot project in Ludwigshafen, the integrated broad-band optical-fiber regional telephone system in Berlin (BIGFON), and the construction of an Integrated Services Digital Network offer possibilities for the introduction of a comprehensive telecommunications network that will be both commercially and privately used. The full technical maturity of transmission and terminal facilities in the electronic workplace will give it a great versatility. This can be seen from its development in the United States, where a great variety of possible uses have come into being. Tippmann (1984) has categorized these forms of use, distinguishing among four types of tele-work:

1. Decentralised workplaces, shifted to the home as a result of rationalization, are the site for specialized and monotonous processing of texts.

2. In the form of tele-work utilized chiefly by insurance and mail-order houses, the relevant workers are given the opportunity to communicate with their central offices in the presence of "their" clients.

3. In the case of managerial work with substantial independent input, isolation is wished for because it enables the worker to concentrate his or her attention on specific problems and not be distracted by day-to-day routine.

4. This type, used principally by programmers, can greatly reduce programmers' stand-by time because they can operate from their homes, while regular work can still be carried out in the office.

The number of workers in the tele-home-workplace is variable. Besides individual electronically based home workplaces, the FRG is also experiencing its first encounter with the so-called electronically supported satellite or neighborhood office. Such collectively run offices are established to accomodate employers' wishes to cut down workers' travel costs. The possibility of cheaper rents outside commercial centers can also be a deciding factor in the setting up of such offices. In many instances such electronically based neighborhood offices are well suited to the needs of programmers.

The following section centers on the impact of the electronically based workplace on the individual in his or her home. It concentrates on these forms of workplaces because they have a very high conflict potential, thus necessitating that they be regulated as soon as possible. This does not mean that such workplaces have reached the limit of their market penetration in the FRG. Given the fact that data hardware and software, as well as the communications network as a whole, are not yet mature, the amount of capital investment required at this time is much greater than it will be when they reach full maturity. Thus one must agree with Zerdick's hypothesis:

> The introduction of electronic homework will be relatively expensive, thus making the electronic workplace itself highly priced. This mechanism will be used to promote a general social acceptance of these workplaces in much the same way that the possible establishment of pilot projects for the handicapped has been used as an example of the meaningful application of such techniques to work practices. This was very much the case during the parallel period of development of these techniques in the United States. (Zerdick, 1984, p. 176)

The successful dissemination of electronically supported home workplaces throughout society following the above pattern could be sociopolitically explosive. A wide social acceptance of telework could promote its image as a well-paid job with good prospects. Those expectations would come into conflict with all experiences of the trickle-down effect of technology, which, in general, have led to lower product standards. There is no reason to doubt that this will be any different with the advent of the tele-home-workplace. None of the great mass of facts and figures on the high social acceptance of tele-home-workplaces in the FRG is based on solid and valid research. This in itself represents a large and alarming gap. Such statistics also hide a basic methodological problem within public opinion research: how to evaluate material collected from people who have no professional relationship to what they are being asked.

Two definite conclusions can be drawn from public opinion research into the social acceptance of various new ITs in the FRG in the last 10 years: (1) their social acceptance has been mostly overestimated; (2) the more detailed the questions concerning the desirability of particular new IT techniques, and the more the individual was confronted with the enormous cost of implementing these techniques, the lower their social acceptance. Hermann Wiesenthal and his colleagues demonstrated this effect in research on the desirability of reducing individual working hours per week. Fifty percent of all fully employed workers supported this idea in general, but when they were confronted with the fact that reduced working hours would mean a reduction in pay, the percentage dropped to 10 percent (Wiesenthal et al., 1984, P. 118).

Siemens Independent Text-Comprehension Project with Teletypists

From January until 30 September 1982, Siemens, Inc., conducted a pilot project in which three secretaries were equipped with a text station and a dictaphone with telephone adapters in their homes.[2] Handwritten materials or material dictated on cassettes was sent to the secretaries by mail. Texts could also be dictated directly to the dictating machines by telephone. The text was transmitted to the text station after processing, though in the case of more extensive texts this was done in parts. As with dictation, the secretary, called the "teletypist" in this project, could receive the text by headphone. When it was fed into the text station, the written text was then transmitted to the given teletex number and reached the recipient within 20 minutes. As the text was stored, it could be corrected or further processed. Manuscripts received by mail were sent back via the same channel. Employees of this company were advised to transmit texts by telephone. This pilot project was evaluated as follows:

The organisational model met Siemens' expectations.

In comparison to similar offices, work quality and productivity were higher.

The officials in charge at Siemens headquarters were content with the promptness and quality of the texts.

The processing time for the completion of documents was reduced to some extent.

The basic working hours were from 10 a.m. to 1 p.m. and from 7 p.m. to 9 p.m. It is within these very hours that the company's processing capacities were lowest. Employment of teletypists during these periods thus led to a more balanced use of the potential of the system as a whole, and thus to a reduction of expenditure.

Taking various profitability criteria (such as write-off, interest,

2. This pilot project produced only two brief articles. A request to Siemens for a comprehensive report was not acknowledged. Because of this, the scientific worth of the project's results cannot be verified. It is particularly unfortunate that a critical evaluation of the social scientific methodology with which the high positive acceptance rate was calculated cannot be undertaken. Wegener 1982, 1983.

fixed costs, and output-oriented expenses) into consideration, the teletypists were cheaper than comparable skilled workers. A fee of DM 4.00 per page meant that a monthly output of 500 pages cost Siemens DM 5.82 per DIN A4 page (a format that is a little bit larger than a standard U.S. sheet of paper). This amount is significantly less than their previous expenditure of DM 9.40 per DIN A4 page for office-produced material.

No great problems were reported from the homes of the teletypists, and the reimbursement was regarded as sufficient.

Their working conditions were well received, and many secretaries and housewives sought to participate in this project.

Without a detailed knowledge of the project's design, its performance, and its criteria for success and acceptance, one cannot comment upon these results. It is impossible also to generalize in this instance. In comparison to office work, the quality of the product was higher, the expenditure less, and the secretarial staff were content.

Despite the positive reception of the Siemens project, the comments of a programmer who had been involved in a different Siemens project give rise to skepticism. it is impossible to say whether this case is representative or not, though it drastically reflects the great potential for social conflict inherent in this technology.[3] This woman worked for a number of years as a programmer with Siemens until her pregnancy. Her present electronically based home workplace is a windowless room of six cubic meters beside the bedroom. Today she is a "self-employed businesswoman" without a company contract. She received DM 36.00 per hour,[4] which has to cover all extra expenses. She receives no rent compensation, health, or social insurance contributions from the company. Her solution to the problem of pension contributions was to cease payment after 16 months. As a self-employed person, she is entitled to neither sickness benefit nor holiday pay. She is, in fact, entitled to absolutely no company benefits.

Siemens pays DM 700 to the federal post office for a leased online connection. Through this leased line, she can at any time be con-

---

3. The text of an interview with a programmer was given to the author by the German Congress of Trade Unions. The woman in question wishes to remain anonymous for personal and data-protection reasons.

4. After the tax payments and social welfare deduction that are normally met by the employer have been taken into account, this gross hourly wage has a net value of DM 11.00 (about $3.60). A contract firm would receive a gross hourly fee of at least DM 100.00 for such programming.

nected to any of the three Siemens computers between 8 a.m. and 5 p.m. She works 18 hours per week between 8:30 and 12.30. These hours are suitable for her because her son is asleep for at least half of this time. The Siemens workers' council had not been consulted when her workplace was installed.

She believes that her work is now more intensive than in the office. Without many of the normal activities in large offices (answering the telephones, questioning colleagues, etc.), her worktime became more concentrated, but also more monotonous, and demanding less of her qualifications. She sees herself becoming less qualified because she is involved in programming itself, while the development of new programs and languages and the use of new machines are passing her by. She misses the interaction of the office and is aware of her legally uncertain position. When her son is older, she intends to work full time again.

The Creation of Decentralized Workplaces Through the Use of Teletex: A Project in Baden-Württemberg

Supported by a number of expert commissions and personally sponsored by Prime Minister Lothar Späth, the region of Baden-Württemberg, which has the highest number of middle-sized firms in the FRG, is actively encouraging the introduction of new ITs. The group of experts who make up Die Förderung neuer Kommunikationstechniken (EKOM) suggested a pilot project with electronically supported home workplaces in their final report (1982). In a statement to the Landtag (regional parliament) of Baden-Württemberg, the government stated the aim of the project as follows:

> The project is to establish how decentralized workplaces can be created through the application of new communication technologies. Technical, economic, organizational, and social advantages as well as disadvantages resulting from the application of, for example, teletex shall be explored and possible solutions arrived at. Target groups are mainly women who are bound to the home for family reasons and especially handicapped people whose mobility is restricted. Work in the home or in near proximity to them is their sole opportunity to participate in the work process.
>
> Within the framework of this project, written text will be transmitted to the decentralized worker through telephone dictation, courier, or mail via the company headquarters in, for example, Stuttgart. The worker will decide freely when he or she will transmit the given text to the teletex. The newly stored text will be transmitted very shortly afterwards to the teletex network headquarters at very low cost and

> then can be processed according to the technical possibilities there or, if desired, sent to a third recipient by teletex. In this context the spatial distance between the workplace and the headquarters loses its meaning to a large extent. The decentralized workplace can exist within the home, in a neighborhood office for a few women, in a decentralized office in rented rooms functioning as a branch office, or in a small independent office. In this project the decentralized workplaces will be manned almost exclusively by workers who formerly had been employed in company headquarters. (Landtag von Baden-Württemberg, 1983.

This project in Baden-Württemberg encountered great difficulties right from the beginning on a number of levels. Above all, the basic assumption formulated by EKOM in 1982 regarding shortages in the labor supply that would ensure the attractiveness of the scheme to women who are interested in working half-days proved to be false. The lack of information passed on to the workers' councils of public and private concerns participating in the project caused the trade unions, particularly Öffentlicher Dienst, Transport und Verkehr (ÖTV), the public sector union, and Handel, Banken und Versicherungen (HBV), the union concerned with trade, banking, and insurance workers, to be particularly critical of the project's aim. The unions feared, above all, the effects of the rationalization of workplaces, the undermining of workers' rights, and the resulting negative consequences.

Some industrialists also expressed hesitation in becoming involved in the project because their hopes of government funding for the necessary infrastructural changes were left unfulfilled. This has given their badly strained relations with the trade union movement a much needed boost. On these grounds the regional institute for insurance and the regional building society, from the public sector, as well as the firm Schwarz, Bauer & Bökeler and the publisher Klett Verlag (the printers of all the regional parliament's published material), have withdrawn from the project.

The project began on 1 January 1984 and terminated on 31 December 1985. The participants were 12 representatives from private enterprise and the services sector, five regional ministries, one local government department, one chamber of commerce, one trade association, two large producers of teletex, one manufacturing company, one engineering office, two translation offices, one printer, one news service, and one research institute. The target group for these decentralized workplaces were women; the majority of projects involving handicapped people failed to materialize. Most of the workplaces were in private homes; some were in the offices of local government authorities; and one was in a neighborhood office.

The contractual status of these workers was governed by an Aussenarbeitnehmerverhältnis (field service contract). Two or three participants were covered by Heimarbeitsrecht (homework law) or by a Werkvertrag (work and labor contract). The scientific study carried out by the Fraunhofer Institut für Arbeitswirtschaft und Organisation (IAO) in conjunction with this project observed that:

> From the very beginning it seemed as if there were not enough qualified personnel in the centers of business and finance. Groups such as the handicapped, the housewife who is restricted to her home, or in particular those who live in outlying areas should be given the opportunity to participate in the project. This pilot project should discover and demonstrate how much the teletex can ameliorate the situation of those people. (Kern and Warwzinek, n.d., p. 6)

The empirical surveys done in connection with the project took the form of case studies. The restrictive methodology employed by the pilot project meant that participants were not (or could not be) selected according to scientific criteria and that the results could not be representative, even if it were possible to empirically predict emerging trends in this area. Technical, organizational, and managerial considerations dominated the IAO's project design, at the expense of social implications.[5]

Although the scientists involved in this parallel research project distinguish various kinds of electronically decentralized workplaces, the home workplace accounts for more than 50 percent of the case studies. Homework's positive qualities are stressed—for example, the flexibility toward working times that enables workers to mix work and leisure. "No negative side effects have been, as yet, encountered by the pilot project study" (Kern and Warwzinek, 1984, p. 440).

In opposition to these findings, the public service trade union ÖTV uncovered serious social problems experienced by individual participants in the Baden-Württemberg project, although no labor law seems to have been violated. The union was concerned with the possible wide-ranging consequences of this pilot project for the social conditions of work. An interview with a participant uncovered the fol-

5. Both the Ministry for Economics, Small Industry, and Transport in Baden-Württemberg, the project coordinator, and the IAO were secretive about project materials. Thus, as in the case of Siemens, this project only can be tentatively judged.

lowing problems that surfaced during the course of the project, but again it must be stressed that this example cannot be generalized:

> Work requiring concentration was possible only when both husband and children were not at home; otherwise disturbances were unavoidable.
>
> Telework demands a great deal of self-discipline.
>
> Because of pressure applied by her husband, the teleworker could not work in the evening or at weekends. This meant that she had to work between 7 a.m. and 7 p.m., and during this time she was not able to look after her children.
>
> Telework and the rearing of babies are incompatible.
>
> The teleworker missed social interaction with her colleagues and thought of herself as isolated.
>
> Telework is possible only in a separate room, but this is usually not available in small rented apartments.
>
> Telework can, in certain instances, lead to a strengthening of one's self-confidence (*ÖTV-Heute*, 1984, p. 2).

The Telework Study Conducted by the Batelle and Integrata Institutes

The study entitled *Studie über Auswahl, Eignung und Auswirkung von informationstechnisch ausgestalteten Heimarbeitsplätzen* (Ballerstedt, 1982) is by far the most extensive work in this field available in the FRG. It was commissioned by the Federal Ministry for Research and Technology and conducted by both the Batelle Institute in Frankfurt and Integrata in Tübingen. Individual contributors have meanwhile published a range of articles on specific aspects of this study. Only a general outline will be dealt with here.

I have already mentioned the study's conclusion that no electronically based home workplaces exist in the FRG. However, there are more important conclusions than this erroneous finding. Representatives from the following branches of industry were interviewed on their attitudes to tele-home-workplaces: banking, insurance, building societies, the energy industry, mechanical engineering, legal administration, word-processing concerns, and companies using computer-assisted design. Among the important results obtained from this empirically structured questionnaire was the fact that employers saw no need to introduce tele-home-work-places in the immediate future for the following reasons:

The danger of the abuse of data

Technical drawbacks caused by the methods of procuring work materials

The fact that the general automation of the office would make simple and integrated typing work obsolete, that is, the internal conversion to computer-oriented work would make tele-homework redundant.

The effects of the tele-home-workplace were seen as controversial. In the event of the full implementation of such technologies, the authors predict the following consequences:

The quality of work would rise when individual needs were taken into account, and fall with the drop in communication with one's colleagues. As efficiency rises, so will the potential social isolation of the teleworker.

The teleworker undermines job security and gives the employer a greater flexibility in choosing workers.

From the point of view of the ergonomist, tele-homework may reduce conditions in the workplace.

It is impossible to predict the worker's job satisfaction.

Great cost-effectiveness can be achieved by employers in many branches of industry.

Productivity will rise.

The employer will be confronted with the problem of controlling teleworkers.

As a result of these individual findings, the study reached the following important conclusions: (1) telework in the next 20 years will remain an exceptional form of work, and its large-scale implementation cannot be seen as likely; (2) there is therefore at present no need for state regulations or innovations in this area.

CONCLUSIONS

As already argued, it seems that the possible consequences of the electronically based home workplace will act to reinforce—but probably only peripherally—a process of social change that will, in any case, come to pass on a much higher structural level. It is thus necessary for scientific researchers and policy-makers to concentrate, from the very beginning, on the social dimensions of this technically oriented process of change. The technical changes brought on by the advent of the so-called information society can, in socially oriented market economies, be regulated only to a limited degree by the state. Furthermore, because potential conflict will arise in the social rather than the technical realm, social compensation strategies must be developed.

In the development of such strategies, the speed at which electronic homework is disseminated must be taken into account. In opposition to the research material emanating from the trade unions and the predictions of the economist Axel Zerdick, it is possible to discern a slow expansion of electronic homework, which concurs with the findings of the Batelle and Integrata institutes. The slowness of this diffusion process (Becker, 1983) is a result of uncertainty and a conflict of interests on the part of the producers. The most important uncertainties for the employer emanating from the electronically based home workplace can be summed up as follows:

The danger of the abuse of data

Technical disruption of the electronic infrastructure

Lack of experience in decentralizing organizational structures and meeting ensuing costs

Uncertainty about and inexperience in the quality control of decentralized work.

On top of these arguments, which can, in general, apply to other western countries, there are two arguments that apply specifically to the FRG in comparison with the United States and the United Kingdom:

The difference in wages and office rental costs between urban and rural areas is much smaller in the FRG.

The cost of commuting between the home and the workplace is significantly lower.

Taking these facts into account, the introduction of new ITs offers fewer incentives to the producer in the FRG than to his counterpart in the United States or the United Kingdom.

In contradiction to the stated findings of the Batelle and Integrata institutes, there is a need for state regulation in this area though the diffusion of this technology is rather slow. The social consequences of electronic homework will be so great that guidelines are needed immediately. It is still possible, at this time, to introduce legislation that will anticipate the changes brought about by new ITs. If this chance is squandered now, it will not be possible to implement such legislation in the future, because resistance to social regulation will have become too great and too homogeneous. The following emerging social problems have not been satisfactorily solved. With the further development of electronic homework, they must find a definitive solution.

Industrial Law. The legal position of the electronic homeworker is unclear. Work contracts that give the electronic homeworker "self-employed" status are to be discouraged, since under them electronic homeworkers would experience a large decline in comparison to the legally protected general standards of social security, becoming responsible for their own social welfare, pension, and supplementary benefit contributions. For similar reasons the application of the homework law to the electronic home-workplace is also to be discouraged. The 1951 homework law and its 1974 amendment cannot cope with the new conditions created by electronic home workplaces.

From a legal point of view, it is also doubtful whether telework can be defined as homework. Under the current legal definition, homework is organized independently, which means that the employer has no control over the pace of work and can impose no time limits or external controls on the worker. When the teleworker's terminal is connected to the employer's data-processing system, exactly the opposite is the case.

The Protection of Labor. The protection of labor has a special place within industrial law. This is not so in the case of traditional homework, where job security is often not guaranteed. Job protection will also play an important role in electronic homework. Child labor night work, the safety of pregnant workers, the ergonomy of the workplace, and remuneration policy will all become potential areas of conflict. Just how much guidelines and, above all, better and more effective controls are needed can be seen from the following two examples. The Board of Industrial Inspection in Baden-Württemberg has reported that out of 11,000 checks carried out on payment to traditional homeworkers, 22 percent uncovered irregularities in the payment of wages and bonuses (Gewerbeaufsichtsamt des Landes Baden-Wurttemberg, 1982). Ergonomical research undertaken by the Ministry of Labor, Environment, and Social Affairs in Hessen on working conditions in approximately 2,300 jobs in sectors of industry that used terminal screens uncovered some serious discrepancies. In 31 percent of all cases the operator never underwent an eye test. In 29 percent of all cases the monitor itself was not properly positioned; in 31 percent the table on which the monitor was mounted did not conform to the legal minimum size (Hessische Minister für Arbeit, Umwelt, und Soziales, 1984).

It can be concluded from these statistics that the abuse of the tele-home-workplace will increase and, after it is introduced into the private home, will become very difficult to control. This in itself shows the need for strengthening government supervision in this area.

Insurance Law. It is at this point unclear under what conditions and to what extent the teleworker is responsible for the hardware left in his or her care. It is also unclear whether, for example, in the event of a failure to transmit data, the teleworker is liable to have a portion of his or her wage deducted as compensation for this failure. These areas of insurance law must be clarified so that the teleworker will not be put at a disadvantage.

Data Protection Law. The federal law dealing with data protection, passed in 1977, is no longer adequate to deal with the recent developments in the area of data and telecommunications networks. Specific laws must be developed to protect the telework place that is a part of these networks and to ensure the protection and the security of data.

Co-determination Law. The laws under which workers' councils operate provide teleworkers with no precise mechanisms through which they can promote their own individual or collective interests. There is also no co-determination process for the issuing of contracts or the decentralization of work.

Women and Family Politics. If we consider the area of social compensation, teleworking will have tolerably positive social consequences only if it is influenced by an active feminist and family politics. Unfortunately, the dismantling of the social security system demonstrates exactly the opposite tendency in this area. Only with a general provision of child allowances and better council housing and childcare facilities can the tele-homeworker achieve emancipation from the negative consequences of her multiple roles as mother and provider. Only when these conditions are realized will the tele-homeworker really begin to enjoy the advantages of the electronically based home workplace. Implementation of these women- and family-oriented policies should be given the greatest priority in determining the future shape of telework.

There is a great need for research in all of the above-mentioned areas, and the social component of this research must become stronger. It is particularly important to carry out qualitatively and empirically based studies of the situation of female teleworkers.

The phenomenon of the transborder application of this technology also needs to be researched and relevant working guidelines drawn up. Because of the advantages of low wages and tax compensations offered by the Caribbean Basin Initiative of 5 August 1983, there are now transborder tele-home-workplaces in the Caribbean that supply producers on the U.S. mainland. (Both American Airlines and Satellite Data Corporation have tele-home-workplaces in Barbados.) The consequences of such transborder teleworkplaces should be researched so as to prevent the implementation of north-south conflict based on this model inside Europe.

A study recently published in London by the National Economic Development Office (*Frankfurter Allgemeine Zeitung,* 1986, p. 13) concluded that by the year 2010, 20 percent of all English employees will no longer have a place of labor in the traditional sense but will operate instead from teleworkplaces at home. West German experiences suggest that electronic homework's process of diffusion will be much slower in the FRG. Even if one acknowledges the necessary and, indeed, politically justified concern about deterioriation in the worker's economic, legal, and political status through the introduction of electronic work, one must stress that the almost incalculable risk for capital inherent in the total reorganization of office structures is the principal reason for the slow diffusion of electronic homework.

On the political and theoretical levels, the phenomenon of electronic homework clearly demonstrates the explosiveness of current patterns of social change. How can the public sector be reconstructed when, at the same time, it is being systematically reduced and restricted by the internal conditions inherent in the current development of ITs? If no answer to this question is to be found, then the so-called alternative use of ITs is, on a political level, of a symbolic emancipative value at best; at worst, it may be the unwitting trailblazer for corporate industrial interests.

REFERENCES

Adorno, T. W., and M. Horkheimer (1972). *Dialectic of Enlightenment.* New York: Seabury.

Ballerstedt, E., et al. (1982). *Studie über Auswahl, Eignung and Auswirkung von informationstechnisch ausgestalteten Heimarbeitsplätzen.* Report of the Batelle-Institute and the Integrata-Institute. Bonn: Federal Ministry for Research and Technology.

Becker, J. (1983). "Contradictions in the Informatization of Politics and Society." *Gazette*, 32, pp. 103–18.

Bell, D. (1973). *The Coming of Post-Industrial Society.* New York: Basic Books.

Frankfurter Allgeméine Zeitung (1986). 14 June.

Gewerbeaufsichtsamt des Landes Baden-Württemberg (1982). *Jahresbericht 1981.* Stuttgart.

Habermas, J. (1969). *Strukturwandel der Öffentlichkeit.* Neuwied: Luchterhand.

Habermas, J. (1979). "The Public Sphere," A. Mattelart and S. Siegelaub (eds.) in *Communication and Class Struggle*, Vol. I. New York: International General.

Hessische Minister für Arbeit, Umwelt, und Soziales (1984). "Überprüfung von Bildschirm-Arbeitsplätzen." Manuscript. Wiesbaden.

Kern, P. and S. Warwzinek (n.d.). *Homework—Dezentraler produktiver arbeiten*? Stuttgart: Institut für Arbeitswirtschaft und Organisation.

Kern, P. and S. Warwzinek (1984). "Dezentrale Schreibarbeitsplätze im Verbund mit der Zentrale." *Office Management*, 5, pp. 436–41.

Landtag von Baden Württemberg (1983). *Printed Matter 8/3460*. 11 January.

Mäckle-Schäfer, V. (1984). "Gleicher Lohn für gleichwertige Arbeit—ob es diesmal klappt?" In E. Vogelheim (ed.) *Frauen am Computer*. Reinbek: Rowohlt.

ÖTV-Heute (1984). "Heimarbeit zerstört kollegiale Beziehungen,' *ÖTV-Heute: Bezirk Baden-Württemberg* 2, p. 2.

Piaget, J. (1974). *Die Bildung des Zeitbegriffs beim Kinde*. Frankfurt: Suhrkamp.

Popitz, H., et al. (1957). *Technik und Industriearbeit*. Tübingen: Mohr

Postman, N. (1982). *The Disappearance of Childhood*. New York: Delacorte.

Prognos, Inc. (1978). *Längerfristige Wirtschafts- und Arbeitsmarktentwicklung in der Bundesrepublik Deutschland und Baden Württemberg*. Manuscript. Bâle: Prognos.

Rauch, W. (1982). *Büro-Informations-Systeme*. Vienna, Cologne, and Graz: Böhlau.

Riesman, D. (1950). *The Lonely Crowd: A Study of the Changing American Character*. New Haven: Yale University Press.

Siemens, Inc. (1976). "Büro 1990." Manuscript. Munich: Siemens.

Tippmann, M. (1984). "Arbeitsflexibilisierung durch Telearbeit," *Der Arbeitgeber*, 30 March, pp. 236–38.

Toffler, A. (1981). *The Third Wave*. New York: Bantam.

Volmberg, U. (1978). *Identität und Arbeitserfahrung*. Frankfurt: Suhrkamp.

Wegener, H. U. (1982). "Advent der freien Texterfassung." *Der Erfolg*, 12, 15–21.

Wegener, H. U. (1983). "Telearbeit für das Büro," *data report*, 1, pp. 4–7.

Wiesenthal, H. et al. (1984). "Flexibilisierung der Arbeitszeit oder garantierte Normalarbeitszeit?" In E. Jacoby (ed.) *Arbeitszeit ist Lebenszeit*. Frankfurt: Büchergilde Gutenberg.

Zerdick, A. (1984). "Mehr Arbeitsplätze durch neue Medientechnologien?" In J. Rau and P. von Rüden (eds.) *Die neuen Medien—eine Gefahr für die Demokratie?* Frankfurt: Büchergilde Gutenberg.

13. Information Technologies For The ASEAN Region: The Political Economy of Privatization

Gerald Sussman

When Malaysian airline clerks go online with computers via Intelsat to Dallas to move passengers from Kuala Lumpur to Kansas City, when Filipino traders receive telexed commodity prices over a submarine cable link from Hong Kong, when a Jakarta-based U.S. energy subsidiary receives data over "Palapa" from an oil rig off the coast of Sulawesi, when Singaporeans access financial information from Belgian data banks, or when Thai students watch live broadcasts of international soccer playoffs from Germany, the utility of telecommunication in varying locales is easily and instantly appreciated. Telecommunication has linked peoples and places in some of the remotest corners of the earth, and beyond, and reorganized vistas in ways incalculable. Breakthroughs in electronic information science are occurring at a moment when even newer, communicative dimensions are likely to be soon uncovered through laser technology.

Adopting the lexicon of their western mentors, many Third World elites have been no less enthusiastic in repeating the marvels of the "information age" and offering their own citizens a creolized version of the "postindustrial" society. The rapid pace of technological change indeed challenges the pundits of the past to rethink their understandings and doctrines of history, science, and development. However, in sweeping aside the relevance of organized political-economic power, technocratic ideology, fostered in the 1970s by McLuhan, Bell, Galbraith, and others, has provided authoritarian systems a rationale for repressive governance shed of personal accountability. Economism, with little reference to the social costs of "development" and augmented by advanced electronic instrumentalities, is among the most powerful weapons in the arsenal of the elite.

Operating out of one well-tutored former colonial outpost, the Philippines, U.S. military planners spent the last years of the war in Indochina designing a fully regional east Asian "EASAT" communication satellite to help salvage the electronic battlefield strategy in South Vietnam. As host to Defense Department's first international satellite ground station in Asia, President Ferdinand Marcos of the Philippines seized the opportunity to begin to confiscate the country's entire communication/information apparatus while speaking publicly of a need for state-of-the-art communication technology "to achieve material advancement within the context of the world political economy . . . what McLuhan calls the 'global village' " (Marcos, 1974, p. 3).

Though the immediate impetus for more advanced telecommunications in the region may have been the logistical demands of U.S. counterinsurgency in Indochina, transnational communication systems had long been a fixture of the colonization process (e.g., the British Austral-Asia submarine cable network). The colonizing powers introduced telegraph and later telephone to their remotest outposts as a way of facilitating their production, trade, security, administrative, and political activities. Neither political nor practical conditions at that time allowed Southeast Asian or any other colonies to participate in the production or employment of these new technologies, though they were very deeply affected by them. Currently, most less-developed-countries (LDCs) are harnessed with a communication infrastructure inappropriate to the contemporary demands of international trade and investment.

Among them, however, the countries of the Association of Southeast Asian Nations (ASEAN)—principally Indonesia, Malaysia, Philippines, Singapore, and Thailand, Brunei having joined only in 1984—have distinguished themselves by their commitment to modern communication development, at the level of both manufacture and information infrastructure. It is not coincidental that ASEAN, currently the fastest capital-expanding region in the Third World, is widely regarded both as a prototype for modern communications and as a model for economic growth. In the 1970s all of the ASEAN states experienced remarkable economic growth at annual rates of 6 percent or higher, well above the LDC average, and committed a significant proportion of their GDP to telecommunications investment toward sustaining the expansionary trend.

Although local prestige, political power, and consumer demand were factors in pushing the importation and, to some extent, the manufacture of digital telecommunication equipment, the strongest impetus has come from the developed market economy (DME) business community. A wave of new transnationalized export-processing (free trade) zones and other "offshore" investments in the region, starting in the late 1960s, brought with them increased demand for advanced communication equipment and services, without which the coordination of transnational corporations' (TNCs) far-flung enterprises and operations, often in the remotest Third World hinterlands, would be difficult if not economically infeasible. World Bank–supported export-oriented industrialization (EOI) was promoted by the leading Organization for Economic Cooperation and Development (OECD) countries as the most appropriate means for attracting foreign capital, which in turn was accepted locally as the best solution to technology gaps, balance-of-payments problems, the need for greater and more skilled employment and improved trade potential, the problem of "nation building," and so on. For their part the western business community saw these investment openings as a way of expanding their horizons and as opportunities for increased productivity, lower production costs, wider markets, access to raw-materials, stable capital-labor relations, and other profitable exchanges. The availability of a communication satellite, submarine cable, telex, high-speed data transmission, reliable telephone circuits, and other communication technologies is part of the infrastructure that the ASEAN states as a whole have been led to believe is a precondition for attracting investment.

Telecommunications, of course, affect more than the strictly commercial side of life. A satellite dish antenna, for example, can bring important information, such as health care education, as well as metropolitan culture to locations otherwise cut off from some of the dynamic centers of human activity. The absence of paved roads, bridges, or airports, once the major concern of developmentalists, now poses no natural barrier to information access. The barriers to communication that seem to be more imposing are not so much physical as political-economic and historical, such that the *means* of communication, either for business or for general welfare, are largely restricted to global routes previously established by the circulation of commodities and capital. The ultimate uses and designs of telecommunication systems are, thereby, best understood not as much through idealized conceptions of their potential as through their actual social appropriation and application. This paper analyzes the effects of new technologies and the promotion of privatized structures on one of the most open sanctuaries for both foreign capital and telecommunication transfers—the ASEAN region.

Toward this end, the principal objective of this essay is to review recent transformations in the telecommunication sector of the ASEAN countries by: (1) outlining the major policy trends and projects taking place in the region; (2) discussing the intended or likely primary end-users of these new technologies; and (3) considering the implied structural changes affecting the area within the framework of what transnational finance and industrial and developmentalist institutions see as the value of a globally integrated production and service economy and new international division-of-labor requirements.

MAJOR TELECOMMUNICATION PROJECTS WITHIN ASEAN

The convergence of what were once discrete categories of telecommunications and computers makes it somewhat difficult to delineate the two sets of technological parameters, inasmuch as digital transmissions standards, local area networks, private branch exchanges (PBXs), switching at the site of the terminal equipment, and so on, have brought about a common systems architecture. This convergence is, in fact, now recognized under the recently coined rubric of "telematics." In this chapter I consider three specific categories of telecommunication equipment and related services:

1. Terminal equipment (e.g., telephone sets, telex terminals), a category that includes those points on the communication network usually located on the end-user's premises, where the signal is originated or finally received
2. Transmission equipment (e.g., co-axial cable, microwave radio, communication satellite, fiber-optic cable), which carries signals between terminal stations and switching centers
3. Switching equipment (mechanical, electro-mechanical, electronic, digital), usually located in telephone central offices, which interconnects multiple communicating circuits and transfers traffic among them

ASEAN's communication infrastructure has been welded into a common unit by two recent and massive undertakings. One is an Indonesia-based communication satellite system called "Palapa" (a term symbolizing national unity), whose "footprint" covers its 13,000-island archipelago together with the rest of the region and which has subscribers from among all the other ASEAN members. Palapa is sanctioned through agreement with the international satellite consortium, Intelsat (of which the United States is the largest voting member and user), which delineates its rights of usage. The Palapa system's total costs were initially estimated to be as high as $1 billion, at a time when Indonesia's annual per capita income was about $120. Tainted by reports of massive TNC bribes, the system was originally built and launched in 1976 by a consortium that included Hughes Aircraft (the vehicle and ground equipment), Ford, ITT, Siemens (ground equipment), NASA (the launch), and a few other OECD transnationals (Jones, 1976; *New York Times*, 1977).

Within Indonesia, initial outlays were for 50 ground stations (as of late 1984 that number was up to 197), delivering broadcasts exclusively from Jakarta to some 5.5 million television sets, along with telephone, record, data, and other services. All of the other ASEAN countries now lease circuits on the system, mainly for television transmission but also for military use (as in Thailand) and for other government administrative functions. The Philippines' use of Palapa for domestic communication, affected by poor internal administrative coordination, corruption, and general economic decline, was drastically cut back in 1985 after the country had failed to pay the annual lease agreement ($1,125,000) to the Indonesia authorities for three consecutive years. Palapa appears to be expanding, primarily for television usage, but its future is far from certain.

For one thing, Palapa is restricted (by Intelsat) almost entirely to domestic applications, and at least one country in the region, Thailand, is considering a satellite for its own domestic traffic. Also looming is the development of the direct broadcast satellite (DBS), which when technically perfected and cost-effective, possibly as early as 1990, will be able to bring television broadcasts directly to homes using small rooftop dish antennas, thereby making Palapa obsolete and perhaps something of a white elephant. There remain serious political problems with DBS, however, apart from the technical (e.g., frequency allocation) and economic ones (e.g., competition with cable), not the least of which has been national concern over the problem of broadcast "spillover" across state boundaries. Spillover is already an issue along the ASEAN borders as well as between Thailand and Laos. Apart from unauthorized program transfers, there is the vexing debate over advertising, which, for example, is banned on Indonesian television but not in next-door Singapore or Malaysia.

Internationally, each of the ASEAN countries is linked to the others and to the rest of the world through Intelsat, which is used in the region mainly for overseas telephone, telex, and television services. A second set of overseas linkages is offered via various submarine cable systems. These include the British Commonwealth Pacific network, linking Southeast Asia to Australia, New Zealand, Canada, Fiji, with through passage via the U.S. transpacific system that joins Guam with Japan, Hong Kong, and additional points in East and Southeast Asia. Also in planning is a controversial $733 million transpacific fiber-optic submarine cable connecting the United States with Southeast Asia via the Philippines. Led by AT&T, which holds 85 percent of the U.S. share, the system offers increased competition to Intelsat operations, advanced technology for end-users, and tighter security for U.S. military transmissions, even though it is highly questionable whether the additional cable system can ever come close to filling its capacity.

Among the ASEAN and adjoining states, five recent submarine cable systems have also been established, connecting all of them and run by state entities in all but the Philippines. These are classified as follows:

ASEAN I System: Philippines-Singapore

ASEAN II System: Indonesia-Singapore

ASEAN III System: Malaysia-Singapore-Thailand

ASEAN IV System: Malaysia-Indonesia

ASEAN V System: Philippines-Malaysia-Thailand (construction delayed)

For most LDCs, including ASEAN, the main thrust of telecommunication development in the next decade will consist of instituting public switched telephone systems and replacing vintage step-by-step mechanical equipment with less-than-advanced but reliable semiautomatic crossbar equipment that makes available direct-distance-dialing and central office switching (centrex). Switching facilities vary greatly among the LDCs; Singapore is moving toward a stored program control (SPC), all-digital system with push-button dialing; Gambia is still using first-generation switching for its national network. The latter is closer to the LDC standard. Inasmuch as the telephone system represents the most essential and most expensive input in the overall telecommunication infrastructure, it is here that TNCs will concentrate and compete in the LDC markets.

Singapore

Within ASEAN there are wide differences in the availability and quality of telephone service and, hence, its relative attractiveness to business users. Singapore has overcome most of the problems that typically plague Third World telephone systems and has set itself on a mission to offer services of "world-class" standard, planning to spend $1.5 billion for 1985–89 to make the island state an international telecommunication center. Already second (behind Japan) in Asia in telephone density (currently about 25 main lines per 100 people, compared with 40 or over for most leading industrial countries), the Lee government seeks to maintain its position as the telecommunication hub of Southeast Asia despite a population base of less than 3 million.

Singapore is already fourth in telecommunications traffic among Commonwealth countries, is first per capita worldwide in communication satellite usage, has telephone and telex service to 207 and 198 destinations respectively, is an important data communications service provider, and is a key international submarine cable hub—for the Southeast Asia Commonwealth system (SEACOM), the ASEAN network and ultimately (the project is currently in the implementation stage) for three new systems connecting Singapore to northern Asia, Australia, and the Middle East–western European routes (Arthur D. Little, Inc., 1980, vol. 4, p. 237; U.S. Department of Commerce, 1983, pp. 171–76).

Singapore connects international telephone users to two-thirds of the world via links to the Indian Ocean and Pacific Ocean Intelsat, offers a "Telepac" database-access service to 200 specialized databases in the United States, and leads ASEAN in its rapid stride toward an integrated-services digital network (ISDN), based on all-digitalized telecommunication networks and exchanges and expected to be fully operational by the 1990s.

Whether Singapore will retain its role as an important communication subcenter has only recently become problematic. Following the high growth rate of 1981, the economy has more recently been in an uncertain state, with real gross domestic product for 1985 showing a decline of 1.8 percent, followed by a weak recovery to 1.9 percent in 1986. Two trends with direct implications for telecommunications development are the layoffs in the industry and a weakening banking sector, typically the biggest long-distance communication end-user. The U.S. transnational General Electric, one of Singapore's largest private employers, laid off 4,500 television employees in 1985, reducing its total workforce there from 14,000 in 1980 to 5,000 in 1986. The Singapore International Monetary Exchange (Simex), which uses satellite and submarine cable in linked trading transactions with the Chicago Mercantile Exchange, has developed very slowly, while the Bank of America closed two of its four Singapore branches in 1985, reducing staff from 797 to 100 (Economist Intelligence Unit, 1986). In the same year the Development Bank of Singapore experienced a 70 percent drop in profits. Additionally, there have been recent fissures in the erstwhile political monopoly of Prime Minister Lee Kuan Yew. Glib projections for this recent Third World "miracle economy" must therefore be tempered by the grave uncertainties that now face ASEAN's preeminent economic entity.

Malaysia

Following the lead of Singapore, Malaysia also has ambitious plans to transform itself into a modern "information society." In its development plan for 1981–85, Malaysia committed itself to spending the princely sum of $2.2 billion for telecommunications (on a population base of about 14 million). The plan called for doubling the number of telephones installed by 1985 (up to 8.7 main telephone lines per 100 people). Those projections are currently far from being met, however, and telephone-line density remained well behind at 5.7 per 100 at the end of 1984 (*Business Times*, 1985, pp. 1, 36; *Far Eastern Economic Review*, 1984, pp. 78–79).

In the current 1986–90 Five Year Plan, the major thrust is toward privatization of the state telecommunications organization with planned spending up to $4 billion. The first formal step in this direction was taken in 1985 with the creation of a private firm, Syarikat Telekoms Malaysia Sdn. Bhd., that was to absorb the assets and responsibilities of running the system. Not until early 1987 was the organization in private hands, but in the meantime several other planned private telecommunication enterprises were also announced. One of the most recent is a four-way, equal-share joint venture, Britarafon, set up among three local companies and British Telecommunications PLC, a 25 percent stakeholder and itself in the process of being denationalized under the Thatcher government. The merchant bank Kleinwort Benson, which assisted in the privatization of British Telecoms, is also an advisor to the Malaysian government's telecommunication privatization plan.

As elsewhere in the region, the heavy commitment in this sector involves turnkey contracts favoring some of the largest global telecommunication firms, including Nippon Electric (Japan), L. M. Ericsson (Sweden), ITT (United States), Philips (Netherlands), Marconi (Italy), and British Telecoms. Initially, Malaysia has contracted for new digitalized switching systems, fiber-optic cable, and microwave relay stations and eventually hopes to move toward packet switching and extensive use of cellular mobile telephone systems.

Thailand

The Telephone Organization of Thailand (TOT) is also investing heavily in revamping its telephone and telex transmission and switching systems as a way of making the country more attractive as a business and financial center. Foreign equipment imports make up 96 percent of total projected 1988 costs ($220 million) in these two key markets. Currently, Thailand is replacing older-generation crossbar switching equipment with an automatic digital store-program control system, which will increase the convenience of overseas calling. Its investment in the Singapore-Malaysia-Thailand submarine cable is 1.16 billion *baht* ($50.5 million), or 44.4 percent of the total, on a system still only 20 percent utilized and one that competes for international service with Intelsat. Thailand also has a national microwave network, a high-frequency radio transmission system, and a lease on Indonesia's Palapa satellite for domestic television transmission (*Far Eastern Economic Review*, 1984, p. 76).

The expanding use of satellites, especially by the military, has led Thai authorities to invest in a proposal to have their own satellite by 1987. The satellite would be 49 percent privately owned, 49 percent public, and 2 percent "crown property," and a $1.5 million feasibility study toward this end has been undertaken by Hughes Aircraft Corporation. The satellite project was later dropped for lack of demand.

Thailand now has 52 ground stations, used mainly for commercial (BBTV) and government television broadcasting and for the military. The Thai army itself leases Palapa channels for national security functions, employing 12 ground stations; 8 transportable stations are planned for the Thai navy. The army also dominates nationwide television through two of its own stations in Bangkok, provides a sublicense to BBTV, and otherwise directly oversees government radio and television broadcasting, including those stations of the state "Public Relations Department" (U.S. Department of Commerce, ITA, 1983b, p. 7).

Thailand is also presently accelerating the pace of telephone development in rural areas under a recent $72.6 million loan from the Asian Development Bank and $13.2 million from Japan's Overseas Economic Co-Operation Fund (*Asian Research Bulletin*, 1985a, p. 1280). Overall costs of the TOT's 1982–85 investment program were projected at $1.3 billion, of which the World Bank was to provide $230 million, the OECF $60 million, and other foreign sources $580 million (World Bank, 1982). This spending level was raised to $1.8 billion for 1984–88. Aimed ostensibly at improving long-distance and local telephone service in the 72 provinces and boosting the country's low rate of access (about 1.1 telephones per 100 people), the government's plans remain far behind schedule. In addition, proposals to privatize TOT were postponed.

In early 1986 it was reported that when TOT resisted the World Bank's demand for "substantial" telephone rate increases, the Bank suspended the loan offer and threatened that it "will be obliged to inform other lenders of TOT's financial situation." By 1987 all foreign bank telecommunications lending was in abeyance, and seven foreign chambers of commerce, acting on behalf of their home corporations, formally protested about the quality of telephone service to the Thai government.

Indonesia

For Indonesia the premier telecommunication project and focus of investment has been the Palapa satellite system. Within the country the business sector has continually expressed dissatisfaction with the quality and extent of telecommunication services, which are said to have failed in their capacity to meet the demand for advanced technological services (Crawford, 1984, p. 47). This has led the government agency that runs the telecommunication system, Perumtel, to grant special concessions to private companies and permit government bodies to run their own networks. Among the recipients of such special concessions are oil and gas enterprises, other TNCs, state enterprises, and trading companies (ibid., pp. 47–48).

Terrestrial telephone lines maintained by Perumtel have been a source of considerable frustration, with waiting periods of three to four years for lines, local service of poor quality, especially in Jakarta, and an access ratio of less than one per 100. Government offices and business, on the other hand, have access to Palapa for sophisticated intercity packet switching services and to a Government Information Network of fiber-optic cables in the capital for high-speed data transmission. The second and more powerful Palapa-B series of satellites, doubling the capacity of the original vehicles to 24 transponders, are expected to handle anticipated traffic increases from some 200 in-country ground stations and new ASEAN users. Smaller ground stations are now possible, and the more powerful signal of Palapa-B allows such corporations as Conoco and Marathon Oil to access the satellite from remote offshore drilling and exploration locations. Should the Indonesian government opt for a direct broadcast satellite, as it is now considering doing, much of the heavy investment in ground station equipment would be lost.

Meanwhile, to alleviate telephone congestion, Indonesia initially planned a joint venture with the Siemens Corporation of West Germany, its largest foreign supplier, to domestically produce 200,000 new telephone lines per year and an international exchange that can handle 74,000 lines, both based on an older-generation analog system. This choice of direction would represent an exception to the general preference for state-of-the-art turnkey purchases among the other ASEAN states, reducing Indonesia's dependence on foreign telecommunication imports from 70 percent in 1978 to about 50 percent for 1986 (U.S. Department of Commerce, International Trade Association, 1983a). In actuality, however, these plans were never fulfilled. The analog project was abandoned, and in 1987 Indonesia invited foreign corporations to "build-own-operate" private in-country digital telephone systems.

Philippines

In the early 1970s the Marcos regime expected to make the Philippines the communications hub of East and Southeast Asia, the only system in the region under virtually fully private ownership. A British-Philippine joint venture set up submarine cable links as part of the ASEAN cable system to Singapore, Taiwan, and Hong Kong in the late 1970s and early 1980s. The Philippine portion of the venture was directed by a government official and intimate business associate of Ferdinand Marcos. This associate, Roberto Benedicto, was also, until the Marcos ouster in February 1986, the major owner of the country's mass media system (television, press, radio), together with the domestic satellite company (Domsat) linkup to Palapa, a second satellite company connected to Intelsat, and a joint (with Japan) venture corporation that assembles imported television sets. Among his many holdings, Benedicto also ran the country's sugar-producing and -trading monopolies and owned a major nationwide banking establishment (Sussman, 1982, pp. 381–86).

As in Indonesia and Thailand, Philippine telephone density is very low, about 1.2 telephones per 100 people. In the late 1970s the country's largest telephone company was PLDT; though one of over 60 private telephone operations, it had 90 percent of sales. In that decade PLDT began a planned phased-in digital telephone transmission and switching project, undertaken with Siemens as primary contractor (again with Marcos as silent partner). The project, expected to cost $944 million, virtually ground to a halt after 1983 because of severe downturns in the economy, the country's balance-of-payments situation, and, reportedly, a multi-million-dollar bilking of PLDT by Marcos personally (*Columbus Dispatch*, 1986). Siemens did complete a digital international exchange for Manila in early 1985, and PLDT fulfilled the major part of a project to introduce 220,000 stored-program-control lines for Manila and surrounding areas. There are additional plans for an "integrated digital network" with modern signaling and transmission equipment, now postponed until at least 1988, because of limited foreign currency reserves and a foreign debt crisis. Foreign debt amounted to $28 billion by early 1987. Moreover, there have been two shake-ups in the Ministry of Transportation and Communication since Corazon Aquino came to power.

In principle, however, the Aquino government remains committed to the essentials of the World Bank–sponsored "national telecommunications plan," and TNCs stand poised to benefit from lucrative contracts once the economy begins to show signs of "stabilization." Japanese firms are involved in planning rural telephone, telegraph, and radio services for northern Luzon, a project estimated at 7 billion pesos ($350 million) (*Asian Wall Street Journal Weekly*, 1985b; Joint Publications Research Service, DZDL radio (transcript), 1985) Of the country's $250 million market for telephone, telex, and transmission equipment in 1981–83, almost all was imported, mostly from Germany (U.S. Department of Commerce, International Trade Association, 1985a). Off-the-shelf purchases will remain the pattern in the years ahead.

The failure of the Domsat project, virtually grounded in early 1985, also set back development of the national television broadcast networks. The private broadcast industry, already in poor economic condition, had to accept "rationalization" measures by the government in 1985, which some opposition groups interpreted as a means to enforce tighter control and censorship (*Business Day*, 1985, p. 5). After the imposition of martial law in 1972 (formally lifted in 1981), the broadcast industry suffered from overconstruction and undersubscription (advertising), with, from a local standpoint, very high rates for satellite usage—for example, 4,000 pesos ($455) per minute during evening hours, described as "prohibitive" for most domestic sponsors (Rosario-Braid, 1983, pp. 171–75). Moreover, according to one study, many of the communication technology transfers are geared mainly for prestige, with little regard given to long-term or social benefit, and tied to an over-dependence on transnational corporations.

USER PATTERNS

Most of the literature on advanced telecommunications is infused with such reverence for new and specialized communicative potential that the actual social utility of such technology is rarely carefully scrutinized. A number of the more formal studies on international telecommunication transfer have typically and simplistically assumed on the basis of correlation that a "nation's industrial development is related to the scope and quality of its telecommunication system" (P. D. Shapiro, quoted in Hudson, 1984, p. 39). The problem of this formulation lies not only with faulty methodology, however. A 1983 study by World Bank telecommunication-sector policy-makers argued: "Were the economic efficiency aspects of development [alone] the sole goal . . . evidence of market forces would in economic terms be sufficient to justify a rapid expansion of the [telecommunication] sector" (Saunders et al., 1983, p. 14). Furthermore, Saunders and his colleagues argue, a reliable telecommunication system gives rise directly and indirectly to new productive communication patterns and new commercial efficiencies (ibid.).

What is absent in this rationale, as in most mainstream institutional writing on social change, is historical and political context, here replaced by unselfconscious technical and technological determinism merged with economic mystification. These latter tendencies downplay or ignore the critical role of *actors* in development issues in favor of a rationality lacking recognition of either basic human needs or organized (power) interests. Such a mode of analysis is common, as we see, not only in trade literature but also in the reports of putatively socially oriented development institutions such as the World Bank.

A Third World scholar at Stanford University warned of the dangers of approaches that are ahistorical, technologically linear, and dependent on First World "advance goodwill":

> Twenty years ago, radio and TV were to make the deserts bloom, eradicate disease, promote literacy and integrate all these well fed healthy educated citizens into a single body public. They did not: in fact, those who were well off gained more, as usual. In the 1980s today, there is talk of the "barefoot chip" and the promise of a computer terminal for every farmer, unqualified by the lessons of the 60s and 70s. (Mody, 1984, p. 88)

In research conducted earlier on telecommunications usage in the Philippines, I found that in contrast to the development rationale espoused by public policy officials in that country, *actual* end-usership of expensive new systems showed little evidence of generalized social utility. Furthermore, despite some $1 billion already committed to upgrading large business-user telecommunication functions, there has been no corresponding commitment on the part of foreign corporations toward new or even retained investment, particularly since the wave of transnational withdrawals starting in 1983. Of the foreign investments in the Philippines registered in recent years, a growing percentage are being financed from local sources (Bello et al., 1982, p. 155).

How much of a role telecommunication plays in siting capital in or out of a country is difficult to determine. What is more determinable is the extent to which telecommunication investment relates to the needs of foreign investors as opposed to local ones, such that satellites, submarine cables, modern toll switching systems, fiber-optic cables, and so on make it far easier for TNCs to maintain a global basis of production and circulation of goods and services. Among the ASEAN countries, it is only in Singapore that telephone service is available to a relatively high percentage of ordinary users, although 70 percent of the island's Telecommunication Authority revenues depend on international service (*Asian Wall Street Journal Weekly*, 1985b). Here the specific historical and demographic characteristics of the island state's entrepot function in the circulation of capital suggest exceptional circumstances. Even in the much touted case of Singapore, however, recent unstable economic conditions raise questions about its dependence on foreign markets and the resilience of its growth model.

The correspondence of telecommunication and general foreign investment in LDCs suggests, if not a causal relationship (i.e., that telecommunication induces investment), then at least that TNCs, which require advanced communication infrastructure as a precondition, constitute the only important demand sector for modern equipment and services. Consider Table 13.1, which suggests, albeit inconclusively, the general political-economic structure of global telecommunication. The close correspondence of the leading (GNP) OECD countries in terms of overall investments in and telecommunication equipment exports to the Third World, together with their contrality in the flow of LDC voice communication, is indicative of the focus and rationale for the latter countries' telecommunication spending policies. The linkages display both colonial-era and more recent patterns of power configurations. For example, Spain, though not a leading OECD industrial power, still serves as a leading terminal point for many South American countries, as Portugal does for Brazil. At the same time, the United States and Japan, the postwar economic superpowers, enjoy a status among the majority of LDCs commensurate with their present-day level of global domination.

With respect to telecommunication exports, Asia is expected to be the fastest-growing market in the 1980s for overall sales (29 percent of total share in 1986–1990, compared with 24 percent for Europe and 41 percent for North America), with an average 10-fold increase (sevenfold for Europe and eightfold for North America) spread over the current decade. Telephone equipment is seen as the principal global market by 1990 (82 percent in 1980, 80 percent in 1986–1990), with the fastest growth rate again occurring in Asia (a 10 percent expansion of total share in 1986–1990 compared with 1981–85; a 10 percent decrease in the total for Europe; and no percentage growth for North America; see Arthur D. Little, Inc., 1980). Telephone sales, therefore, would appear to be a good indicator of telecommunication usage over the next five years.

Apart from market distribution, regional distribution of telephone access gives evidence of the high degree of producer and service con-

Table 13.1. Comparative Ranking of Overall Investment by Members of the Development Assistance Committee[a] in and Telecommunications Exports to LDCs and Long-Distance Telephone Terminal Points, 1979[b]

	From DACs					
To LDCs	US	UK	FRG	Japan	France	Italy
Investment[c]	1	2	3	4	5	6
Telecommunication exports[d]	2	5	3	1	4	[e]
Long-distance telephone terminal points[f]	1	2[g]	3	6	5	4

[a] Of the OECD.

[b] Based on a survey of 64 reporting LDCs.

[c] The strongest DAC countries in terms of GNP in 1979 were, in rank order, the United States, Japan, West Germany (FRG), France, United Kingdom, Italy.

[d] 1980 equipment data.

[e] The sixth was Sweden; Italy was eighth.

[f] 1979 overseas calls from LDCs.

[g] Including the Crown Colony of Hong Kong.

Sources: AT&T (1980–83); OECD (1983, p. 135); UN Center on Transnational Corporations (1983, p. 55).

centration, which corresponds with most other economic concentration indicators. With 71 percent of the world's population, LDCs together held only 7 percent of its telephones and 17 percent of its total income in 1981. Even these figures overstate the status of most LDCs, as Asian (and African) access rates show typical densities of less than one telephone per 100 people, compared with about 5 per 100 for Latin America. Furthermore, concentrations of LDC telephones almost always occur in large urban areas and especially the capital (and premier international trading) city. Within ASEAN, Bangkok has 70 percent of Thailand's telephones (and 81 percent of its telex machines), with 15 percent of the population. Telephone densities among the ASEAN countries as of 1981 were as follows: Indonesia 0.3 (ranked number 147 globally); Malaysia 3.3 (92); Philippines 1.3 (116); Singapore 20.4 (37); and Thailand 0.9 (124). (See Kurian, 1984.)

The median telephone density for all countries is 4.9, and the average is 10.5. North (including Central) America leads the rest at 53.1 (the United States at 77.0, has about 38 percent of the world's telephones), with Europe at 30.0 and Japan at 42.4 (16th-ranked globally). Ten countries (all in the west) have almost 80 percent of all telephones (ibid.). Considering the very low access rates among four of the five ASEAN countries, the speed with which they are opting for advanced electronic and fiber-optic systems raises questions about who stands to benefit from such sophisticated and costly imports.

Low access rates are frequently cited by the World Bank, among others, to justify heavy LDC expenditures in telephone systems, but the cost-recovery requirements of fiber-optic cable, communication satellites, pulse-code modulation transmission, digital switching, push-button dialing, packet-switched networks, and telex and data terminal equipment mean that such technologies are not likely to give priority to lifting peasants from their communicative isolation. Yet these technologies represent the direction of investments toward which the ASEAN countries are committed. By all available evidence, privatization of communications in the region almost assuredly means promoting services for a specialized set of users and postponing access for the rest. Thailand's World Bank–funded fourth telecommunication project (FY 1982–85), costing $492.2 million, aimed to expand and improve telephone service primarily in Bangkok (42.4 percent of total project cost distribution) while providing access to only 6 percent of rural settlements still without telephones (World Bank, 1982).

In a previous study I discussed how the "ability to pay" principle is inscribed in the choices of telecommunication imports in the Philippines, which has led to a heavy concentration of transnational corporate and military users within the long-distance telephone, telex, data transmission, and satellite television infrastructure (Sussman, 1982). The high cost of international telephone service makes it prohibitively expensive for Filipinos to telephone or wire overseas relatives, while TNCs use private leased lines to transmit volumes of far less expensive per word/character telex and data transmissions. Long-distance tolls constituted 52 percent of the revenues of the main telephone operating company, and the list of primary end users reads like an international Fortune 500. Government-operated telephone and telegraph systems, meanwhile, have been in a steady state of disrepair and have gradually been phased out in favor of private joint-venture operations. Television, too, favored corporate users: 75 percent of airtime advertisers are TNCs, and 50 percent of programs are imported (Sussman, 1982, pp. 386–88). Imports dominate television programming in other ASEAN countries as well: Singapore, 60–66 percent; Malaysia, 50 percent; Thailand, 50 percent; and Indonesia, 20–30 percent (Lent, 1982, pp. 174–75)

Telecommunication also provides vital links for the whole realm of data storage, transmission, and retrieval operation. According to one study, PLDT, the private telephone giant in the Philippines, "serves the banking community, the government institutions, the business establishments for their on-line data communication requirements and information exchange both local and foreign." This, the study argues, led to investment in a $300 million submarine cable project "that will link the Philippines with other countries in Asia, Europe and North America" (de la Cruz, 1980, pp. 426–27). New technologies, especially with the convergence of telecommunications and computers, are rapidly changing telecommunication parameters, leading to the integration of terminal transmission and switching operations. This is one of the major developments, in fact, in the modern large business office, which is increasingly using key telephones and digital private branch exchanges (PBXs) to handle interoffice telephone communications and local area networks (LANs) to interconnect and switch interoffice data communications.

Demand for specialized applications like interoffice communications has led to proposals between Malaysia and Indonesia to set up a private company (headed by businessmen close to the respective heads of state) to handle ASEAN-wide uses of Palapa, similar to the trend in the United States, and more recently in Japan, of opening voice and data services to nonregulated operators. The Malaysia-Indonesia joint venture would have exclusive rights anywhere in the region outside Indonesia to market digital-based services, particularly to prospective business and banking clients not satisfied with public switched networks. For Malaysia this step represents a departure from government monopoly of telecommunication in the direction of privatization of its former state telecommunication organization, Jabatan Telekom Malaysia (JTM), and is currently included as a highlight of the 1986–1990 Fifth Malaysia Plan.

At the present stage of communication development in Malaysia and Indonesia, it remains to be seen whether privatization will mean postponing telephone availability for the majority. In the Philippines, where telephone operations have long been privatized, the largest projects in technical upgrading are in the suburban Manila business district of Makati and surrounding areas, where digital switches and new cable are expected to provide fast and reliable service to the high-demand sector: banking, tourism, airlines, insurance, trading, transnational manufacturing, shipping, media, and so on. Proposals to develop a fully national telecommunications system remain deferred since early 1985.

While the leading industrial countries (already with high telephone/population density rates) are moving toward all-electronic switching and transmission systems and have sufficient planning know-how to utilize them, LDCs are faced with the quandary of whether to implement the latest "off-the-shelf" technologies, postpone the decision, or opt for older electromechanical systems or even earlier-generation equipment, the long-term costs of which may appear to be higher if one takes into account, for example, circuit capacity and flexibility. At the same time, few LDCs have the means to pay the terrestrial costs of building their own systems (e.g., cable, construction, local switching centers). One interim solution may lie in available cellular radio technology, which allows the bypassing of much of the expensive infrastructure and which potentially could provide every village with at least one public telephone interconnection to every other village in a relatively inexpensive way. Such a project would require the active involvement of the state; and at the moment such grassroots communication does not appear to be high on the agenda within ASEAN.

IMPLICATIONS FOR ASEAN'S TELECOMMUNICATIVE SOVEREIGNTY

Self-reliance in telephone manufacturing also does not appear to offer a solution to the ASEAN countries at this time, at least not individually. Although LDC investment in telephone sets and electromechanical private automatic branch exchanges (PABXs) are relatively amenable to efficient small-capacity utilization, electromechanical transmission and switching equipment require high-precision mechanical and installation skills and production facilities. The CCITT (Consultative Committee on International Telephone and Telegraph), a technical standard-setting agency of the International Telecommunication Union, advises that such a production investment would require a market able to absorb at least 50,000 new subscriber lines per year as well as well-trained personnel able to exploit value-added potentials. Moreover, sophisticated testing and manufacturing equipment are necessary. For digital electronic switching, a high degree of automation is needed to make production costs competitive. CCITT estimates that such a telephone production system, based on substantial imports, is possible in a growing economy with one million telephones or more (International Telecommunication Union, 1983, pp. 12–13). On this basis alone, none of the ASEAN countries yet qualifies, though this could change before the turn of the century.

Singapore, too small a market to produce its own telephones, will be manufacturing them for the U.S. market. AT&T has moved its residential telephone manufacturing operations to Singapore under "pioneer status," laying off 875 American workers in its Shreveport, Louisiana, plant in 1985, and plans to invest $70 million in its new site over the next five years (1985–89), with employment for 1,000 people and production levels projected at 4 million sets by the end of 1987. Hourly wages are less than one-fourth those in the United

States. AT&T cordless phones are already totally manufactured abroad, by suppliers in Hong Kong, Taiwan, and Japan (*Asian Computer Monthly*, 1985, p. 72; *Asian Wall Street Journal Weekly*, 1985, p. 10).

In the service sector, the shift toward privatization of services, already existing in the Philippines and slated to soon appear in Malaysia, Thailand, and Indonesia, is associated with increased TNC demand for "value-added" networks. Telecommunication provides the essential link between users and online data service providers, but cost factors will distance most of ASEAN's business users out of major information markets. For international telecommunication, service charges usually include separate hourly current rates and amount of characters transmitted, in addition to minimum monthly password per-use charges, subscription fees, printing costs, user aids, and other pricing arrangements. One study indicates that in 1983 transatlantic transmission costs alone usually ranged from $20 to $40 per connection hour; equipment cost about $4,000 to $10,000 a year per unit in western Europe and $4,000 to $5,000 in the United States. For LDC users there are usually the added expenses of travel for training purposes (United Nations Center on Transnational Corporations, 1983, pp. 17–19). Moreover, even in the few LDCs where specialized telecommunication facilities exist, their databases tend to be outdated or incomplete; detailed data on technology, licensing, or costs are generally unavailable (ibid., p. 108).

In the high-value-added areas of high-speed data transmission, satellite teleconferencing, facsimile, and other key applications of international telecommunication, TNCs clearly monopolize the demand sector. The communication satellite represents a supratechnology that ties together central and peripheral production and circulation centers, with the consequences, according to one writer, of disappropriating data from local areas, concentrating information in a few locations, bypassing public networks and control systems, creating a redundancy of public investment in public networks, and concentrating (economic and political) power (Locksley, 1982, p. 199).

TELECOMMUNICATION AND ASEAN'S DEVELOPMENT

TNCs are also the most important source of new telecommunication technology transfers to LDCs. Most LDCs have no scientific and technological base to speak of in this sector and will continue to rely on TNC transfers far into the future. In the services area, virtually all LDC telecommunication administrations follow the European PTT (Postal, Telegraph and Telephone) approach but, again, rely on

TNCs and foreign loans and assistance to provide the wherewithal to communicate across borders. A few regional organizations have been formed, such as PANAFTEL in west Africa and ASEAN in Southeast Asia, to standardize and facilitate communications among their members, but these organizations have not developed what could be called a self-reliant basis for regional cooperation in information transfers. Even an ITT corporation publication acknowledges, in rare candor, that telecommunication equipment transfers provide no assurances of self-directed development and that such technologies may increase urban-centeredness. It also cites the asymmetrical advantages favoring elites, the great costs involved from capital, human, and material standpoints, and the fact that the benefits of such transfers are likely to be "intangible." It further concedes that "the problem with these correlation studies" (i.e., those that imply that telecommunication produces development), espoused by development-oriented institutions such as the World Bank, "is that the statistical analysis does *not* prove causality" (1980, p. 15).

The ASEAN states are at present among the few LDCs with heavy new investment commitments in the telecommunication sector although actual disposition of such funds is still largely incomplete. These commitments have followed largely from decisions taken earlier to integrate their economies more fully into the transnationalized division of production and labor. One of the results of export-oriented industrialization is a rather impressive new capacity for international communications, but attention to the basic or communicative needs of the rural and urban underclasses dwindles. World capitalism appears capable in the next decade or so of absorbing a limited number of newly enfranchised, socially mobile subgroups in such locales as South Korea, Taiwan, Brazil, and Singapore, yet little evidence is shown by its advocates that "trickle down," "supply-side" economics will significantly improve the lot of the majority. International competition, recession, and the drive to cut labor and other production costs have already eliminated or automated much of the would-be new manufacturing employment. Hence, the withdrawal of thousands of General Electric jobs in Singapore and the general export malaise in the rest of ASEAN. The combination of the billions of dollars projected for ASEAN's telecommunication investment over the next five years and the related demands by the World Bank and International Monetary Fund for government "austerity" measures appears to be a risky formula encouraging political polarization and possibly increased antilabor repression by the military and police.

For LDCs as a whole, the most significant reality is the fact that

90 percent of the $45 billion invested in worldwide telecommunication equipment production in 1981 came out of the advanced industrial countries (Eckelmann, 1983, pp. 14, 15, 18). Pressures to protect these supplier markets will discourage technology transfer to LDCs on terms advantageous to the latter, while other pressures will be placed on LDCs to become larger net importers. Some LDCs may be partially successful in domesticating production, but the overall costs to their economies in shifting to advanced technological production on a subsidiary basis (e.g., with respect to employment, agriculture, and other industrial and infrastructural investments) could very well be far greater than anticipated.

At the same time, it cannot be presumed that the current trend toward privatization has an inevitable direction or outcome. In early 1986 the Marcos dictatorship came to a dramatic finale, and many of its economic institutions, priorities, and policy-makers have since been jettisoned or subjected to intense public criticism. There is no telling what effects the shakeup may have on the rest of the region. The long political stability of the UMNO ruling coalition in Malaysia is also now in question, and even in politically regimented Singapore, signs of opposition have reappeared.

The exuberance expressed by ASEAN patriarchs in the 1970s has in the 1980s turned more cautious and circumspect. Underneath a veneer of political order in the region lies what some see as a social volcano waiting to be ignited. Landlessness and poverty among the region's workers and peasants are growing as political tensions increase. There is little indication that telecommunication developments have guiding principles other than those of privileged capital accumulation, at a time when labor's accumulation is eroding. Projections about the likelihood of technological change can perhaps be more wisely undertaken when grounded in an understanding of historical events and broad political-economic transformations.

REFERENCES

American Telephone & Telegraph (1979–83). *The World's Telephones*. Morris Plains, N.J.: AT&T.

Ang Pahayang Malaya (Manila) (1985). 25 April.

Arthur D. Little, Inc. (1980). *World Telecommunications*. 4 vols. Cambridge, Mass.: Arthur D. Little, Inc,

Asian Computer Monthly (1985). "Another $30 Million for Singapore." August, 72.

Asian Research Bulletin (1985a). 31 March, 1264.

Asian Research Bulletin (1985b). 30 April, 1280.

Asian Wall Street Journal Weekly (1985a). "AT&T to Make Home Phones in Singapore." 15 July, 10.

Asian Wall Street Journal Weekly (1985b). "Telecom 85" (Special Supplement), n.d.

Bello, W.; D. Kinley; and E. Elinson (1982). *Development Debacle: The World Bank in the Philippines*. San Francisco: Institute for Food and Development Policy.

Business Day (Manila) (1985). 22 May.

Business Times (Kuala Lumpur) (1985). 17 June.

Columbus Dispatch (1986). "Marcos Shared Profits from Phone Company." 18 June.

Crawford, M. H. (1984). *Use of Information Technology in Third World Industrial Policy: The Case Study of Singapore, Malaysia, and Indonesia*. Cambridge: Harvard University Center for Information Policy Research.

de la Cruz, M. O. (1980). "Informatics for National Development: Philippines." In Intergovernmental Bureau for Informatics, *Transborder Data Flow Policies*. New York: Unipub.

DZDL Radio (1984). 21 December. Transcript of radio report in Joint Publications Research Service (TTP-85-001), 14 January 1985.

Eckelmann, R. (1983). "A Study of the International Competitive Position of the U.S. Telecommunications Equipment Industry." In U.S. Department of Commerce, *The Telecommunications Industry*. Washington, D.C.: Government Printing Office.

Economist Intelligence Unit (London) (1986). *Quarterly Economic Review of Singapore*. No. 1.

Far Eastern Economic Review (1984). 6 September, p. 76–79.

Hudson, H. (1984). *When Telephones Reach the Village*. Norwood, N.J.: Ablex.

International Telecommunication Union, Consultative Committee on Telephone and Telegraph (1983). "Conditions Required for the Establishment of a National Industry for the Manufacturing of Telecommunication Equipment (Especially Switching Equipment)." GAS 5 series, no. 3. Geneva: ITU.

International Telephone and Telegraph (1980). *Telecommunications and National Economic Development* (Report). New York: ITT.

Jones, R. (1976). "Satellite Communications: Indonesia's Bitter Fruit." *Pacific Research and World Empire Telegram*, May/June, p. 1–7.

Kurian, G. T. (1984). *The New Book of World Readings*. New York: Facts on File.

Lent, J. A. (1982). "ASEAN Mass Communications and Cultural Submission." *Media, Culture and Society*, 4, 2, pp. 170–80.

Locksley, G. (1982). *The EEC Telecommunications Industry: Competition, Concentration and Competitiveness*. Brussels: Commission of the European Community.

Marcos, F. E. (1974). "An Ideology of Development." In F. Tatad (ed.) *The Ascent*. Manila: Department of Public Information.

Mody, B. (1984). "Technological Options for Third World Countries: Do We Have the Freedom to Choose?" *Media Asia*, 2, 2, pp. 85–89.

National Review (Bangkok) (1984). 30 October.

New York Times (1977). "Hughes Aircraft Faces Allegation That It Used Bribery in Indonesia." 25 January.

Organization for Economic Cooperation and Development (1983). *Telecommunications: Policies and Pressures for Change*. Paris: OECD.

Rosario-Braid, F. (1983). "Information Technology Transfer: The Philippines." In D. Wedemeyer (ed.) *Pacific Telecommunications Conference Proceedings*. Honolulu: Pacific Telecommunications Council.

Saunders, R.; J. Warford; and B. Wellenius (1983). *Telecommunications and Economic Development*. Baltimore: Johns Hopkins University.

Sussman, G. (1982). "Telecommunication Transfers: Transnationalizing the New Philippine Information Order." *Media, Culture and Society,* 4, 4 pp. 377–90.

United Nations Center on Transnational Corporations (1983a). *Salient Features and Trends in Foreign Direct Investment*. New York: U.N.

United Nations Center on Transnational Corporations (1983b). *Transborder Data Flows: Access to the International On-Line Date Base Market—A Technical Paper*. New York: U.N.

U.S. Department of Commerce, International Trade Association (1983a). *Telecommunications Equipment: Indonesia*. Country Market Survey. Washington, D.C.: Government Printing Office.

U.S. Department of Commerce, International Trade Associatioon (1983b). *Communication Equipment: Malaysia*. Country Market Survey. Washington, D.C.: Government Printing Office.

U.S. Department of Commerce, International Trade Association (1983c). *Telecommunications Equipment: Singapore*. Country Market Survey. Washington, D.C.: Government Printing Office.

U.S. Department of Commerce, International Trade Association (1985a). *Telecommunications Equipment: Philippines*. Country Market Survey. Washington, D.C.: Government Printing Office.

U.S. Department of Commerce, International Trade Association (1985b). *Telecommunications Equipment: Thailand*. Country Market Survey. Washington, D.C.: Government Printing Office.

U.S. Department of Commerce, National Telecommunications and Information Administration (1983). *Telecommunication Policies in Seventeen Countries: Prospects for Future Competitive Access*. Washington, D.C.: Government Printing Office.

World Bank (1982). *Staff Appraisal Report: Thailand, Telephone Organization of Thailand (TOT), Fourth Telecommunication Report*. Washington, D.C.: World Bank.

14. The Intergovernmental Bureau For Informatics: An International Organization Within The Changing World Political Economy

Eileen Mahoney

The transformation of a few of the most advanced industrialized nations into sophisticated information-using societies is a complex, confusing, at times contradictory, and far-from-completed process. It is to be expected that reorganization of the advanced market economies of the United States, Japan, and Western Europe would have powerful impacts throughout the global arena affecting, in particular, the Third World developing nations that constitute the vital periphery of the world business system. Within this process, the Intergovernmental Bureau for Informatics (IBI) assumes special significance. Restructuring the central activities of the world economy, by its very nature, overshadows national activities and interests and thus creates the conditions wherein a variety of institutional mechanisms must be created to respond to new requirements and to ensure the overall stability of the system. The emergence of the IBI provides a unique prism through which analysis of the social and technological forces, economic actors, and political maneuvers fashioning the role of an international organization within the emerging world political economy may be undertaken.

The IBI entered the international political regime as a small organization with a big plan. The central objective of the organization, as set forth in its official 1978 convention, is to "undertake all action—including policy formation—[to] promote the development and diffusion of informatics" (Intergovernmental Bureau for Informatics, 1978a).[1] Special attention, according to the organization's mandate, is to be given (member) nations with "limited resources" (ibid.).[2] In

1. "Informatics" is the neologism used by the IBI to refer to the new information technology—primarily computing—and expertise in its use.

2. In 1978 the IBI comprised members from 25 countries: Algeria, Argen-

short, the IBI is a multilateral organization devoted to the promotion of Informatics in the Third World. What accounts for the emergence of this organization? Moreover, how does the unfolding international political economy of information influence the IBI and its agenda?

Three dynamic forces profoundly affected the development of the IBI and the postwar political-economic environment within which it was created and continues to operate. (Mahoney, 1987). First, the centrality of new information technologies (ITs) to the basic operation of expanding business activity fueled the development of a new economic sector devoted to the production and provision of new information technologies, software, and services. This new information instrumentation and related information-based services have become central components of the business activities of the advanced market economies.

Second, as the postwar economic expansion began to slow in the early 1970s and the rebuilt economies of Western Europe and Japan began to compete with once uncontested U.S. businesses for lucrative international markets, the rapidly emerging information business has assumed ever more significance. Intensifying competition among the advanced market economies has spurred policy disputes in the new IT field and increased pressure to ensure unrestricted access to the resources and markets of the Third World.

Third, the entrance of many newly independent nations into the global business system and international political arena presented both new opportunities and new obstacles to the commercial imperatives of the advanced market economies. Extensive business opportunities, including markets for new IT, could be promoted in the Third World. Yet national independence and the political-economic determination of Third World development programs, including the role assigned communications and new IT resources, created uncertainties for the expansion plans of transnational businesses and the economic strategies of the advanced market economies.

To the extent that the IBI was assigned or claimed a role in the crucial domain of new IT, it would be subject to the dynamic interplay

---

tina, Bolivia, Brazil, Cameroon, Chile, Cuba, Equador, France, Gabon, Ghana, Iraq, Iran, Israel, Italy, Jordan, the Malagasy Republic, Morocco, Mexico, Nigeria, Senegal, Spain, Swaziland, Tunisia, and Zaire. In 1984, at the time of the Second World Conference on Transborder Data Flows, the IBI's membership had increased to 40 members. The additional members were all developing nations. Brazil withdrew from the IBI in the aftermath of the 1980 TDF Conference, and in January 1985 France withdrew from the organization.

of these powerful transnational and national economic, political, technological, and cultural forces. Structural reorganization of the transnational business system, while it opened up new opportunities for core market economies, ruptured previous economic arrangements and policy regimes and thus produced new requirements, new issues, and new contradictions. The IBI grew out of, but was constantly forced to interact with, the potent and often mutually antagonistic forces that were shaping the postwar global political economy.

That the IBI could assume a position, however briefly, to negotiate these dynamics is also attributable to another condition influencing this period. It can be described loosely as an organizational vacuum. The rapidly changing global political economy in the postwar period went beyond the parameters of older and even newly created international organizations. The International Telecommunication Union, for example, and the United Nations and its affiliated bodies, had not identified the computer-telecommunications sector as a dynamic component in the world economy that was developing rapidly but almost invisibly. (H. Schiller, 1981). It was into this increasingly vital, yet organizationally unoccupied, arena that the IBI later projected itself. Yet even its initial institutional formation did not suggest its future.

ORIGINS OF THE IBI: THE INTERNATIONAL COMPUTATION CENTRE AND THE COMMERCIALIZATION OF COMPUTING

Originally established in 1951 under the auspices of the United Nations Educational, Scientific, and Cultural Organization (UNESCO), the IBI's predecessor, the International Computation Centre (ICC), was created to introduce rapidly developing—methods and technologies of computing in Western Europe.[3] Throughout its arduous development, conflicting national interests and private sector objectives embroiled this organization in a continuous battle over the functions it would perform. Was the International Computation Centre (ICC) to be a scientific organization devoted to research or a center designed to provide computing services?

Two models emerged. An early and very influential American proposal envisaged the ICC as a research-oriented organization that could provide a means for Western European scientists and mathematicians to keep informed of innovations and practices under development in the heartland of computerization at the time—the United

3. For an extensive discussion of the development of the ICC, see Mahoney, 1987.

States. Major Western European proposals, in contrast, saw the ICC as a well-equipped computation service center that could provide information-processing services to European private and public sector organizations while also assisting the development of national computing industries.

The debate that engulfed the ICC, stalling its development for many years, centered on a fundamental issue that would forecast the direction of the unfolding international political economy of information. How would the new technologies of information be organized and utilized? Would they afford the instrumentation for a strong and expansive public sector, or would they be the means whereby the private sector would find new strength and vitality?

The ICC, if developed into a viable international organization devoted to the provision of information services, would have worked in favor of the first alternative. Yet the strength of private economic forces in the United States and, to a lesser, but still not inconsequential, degree, in Western Europe made this unrealistic. The ICC found itself, of necessity, occupying the interstices within an explosively expanding commercial computing industry. Ill-equipped and underfinanced, the ICC was reshuffled, reorganized, and finally recast into a short-lived academic forum whose activities were designed to facilitate private sector development of new information technology and related services in the advanced market economies.

It was not until 1969, by which time the ICC was ineffective, that an imaginative and entrepreneurial nucleus formed within the organization. Under the activist leadership of the Argentinian mathematician Fermin A. Bernasconi, new life was breathed into the ICC. Reconstituted, the new organization would not engage in scientific research or provide computation services.

Following several years of bureaucratic reorganization and preparation, the IBI emerged in the mid-1970s, a *UNESCO*-affiliated organization whose main objective was to promote the introduction and use of new IT in the Third World. More specifically, the IBI's aggressive new strategy called for "government leadership" in the informatization of the Third World. Accordingly, the IBI called for the establishment of government ministries of Informatics and the formation of national Informatics policies designed to spearhead the introduction and implementation of new IT in developing nations. Members of Third World professional elites thus constituted the new organization's target audience.

To its newly chosen audience of policy-makers, the IBI's directorate argued that the new IT and related information management techniques that were being increasingly employed in the transformation of advanced market economies could be expected to produce similar results and thereby accelerate national development in the Third World. Through national Informatics strategies, designed and implemented with the IBI's assistance, developing nations could employ new IT to effect more efficient public administration, open up new economic and educational opportunities, and improve basic services such as health care and telecommunications. In essence, the IBI claimed, Informatics was "essential for social and economic development" (Intergovernmental Bureau for Informatics, 1975, p. 3–4).

The full significance of the IBI's activities in these formative years was not derived from—to borrow a phrase used by Karl Sauvant to describe a different subject—"the novelty of the ideas, but [from] the historical context in which they were advanced and the political support that was given to them" (quoted in Kuitenbrouwer, 1980, p. 11). Although the technology-based modernization scheme advanced by the IBI offered an early indication of its leaders' objectives, it was the larger historical context and the shifting relations of forces therein that would shape the organization's future. In this regard, the seminal aspect of the IBI's early activities lay in its calling the attention of Third World policy-makers to the increasingly crucial, but largely unacknowledged, domain of new information technology.

THIRD WORLD ACTIVISM AND THE IBI

Increasingly throughout the 1970s, the formative years of the IBI, international and national political-economic agendas were influenced by the widespread mobilization of Third World nations. National independence and the formation and activities of the Non-Aligned Movement challenged longstanding political, economic, and cultural relations between advanced industrial countries and the developing nations. Third World demands for economic independence and cultural autonomy—the basic constituents of genuine political sovereignty—sparked great controversy in the major multilateral international organizations, especially the United Nations and its affiliated bodies.

The core issue of the debates that ensued was the continuing, indeed deepening, inequality in the international distribution of the world's resources. New nations in particular found that their development in the post-independence period remained largely conditioned by a system of global market relations over which they had little or no control. Third World demands for a new International Economic Order and, later, a New International Information Order (NIIO), while never fully articulated into specific policy measures, critiqued the dominance of free enterprise as the sole arbiter of national and international development.

In the communications and cultural sphere, an area of special interest in this discussion, the call for a NIIO challenged the prevailing "free flow of information" doctrine, as well as the preponderant Western control over Third World communications and cultural industries that had been built up under its protection. Although the NIIO drew critical attention to the cultural component of continuing dependency in the Third World, at the same time it generally failed to take into account the recently formed new IT networks, which would create conditions of even greater informational and economic inequality. Nonetheless, the NIIO provided an important focal point around which Third World scholars and policy-makers concerned with vital communications issues could organize and mobilize. Galvanized by the NIIO, Third World activism in the field of international communications set the stage, in many ways, for the emergence of the IBI.

The response in the decision-making circles of the advanced market economies and transnational corporations to the challenge posed to the free flow of information revealed the gravity of the problems raised by the NIIO. At the structural level, Third World activism in UNESCO had, in effect, transformed an institutional mechanism created and previously controlled by the Western powers into a forum in which the West could be isolated and outvoted. This suggested the far-reaching ramifications of the exercise of one-nation, one-vote throughout the international political regime.

This shift in the power relations within international organizations—UNESCO in particular—made it possible for an issue that Western policy-makers considered beyond question to be subject to policy debate, negotiation, and possible reformulation. The free flow of information, always crucial to Western media conglomerates and government ideologues, assumed ever greater significance as the introduction of new IT became ever more central to the functioning of the advanced market economies. For this reason, the United States remains immovable in its position that the free flow of information is nonnegotiable. Threats of American withdrawal from UNESCO (carried out by the Reagan administration) were a clear signal that multilateral decision making—to the extent that it departs from American interests (through, for example, advocacy of national or international public sector organizations to monitor or govern "free enterprise")—would not be tolerated (Nordenstreng, 1984).

It was in this volatile period in international communications that the IBI entered into the international political regime. At the IBI's first major international meeting, the Intergovernmental Conference on Strategies and Policies for Informatics (SPIN), which it cosponsored with UNESCO in 1978, the director general welcomed the

Conference participants—many of whom were representatives of developing nations—with the following powerful, if flawed, argument:

> The time is favorable for a great freedom of choice. Today's developing countries are those which missed out on yesterday's industrial revolution; those of tomorrow may well be the countries which will miss out on the Informatics revolution which is taking place today. (Intergovernmental Bureau of Informatics, 1978b, p. 66)

Invoking the perils of "missed" opportunity and the "great freedom of choice" for modernity promised developing nations by the unfolding Informatics revolution, Bernasconi heralded the IBI's brief attempt to construct a new world order. The IBI materials and its directorate promoted Informatics as a means for both developing nations and advanced industrial ones to transcend the structural realities impeding their economic growth. Despite the continuing concentration of wealth, power, and technological know-how among a few advanced industrial societies, and the failure of prior modernization schemes, Informatics, argued the IBI, promised developing nations the means to overcome historical dependency and assume the full proportions of modernity as sovereign nations. To advanced market economies, confronted with deepening Third World political resistance to unchecked business expansion and mounting competition for markets, the IBI claimed that financial support for the organization's Third World Informatics projects would secure the sought-after political cooperation and markets for new IT in developing nations. Trying to procure the interest and financial support of both constituencies, the IBI improvised an international political economy of information that could accommodate the different—and often profoundly conflicting—interests of the advanced market economies and transnational corporations and the developing nations.

Widespread Third World participation at the conference introduced, at times with uncompromising candor and resentment, descriptions of the international information business that differed significantly from those of the IBI's directorate. "Repeatedly," according the final conference report, "delegates from developing countries expressed concern about the monopoly of multinational companies in the Informatics field" (Intergovernmental Bureau for Informatics, 1978 b. p. 9). Additionally, "most of the delegates from developing nations" claimed that "procurement of Informatics based solely on a trading relationship with manufacturers [had] created more problems that it solved" (ibid., p. 9). Given these conditions, there was general concern among members of the developing community that "any dependence in the realm of Informatics could give rise to a host of servitudes which could place the attributes of national sovereignty in jeopardy" (ibid., p. 59).

Notwithstanding the potent criticism of the existing international information business, developing nations indicated their interest in gaining access to new IT in the hope of deriving some of the benefits that remained the sole province of certain sectors within the advanced market economies. In order to overcome in some measure their disadvantaged position within the global market economy, Third World nations sponsored many recommendations calling for a variety of corrective measures or reforms (standardization of software, a code of conduct for technology transfers; the study of transborder data flows, among others, see Intergovernmental Bureau for Informatics, 1978b). The tension between Third World criticism and acceptance of new IT afforded the IBI space to promote itself as a vehicle through which developing nations could acquire new IT without sacrificing their national sovereignty in any respect.

The serious concerns raised throughout the conference seemed to dissipate as the IBI offered this concluding summary.

> The full extent of the Informatics revolution was considered much wider since it hasten(s) the process of economic, social and cultural development. This is why its mastery can be viewed as a lifebelt for many developing nations and as one of the most powerful ways of reducing the gap between different countries' stage of development. (ibid., p. 33)

Thus, as the United States countered the NIIO with the proposal that greater access to technology through the International Program for Development of Communications was the solution to the problems raised by the debates, the IBI was positioned to launch itself into the mainstream politics of international communications.[4]

The IBI took advantage of the enhanced awareness that the NIIO had created and attempted to channel this concern in the direction of utopian technological "solutions." For the industrial countries, whose business enterprises increasingly needed sophisticated new information technology networks on a global scale, and expanding

4. The U.S.-proposed International Program for Development of Communications introduced what would become the dominant model in telecommunications "development assistance." The funding for the IPDC was to be derived from voluntary contributions, ostensibly from private sector sources. And the distribution of the monies was designed on a bilateral basis. For an excellent discussion of the IPDC within the politics of international communications, see Bascur, 1981.

markets, the promotion of new IT as the guarantor of national development in the Third World was a nice dividend, as well as an escape from the troublesome NIIO debate. Thus demands of the nonaligned and developing nations for a more equitable information system provided a propitious platform from which the IBI recommended new IT as a way of rectifying global informational inequality.

SHIFTING TERRAIN IN INTERNATIONAL COMMUNICATIONS POLITICS

Although the IBI's plan to fuse Third World development aspirations with the commercial interests of the advanced market economies may have appeared neatly designed on paper, a developing dynamic made this equation less attractive to the most powerful actors in the international arena. The great expansion of the transnational business system and its deepening reliance on unrestricted utilization of computer-communication networks might have been expected to generate positive support for an international organization that could defuse Third World resentments and channel Third World government policies into full acceptance of, and participation in, the new information technologies. Yet a countervailing development interceded.

A powerful movement to deregulate the corporate sector, and the communications component in particular, succeeded in the United States. (D. Schiller, 1982; Tunstall, 1986). Quickly thereafter the movement traveled overseas, to Western European industries first, and in its most far-reaching form to Thatcher's England. In addition to dismantling the means of ensuring social accountability, deregulation meant an assertion of unilateralism and an unwillingness to accept multilateral fora and decision making of almost any kind — especially any kind that might inhibit corporate activity even minimally (H. Schiller, 1984, 1985).

In this new climate the IBI's activities suffered total derailment. Although it continued to proclaim its ability to represent Third World interests, its space for maneuvering abruptly disappeared. National policy making in the field of transborder data flows (TDF), which could be regarded as *the* vital issue in the electronic international information order, was considered intolerable by the powerful groups the IBI was trying to cultivate. Accordingly, from its early pronouncements that national "Informatics authorities . . . should have a major role in planning and implementing TDF policies," the IBI confronted, and was forced to accommodate, the *actual* dynamics of the international political economy of information (Intergovernmental Bureau for Informatics, 1980a, p. 15).

TRANSBORDER DATA FLOWS: FROM POLICY TO PRIVATIZATION

This confrontation took the form of the TDF debate. Technically defined as the transfer of machine readable data across national borders, TDFs carry information (e.g., production schedules, inventory and personnel records, tax and legal information and currency transactions) that is vital to the basic operation of the transnational business system. Transnational corporations are totally dependent on TDF, as are entire service industries, such as banking and tourism. TDF allows transnational businesses to take advantage of international wage and tax differentials and resources and market availabilities (H. Schiller, 1981). It is this enhanced mobility of capital—largely derived from TDF and the new information instrumentations that carry it—that has spurred serious debate regarding national jurisdiction and well-being.

In its largest dimension, TDF threatens national prerogatives in economic decision making and cultural production, and even political independence itself. This was recognized very rapidly in Western Europe and not long after in Third World nations as well. Early concerns regarding the protection of privacy quickly yielded place to the fundamental question of power—the core issue raised by the unchecked use of new IT. Louis Joinet aptly framed the issues:

> Information is power, and economic information is economic power. Information has economic value, and the ability to store and process certain types of data may well give one country political and technological advantage over other countries. This in turn may lead to a loss of national sovereignty through supranational data flows. (OECD, 1979, p. 208)

The debate sparked by the actual and potential ramifications of TDF marked the reappearance of concern regarding national sovereignty—no different in essentials from the debate over the NIIO, but now tied to the vastly more important issue of electronic data flows.

Challenges to the emergent political-economic and technological hierarchies based on TDF found their earliest expression in Western Europe and soon thereafter involved Third World nations. In France, for instance, a presidentially commissioned study called for the mobilization and protection of national resources in the new IT sector. National development of new IT and related information-based services, especially databases, argued the report, represented the *sine qua non* of economic independence and cultural autonomy in the information age. Moreover, the report claimed that "the sovereignty stakes have shifted to control over networks, which condition both communications control and the direction of the computer market" (Nora and Minc, 1979; p. 71). In order to stimulate the growth of national industries in the rapidly developing and intensely competitive international information business, national control over the basic communications infrastructure and TDF was also given favorable attention in the major Canadian study, *Telecommunications and Canada* (Consultative Committee on the Implications of Telecommunications for Canadian Sovereignty, 1979). And calls for the development of a pan-European market for European companies also indicated a strategy of market protection emerging, with some variation, among the second-tier Western market economies.

These proposed actions sounded the alarm in threatened American transnational quarters. Writing in 1978, John M. Eger, then a Washington, D.C., attorney and recently senior vice-president of CBS, International, cautioned that these efforts presented "an imminent threat to the world economy and to all nations increasingly dependent upon the free flow of information across national borders" (Eger, 1978, p. 50). Fearing that national legislation "could actually cut off the flow of information, the central nervous system of transnational communications, which [is] vital not only to the U.S. but also to the far-flung activities of multinational corporations," Eger among others, called for a forceful American response one that reflected the centrality of unrestricted international information flows to the basic operations of the changing U.S. economy.

The overriding objective of U.S. private and public sector interests was to stymie any attempt to monitor or regulate international data flows. The implacable opposition of transnational business and its governmental representatives in the United States to any effort to establish national oversight of TDFs gave an early indication of how these groups would respond to the continued strong participation, or even the mere presence, of the IBI in the TDF debate. For the United States, the opening of another arena for TDF policy debate, especially one that could involve Third World countries who were already engaged in international communication policy disputes, was a dangerous turn of events.

It was into this opening that the IBI inserted itself. In its efforts to establish itself as a member of the international political regime, the IBI organized a series of major international conferences on TDFs, the first of which was held in 1980. In so doing, the IBI presented itself as a forum in which the currents of disaffection could be harmonized. Conference materials for the 1980 meeting, for example, urged that "special attention be paid to the compatibility between the principle of free circulation of information and the necessary regulations" governing such circulation (Intergovernmental Bureau for Informatics, 1980b, p. 77). However, the organization's attempt to appease both constituencies—its Third World membership and the transnational business community—quickly revealed the limitations of its mission.

In his opening address to the 1980 meeting, Bernasconi, hoping to allay Third World concerns, conceptualized TDFs as a means of gaining access to the huge stocks of datas owned by the advanced industrial countries. "The convergence of computers and telecommunications . . . linking data banks via ground and satellite facilities," he said, "can accelerate access to sources of information in different countries" (ibid., p. 15). Unable to ignore the existing political-economic forces governing technical and informational resources, Bernasconi simply discussed them in a way that supported the IBI's basic goal—the promotion of Informatics in the Third World:

> Being realistic, we recognize that ownership and control of information is a source of economic and political power. Technical progress cannot be isolated from considerations of this nature. Therefore, a redistribution of technological capabilities and information resources is *ESSENTIAL* in achieving a New International Economic Order." (ibid.; emphasis in original)

By calling for a redistribution of technological resources as a means of achieving the NIEO, Bernasconi dressed the IBI's promotion of new information technology in the Third World in political terms considered attractive to that constituency.

The forum provided by the conference, however, heard views both similar to and different from those expressed by the director general. The impact of TDFs on national sovereignty, economic opportunities, and cultural autonomy constituted the core concerns addressed by many representatives of developing nations, as well as by delegates of a few second-tier advanced industrial countries. In contrast, the free flow of information was stressed by speakers from the advanced market economies of the United States and England and members of the private sector generally.

The response of the IBI's directorate to the inescapable polarization in the TDF debate began to reveal the alliances of the organization's leadership. In addition to his routine assertions regarding the efficacy of new information technology to meet development needs,

Bernasconi's closing conference remarks urged maximum restraint in national TDF policy making:

> transborder data flow offers great opportunities, but to benefit from them it is necessary that the regulatory conditions at the national level are not unnecessarily complicated and that a high grade of harmonization exists at the international level. (Intergovernmental Bureau for Informatics, 1980a, p. 52)

Following the claim in his opening address to the same conference that developing nations "should have a major role" in TDF policy making, the above indicates the kind of conflicting responses the IBI's leadership was forced into in its attempt to "harmonize" fundamentally opposed positions.

Under increasing pressure from both constituencies—the Third World pushing for TDF policy formation and the advanced market economies and their transnational corporations ever more dependent on the free flow of information, the IBI could no longer mask its allegiance in rhetoric. Interviewed shortly after the 1980 TDF conference, Bernasconi reiterated the position of transnational business. "Let me underscore," he said, "our [IBI's] belief in an open flow of information between countries and the requirement for a free flow of information in these times of an international economy" (*Transnational Data Report*, 1981, p. 27).

Despite the IBI's two-sided effort to make it appear as though Third World needs and aspirations and the objectives of the international business system could be reconciled, the very articulation of these questions in an international forum that was not totally controllable created increasing uncertainty and doubt in the market economy decision-making centers. This is evident in the efforts, beginning as early as the IBI's 1980 TDF meeting, to move the TDF discussion out of the larger political context into a far more narrow and restricted (and inaccessible to general comprehension) economic framework.

Interviewed at the 1980 TDF Conference, Harry DeMaio, IBM director of data security programs and regular IBM representative at TDF meetings, reportedly suggested that "putting aside purely national concerns of protecting native DP [data processing] and telecommunications industries and restricting data flows to counter perceived threats to national sovereignty" could facilitate a more productive discussion of "overall economic policies" (Kirchner, 1980). Efforts to separate *certain* economic interests from broader sociopolitical concerns informed the political maneuvering undertaken by the U.S. government throughout the early 1980s.

The strategy aimed at establishing new, circumscriptive parameters in the TDF debate that would make it more amenable to private sector interests while at the same time narrowing the range and number of national actors able to participate in policy negotiations. Ambassador Diana Lady Dougan, U. S. State Department Coordinator on International Communication and Information Policy, speaking in 1983 before a symposium sponsored by the Organization for Economic Cooperation and Development (OECD), offered this obfuscatory rationale for the policy shifts underway. "If the countries who are first to experience the implications and impact of the new technologies cannot resolve their differences," she said, "there is little reason to hope that these issues can be successfully dealt with in other arenas" (quoted in Pipe, 1984, p. 1). This rendition, ignores the profoundly *international* impacts of the ongoing transformation of the advanced market economies resulting from the increasingly widespread application of new information technology and transborder data flow.[5] Underlying this weak attempt at mystification is, as Schiller points out, a desire on the part of transnational companies and their government representatives in North America, Western Europe, and Japan to maintain TDF "as as private preserve, shielded from scrutiny and accountability, engaging the attention of a small number of policy makers in the developed market economies" (H. Schiller, 1985, pp. 31–32).

STRATEGIC INTERVENTION: PRIVATIZING THE TDF DEBATE

In a context wherein TDF issues were also being addressed in "other arenas," re-establishing exclusive control over policy negotiations required the "depoliticization" of TDFs. By arguing that TDFs entail the rendering of data services—that is, data processing, software, storage and retrieval, and telecommunications services—members of transnational business and governing circles effectively redefined them as "trade in data services" (Sauvant, 1986). Redefined in this way, TDF issues were subsumed under the "nonpolitical" rubric of trade.

Accompanying the imposition of the terms of trade on TDF, U.S. initiatives spurred the mobilization of two institutional mechanisms—the OECD and the General Agreement on Tariffs and Trade (GATT)—that could be entrusted with the general interests of the advanced market economies. The "free flow of data" declaration pro-

5. It is useful to point out that several private sector publications and studies were highlighting the importance of the global nature of transborder data flows at the same time Dougan tried to minimize it. (e.g., Business Roundtable, 1985)

posed in 1982 by the United States for adoption among OECD countries and the extension of the GATT to cover "trade in data services" were the principal policy instruments used to transform the TDF debate into advocacy for trade liberalization in the crucial field of new information technology and services.

The U.S.- sponsored OECD Declaration on Transborder Data Flows was designed to "promote access to data and information and related services, and avoid the creation of unjustified barriers to the international exchange of data and information" (Organization for Economic Cooperation and Development, 1985, p 2.). Initial discussion of the declaration within OECD circles led one participant to observe critically that "the economic and trade dimensions of these [TDF] issues have squeezed out the human rights, legal and policy aspects" (Transnational Data Report, 1982, p. 58). This, of course, was one of the central objectives of the strategy. As the *Chronicle of International Communication* reports, "Western commitment to open practices," as established in the declaration, was designed "to blunt the impact of any transborder data flow proposal advanced by the developing world" (1984, p. 5).

GATT AND THE TDF NEGOTIATIONS

The OECD Declaration on Transborder Data Flows set the foundation for an even more far-reaching initiative intended to "improve the U.S. competitive posture" in the international political economy of information (Congressional Research Service, 1983 p. 13). In this effort, the United States called for the extension of the GATT, which currently covers only trade in goods, to include trade in data services. Incorporation of services into the GATT regime represented another breakthrough for those attempting to block any public sector involvement in TDF negotiations "because the free-trade persuasion underlying the institution's Articles of Agreement suits their interests perfectly" (Sauvant, 1985, p. 102).

Although services accounted for only one-fourth of the total export of goods in 1980, these service exports exceeded $350 billion, and they are expected to continue to grow at a much higher rate than trade in other sectors. While advanced market economies engage in fierce competition for the international service business, the majority of the developing nations have "relatively weak indigenous services sectors" (Sauvant, 1985, p. 102). Development of service industries in the Third World would, in one researcher's view, require "active state involvement." According to Chakravarthi Raghavan, "the U.S. effort to bring 'services' into GATT by prefixing 'trade' before it, is really aimed at reducing, if not eliminating, Third World options in this [sector]." It is, moreover, designed to obtain for transnational corporations the full freedom to invest and disinvest "without the government of the host-country being able to exercise any effective control" (Raghavan, 1986, pp. 59–60). The Business Roundtable concurs with this assessment, cautioning policy-makers that "any international agreement [e.g., GATT] in this area (trade in data services/TDF) must not rely upon the kind of government monitoring and regulation of information flows that we are seeking to avoid" (Business Roundtable, 1985, p. 37).

IBI AND FREE TRADE PRINCIPLES

The depoliticization of the TDF debate and the mobilization of Western-controlled, trade-oriented organizations to establish the terms for trade in data services were not welcomed by the developing community. Significant opposition to the inclusion of services in the GATT was waged from 1982 to 1984 (Raghavan, 1986). In the IBI as well, developing nations continued to call for the formation of policies to deal with the full range of TDF issues. In a survey conducted by the IBI in the early 1980s, the results show that fully 72 percent of the 70 nations that participated "favoured establishment of basic international principles for TDF." Additionally, a 63 percent majority felt that "special programs and mechanisms were necessary to deal with TDF," and 52 percent registered support for "a legal framework governing the international circulation and trade of data" (Intergovernmental Bureau of Informatics, 1983, pp. 7–9). How would the IBI respond to these demands for policy making within the environment thrust upon it by far-reaching deregulatory trends?

By the Second World Conference on Transborder Data Flows, sponsored by the IBI in 1984, the organization was mired in a real quandary. Its largest, yet in terms of power weakest, constituency called for policy measures that the advanced market economy and transnational business groupings the IBI had continuously tried to please would clearly not tolerate. It is within these polarized conditions that the IBI made its intentions known.

Regardless of the support shown for TDF policy making in its own study, the leadership of the IBI did not allow the organization to engage in even the smallest attempt to slow the march of private interests. In his opening address, Bernasconi announced to a conference convened to study and perhaps undertake formulation of universal principles to govern the use of TDFs that "it would hardly appear realistic to undertake world regulation efforts," but would instead "be more opportune to promote dialogue." Behind the directorate's attempt to jettison any real policy negotiations at the 1984 meeting was a decision already taken prior to the meeting and presented as an organizational position in the Conference Working Document. Under the heading "TDF and Economic Development," the following paragraph indicates the principles that the organization's leadership embraced:

> For forty years, the free trade doctrine has prevailed among the countries of America, Asia, Europe and Oceania. This freedom in the trade of goods and services has certainly fostered the growth of many countries. But freedom of trade also requires the free trade of information associated with international trade. (Intergovernmental Bureau for Informatics, 1984b, p. 25)

Thus, in the end, the IBI, which has presented itself as an organization capable of advancing the interests of developing nations within the unfolding international political economy of information, simply yielded to the powerful demands of the transnational corporate sector.

Ironically, the IBI's other promise—to provide markets in the Third World for the big equipment and software producers of Western Europe, the United States, and Japan, would also fall victim to the exigencies of free trade policies. The imposition of free trade rules in the new IT sector would spread beyond the parameters of the TDF debate to facilitate the privatization of new IT sectors throughout the international community. Private sector development of the telecommunication and new IT industries in the Third World threatened to eliminate the IBI's main constituency, Third World government elites. Thus, as the IBI retreated to pronouncements of the need for continued study at its last major meeting it announced, in effect, its inability to play a substantial role in the international political economy of information.

CONCLUSION

The history of the emergence and brief prominence of the IBI suggests these conclusions for those interested in the modern trajectory of international communications. First, the international business system is totally dependent on information channels and technologies; and, if it can help it, it will not allow this vulnerability to be exploited by international organizations over which its control is limited. Second, stability in the international political economy cannot be secured by an organization that tries to reconcile the irreconcilable: the needs of less industrialized nations and the profit seeking of transnational businesses. Third, international and national organizations are created to accomplish objectives that sometimes can be harmonized. But when great power exists outside the international organization, it may be expected that multilateral decision making will be disregarded. Finally, the processes described in this paper are themselves still undergoing changes, and innumerable factors are operating. Hence, definitive predictions are hardly a reasonable objective. The best that can be done is to attempt to sketch the dominant forces and to take into account the numerous conflictive groupings that make unexpected outcomes always a possibility.

REFERENCES

Bascur, R.S. (1981). "IPDC: International Cooperation or Neo-Colonialism," Manuscript (Chile).

Business Roundtable (1985). *International Information Flow: A Plan for Action*. New York: Business Roundtable.

Chronicle of International Communication (1984). "Tale of Two Cities." vol. 5, 6, pp. 1, 5.

Congressional Research Service (1983). *International Telecommunications and Information Policy: Selected Issues for the 1980's*. Washington, D.C.: Government Printing Office.

Consultative Committee on the Implications of Telecommunications for Canadian Sovereignty (1979). *Telecommunications and Canada*. Toronto: Federal Department of Communications.

Eger, J. (1978). "Transborder Data Flows." *Datamation*, 15 November, pp. 50–54.

Intergovernmental Bureau for Informatics (1975). "The IBI." Rome: IBI.

Intergovernmental Bureau for Informatics (1978a). *Convention of the Intergovernmental Bureau for Informatics*, Rome: IBI.

Intergovernmental Bureau for Informatics (1978b). *Analytical Report of the Results of the SPIN* (Intergovernmental Conference on Strategies and Policies for Informatics). Rome: IBI.

Intergovernmental Bureau for Informatics (1980a). *Final Proceedings, World Conference on Transborder Data Flow Policies*. Rome IBI.

Intergovernmental Bureau for Informatics (1980b). "Transborder Data Flow: Its Environment and Consequences." Rome: IBI.

Intergovernmental Bureau for Informatics(1983). *IBI World Survey of National Policies and Company Practices Concerning Transborder Data Flows*. Rome: IBI.

Intergovernment Bureau for Informatics (1984a). *IBI, Informatics, and the Concern of Nations, Simultaneous Growth*. Rome: IBI.

Intergovernmental Bureau for Informatics (1984b). *Working Document*. Second World Conference on Transborder Data Flow Policies. Rome: IBI.

Kirchner, J. (1980). "Transborder Data Flow Meet Opens." *Computerworld*, 14, 25, p. 2.

Kuitenbrouwer, F. (1980). "Legal and Regulatory Issues: A Main Focus of the TDF Conference," *Transnational Data Report* (Amsterdam) 3, 3/4, p.2.

Mahoney, E. (1987). "Negotiating New Information Technology and National Development: The Role of the Intergovernmental Bureau for Informatics." Ph.D. Dissertation, Temple University.

Nora, S., and A. Minc (1979). *The Computerization of Society*. Cambridge: MIT Press.

Nordenstreng, K. (1984). *The Mass Media Declaration of Unesco*. Norwood, N. J. : Ablex.

Organization for Economic Cooperation and Development (1979). *Transborder Data Flows and the Protection of Privacy*. Paris: OECD.

Organization for Economic Cooperation and Development (1985). *Declaration on Transborder Data Flows*. Document no. ICCP (85) (10). Paris: OECD.

Pipe, R. (1984). "Searching for Appropriate TDF Regulation," *Transnational Data Report* (Amsterdam), 7, 1, pp. 1-10

Raghavan, C. (1986). *"A Rollback of the Third World?"* IFDA Dossier, no. 52 Rome: International Foundation for Development Alternatives.

Sauvant, K. (1985). "The International Politics of Data Services Trade," Springfield, Va.: Transnational Data Reporting Services.

Sauvant, K. (1986). *International Transaction and Services: The Politics of Transborder Data Flows*. Boulder, Colo.: Westview Press.

Schiller, D. (1982). *Telematics and Government*. Norwood, N.J.: Ablex.

Schiller, H. (1981). *Who Knows: Information in the Age of the Fortune 500*, Norwood, N. J.: Ablex.

Schiller, H. (1984). *Information and the Crisis Economy*. Norwood, N.J.: Ablex.

Schiller, H. (1985). "Expanding the Club: New Vistas for TDF." Springfield, Va.: Transnational Data Reporting Servies.

Transnational Data Report (1981). "Rules to Facilitate TDF Envisioned," Transnational Data Reporting Servies, Inc. Amsterdam. 4, 3.

Transnational Data Report (1982). "OECD Data Declaration Stalled," 5, 2, pp. 57–58.

Tunstall, J. (1986). *Communications Deregulation*. Oxford: Basil Blackwell.

Contributors

BENJAMIN J. BATES is assistant professor of communications studies and Director of the Institute for Communications Research at Texas Tech University. Drawing from a background in economics, statistics, and communication, Dr. Bates' research addresses issues of value in information and information systems.

JÖRG BECKER is Heisenberg Fellow of the German Research Fund and professor for political sciences at the Institute for Political Sciences at the Technical University of Darmstadt, and research director of the Center for Communication and Technology Research Ltd. in Frankfurt, FRG. His recent publications include *Informationstechnologie in der Dritten Welt, Massenmedien im Nord-Sud-Konflikt, Papiertechnologie und Dritte Welt*, and is coeditor of *Communication and Domination: Essays to Honor Herbert I. Schiller.*

ANDREW CLEMENT is assistant professor of library and information science at the University of Toronto. His research includes a study of computerization and management of work in a large insurance firm, a survey of electronic monitoring in the workplace, and analyses of how workers are affected by and make use of computer technology.

TERRY CURTIS teaches in the College of Communications at California State University, Chico. He has a law degree from the University of Chicago, a degree from Annenberg School of Communication, University of Southern California and is a consultant in the areas of communications law and policy.

DONNA A. DEMAC is an attorney specializing in telecommunications and also teaches courses in the areas of intellectual property, domestic communications policy, and satellite applications and regulation at New York University. She is the author of *Keeping America Uninformed: Government Secrecy in the 1980s*, numerous articles on federal government information policy, and is the editor of *Tracing New Orbits, Cooperation and Competition in Global Satellite Development.*

ANITA R. SCHILLER is a reference librarian/bibliographer at the University of California, San Diego. She has served as Ralph R. Shaw Visiting Scholar at Rutgers University where she lectured on libraries and national information policy.

DAN SCHILLER is associate professor in the School of Library and Information Science at University of California, Los Angeles. He is the author of *Objectivity and the News: The Public and the Rise of Commercial Journalism, Telematics and Government*, and has published numerous articles on the history and political economy of communication and information technology.

HERBERT I. SCHILLER is the author of *Mass Communication and American Empire, The Mind Managers, Communication and Cultural Domination, Who Knows: Information in the Age of the Fortune 500*, and *Information and the Crisis Economy*. He is professor of communication at the University of California, San Diego.

GERALD SUSSMAN is assistant professor of political science at Emerson College. His research has focused on issues of third world development, communication technology transfer, and Southeast Asian politics.

TONY TINKER is professor of accounting at Baruch College, the City University of New York. He is the author of *Paper Prophets: A Social Critique of Accounting*, and *Social Accounting for Corporations: Private Enterprise and the Public Interest*. He has published in a variety of fields including sociology, finance, accounting, cybernetics, organization theory, and systems theory.

JANET WASKO is associate professor in the Department of Speech at the University of Oregon. She is the author of *Movies and Money: Financing the American Film Industry*.

FRANK WEBSTER is chair of sociology at Oxford Polytechnic. He is the author of *The New Photography: Responsibility in Visual Communication*, and is co-author, with Kevin Robins, of *Information Technology: A Luddite Analysis*.

Oscar H. Gandy, jr., is associate professor of communication at the Annenberg School of Communications, University of Pennsylvania. A former television writer/producer, his research and writing has been primarily in the area of information and social power.

Cheryl R. Lehman is assistant professor of accounting at Hofstra University. She is serving as chair of the Public Interest Section of the American Accounting Association and chair of the Women Faculty Development Committee. She is editor of *Advances in Public Interest Accounting*, and has published her research in the journals of *Accounting, Organizations and Society*, and *Advances in Public Interest Accounting.*

Eileen Mahoney is assistant professor of communication at City College, City University of New York. Her research and teaching interests include international communications, new information technology, national development, and media analysis.

Eileen R. Meehan teaches in the Department of Communications Studies at the University of Arizona. Her research interests include the political economy of mass communication, especially in terms of the television ratings industry, and the impact of economic constraints on the manufacture of popular culture.

Vincent Mosco is professor of journalism at Carleton University, Ottawa, Canada. He is the author of *Broadcasting in the United States: Innovative Challenge and Organizational Control* and *Pushbutton Fantasies: Critical Perspectives on Videotex and Information Technology.* He is the editor or coeditor of four books on communication, three of them with Janet Wasko.

Marilyn Neimark is associate professor in the department of accountancy, Baruch College, the City University of New York. She is the editor of *Advances in Public Interest Accounting.* Her research into the social and historical origins of accounting theory and practices has appeared in *Accounting, Organizations and Society,* and the *Journal of Accounting and Public Policy.*

Kevin Robins teaches mass communication at Sunderland Polytechnic, England, and is working in the Centre for Urban and Regional Development Studies at the University of Newcastle upon Tyne. He is the coauthor, with Frank Webster, of *Information Technology: A Luddite Analysis.*

Author Index

Subject Index